TROUBLESHOOTING & REPAIRING
PERSONAL COMPUTERS

TROUBLESHOOTING & REPAIRING
PERSONAL COMPUTERS

BY ART MARGOLIS

TAB BOOKS Inc.
BLUE RIDGE SUMMIT, PA. 17214

FIRST EDITION

FIFTH PRINTING

Printed in the United States of America

Reproduction or publication of the content in any manner, without express
permission of the publisher, is prohibited. No liability is assumed with respect to
the use of the information herein.

Copyright © 1983 by TAB BOOKS Inc.

Library of Congress Cataloging in Publication Data

Margolis, Art.
Troubleshooting and repairing personal computers.

Includes index.
1. Microcomputers—Maintenance and repair. I. Title.
TK7887.M37   1983   621.3819′58   82-19342
ISBN 0-8306-0139-2
ISBN 0-8306-1539-3 (pbk.)

Cover photograph courtesy of
Michael Gorzeck

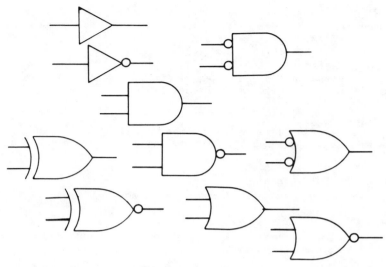

Contents

Introduction   vii

1 Trouble Symptom Analysis   1
After the Fact—Exercising the Circuits—Isolating the Seat of the Trouble—Block Diagram of a Typical
Computer System—Microcomputer Block Diagram—How the Block Diagram Works—Eyeball Analysis

2 Breaking the Factory Seal   16
Different Style Computers—Step-by-Step Disassembly—Fixing it Just by Disassembly—Visual Inspection and Cleaning—Static Electricity Precautions—Checkout Before Reassembly—Step-by-Step Reassembly

3 The Chip Location Guide   27
Service Note Prints—Drawing Your Own Guide—The Socket Controversy—The Important Parts of the
Guide—Using the Guide for Replacements

4 The Main LSI Chips   39
Typical LSIs—The CPU—The PIA—The VDG—The SAM Chip—The ACIA

5 The RAM and ROM Chips   60
The Read-Write Memory—The Read-Only Memory—All the Confusion—ROM and RAM Rows and
Columns—Wired Memory—PROMS and EPROMS—Upgrading Memory

6 The Rest of the Chips   81
Internal Wiring—Buffers—Latches—The Octal D Flip-Flop—Encoders—Decoders—Logic Gates—The
Video Mixer—Modulator—Regulators

7 Techniques Needed for Changing Chips   99
TTLs, DTLs, and RTLs—MOS Chips—The Chip in Your Hand—IC Extraction Technique—IC Insertion
Technique—Soldering Precautions—Resoldering the Replacement

8   Computer Block Diagram   113
A Simple Computer—The CPU—RAM—ROM—Input-Output Chips—The Computer in Action—
Addresses in the Block Diagram

9   Servicing Logic Gates   132
The Three Logical States—The YES Gate—Inverters—Logical AND—Logical OR—Exclusive OR
The NAND Gate—The NOR Gate—Exclusive NOR—Gate Testing

10   Digital Registers   160
The R-S Flip-Flop—The Basic Flip-Flop Circuit—The Counter—Counting Higher Than 1—
Hexadecimal—Shift Registers—Clearing and Complementing—Incrementing and Decrementing—
ANDing and ORing

11   Checking Out the CPU Workhorse   176
Inside the CPU—The Instruction Set Layers—Assembling a Program—Hand Assembly—Assemblers

12   The Memory Map   198
The CPU Addressing Circuits—Relative Addressing—Index Register Addressing—The Stack—
Addressing with other Registers—The Memory Map Itself

13   The Clock   205
A Clock Circuit—The Frequencies—What the Clock Does—The Clock Signal in Action—Testing the
Clock

14   The Address and Data Buses   215
Connecting Data Lines—Digital Components in the Data Bus—The Components in the Address
Lines—Assigning Addresses—Testing Address and Data Buses

15   The SAM Chip   226
The SAM Schematic—The SAM Block Diagram—System Timing—Device Selection—Checking Out the
SAM Chip

16   The PIAs   244
Addressing PIAs Six Registers—Choosing Between PDR and DDR—The Control Register—The PIA
Pins—The PIA in Action—A Different PIA Application—Checking the I/O Bytes—The Chip Pin Chart

17   The Video Display Generator   258
Typical VDG Inputs—VDG Character Set—Video RAM Involvement—The Other Modes—The Semigraphic Mode—The VDG Video Output—Checking Out the VDG—The VDG Output

18   The Digital to Analog Devices   270
Computer Audio—Checking Out the Sound Circuit—The Joystick Interface—Checking Out the Joystick
Interface

19   The Cassette and RS-232 Interfaces   279
The Cassette Interface—The RS-232C Type Interface

20   Reset and the Power Supply   288
The Reset Circuit—The Power Supply—Power Supply Repairs

21   The TV Display   295
The Video Circuit Board—The Video Driver Circuit Board

Index   309

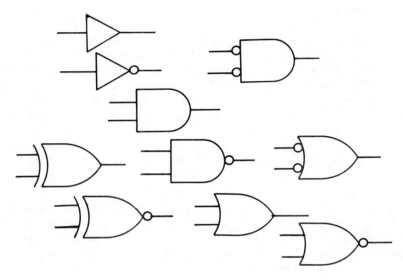

Introduction

A few years ago, in my TV repair shop, a customer brought in a home computer that had stopped working. There were very few of these instruments around at that time and it quickly attracted the technician's interest. One of the benchmen took over the repair. The computer owner had brought in a service manual with the unit. My star benchman went to work on the trouble. After a while he waved me over. He had a scared look on his face. "Well, I'll be darned Art," he said as he pointed to the service notes, "I don't understand a word that is written here."

As it turned out, the computer was dead because there wasn't any +5 volt power on any of the chips. The trouble was traced quickly in the analog style power supply, a little filter capacitor had shorted to ground. It was replaced and the computer started computing again. However, I began thinking about the shock my experienced TV man had as he tried to comprehend the computer service manual.

This book is a result of that experience. The computer has introduced a whole new dimension to electronic servicing in the home. In years past, technicians and knowledgeable TV and radio owners were able to change tubes, change transistors, and do all the various repairs that were needed on electronic equipment. They learned, over the years, all about the way the equipment worked and failed. All of these repairs were invariably performed on what is known as analog circuits.

The computer has changed all that. Computers have a few old-fashioned analog type circuits, like the power supply, but the great majority of the computing circuits are digital. Digital circuit troubleshooting is a different ball game. The digital circuit theory of operation in the computer service manual is what threw my star benchman off his perch. Even after being an expert on analog circuits for years, understanding what the digital operation was all about was beyond him at first reading. Today the situation is different. He repairs home computers one after the other in a professional expert manner.

This book covers the knowledge the authors of

factory service manuals assume you know when they prepare those notes and schematics. Up to and including the present, there are unfortunately, very few technical schools that teach courses in digital electronics. Of course, electrical engineering schools cover the material from an engineering point of view, but the training on a technician level is hard to come by. I hope the information in this book will help you close the gap.

The first eight chapters of the book deal with chip changing. This is roughly like old-fashioned tube changing. Chips are often socketed and can be tested by direct substitution. The technique required is the ability to analyze the trouble, be able to take the computer apart, look for suspect chips with the aid of a chip location guide, and then gingerly remove the chip with one tool and replace the chip with a second tool. A cursory acquaintance with the different chips is needed as well as a block diagram idea of what's happening. The techniques in the first eight chapters should enable you to repair about 50 percent of home computer troubles.

Chapters 9 and 10 launch you into the digital world of the computer. Digital electronics from the technician's point of view is discussed. Chapter 11 begins the more technical repairs. From there to the end of the book the bench repair techniques that are required are covered. The majority of the circuits in the computer are digital.

The last few chapters deal with the computer signal leaving the digital world, getting converted from digital to analog, and entering analog peripheral devices such as the cassette recorder and the video output. The complexion of the repairs in the conversion process is a combination of digital and analog techniques.

Electronic repairs, whether digital or analog, require a combination of tools, technique, and theory of operation knowledge. The theory is very important since it is often impossible to figure out how something failed, unless you know how it works. The repair technician does not have to know the way a piece of equipment works from a design engineer's point of view. He only has to understand the operation from a servicer's viewpoint. This is admittedly much easier than what the engineer must learn. In addition the technician does not have to be an expert programmer to fix a computer. Programming in high-level languages does little in locating defective components, when the computer goes down. Some rudimentary machine-language programming can be used during a repair, but this is minimal and is usually provided by the manufacturer if needed. The computer troubleshooting job requires its own point of view not to be confused with design or programming.

It turns out that in order to be able to troubleshoot and repair a computer you must learn about the hardware. Once you can handle the hardware, an extra bonus is provided, all the other dimensions of computers become easy to learn. Design and programming is approached from this hardware view and quickly will make a lot of sense.

I would like to take this opportunity to personally thank Jon Shirley, Vice President, Radio Shack Computer Merchandising; David S. Gunzel, Director, Technical Publications, Radio Shack Research and Development; F. Wiley Hunt, Publications Development Supervisor of the Heath Company; and Barry A. Watzman, Product Line Manager of Zenith Data Systems, for their kind cooperation in providing me with material for the book.

Chapter 1

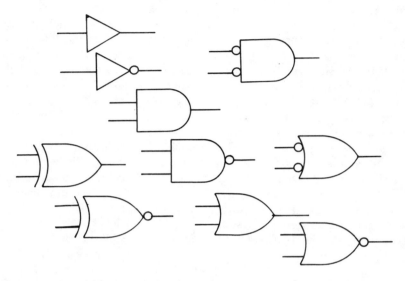

Trouble Symptom Analysis

Years ago, there was a sci-fi movie called *The Incredible Shrinking Man*. If you don't remember, it was about this fellow who was poisoned by a mysterious fog and began to slowly shrink. By the end of the picture, he could literally walk through the eye of a needle. I don't remember him needing any doctoring, but if he had, the doctor, as you can imagine, would have had a dickens of a time running medical tests on the germ size man.

While the movies were showing the flick, in real life scientists were actually creating the Incredible Shrinking Computer. First Bell Tel produced transistors. A generation of computers were born that were only a fraction of the size of vacuum tube based computers. They required slightly different techniques for servicing, but the changes were not too drastic. Then companies like Texas Instruments introduced integrated circuits, and as they started to be used in computers, the revolution was on. Computer costs and sizes shrunk as if they had been placed in that mysterious fog.

Like the shrinking man, the entire computer shrunk. All the capability, memory, and power of

the computer is still there. Only the cost and physical size has shrunk. In fact, the new computers are more powerful and faster than similar ones from the earlier generations. These computers are finding their way into the home. This means, when the computers need doctoring, the repair responsibility becomes the homeowner's problem. This book will wind it's way through the typical home computer's microscopic circuits showing how the circuits fail and what techniques are needed to repair them.

AFTER THE FACT

The servicer arrives on the scene after the failure has taken place, or as detectives call their situation "after the fact". You as a repairman, are charged with this responsibility. You must examine the failure, and by logical means, piece together all clues, working the repair puzzle out and thus pinpoint the defective part. Then that part must be replaced or repaired to get the computer back into operation once again.

Years ago, during the vacuum tube age, about 80% of repairs consisted of finding a bad tube. Most of the time tubes just burnt their filaments. Locating an unlit shorted or open tube was a snap. In the other 20% of repairs, the servicer brought into play his test equipment, and readily pinpointed shorted or open capacitors, resistors, coils, connections and the like. All circuits were relatively large and accessible. The schematic showed every component and connection in the circuit.

During the transistor heyday not too much changed on the servicing scene, except a lot of the transistors, which replaced the vacuum tubes, were soldered in, instead of being plugged in. This caused the servicer to do a lot of extra squirming during testing and a lot of soldering during transistor replacing, but the testing and tracing was straightforward since the schematic exhibited every part and connection. There were no mystery or "black box" type units, that held unknown circuits (Fig. 1-1).

Today in the chip age, while there are a lot of resistors, capacitors, etc., in plain sight, these discrete components, are a minority compared to the chips. This fact turns troubleshooting techniques into different areas. Add to the situation that in each chip are transistors, diodes, resistors, and capacitors. These internal components are wired inside the chip and in many cases there is no way you can put a probe on these components. You must rely on the external input-output connections.

There is another major servicing difficulty that came along with chips. While bad vacuum tubes were the major source of failure in vacuum tube circuits, it was easy finding and plugging in a new tube. Transistors, while not as failure prone as tubes, did represent a majority of the troubles in transistor circuits. Chips on the other hand are quite rugged, and are usually not the seat of a trouble. Chips are often wired into a circuit and can't always be readily tested by direct replacement. When chips are plugged in they, of course, can be easily replaced but unfortunately quite often do not effect the repair.

All is not lost however, the plug-in chip, during advanced troubleshooting, as described in later chapters, plays a large part in narrowing down troubled areas. What happens is, you remove the clip and then perform a test. The results of the test then provides valuable information that points out suspects.

EXERCISING THE CIRCUITS

I was in an auto repair shop awhile back. My

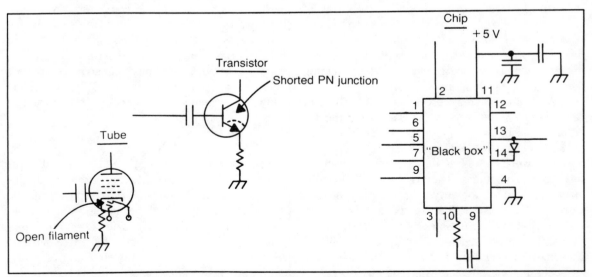

Fig. 1-1. Troubles in tubes and transistor circuits were traced easily with straightforward tests. Troubles in chips are identified with indirect input-output measures because of the chip's "black box" nature.

Fig. 1-2. Diagnostic type programs can be used to enable the computer to figure out what is wrong with itself (courtesy of Michael Gorzeck).

generator indicator told me I had electrical trouble and I wanted the problem fixed. The mechanic disconnected the battery terminals and attached a pair of cables from a test machine. The machine blinked a few times then displayed "alternator defective". Sure enough, a new alternator cured my problem. The machine was a special computer, full of chips, dedicated to testing auto electrical systems.

The computer is a natural tester and especially so on electrical and electronic gear. Your computer not only can test these pieces of equipment it can put itself through the paces. There are many programs available, that allow you to exercise the computer circuits and give you an announcement at the end of the exercise revealing the defect if it exists.

Unfortunately, there aren't many universal programs available. The test programs have to be tailored to specific computers. Most manufacturers do have tests and with a bit of effort a servicer can get ahold of one that he needs. The tests can't and do not cover all contingencies, and sometimes will give false clues, but used judiciously they are a valuable source of service information. If you are or become a computer programmer you'll be able to write your own test programs.

A good example of a thorough test program is one called *Diagnostics* for the Radio Shack Color Computer (Fig. 1-2). It comes on a plug-in board like a computer game. As we progress through the

book, you'll find that this program and ones like it are an important tool to quickly isolate a lot of hardware failures. For instance, suppose you turn on the computer, the READY message appears so you begin computing. However, when it becomes time to print your results, nothing happens. The failure could be traced to almost every circuit in the computer. How can you narrow the seat of the trouble to a particular area of chip circuit?

To come to your aid, a plug-in program could be used. If the computer doesn't have such an item in it's repertoire, often the manufacturer will sell you a test and debugging tape that you can put into memory that will do the same thing. Perhaps you'll be able to write a test program and install it into memory to do the job. Whatever method you use, the circuits can be exercised to help your diagnosis.

The Radio Shack Diagnostics works like this: Upon experiencing trouble, like I mentioned, where the computer won't print the results, but does sign on OK, the first move is to properly connect the output devices that get tested during the exercising. On the color computer these are the printer, joysticks, and cassette tape recorder. Then the TV monitor is turned on and the program cartridge diagnostics plugged in. Lastly the computer is turned on. A list of the tests appears on the TV screen automatically (Fig. 1-3). If it doesn't you

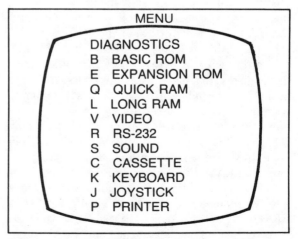

MENU

DIAGNOSTICS
B BASIC ROM
E EXPANSION ROM
Q QUICK RAM
L LONG RAM
V VIDEO
R RS-232
S SOUND
C CASSETTE
K KEYBOARD
J JOYSTICK
P PRINTER

Fig. 1-3. A typical diagnostic program offers a menu of many different tests. Each test checks out a different circuit in the computer.

3

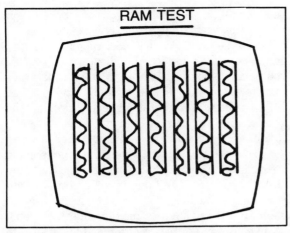

Fig. 1-4. A RAM test could put a vertical stripe pattern like this on the TV screen as it tests each RAM chip in turn.

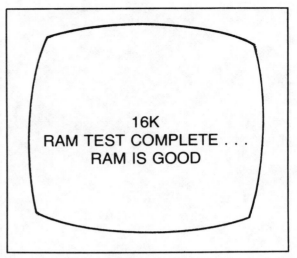

Fig. 1-5. When the test is complete the diagnostic program could give the RAMs a clean bill of health.

have to abandon that approach, but we'll assume it does appear. Incidentally, these lists are called in computerese "Menus". The illustration shows what the Main Menu for this program looks like.

The rest is button pushing. If you want to check out the RAM memory quickly you Press Q. This test figures out how much RAM you have (4K bytes, 16K bytes, 32K bytes and so on). Then the program checks out each byte of memory. It does this by filling each byte with numbers and then as each number is installed the computer checks to be sure the number has been correctly memorized. During the test you are entertained with a constantly changing pattern of vertical stripes (Fig. 1-4).

The RAM quick test takes about three minutes to run through 16K bytes. There is another more thorough test that takes about four hours. We try to avoid that if possible. Anyway, the test program is written to display the results on the TV. If there aren't any defective RAMs then the TV will show RAM TEST COMPLETE . . . RAM IS GOOD. Then your RAM size will appear and should correspond with your RAM (Fig. 1-5). If the RAM size does not match, that could be a clue to trouble. When there is a RAM trouble the computer nicely displays RAM ERROR . . . REPLACE CHIP ---. Then you also receive the chip number and amount of RAM present (Fig. 1-6).

The other tests on the program produce simi-

lar and appropriate results. No doubt, as time goes by we will develop all sorts of diagnostic checks and tests that will guide and aid us in fixing the machines.

ISOLATING THE SEAT OF THE TROUBLE

Like the old fashioned TV repairs, computer failures also use the picture tube display as a test

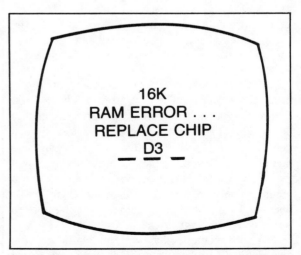

Fig. 1-6. If one of the RAMs should be defective, the program can tell you so and also tell you which chip is the troublemaker.

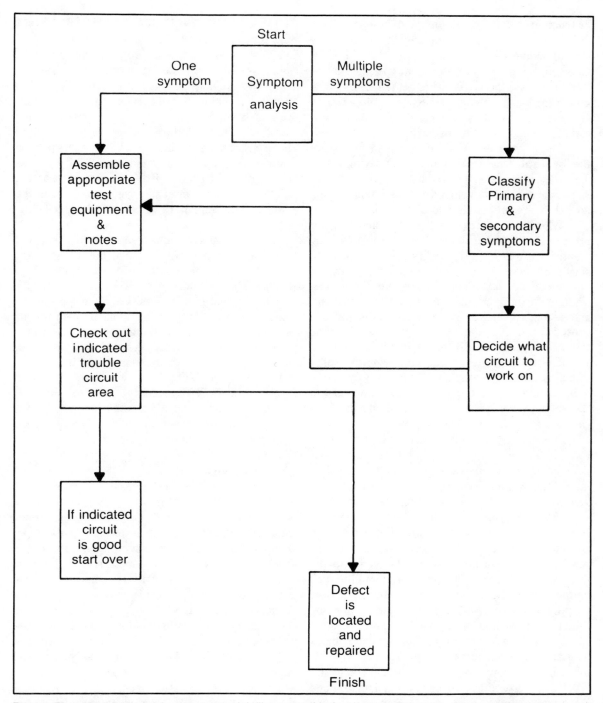

Fig. 1-7. The typical start to finish computer repair is like any troubleshooting task. The start is always symptom analysis and proceeds from there.

instrument. In a large percentage of cases the CRT tells you what circuit is causing the trouble. By careful analysis of what is happening on the CRT face you are told immediately that the video interface is at fault, the keyboard is defective, the sync generator has problems, the ROM is inoperative, etc. Even some of the joystick and cassette troubles can be indicated by the display.

The trick is, of course, an educated analysis of the TV display and what signals are arriving there. This means you need a clear understanding of what signals are being developed in the computer and how they are processed and displayed.

When the professional electronic tech approaches a repair he goes through the following mental warmup (Fig. 1-7). First, he carefully observes the symptom. He classifies the symptom into one of the major computer trouble categories. Then he further classifies the symptom to primary and secondary indications. Often the display will show more than one or two symptoms at the same time. For instance, the picture might be not holding vertical sync properly but also won't display graphics. Sometimes the obvious primary symptom is indicating the bad circuit and other times one of the secondary symptoms is really doing the indicating, and is the primary symptom after all.

Once the tech decides on a circuit to check, he reaches for the proper test equipment and makes the correct service moves as dictated by the calculated observations. There is almost a separate service approach for each major trouble category, 30 or 40 different approaches. Unless the tech takes this route he is probably wasting time. For example, if circuits on the computer board are suspect, he reaches for his logic probe to test states. Should the display look shrunk, he begins working in the high voltage power supply with a voltmeter. When the sound effects are inoperative he begins examining the digital to analog circuit. He can go to the most likely circuit area only if he has a general block diagram of the computer system firmly fixed in his mind and he knows how the digital and composite TV signals are being processed, manipulated and displayed.

BLOCK DIAGRAM OF A TYPICAL COMPUTER SYSTEM

If you look at a typical home computer system in action, you'll see the homeowner typing on what appears to be a portable typewriter. He stares at a color TV screen as he types. Alongside the TV is a printing machine and a cassette tape recorder. Every so often the operator reaches over and punches buttons on the cassette. Almost as often the printer buzzes to life and rolls out some printed copy. A closer look reveals a couple of joysticks plugged into the back of the typewriter near the cables from the printer and cassette. That is the typical home computer system at first glance (Fig. 1-8).

The home computer uses the principles of television receiving exactly like the TV industry does. The computer just has a different product to display. The TV industry produces a composite TV signal, modulates it with entertainment programming and transmits the total signal out over the air or cable (Fig. 1-9). The home computer also produces a composite TV signal, but modulates it with digital logic signals then sends it into the TV receiver for display (Fig. 1-10). The home computer is like both the TV transmitter and the receiver. The typewriter case contains the complete TV signal producer like the transmitter. The keyboard generates the digital logic signal. The joysticks are like a few more keys on the keyboard, generating some more logic.

The cassette tape recorder is a storage device. If the operator wants to save some of the logic signal, a few strokes on the keyboard in the proper code will output the logical signal onto the tape. There are only logic signals sent to the tape, not the composite TV signal. The tape can save the logic since it is in the range of voice frequencies. The TV signals are video frequencies and can't be saved on ordinary cassette tape.

Once a tape has logic on it, the tape and cassette become an input device like the keyboard. You can consider the cassette as both an output and input device, unlike the keyboard and joysticks which are solely input devices.

The TV display is often simply a black and

white or color TV. When the computer is not attached to it the TV can be used for regular programming. In some systems the display is a separate TV monitor. These monitors have no tuning circuits and can't be used for home TV viewing. Then there are the computers with a monitor built right in the case with the typewriter system. All these special computer TV monitors are designed with special care to accommodate digital logic displays. The resolution for lettering is far better than the ordinary TV. Yet the regular home TV is quite satisfactory for computer displaying most of the time. The TV receiver, of course, is only an output device. There is no ordinary way it is ever used as an input.

The typical printer that goes with a computer is an alternative output device. The typewriter keyboard and printer, properly programmed can act just like a complete typewriter. The TV display could even be left off. The printer can print, in hard copy, the same information the TV prints on the screen.

The eye's view block diagram of the equipment therefore shows five types that make up a home system. There is the typewriter and joysticks as input-only units, the cassette as an input-output device and the TV and printer as output-only pieces. The TV, printer, cassette, and joysticks are all called peripherals. Each is discussed in greater detail later in the book. From here to those chapters

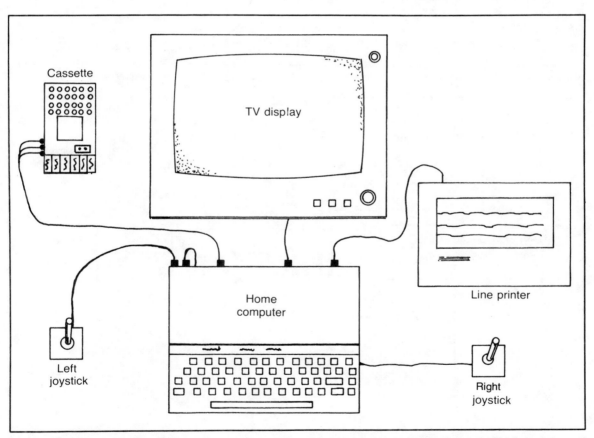

Fig. 1-8. The typical home computer system will have keyboard, joystick, and cassette tape inputs and a TV, line printer, and cassette recorder output.

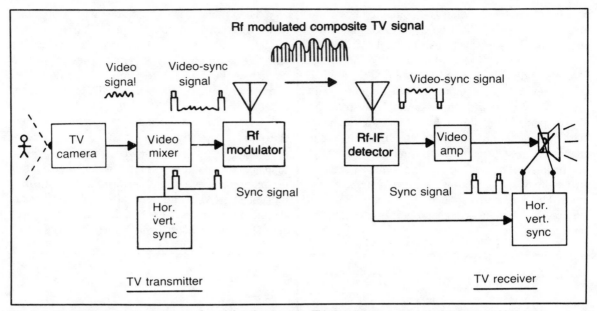

Fig. 1-9. The TV industry produces an rf modulated composite TV signal that contains entertainment video.

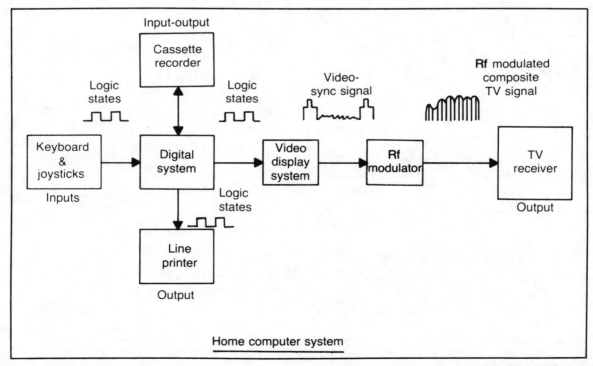

Fig. 1-10. The home computer system can also produce an rf modulated composite TV signal, but it contains digital logic information.

we will go into the typewriter appearing part of the computer, which is not a peripheral, but the computer itself.

MICROCOMPUTER BLOCK DIAGRAM

When you open a computer, all you'll see is a large print board loaded with integrated circuits. The hundreds of thousands of circuits are boiled down to about 50 ICs and associated capacitors, resistors, etc. The block diagram can be roughed out into five major functions (Fig. 1-11).

The heart of the microcomputer is the central processing unit, known as the CPU. It does all the hard work and as you'll see is really what the computer is all about. It is attached to all the other parts of the computer. The CPU, while it is a strong heart, and as you'll see hardly ever fails, needs a pacemaker to beat. The pacemaker is called the clock, and is a crystal controlled oscillator that is hooked into the CPU.

The brains of the computer is not in the CPU. The brains consist of two separate types. The most extensive type is called the *RAM*. RAM stands for *Random Access Memory*, which is not really an easily understandable name. A better description is read-write memory. The RAM consists of rows and rows of memory banks. As you fill the rows of memory with digital logic, it is said, that you are writing to the memory. You can write into the memory reams of coded instructions and data. All

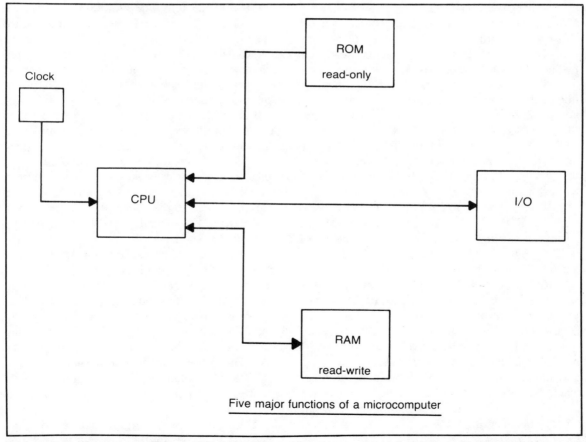

Five major functions of a microcomputer

Fig. 1-11. The microcomputer contains a CPU, RAM, ROM, and input/output ports. A clock keeps the computer working and all components timed together.

the computer programs you devise you can write or type into RAM. The only limitation is the amount of RAM in your computer. A small amount of RAM is 4K while 128K is quite a bit of RAM for a home computer. A good usable amount is 16K.

Once you have written instructions and data into memory then you can go ahead and read the information out of the memory. The information in the memory is like information that you copied into a notebook. Once written in, it can be read whenever you need to use it. That's why RAM is called read-write memory. You can write the information into the RAM, and then read the info out at will. The RAM is just blank pages that can be filled, read or erased as your needs dictate.

The other type of memory inside the typewriter case is called *ROM*. ROM stands for *Read-Only Memory*. This name is easier to understand than the RAM nomenclature. The ROM as its name indicates can't be written into. You can only read from it. The ROM can be thought of as a published book. The pages are not blank like the RAM, they are filled with instructions, data, and addresses. There are ROMs inside the computer case. The cartridges that you buy to play games on the computer are ROMs. The ROM is really the brains of the computer. It takes control when the computer is turned on, and stays in control. The ROM contains a control program.

When the computer starts operation it reads from the ROM. You can't write into a ROM. It's permanently filled. It does a specific job and that's it. The job the ROM does is all it can do. You can't get the ROM to do anything else.

RAM, with its blank pages however, is more versatile. RAM can do everything a ROM can do if you fill the blank pages, or program RAM correctly. At any rate, RAM and ROM are covered in greater detail in a later chapter. RAM and ROM are both needed in a home computer. ROMs are fairly rugged and do not fail too often. RAMs on the other hand, are very susceptible to failure from static electricity. Extraordinary handling precautions must be taken during RAM testing and replacement to avoid troubles.

The fifth major function in the block diagram is

called I/O. This means Input/Output. In order to plug printers, cassettes, etc. into the computer case complex interface circuits must be used. Typical I/O circuits for the home computer, are found behind the plugs in the back and sides of the case. In the circuits are all sorts of components including many chips. The chips can be as extensive and complex as the CPU. For instance, a common I/O chip is the *PIA*. PIA stands for *Peripheral Interface Adapter*. It is a 40-pin unit the same size as the CPU. Another chip in common use is the *ACIA*. That stands for *Asynchronous Communications Interface Adapter*. It is a 24-pin package that is in lots of home computers. These circuits will be covered in detail in later chapters.

HOW THE BLOCK DIAGRAM WORKS

In order to be able to repair a computer you are going to have to know how it works. Throughout the book we'll go over its work process again and again, each time digging into the circuits a little deeper. At this juncture, let's see what the five computer elements do as they operate together.

For instance, suppose you want to write a letter on your home computer. To accomplish the task you need a printer in addition to the typical typewriter-TV arrangement. The first thing you need is a letter writing program. The computer can do very little without being told what to do by a program. You go to the computer store and buy a letter writing program. It's on a cartridge. The cartridge is a ROM.

Next, you go home, sit down with your machine, and plug in the letter writing ROM. You turn on the equipment. The CPU is made to go directly to the ROM as soon as it is energized. That gets all elements ready for action. Here is the lineup. The ROM is in charge. The CPU is pulsing away. The RAM is waiting with open memory banks. The printer is plugged into one output port. The TV display is connected to another output port. You are ready to hit typewriter keys at the input (Fig. 1-12).

You hit a key to begin your letter. The keyboard sends code for the character you pressed to the CPU. The CPU holds the character and sends a plea to the ROM. The CPU in digital logic code asks ROM, "What should I do with this character from the keyboard?"

The ROM answers swiftly, "Store the character in RAM and also display it on the TV screen." The CPU quickly follows orders. It stores the characters, in code, to RAM and also makes a record where in RAM the character was placed. Every RAM now has its own address and the CPU must keep a record of all addresses (Fig. 1-13). Then the CPU outputs the character to the video and you see it on the screen.

Next you press another character on the keyboard. It heads right into the CPU. The CPU has practically no brains. It examines the character and sends a frantic message to ROM. The CPU says, "There is a character here from the keyboard. What should I do with it?"

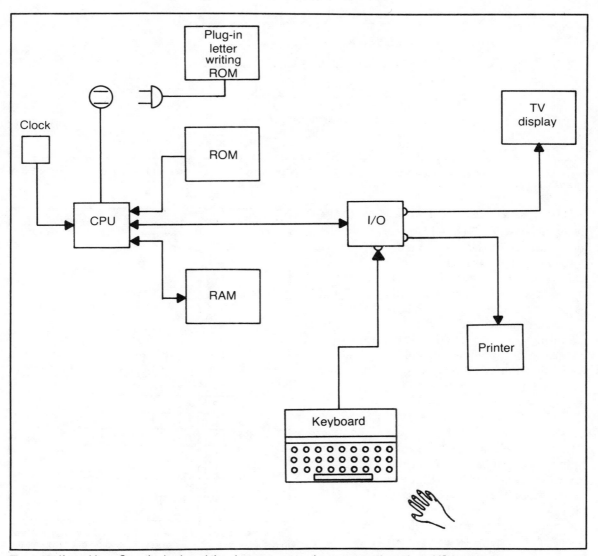

Fig. 1-12. If you hit an S on the keyboard the character enters the computer through an I/O port.

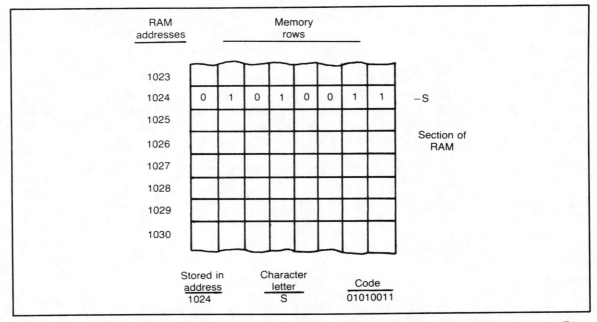

Fig. 1-13. The character letter S gets coded into 01010011. The eight code numbers get placed into a RAM memory row. Every row has its own address.

ROM patiently answers, "Store it in RAM and display it on the TV." The CPU snaps to and quickly follows the command. ROM has to be patient because this same routine is followed over and over and over as you type the letter. Each character is stored in a row of memory and the CPU keeps a record of the address of each character.

Meanwhile you are composing the letter with the aid of the TV display (Fig. 1-14). Finally you get your letter fully written and ready to be printed. In RAM the letter is stored exactly like the TV display. The printer is waiting. You type PRINT and the command goes to the CPU.

The CPU as usual asks ROM, "What should I do with this word PRINT?" The ROM answers, "Read all those characters you stored in RAM, one by one, and send them to the printer." That's what the CPU does. Starting with the first address it remembered it reads that character and sends it to the printer. Then the CPU reads the next character and sends it to the printer. Monotonously it continues till the entire letter has been read and sent on.

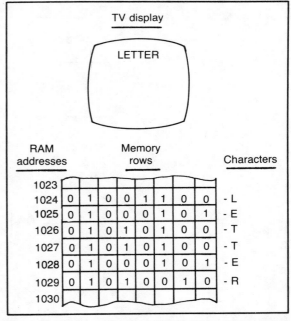

Fig. 1-14. If you type the word "LETTER" it will be installed into successive memory rows and also be displayed on the TV screen.

At the printer, there is a tiny bit of RAM. There is usually enough to hold a line of copy. The printer then waits till a line of copy fills up and then prints the line.

EYEBALL ANALYSIS

When the home computer fails you are faced with one of about a dozen general symptoms. The symptoms are the results of problems in the computer or in a peripheral. If the printer won't print, the cassette stops working properly, the TV won't go on, or a joystick is busted, you have a peripheral trouble. Should the computer be dead, not be able to send sound, video or the display block, send sound but no display, display video but no sound, have no color from a color computer, or have color and sound but display "garbage", you have a computer breakdown.

If you can't decide whether you have a peripheral or a computer defect, you'll have to try substitute units. For instance, if you can't figure whether a loss of color is happening due to the TV or computer, hook the computer to a known good color TV. If the color is still missing then the problem can be blamed on the computer. Should the color return on the substitute TV then the computer is exonerated and the original TV has a No Color trouble.

The computer sends four outputs to the monitor or color TV. (Fig. 1-15) First of all there is

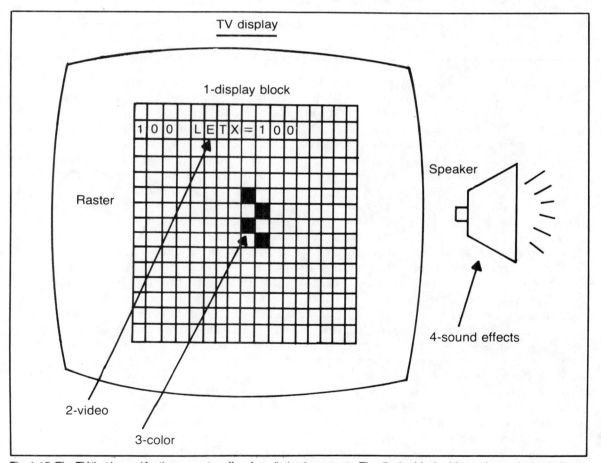

Fig. 1-15. The TV that is used for the computer offers four distinctive outputs: The display block, video, color, and sound effects.

Table 1-1. The General Categories of Computer Troubles All Indicate a Specific Circuit to Begin Testing When Those Troubles Occur.

General Home Computer Troubles	
Symptom	Indicated Circuits
Dead Computer	Power Supply
Display Block OK, No sound or video	Video Modulator
No Display Block, Sound only	Sync Circuits
No Sound Effects	Digital to Analog Circuits Sound Circuits
No Color, otherwise OK	Color TV chips
Garbage	All Logic Circuits

a Display Block. This is like a raster a TV manufactures. However, the display block is imprinted on top of the TV raster. The display block is made mostly with the sync generator in the computer. When you analyze the TV monitor for symptoms, you must clearly distinguish the display block made by the computer, from the raster being made in the TV.

The second output the computer makes is video. This can be in the form of *alphanumerics, alpha semigraphics* or *full graphics*. Alphanumerics are characters such as the alphabet and numbers. Graphics are symbols and pictorial representations, while alpha semigraphics are a combination of the two. Anyway, they are all video which is the main concern of the servicer.

The third output is a color signal. This is produced and delivered along with the video. The fourth output is sound effects. This can be your voice off the tape recorder, game sounds from a cartridge, tones from a special digital to analog circuit or blasts from another little single bit circuit.

When you analyze a TV screen for trouble caused by the computer look for these four outputs. By their presence or their absence you will be clued to begin your repair search at the most likely cir-

cuit. Let's go through the general categories of failures that can beset a computer, both color and monochrome (Table 1-1).

Dead Computer. A large percentage of computer troubles happen because of power supply failure. In the typical home computer there can be a supply that is supposed to produce four highly critical voltages. They are $+5$ V, -5 V, $+12$ V, and -12 V. When all these voltages are missing the computer goes dead and will respond to power supply test techniques.

No Sound or Video but the Display Block is OK. When this set of symptoms appear, the trouble is indicated to be in the circuits that process the sound and video together. This narrows down the suspect areas to the sections starting in the video modulator where the sound input signal is converted to a 4.5 MHz signal to be mixed with the video. It is highly unlikely that separate bad fates could befall both sound and video at the same time. One trouble usually occurs at a time. One trouble that will shoot down both sound and video at the same time can only happen in circuits where they are traveling together. The most likely suspect then is the modulator circuit.

Sound only, No Display Block. This trouble indicates problems in the video processing circuits. The video and color are probably OK, but the circuits that produce the display block (that the video and color are shown in) is in trouble. The circuits that make horizontal and vertical sync are the main display block producers. Beginning your search in the sync generator eliminates checking circuits that are probably good.

No Sound Effects. The sound produced inside the computer, not from the cassette or other peripherals, is made by the digital to analog circuitry and a circuit called "single bit sound output." These are the prime suspects, ready to be tested, and the place to begin the no sound trouble.

No Color, Sound and Video OK. The color signal produced in the computer is almost made exactly like the color in a TV. Color computers will have a complete color video modulator chip. This circuit area is the place to begin the repair search.

Garbage. You'll hear this term used a lot during computer servicing. Garbage in the display block means the display is showing lettering or symbols with no rhyme or reason. The amount of garbage could be a little or a lot, it could be all over the display or only on a portion, it could happen while a program is being run or at any random time. Garbage is garbage and it indicates a major logic function has failed. With experience on the same model machine, the pattern the garbage displays, could indicate particular circuit sections, but most of the time, a garbage trouble just means a long checkout of all the logic circuits in the computer.

Chapter 2

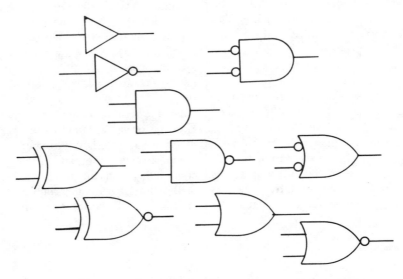

Breaking the Factory Seal

When I first brought home my personal computer, an early 4K TRS-80 Color Computer, I could hardly wait to take it apart. I was a little hesitant to open it up, since it was operating beautifully and I didn't want to lose a chip by poking a screwdriver in the wrong place. Sometimes electronic cabinet designers put holes in places where a long screwdriver can short out circuits or break open a sensitive component. I didn't want to start out with the new piece by doing a repair job.

I held off breaking the seal until I got ahold of the factory service manual. The day the manual arrived though, I waited no longer. I placed the little beauty on my home bench, and prepared it for the exploratory. I opened the manual and there was an exploded view (Fig. 2-1) and step-by-step disassembly/assembly instructions (Fig. 2-2). All of my tentativeness disappeared immediately. I was now treading familiar territory.

The first thing I wanted to find was the so-called factory seals. Following instructions, I placed the case upside down on a rubber mat. The instruction said remove the seven screws. There were eight holes in the bottom of the case. I looked in all eight holes. There were two holes without screws, six with screws. I removed the six screws. Where was the seventh?

Then I noticed a sticker in the center of the case bottom. It read, OPENING CASE WILL VOID WARRANTY. SEE OWNER'S MANUAL FOR WARRANTY INFORMATION (Fig. 2-3). I peeled off the sticker. There it was. Another hole with a screw at the bottom. I removed the seventh screw and turned the case face up. The case then was easily lifted off exposing the neatly laid out print board (Fig. 2-4). The factory seal was composed of one sticker covering a hole. For an experienced tech breaking this seal was not really an earthshaking problem.

If you compare opening up a home computer to taking a back off a TV, it's a bit different, but not more difficult. In the typical TV the back is removed while the chassis remains in the cabinet. The home computer chassis and innards all remain intact as

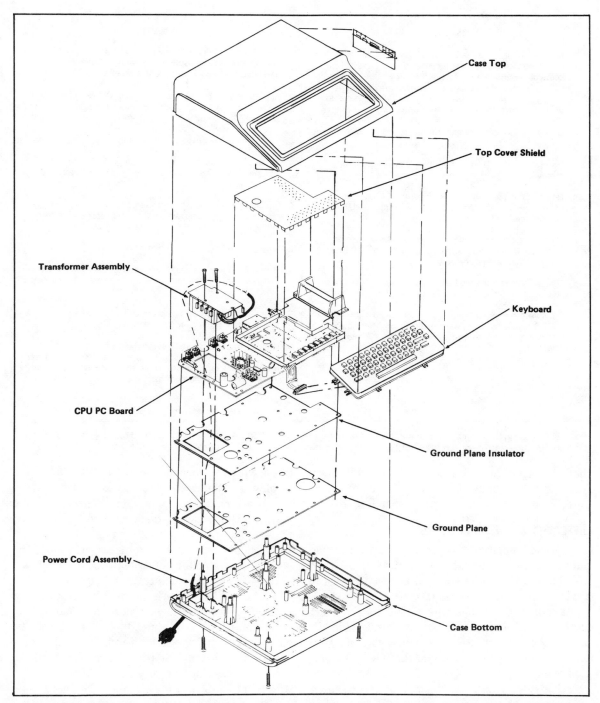

Fig. 2-1. The exploded view of a home computer takes all the fiddling and guess work out of how a computer is assembled (courtesy of Radio Shack, a division of Tandy Corporation).

DISASSEMBLY	REASSEMBLY
1. Make sure all cables (also power cord) are disconnected. Place the Color Computer face down on a padded or non-scratching surface and remove the seven screws from the Case Bottom. (Because the screws are positioned so deeply, you may not be able to actually remove them until the Computer is turned face up.)	1. Replace the Ground Plane and its Insulator on back of the PC Board and install the sixteen fasteners. You may need some pliers to close the tips together and then insert.
2. Carefully place the Computer face up and lift off the Case Top and set it aside.	2. Replace the PC Board onto the plastic bosses. Be sure that the ends of the Power Cord are pulled through the square cutout in the Board where the transformer is positioned.
3. Carefully lift the Keyboard off the plastic bosses and remove the Keyboard Cable.	3. Fasten the PC Board in place using ten No. 6 × 1/2″ screws.
4. Remove the Top Cover Shield and set it aside. You may have to remove the top cover of the modulator (U5) to get the shield off.	4. Connect the transformer jumper cables, E1 through E4 and the Power Cord jumpers, E6 - white, E5 - green, and E7 - black.
5. Remove the three screws supporting the transformer assembly (two on transformer, one on the board) and disconnect all jumper cables.	5. Position the Transformer assembly and attach jumper cable E8. Fasten using two No. 6 × 1 1/2″ screws (on Transformer) and one No. 6 × 1/2″ screw (on board).
6. Remove the ten screws fastening the CPU PC Board and lift the Board off its plastic bosses.	6. Replace the Top Cover Shield.
7. Remove the Ground Plane and Insulator from the back of the PC Board by using a screwdriver or other small, thin tool to pry off all sixteen fasteners from the rear of the Board.	7. Reconnect the Keyboard Cable and Cable Shield if used. Replace the Keyboard onto the plastic bosses in the case bottom.
	8. Replace the Case Top onto the Case Bottom and carefully turn the entire unit over (face down).
	9. Replace the seven screws in the Case Bottom (Two No. 6 × 7/8″ toward the front and five No. 6 × 1 1/4″ toward the rear). **Do not put the longer screws in the front positions, it could dent the Computer Case Top.**
	10. *Don't forget to put on the Radio Shack authorized seal to maintain the warranty.*

Fig. 2-2. Following the step by step assembly and disassembly instructions is the best way to avoid causing trouble on top of the trouble already present (courtesy of Radio Shack, a division of Tandy Corporation).

the cabinet is removed and all of the circuits are exposed and quite available. This makes the computer more accessible than the usual TV.

DIFFERENT STYLE COMPUTERS

Home computers, in general, are built in two different styles. The first type has the keyboard and TV display all in one case. The second has the keyboard in a separate case while the TV display is on its own. The all in one type is a bit more compact and examples are the TRS-80's models, I, II, and III and the Heathkit H-89A. Separate keyboard examples are the Apple, Atari, and the TRS-80 Color Computer.

The reason for the keyboard only style is obviously to save the cost of the built-in TV display. For commercial usage the TV display cost can be jus-

tified with the higher resolution available if the display is designed to match the keyboard activity. For the home, with plenty of TVs around, the built-in display can be dispensed with. However, there are still plenty of both being sold and a servicer should be prepared to take apart both.

In the computer with a built-in TV, when you get inside, you must exercise the same care you'd use in any TV. There is more in there than low voltage logic components. There is a picture tube with high vacuum pressure, high voltage circuits, sharp edges and possible X-radiation. All safety applications that are used on ordinary TVs must be used when working on these units (Fig. 2-5).

In the keyboard only machines the safety situation is much easier. The voltages, aside from the line voltage are harmless. You can get across 12 volts and not even know it. The only voltage danger inside these computers is where the 120 volts from your house plug enters the computer. Your main concern when working on these keyboard only types, is accidentally shorting some voltage into a sensitive chip.

The keyboard only types produce a composite TV signal. The signal contains four parts as described in Chapter 1. To repeat they are, the display block, the video, color, and sound. The signals can all be seen on the scope easily (Fig. 2-6). The display block is composed of mostly horizontal and vertical sync pulses. The video is like the conventional TV Y signal. The color is like the TV Red,

Green, and Blue signals. The sound is 4.5 MHz intercarrier sound. All these signals are handled easily by TV video and audio circuits. However, there is no carrier for these four signals. These signals can be injected via a 72 ohm piece of coax into video and audio circuits of a TV but not into the tuner's antenna terminals.

If a computer has a built-in display there is no problem, the signals are injected into the video and audio circuits of the monitor. Should a separate monitor be designed for a specific computer, again there is no problem as the signals are applied correctly. What about using a home TV? How can these signals be applied?

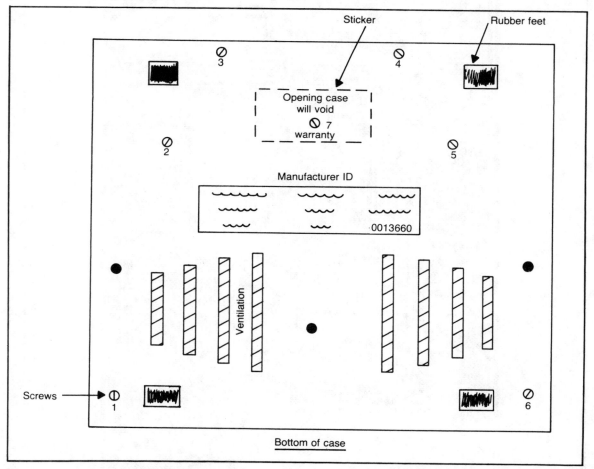

Fig. 2-3. The factory seals that are placed on home computers are usually stickers that can be located with the aid of the factory service notes.

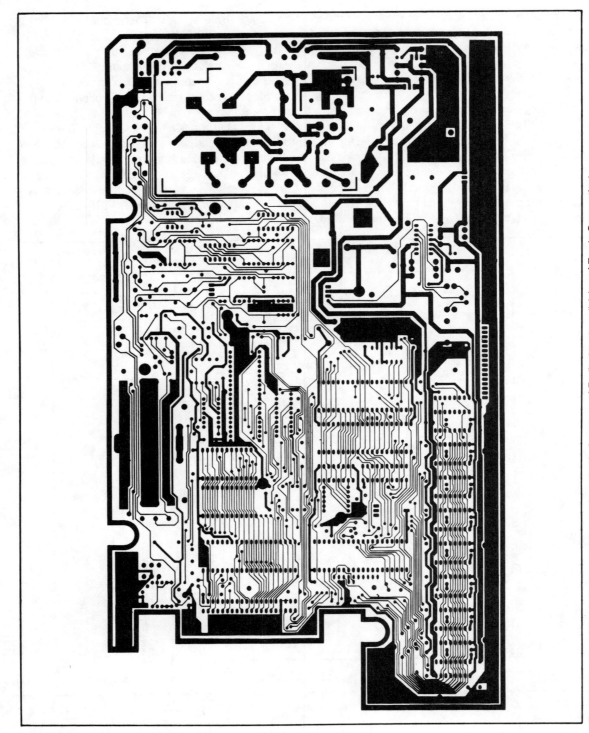

Fig. 2-4. Once the print board is exposed the repair can begin (courtesy of Radio Shack, a division of Tandy Corporation).

CABINET REMOVAL

Whenever you need to remove the cabinet top:

- Refer to the inset drawing on Pictorial 3-1, insert the blade of a small screwdriver into the notch in the latch plate, and then, as you lift upward on the front, slide the latch plate toward the front of the Computer about 1/4".

- Likewise, open the latch plate on the other side of the cabinet top.

- **WARNING:** When the line cord is connected to an ac outlet, hazardous voltages can be present inside your Computer. See Pictorial 3-1.

- Carefully tilt the cabinet top back.

- Unplug the fan.

- When the top is tilted straight up, carefully lift the hinges out of the rear panel.

Simply reverse this procedure to close and lock the cabinet top back on the Computer.

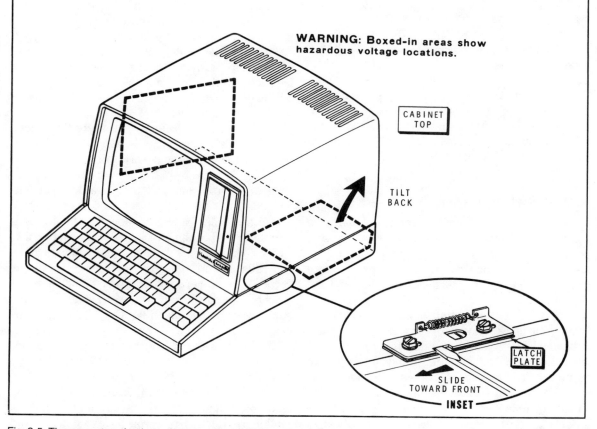

WARNING: Boxed-in areas show hazardous voltage locations.

CABINET TOP

TILT BACK

SLIDE TOWARD FRONT

LATCH PLATE

INSET

Fig. 2-5. The computers that have their own display TV have hazardous high voltage circuits like a TV receiver. Care must be taken that is not necessary on the keyboard-only types (© 1981 Heath Company, Reprinted by Permission of Heath Company).

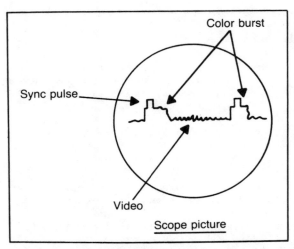

Fig. 2-6. The output of a computer, before it is modulated with an rf carrier, looks exactly like the composite TV signal in a color TV, on the ordinary TV service scope.

Another circuit must be used, it's called a modulator. Some computers like the TRS-80 Color comes equipped with a modulator. Others like the Apple do not. You can buy a modulator for about $50. When there is a modulator on the unit, the four signals are modulated with a form of carrier wave. Then the output of the computer is a signal that can be tuned for on TV channels 3 or 4. That way you can use an ordinary TV as a monitor.

STEP-BY-STEP DISASSEMBLY

When you want to take a computer apart, an exploded view is worth a thousand words. The step by step text the factory wrote to go with the text is useful too. The importance of the view during a repair goes far beyond just taking the unit apart and then reassembling it.

A computer repair, from beginning to end, consists of a finite number of service moves. Each individual move can be counted like the step-by-step disassembly instructions. If you assign the same repair to two techs, one will probably make more service moves than the other. All things being equal, the fellow who makes the least moves is the more expert repairer. He arrives at the seat of trouble first and cures the trouble with the lesser effort. One of the areas where he saves moves is

during the disassembly. He rarely has to take the gear completely apart. Most of the time he does little more than get the board exposed.

The more you take apart, the more you will have to put back together. The more you take apart, the more possibility "induced" trouble is likely to occur. Good technique dictates, taking apart only what is needed. Further dismantling is not only a waste of time but an invitation to problems that otherwise would never have occurred. The factory illustrations and text, used to their fullest, helps you conduct your repair while avoiding unnecessary work.

FIXING IT JUST BY DISASSEMBLY

During print board manufacturing a form of booby trap can be installed on the board. The boards are soldered with automatic machinery. The machines generate hot gases that expand rapidly and blow liquid solder into the air. Some of the solder may fly over the print board. The solder hardens and drizzles onto the board. The solder falls in little balls. The board has flux on it and some of the little balls stick.

Of course, the factory is aware of this solder raining and has an extensive cleaning procedure to get rid of the excess solder. However, some of the solder balls stick to places where they cause no immediate problems, and pass board inspection. The computer then gets assembled and packaged. The little solder balls get shipped and sold along with their host computer. Sometime down the line, as the computer gets used, a solder ball gets loose and rolls around the innards of the computer. It settles into another spot. This time though, the ball touches two copper runs (Fig. 2-7). The computer stops working intelligently. Only "garbage" appears on the screen.

When you start checking out the computer, the first thing you do is, take it apart. As you remove the case and turn the board up on its side, a tiny solder ball bounces on your workbench. Then when you turn on the unit to check it, you find the thing is working perfectly. Yes, you have completed the repair. You have eliminated the short simply by taking the gear apart.

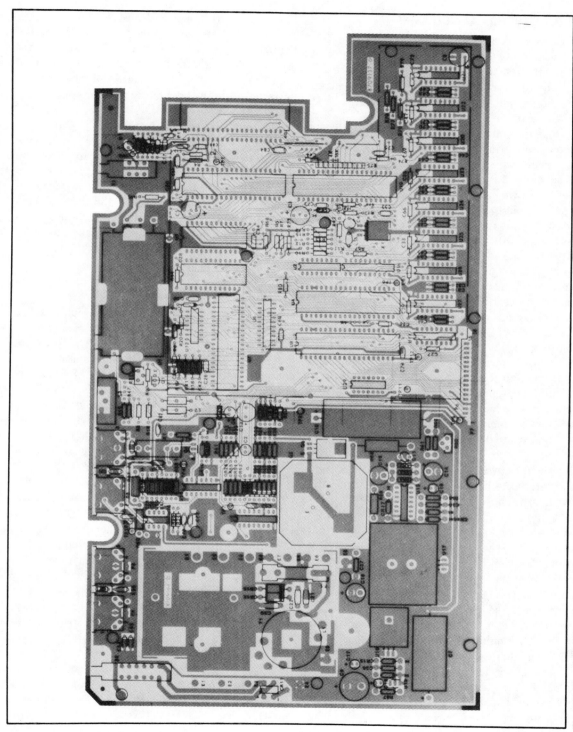

Fig. 2-7. The underside of the computer board has most of the copper lines and circuit connections. A speck of solder there can easily cause a short.

23

VISUAL INSPECTION AND CLEANING

The solder ball short is one of the easiest types of repairs. While you will encounter them, most of the time the repair is not so convenient. There are though, quite a few service moves that you can make without test equipment that can prove fruitful. First of all there is the visual inspection.

Once the computer is apart, you can look over the board for various types of shorts. One common type happens when an IC lead punctures the insulation between the print board and the grounding plane. As shown in the exploded view (Fig. 2-1) the computer is put together in layers. At the bottom is the case, next is the ground plane, on top of that is the insulator, with the print board over it all. If an IC lead is a bit long and receives some pressure, it will poke right through the insulation and short out to ground. You can see the actual short and clear it by snipping and bending the excess lead.

Another quick check should be made on the IC sockets. On occasion a socket pin can get bent under instead of being soldered into its board hole. It can make contact during factory checkout and pass inspection. During customer use the contact opens up. The open can be spotted with a bright light and a close look. Moving the pin into its socket hole and a drop of solder produces a quick fix.

Other board defects can also be found visually. There are 16 copper etch address lines that travel side by side all over the board. There are also eight copper etch data lines that are also traversing the entire board. These 24 etch trails must be continuous. If any of them, at any place, are either shorted together, or broken open, the computer will not work properly. These etchs are a common source of trouble. An open or short in these bus lines can cause almost any type of symptom, according to where the defect occurs. It is good practice to visually inspect the address and data bus lines carefully at the beginning of each repair. Odds are favorable that you might quickly find a solder sliver short or break in an etch right off.

Another service move that produces favorable results when the computer is apart is cleaning. As the computer is used it gathers dust. Dust itself is an insulator and as such won't short out the print board or its components. However, the computer needs ventilation and the dust enters through the ventilation apertures and restricts the circulation of air. In addition the dust impairs the movement of the keyboard, cartridge interface and other moving parts and ports. It is definitely not a desirable product to have in the computer.

A good way to remove the dust is with a thin clean paint brush. The dust removal should be done slowly and carefully. Be especially careful around the RAMs since they are susceptible to static electric charges. It's a safe idea to ground the brush during the cleaning, as described in the next section. Never use any water or cleaning solution on the print board. The idea is not to make the board goodlooking, all you want is adequate air circulation and a clear view of the circuits.

STATIC ELECTRICITY PRECAUTIONS

The two common types of chips you'll find in a computer are *TTL (transistor-transistor logic)* and *MOS (metal-oxide semiconductor)*. The TTLs are fairly rugged and can withstand some static electric charges, but the MOSs are sensitive. Even a tiny spark can rupture one. The MOS performs due to a very thin insulating layer of oxide, which acts as an insulator, between the gates and the active channel in each microscopic transistor in the chip (Fig. 2-8). If any static spark should puncture any of the oxide the entire chip could become worthless.

There are a number of ways static electricity can get to the oxide. First of all, you can carry the chip death charge. At humidity levels of 40% you can develop a static potential of hundreds of volts. If, during a chip replacement you ground a chip in your hand, the volts will course through the oxide and kill the chip as it punctures the silicon dioxide. To avoid this problem you must keep yourself and everything else that contacts the chip grounded. This is accomplished easily with a jumper lead attached to your wristwatch or belt and the chassis you are plugging the chip into.

There are many ways static charges can kill a MOS chip. If you do have to move them around use a conductive tube or conductive foam. Don't let them brush against any materials, such as silk, nylon, or

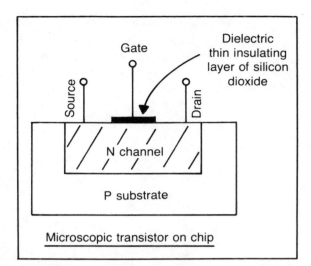

Fig. 2-8. A lot of the chips in a computer are MOS types. These metal-oxide-semiconductor types are subject to having their oxide gate insulators ruptured by static electricity. Great care must be taken during handling of the MOS chips. Be sure to keep plenty of jumper leads around to ground your wristwatch, belt, and any other source of static electricity.

styrofoam. As long as you take care you'll avoid their electrocution.

CHECKOUT BEFORE REASSEMBLY

Once you have found the trouble, removed the short, open, or leak, or installed the new replacement, you are ready to reassemble the computer. It is good technique to test out the gear before you put it together. There is always the possibility that the computer will operate out of the case but not back in the case. If you do not test it before reassembly, and it does not work after being put back together, you'll be missing the service information about its preassembly operation. This is an important piece of the repair puzzle.

For example, suppose you repaired a "garbage" problem by locating a shorted chip, and changing it. Once all the computer voltages read correctly you hooked up all the peripherals, and ran through the "exercise" program. The computer checked out perfectly. Then you put it back together and exercised it again. This time though, you got garbage again!

Your heart sinks, but you stand a chance that this latest trouble is not serious. The unit was working ok before the reassembly. You start to take it apart again. Aha!, you notice one of the screws was not seated properly. You loosen it and seat it correctly. Then you try the exercise program again. To your delight the computer works as it should. The poorly seated screw was shorting something out. Your original repair was still fine. The reassembly had induced a new trouble that was easily dispatched because you suspected it since the open chassis check had been good.

STEP-BY-STEP REASSEMBLY

The ideal computer repair goes something like this. You analyze the trouble and correctly diagnose the keyboard PIA chip has failed. Next you take the case off the computer and lay all cables, screws and other dismantling parts in the neat order you removed them. You locate the bad chip, take a replacement off your shelf, and replace the defective one. Then you exercise the computer, pronounce it fixed, then reassemble it by retracing the disassembly steps. Simple? Easy? Of course. Unfortunately a lot of repairs are not that ideal. More than likely they happen like the following description.

The computer trouble is analyzed and the keyboard PIA is diagnosed as defective. You take the gear apart and sure enough the PIA is bad. However it is not on the shelf. You have to order it. Since you need the bench space you put the disassembled piece on a storage shelf, and put all the chassis hardware in the case. Then you order the chip and go to work on other things. About a week later the replacement chip arrives. You are working on other things so your associate gets the task of replacing the chip and reassembling the computer. He does so. When you look over the computer before returning it, you find two screws and a metal shield left over. The computer exercises out ok, but you are not comfortable and confident with the reassembly. If you are like me you pull the unit apart again and install the shield and two screws. After that you feel confident again.

Step-by-step disassembly and reassembly instructions along with the exploded view are very handy and save a lot of head scratching even among the most experienced technicians. If you are working with the same make and model continually, the instructions become second nature as you memorize them from the constant repetition. When you are operating on all different makes and models though, the best way to go is with as much service information and factory notes as possible. Most of the time you'll hardly do more than glance at them, but those glances are enough to steer you down the correct repair path.

Chapter 3

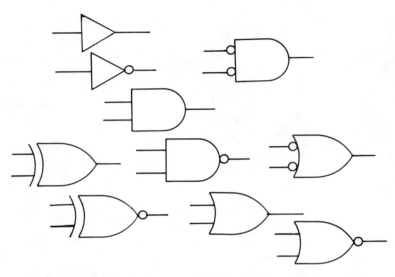

The Chip Location Guide

The first piece of service information a TV repairman consults is the *location guide* that is pasted inside the case of every TV (Fig. 3-1). The guide, as all techs know, shows the location, name, and generic number of all tubes and transistors. The majority of fixes happen as the servicer tests and replaces suspect parts as indicated with the help of the guide. The guide has been likened to a roadmap. A manufacturer would not dare to leave the location guide out of the TV package he produces.

Home computer manufacturers, on the other hand, seem to place little emphasis, on a location guide. Of all the microcomputers I've examined, there hasn't been a sign of a location guide inside any of the cases.

SERVICE NOTE PRINTS

While there doesn't seem to be any location guides anywhere inside the computer casing, the location information is available. First of all, most of the components are labeled clearly right on the print board itself. For example, the drawing of the microcomputer on a board shows a lot of information (Fig. 3-2). All of the chips are identified with manufacturer part and generic numbers. The resistors, capacitors, etc. are also easily identified as to their value and manufacturer. There is all the needed information on the print board. However, the facts are in a jumble and a lot of valuable servicing time will be lost as you try to trace the signal from chip to chip.

Another place you'll find roadmap type information is in the manufacturer's service note package. One of the staples in the notes is a detailed drawing of the print board. The servicing purpose of these drawings is to enable you to relate the symbols on the schematic to the actual components on the print board during signal tracing. There are usually at least two drawings (Fig. 3-3, Fig. 3-4). One showing the topside of the board with most of the components, and another displaying the bottomside with most of the copper traces. Here again the information is all there but in a complex mix of chips, capacitors, resistors, and so on. For signal tracings, voltage and scope readings, short and open tests, the notes are valuable. For visual peeks

Fig. 3-1. The first move a TV repairman does is consult a component location guide that is pasted inside the case of every TV.

and chip changing though, a lot of servicing time is lost as you wend your way through the maze.

A large percentage of repairs are completed quickly by chip changing and visual inspection of traces. The chip checkout and thorough looks would

go much faster if you had a *chip location guide* in addition to the other more complete service notes.

DRAWING YOUR OWN GUIDE

Since the chip guide is not supplied, you can draw your own. It's not really time consuming if you are prepared to draw one. All you need are the simple school supplies, a pencil, ruler, and some graph paper. It shouldn't take more than five minutes. You'll easily save more than that on every repair as you don't have to stumble through a complex drawing when the repair only requires knowing where the chips are. In addition, if the repair does need more servicing information that the chip guide provides, you'll already be briefed by doing the chip guide first and will be able to read the complicated drawing easier.

Once you are embarked on a repair and you have the computer case off, reach for your pencil and graph paper. The first step to draw the guide is

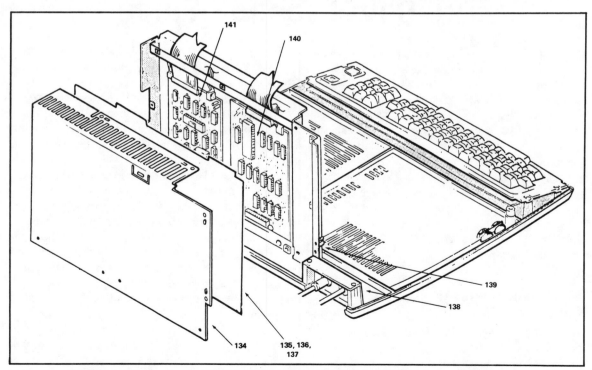

Fig. 3-2. In the service notes a specially prepared photo or drawing provides a lot of location information (courtesy of Radio Shack, a division of Tandy Corporation).

to draw coordinates (Fig. 3-5). All that means is number the blocks on the paper. On my illustration I have the numbers *across* the top of the page going from 0 to 50. The numbers *down* the left side of the page go from 0 to 40. That way every block on the page has a location. For example, you can locate every chip on your page quickly. Suppose you need to find the SAM chip U10. All you have to do is to look at the 40-pin LSI chart. It shows SAM at 36 ACROSS and 30 DOWN. A glance reveals SAM on the paper. From the paper to the actual chip is then only a quick look.

Once you have your coordinates laid out, you can draw in the chips. The sketch need not be exact. The shape of the chips do not have to be proportional rectangles. The location of each chip does not need to be on their precise coordinate. You do not have to put the manufacturer's part number on a chip. You do not even have to put as much information on your guide as I've shown, in order for the guide to save you lots of time.

I usually draw the following information into the guides I sketch. For instance, the illustration (Fig. 3-6) is my location guide for a TRS-80 Color Computer. There are 29 chips. Five of them are 40 Pin Packages. The 40 pin jobs require special attention. I make a little chart for them at the top of the paper. The chart quickly locates any of them as it has across and down for each chip. The chips are identified both by their function and schematic number. For example, the VDG has a schematic number U7.

After I complete the chart I draw the 40 pin chips on the paper. In this case then the CPU, VDG, both PIAs and SAM are placed on the guide paper. The rest of the chips are then sketched in by using the 40-Pin Packages as reference. I usually rough them in the following: the RAMs, ROMs, buffers, latches, decoders, any flip-flops, gates, comparators, separators, op-amps, video circuits, any modulator, and finally power supply chips like regulators.

I'm sure it took you longer to read the last few paragraphs than it will take you to draw up a rough location guide. The first time you encounter a specific microcomputer you will find it useful to sketch out a location guide for yourself. Once you do one though, you can keep it with your service notes for that particular make and model. If you feel magnaminous you can make a copy of your sketch and paste it inside the case to aid the next servicer who has to repair the same computer.

The amount of information required for the quick checks is small. You can assemble these valuable tidbits on the guide you can draw in a few minutes. They are the location of the chips on the board, the function of each chip, the parts list symbol number as designated on the schematic (U7 is the VDG), and the dc voltages in the power supply. With only this tiny bit of information you can complete a lot of repairs, on the order of a TV repairman, using a tube and transistor guide.

THE SOCKET CONTROVERSY

Vacuum tubes, for the most part, use tube sockets to operate. There are a few applications like high voltage rectification that sometimes have the tubes wired into place, but these uses are few and far between. As a direct result of the widespread use of tube sockets, and the fact that most TV troubles were caused by bad tubes, a large percentage of TV repairs could be performed by any mechanically inclined person. Technical training was not required to locate and change a dead tube.

When transistors appeared on the servicing scene, they arrived both ways. Some manufacturers used a lot of transistor sockets while others soldered the solid-state devices in place. There is a good argument for both methods. For the soldered in types, designers saw transistors do not fail as often as tubes. In addition, when a transistor is soldered in place it is much more reliable than if its skinny and flexible leads are poked into a socket. Tubes were especially designed to operate in sockets. Transistors were designed with leads like capacitors and resistors. Would you push a capacitor into a socket?

On the other hand, during servicing, if transistors are wired in, a repair hardship occurs. First of all, the luxury of the quick direct replacement transistor test is not available. If a transistor is a suspect it must be tested in-circuit or desoldered

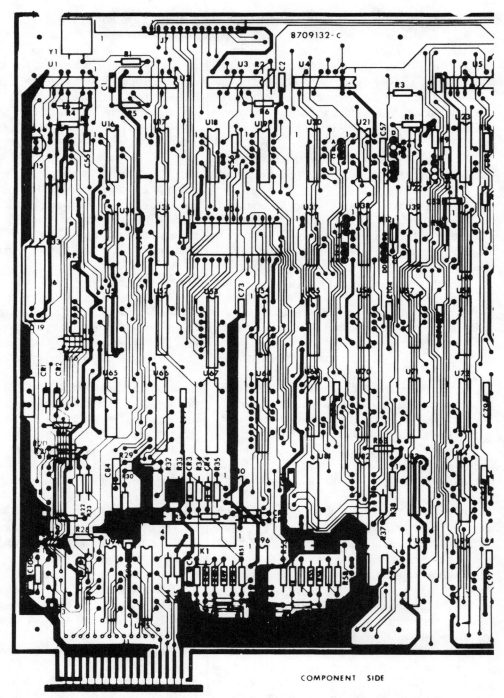

COMPONENT SIDE

Fig. 3-3. Most print boards come with a detailed sketch of the component side of the board (courtesy of Radio Shack, a division of Tandy Corporation).

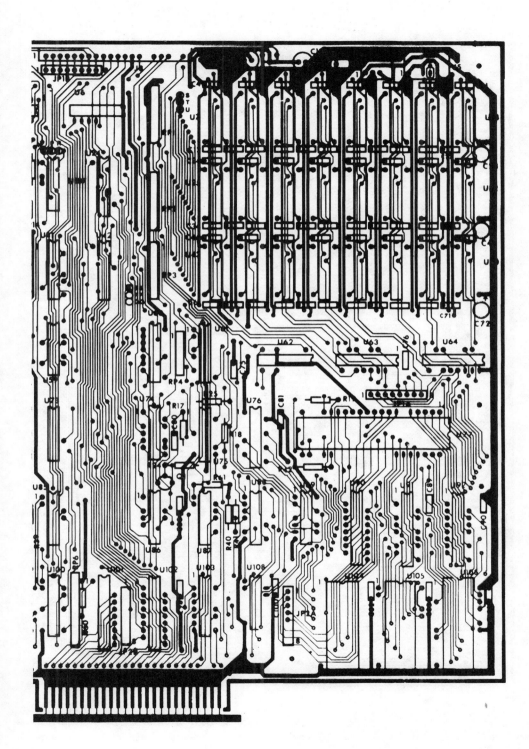

31

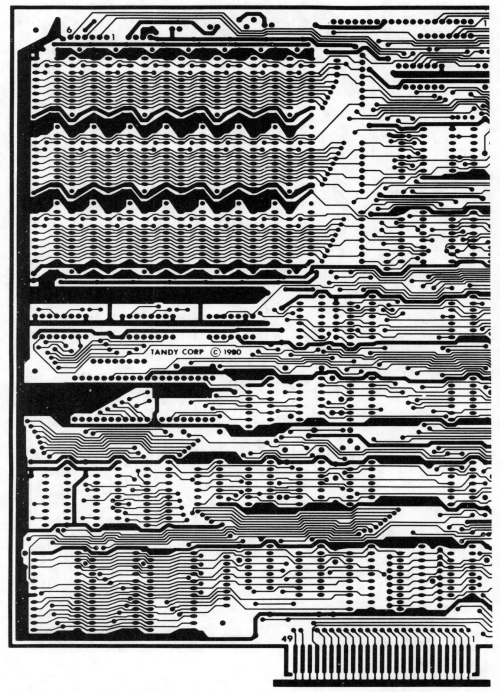

Fig. 3-4. There is also a detailed sketch of the copper etched wiring on the bottom of the board (courtesy of Radio Shack, a division of Tandy Corporation).

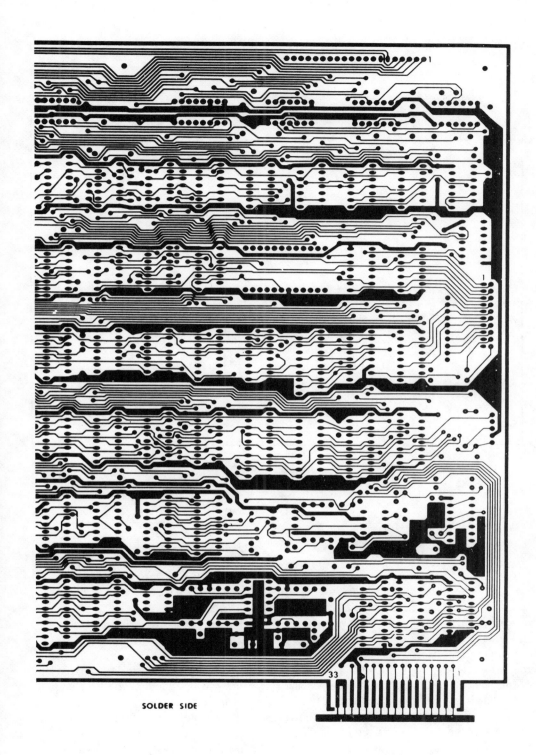

SOLDER SIDE

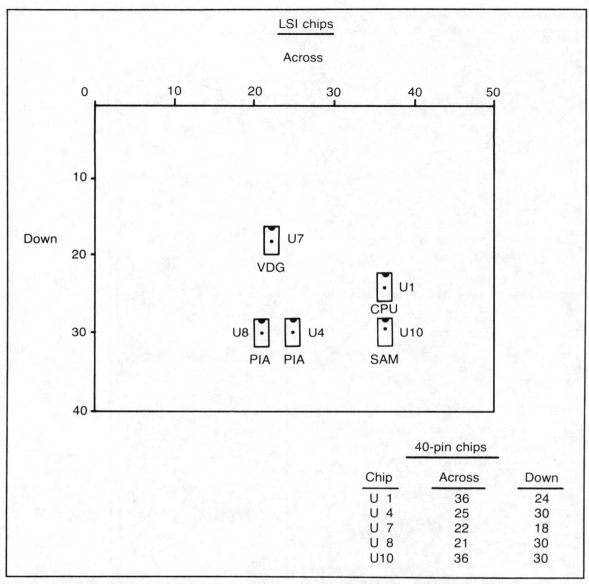

Fig. 3-5. When preparing your own location guide start with a set of coordinates and then locate the large chips.

with a new one resoldered in place. Wholesale replacement, which often effects a repair, is out. To add to the problem, a lot of soldering can induce additional troubles which complicates an already poor situation.

Secondly, a transistor socket can be used as a convenient test point. Even though the transistor is fine, by removing it, the circuit is opened up and all types of signal injection, signal tracing, voltage and resistance tests can be made. If the transistor is wired in, the same tests can be made, but only after the transistor is desoldered with all its attendant difficulties.

Chips, from a socket point of view, appear

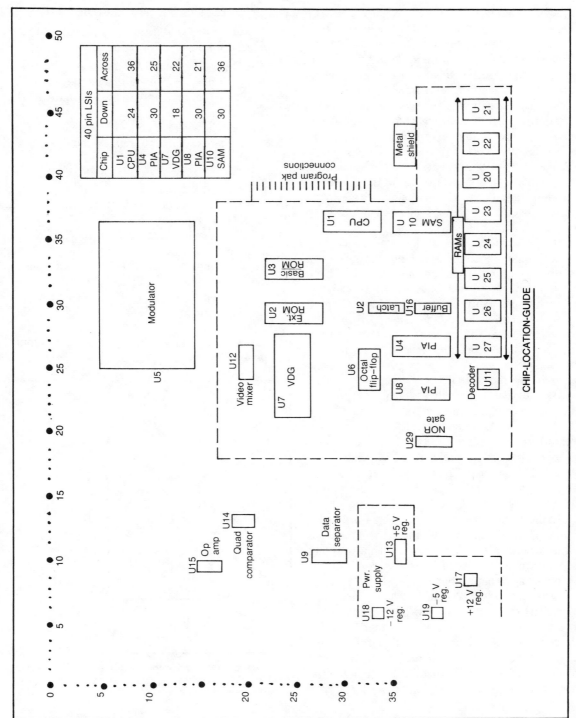

40 pin LSIs		
Chip	Down	Across
U1 CPU	24	36
U4 PIA	30	25
U7 VDG	18	22
U8 PIA	30	21
U10 SAM	30	36

CHIP-LOCATION-GUIDE

Fig. 3-6. This is the location guide that I drew for use on my own computer.

somewhere between tubes and transistors. The chips are tiny and not as easy to handle as a tube. However, they have sturdy little feet, and can be pulled and inserted into little sockets freely if you use the proper techniques. The chip package is designed with a chip socket in mind. The reliability of a chip in a socket is almost as good as a chip that is wired onto a print board. If a manufacturer produces a microcomputer with the large chips soldered into place, rather than socketed, it's because he wants to save the price of the socket. He can't be blamed, because in production the savings of the cost of 10 or 20 chips can come to a lot of money, and we are all anxious to see the price of home computers keep falling.

The rule of thumb among designers concerning chip sockets has been the following. During design and breadboarding, while technicians were hand wiring a new board, sockets are used exclusively. The tech is constantly removing and installing all the components, including the chips, as the design progresses. Once the project is finished and the board goes into production, the sockets are removed, except for maybe the 40 pin packages, and the board has mostly soldered in chips.

As a servicer I naturally would like to enjoy the benefits the design breadboarder has with a board full of sockets. As a computer user I am also interested in buying my equipment at the lowest possible price. The manufacturers are trying to find some middle ground. They would like to satisfy everyone. As a result you'll find some computers with a lot of sockets and others with very few.

Experience is showing that chips are quite rugged. They do not fail with the same consistencies as tubes or even transistors. This tends to lessen the need for sockets. However, if a 40- or 24-pin package, that is soldered in, should fail, you have a considerable replacement job on your hands. In addition the testing of the chip in-circuit is quite a chore too. The socket question is knotty, but as time goes by, and millions upon millions of computers are installed in homes, I would say more and more chip sockets will be used to make servicing easier, and consumer repair bills tolerable.

THE IMPORTANT PARTS OF THE GUIDE

The location guide, that you prepare, should contain the following information.

☐ The location of all the chips. If a chip has a dot or notch on one end, mark that on the guide. Pin 1 will be found immediately to the left of the marking (Fig. 3-7).

☐ The location of any metal shields. This could serve as a reminder to replace the shield after the repair.

☐ The location of any and all plugs, adapters, and other interface circuits.

☐ The location of any extra circuits such as a TV modulator (Fig. 3-8).

☐ A special marking, to show which chips are socketed and which are not.

☐ It's handy to show the location of transistors and the position of their collectors.

☐ The location of the off-on and reset buttons.

☐ The function of each chip and its symbol part number.

☐ A dotted line around the power supply components.

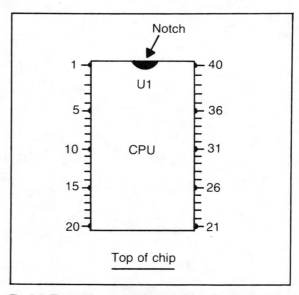

Fig. 3-7. The notch or dot on the end of the chip is the keyway indicator. The pin numbers are counted starting with 1 on the immediate left of the notch.

☐ The voltages of the different power supply components (Fig. 3-9).

☐ A small chart of the 40-pin LSI's.

It is not mandatory that you install all the above information. A more abbreviated version as described earlier in the chapter will be almost as useful. If you do draw up this one though, you'll find it will be all the information you'll need for most jobs. In addition, should you have to go to the schematic for more information, the schematic symbols will appear to be much easier to read since you learned the physical layout so thoroughly as you drew your location guide. Hopefully manufacturers will begin to provide location guides for computers like ones in TVs.

USING THE GUIDE FOR REPLACEMENTS

Let's see how the guide works on a typical easy repair. Suppose you want to repair a home computer that has an intermittent program problem. It works fine on some parts of a large program but produces garbage on other sections of the program. Since it is operating somewhat an exercise program could be useful. You load in the exerciser.

Since the symptom of trouble is only happening on one part of the program indicates the CPU and ROMs are probably good. The problem program is spread all through the RAMs. If one of the RAMs is dead it could cause this particular trouble. You decide to exercise the RAMs as your first test.

The RAM test counts the amounts of RAM and runs a test on every byte. You get the test going and watch the TV screen. There is 16K of RAM in the unit under test. The exerciser takes about three minutes to test all the RAM. A display of vertical stripes starts changing colors on the screen. Then

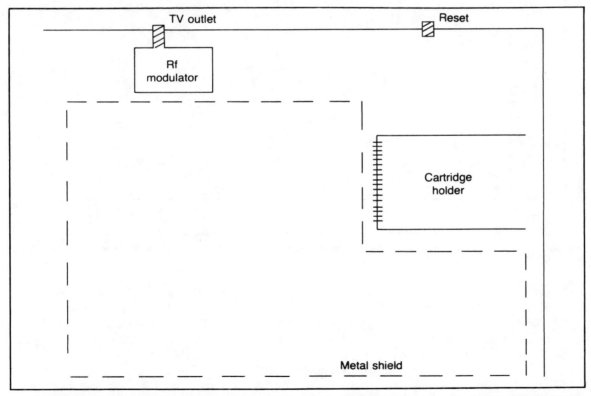

Fig. 3-8. The location of extra circuits in the computer and plugs and adapters, is valuable information during troubleshooting.

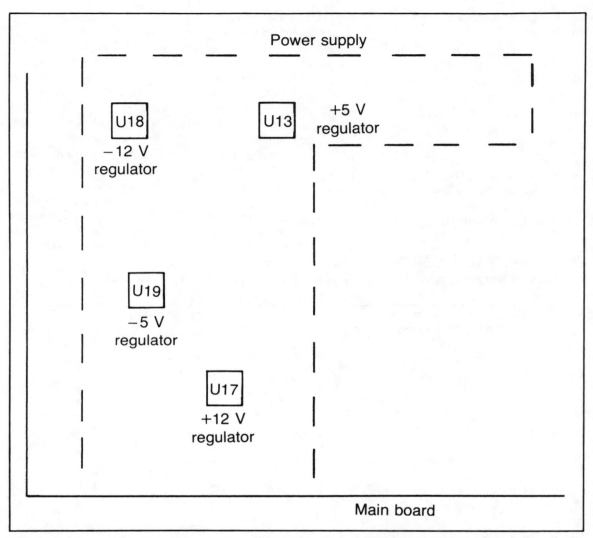

Fig. 3-9. The power supply voltages are among the most tested ones. If a record of them is on the guide, the schematic needn't be consulted.

suddenly the stripes blink and disappear. Some text appears on the TV face. It reads RAM ERROR . . . REPLACE CHIP U24.

Sounds great! But where is U24? There are a lot of chips on the board. Also some of the chips are socketed and others are not. With the location guide U24 is located quickly. It's under a metal shield the fifth chip from the bottom right of the board. Also it does not have a socket. It must be desoldered.

The job turns out to be a soldering chore with extra grounding care needed since you are replacing an MOS chip. All goes well however. The guide was the only service notes you needed. A good guide will provide this type of valuable aid most of the time upstaging the schematic diagram again and again.

Chapter 4

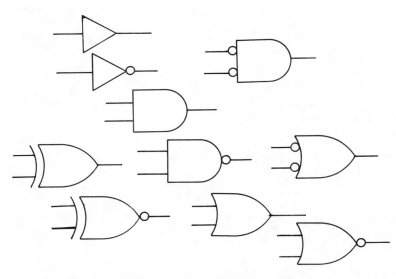

The Main LSI Chips

If you examine the chips on the board carefully you'll see about five in 40-pin packages. All the main functions of the computing are taken care of in these chips. When you see a 40-pin chip you can be quite sure that it contains at least a thousand individual circuits in microscopic form. There is no way you can test these individual circuits easily and even if you could, there would not be any way to repair or replace the defect. To gain service access to the minute circuits you have to analyze the pin voltages and waveshapes. The results of your service moves then indicate whether the chip is good or bad. If all tests work out well then the chip is left in place. When the chip is deemed defective then it must be replaced. There is no middle ground, and those of you who would like to know just what actually failed, will not obtain these facts easily. The chip is a true "black box" and only the original designer and manufacturer knows what happens down to the last detail.

As a matter of fact, to service a home-type computer, it is not a necessity to learn all there is concerning computers. You do not need to know the detailed construction secrets of a large scale integrated chip. It is not necessary for you to be a computer programmer. The servicing skills that are used to repair electronic circuits are the ones that are used to troubleshoot computer circuits. Let's take an overview of the main LSI chips with servicing in mind.

TYPICAL LSIs

Four 40-pin LSIs you will encounter often are known by the initials CPU, PIA, VDG, and SAM. Another common chip in a 24-pin package is called the ACIA (Fig. 4-1). These acronyms stand for *Central Processor Unit, Peripheral Interface Adapter, Video Display Generator, Synchronous Address Multiplexer,* and *Asynchronous Communications Interface Adapter.* Those definitions are a mouthful but as time goes by the mystery of their meanings will clear up. These chips plus some RAM, ROM, and a power supply make up a complete computer that will provide all the computing power a user would need. The only things left to do a computing job is some input-output equipment like a CRT

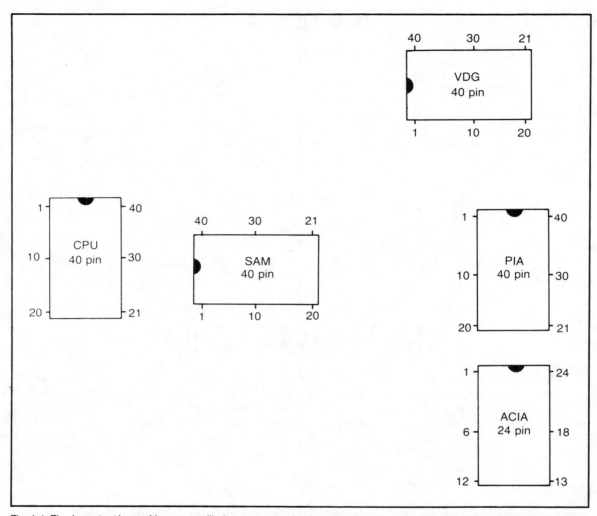

Fig. 4-1. Five important large chips you are likely to encounter in a home computer are the CPU, PIA, VDG, SAM, and the ACIA.

display, cassette recorder, etc. and some interfacing (Fig. 4-2).

THE CPU

The heart of the computer is the CPU. The CPU connects to all of the rest of the chips. It has arteries called address lines (Fig. 4-3), data lines (Fig. 4-4), and control lines, (Fig. 4-5). The CPU really doesn't do that much, but what it does do is the most important part of the computing. Without a CPU a computer is not a computer. You can probably design a computer and leave out any of the other

chips. You cannot leave out the CPU and still have a computer. I'll describe what the CPU, in general, does. It might not have much meaning to you at this stage, but its duties will become clearer as you go.

The CPU, first of all, has the duty to provide and request data. During operation the computer processes data. The data is held in places like ROM, RAM, or cassette tape. The CPU will send a message to one of these places and request the data (Fig. 4-6). The data is sent back to the CPU on the data lines. The CPU then works on the data and sends it back via the same data lines to one of those storage places mentioned. How does the CPU alert a storage place that it wants the data?

The message the CPU sends is an address. The address goes out on the address lines (Fig. 4-7). The way the addressing happens is quite like telephoning. If you want to call someone you dial their number on the telephone. Everyone in the telephone book has a different telephone number. You get your party by dialing their individual number. The telephone lines are like the address lines that connect the CPU to the rest of the computer. The CPU is connected to every major section of the computer. The typical CPU can address over 65,000 individual addresses in the home computer.

Therefore, when the CPU needs data, it outputs an address on the address bus line. Like a dialed telephone number the address goes right to the correct storage place in the computer and opens up that address. As soon as the storage spot opens up the data stored at that address is outputted to the data lines and travels to the CPU. In the CPU the data is then worked upon.

The CPU is capable of doing some limited mathematical and logical manipulating of the data. The nature of that work is covered in greater detail in the chapter on CPUs.

Once the CPU is finished with the data it is ready to send it back to a storage place. It opens up a storage spot by outputting an address. Then the CPU outputs the data. The data travels the data bus lines, arrives at the correct address and gets stored.

The above is basically what the CPU does as it

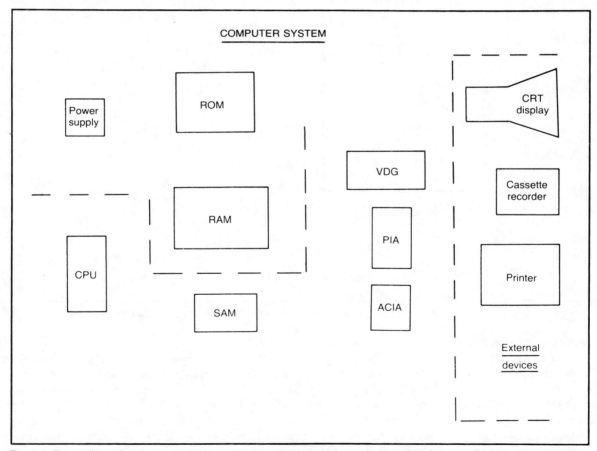

Fig. 4-2. The addition of a power supply, some RAM and ROM, and the external devices is a complete computer system.

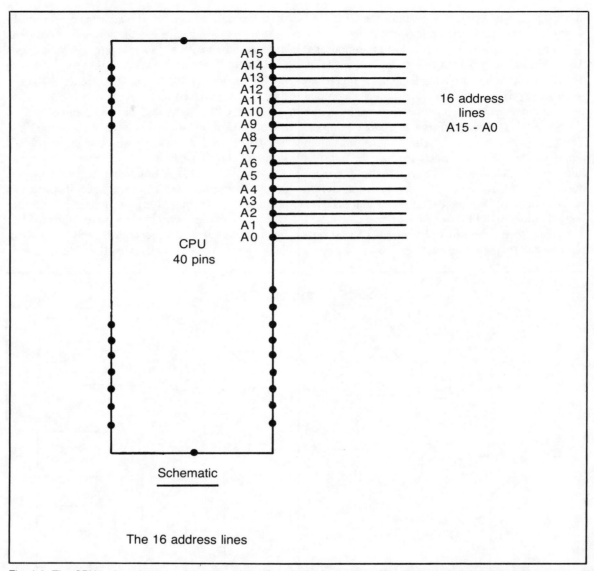

CPU
40 pins

Schematic

16 address
lines
A15 - A0

The 16 address lines

Fig. 4-3. The CPU is the originator of the 16 address lines in the home computer. They are labeled A15 through A0.

works through a program. In computerese this is known as the "fetch and execute" cycle (Fig. 4-8). When the cycle breaks down the computer requires the repairman's services. While it is necessary for you as the repairman to understand the hardware's location and general operation to apply the fix, the ability to write a program has little use here.

THE PIA

Another prominent 40-pin package is the PIA. It has the duty of connecting, or as it's called, interfacing, the CPU with all the external devices (Fig. 4-9). These include the keyboard and joysticks which are input only units, the cassette which is an input-output device and the printer, video and audio

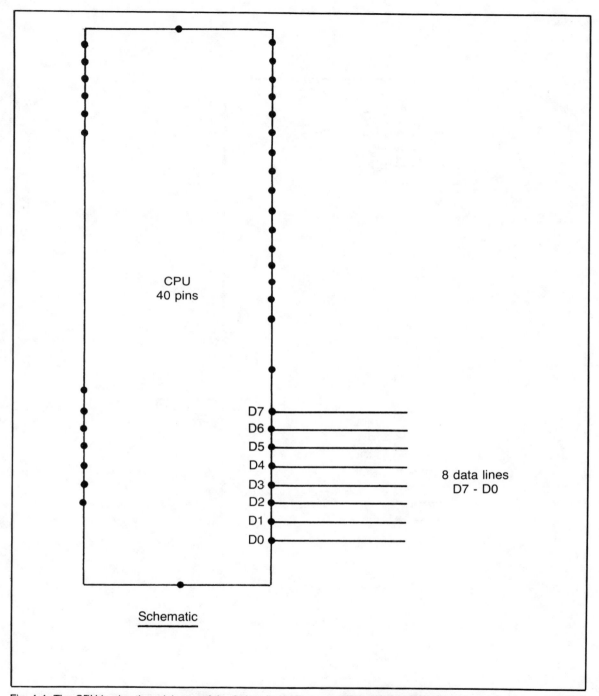

CPU
40 pins

D7
D6
D5
D4
D3
D2
D1
D0

8 data lines
D7 - D0

Schematic

Fig. 4-4. The CPU is also the originator of the 8 data lines. They are labeled D7 through D0.

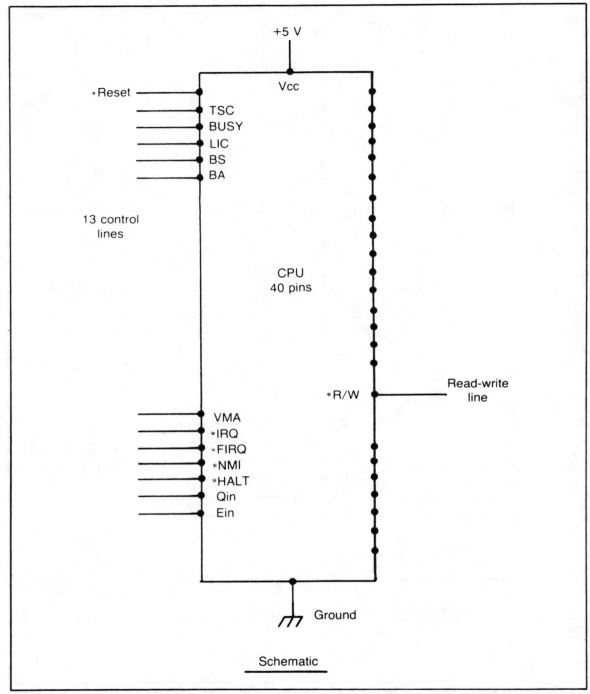

Fig. 4-5. The third set of lines in the CPU are called control lines. There are 13 of them in this CPU and they have a lot of different names.

circuits, which are output only pieces of gear. There is often more than one PIA in a home computer. The PIAs are connected to the CPU through the same data lines that go to all the rest of the chips in the computer. The PIAs have their own addresses. When the CPU desires access to a PIA it outputs the PIA's address and is immediately connected.

One typical use of a PIA is to interface a keyboard to the data lines of the computer (Fig. 4-10). A PIA has two data buses attached to the keyboard. One of the data buses is connected to the rows of keys. The *rows* are the keys arranged one on top of another. In the illustration there are seven rows. The other data bus is connected to the col-

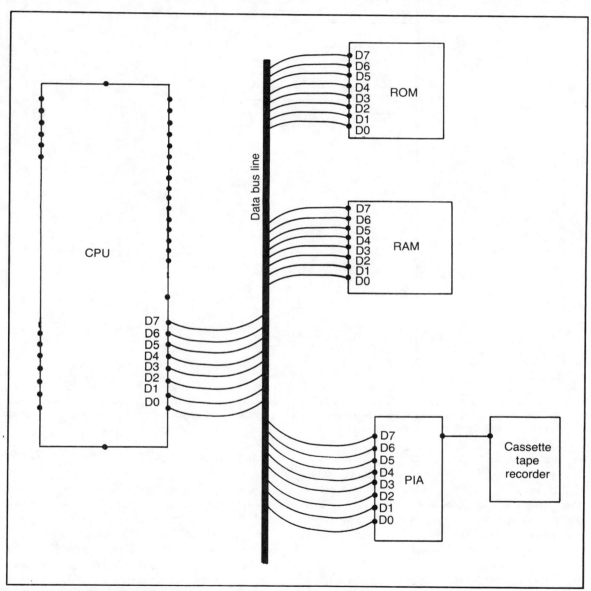

Fig. 4-6. The data bus is able to send data to and from all the data storage places.

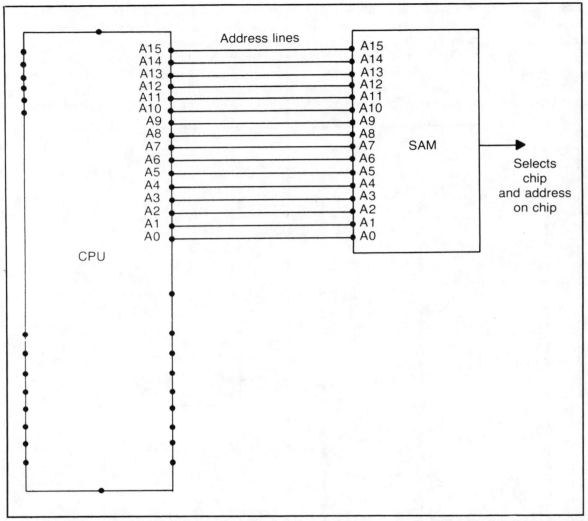

Fig. 4-7. The address lines from the CPU can dial up any data storage place in the computer. It puts out an address that selects a particular chip and the address of the data on the chip.

umns of keys. The *columns* are the keys arranged side-by-side. The illustration shows eight columns.

When you hit a key, the effort presses a switch at an intersection of a row and a column. For example, if you strike Q, you have switched on the intersection of row 3 and column 2. The information that you struck row 3 enters one data bus and the fact that you simultaneously struck column 2 enters the other data bus. This information is combined in the PIA and the letter Q is sent to the CPU for process

over the computer's main data bus. This PIA is doing input only duty.

A second PIA in the computer could perform the output duties (Fig. 4-11). For instance, its two data buses could be connected to the audio and video outputs. One of the data buses could be attached to an audio circuit while the other PIA data bus is connected to an LSI called the video display generator. When audio arrives on the computer's main data bus, at the PIA's input, it is directed

46

inside the PIA to the PIA's audio output bus. From there the audio continues on till it is heard from the speaker. If a video signal like the Q mentioned before should arrive on the main data bus, the PIA sends it to the VDG, from where the Q proceeds till it is displayed on the TV screen.

The PIAs are capable of handling a number of inputs and outputs. For instance, the PIA that is processing the keyboard signals can also handle the joysticks' switches. The keyboard and joysticks are both input only devices. In addition, the keyboard and the joysticks are not used at the same time. Also both are open circuits when not in use. As a result the keyboard and the joysticks can be connected

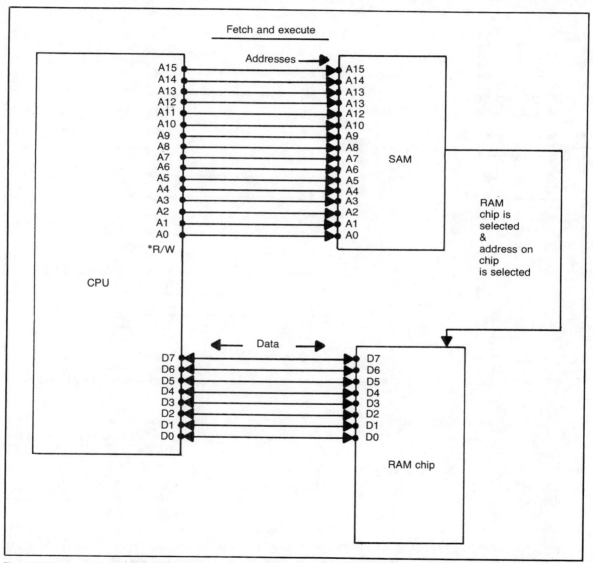

Fig. 4-8. When a program instruction arrives at the CPU, it can tell the CPU to fetch some data. The CPU outputs an address where the data is located. The addressing opens the address and the data then goes into the data bus. The data bus connects the data back to the CPU. The CPU then works on the data. This procedure is called "fetch and execute."

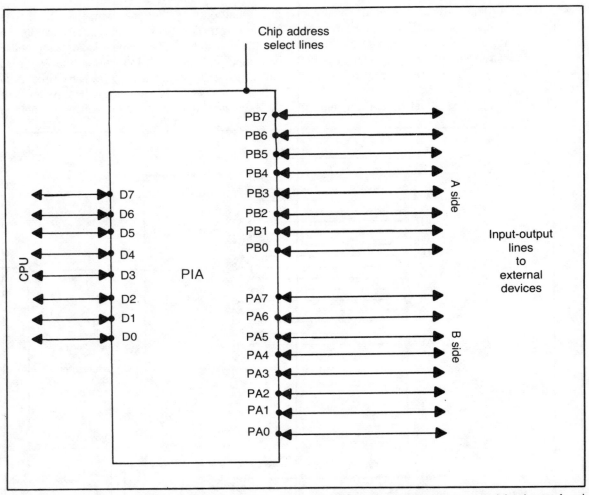

Fig. 4-9. The PIA is connected to the CPU via the data bus. It connects to external devices with two external data buses, A and B.

together to the same PIA pin numbers without interfering with each other.

On the output PIA, in addition to handling the audio and video, the PIA can accommodate other input-output lines too. This will be discussed in greater detail in the chapter on PIAs.

THE VDG

The video display generator type chip is the place where the composite TV signal that appears on the TV screen has all its various signals assembled together. The inputs to the chip are the following. When the computer is capable of displaying color, a 3.58 MHz color TV signal is applied from the clock circuit. A horizontal sync pulse and a vertical sync pulse is injected from the SAM chip. Video is sent over from the RAM (Fig. 4-12).

From a PIA a set of lines bring in control signals that set the mode. What is a VDG mode? In the VDG are a lot of circuits that produce video outputs to be placed in the composite TV signal for display. The video outputs are specified by the individual VDG circuits. Some of the VDG circuits cause the display to be broken up into little areas to show alphanumerics (Figs. 4-13 and 4-14). These are the characters that are on the keys of the keyboard. When these character blocks are shown the VDG is said to be producing the *alphanumeric display mode.*

Other VDG circuits produce a *semigraphic mode.* Besides the numbers and letters, most home computers can show various symbols like little checkerboard displays in the same picture tube areas a character block usually occupies. These are called graphic characters. There easily can be 60 different graphic characters and crude drawings or various graphs and charts can be made with these characters. When the VDG is set to produce graphic

characters it is said to be in one of its semigraphic modes.

The third major mode type a VDG is able to produce, is called *full graphics.* Instead of being confined to one of the areas the size of a character block to display a graphic, the entire TV screen is used. The full graphic mode enables a programmer to be able to turn every picture element on the TV screen off and on. That way a picture could be electronically drawn on the screen. The VDG is able to arrange a lot of these graphic modes.

While the input to the VDG is a group of digital signals, the output of the VDG is a group of TV signals, known as analog signals (Fig. 4-15). The

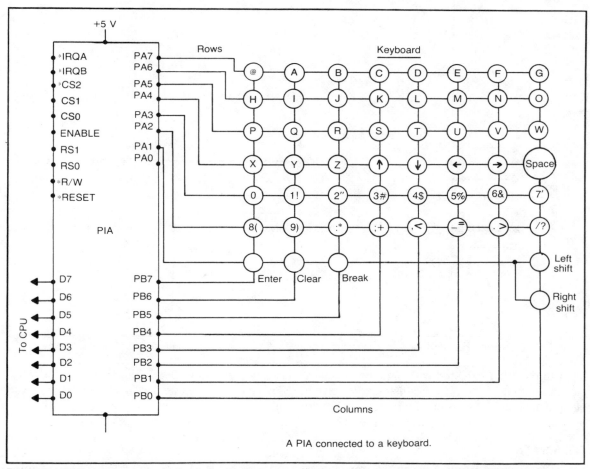

A PIA connected to a keyboard.

Fig. 4-10. A PIA with its two external data buses is able to connect to the keyboard. One bus attaches to keyboard rows and the other to keyboard columns.

49

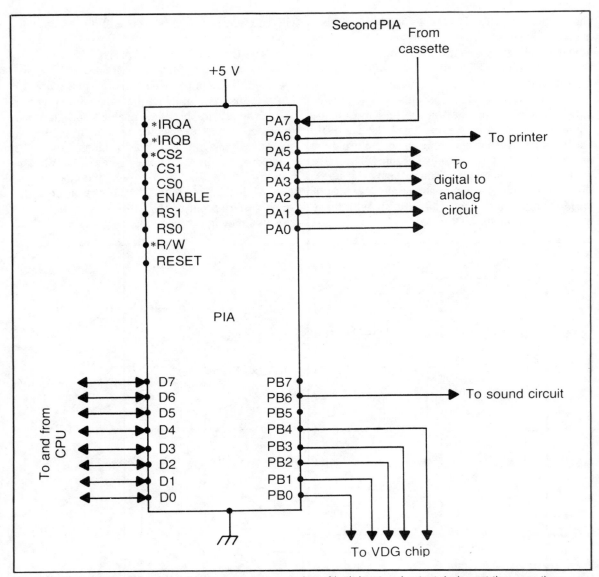

Fig. 4-11. The versatile PIA is also able to connect to a number of both input and output devices at the same time.

input to the VDG is tested with digital techniques and the output of the VDG is tested with analog equipment along the lines of a TV repair. There will be a more detailed discussion in Chapter 17.

THE SAM CHIP

The *synchronous address multiplexer* chip is nicknamed SAM. SAM takes the place of a lot of the circuits that are needed in the output of the CPU. SAM also operates as part of the systems clock. There is a full chapter later on in the book just on SAM (Chapter 15).

SAM is assigned three major duties in the scheme of the computer. All of these duties were performed in separate circuits in early computers. The number one job for SAM is the system clock that originates all of the frequencies needed to run the computer. For instance, in the TRS-80 Color Computer, SAM along with some capacitors, resistors, and a crystal produce a series resonant oscillator circuit that runs at 14.31818 MHz. This is the master clock frequency for the computer. All the various frequencies are derived from the master (Fig. 4-16).

To generate a good color picture a frequency of exactly 3.579554 must be produced. This is ac-complished by 14.31818 divided by 4. The CPU needs two frequencies called E and Q that run at 0.89 MHz and are 90 degrees out of phase with each other. These control frequencies are obtained with 14.31818 divided by 16. The division and phase shifting required is accomplished by internal circuits in the SAM.

The number two job SAM does is called device selection. All this means is SAM chooses some of the devices the CPU wants to communicate with.

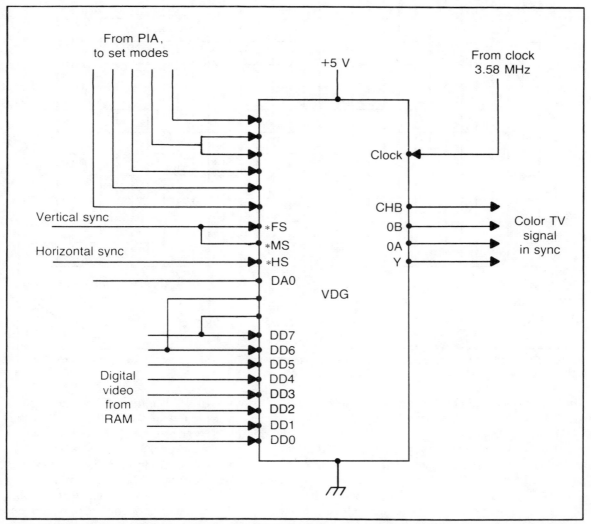

Fig. 4-12. The VDG chip is the place where all signals to be displayed are assembled and readied. The chip inputs are a color oscillator signal, vertical and horizontal sync, video from RAM and controls from a PIA. The outputs are the color TV signals.

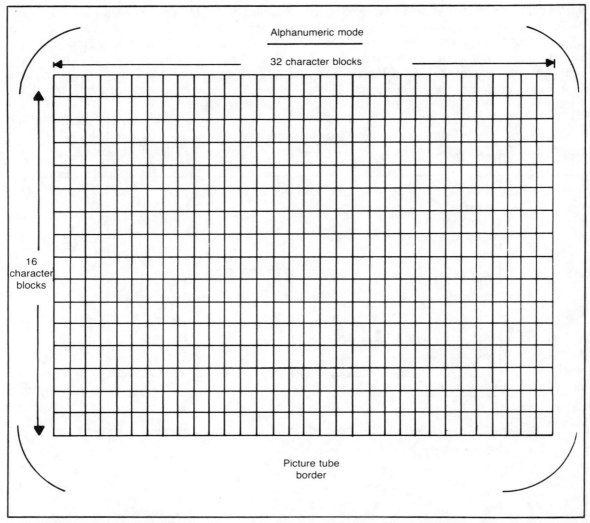

Fig. 4-13. Some of the circuits in the VDG produce an alphanumeric mode. This CRT display can place one character from the keyboard in each character block.

These devices are either the internal registers inside SAM or up to eight external devices like RAM, ROM, or the PIAs.

Let's examine a very important concept at this time that is vital to servicing. Notice in the last paragraph that SAM can select *up to eight* external devices (Fig. 4-17). Why eight? If you look at the sketch there is a chip U11. U11 has three chip select lines coming from SAM. They are S0, S1, and S2. However, there are eight chip select lines exiting

U11, Y0 through Y7. The three SAM lines choose eight chips. How is that done? Well, each of the three SAM lines can be turned off or on. Now if you figure out how many total possible off and on situations three lines can produce you'll see there are eight. That's where the eight comes from.

Inside the U11 there are circuits that turn the eight output lines on or off according to the output from SAM's three lines. To be exact the following can occur. If all three SAM lines are off, then Y0 is

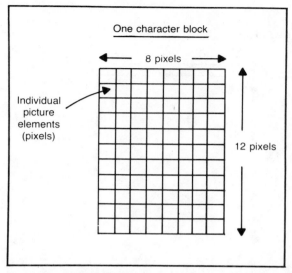

Fig. 4-14. Each character block is made up of 96 picture elements. A special character generator ROM inside the VDG, can turn the pixels off or on to produce the character in the block.

turned on. When S0 goes on by itself Y1 goes on. Should only S1 go on then Y2 is turned on. If S2 only, is on, then Y3 will go on. Figure 4-18 details all eight possibilities. This concept right now might

not appear earthshaking, but learn well how three lines can choose and activate one out of eight lines. It's the basic idea behind a lot of important computer activity that you will encounter as you trace out logic circuits during troubleshooting.

The third big job SAM does is called address multiplexing. Here again is a concept that you cannot learn quickly with a fast explanation. The way to eventually master the idea is to read it over and over again, first from a cursory view and then deeper and deeper as you go. After awhile the idea will be installed in your head. Anyway, SAM performs address multiplexing in this manner. It puts together a final address for the RAM chips. The address desired is composed of the video signals and the CPU address lines. The addresses produced activates the RAMs which in turn activates the VDG and produces the video display. The actual step-by-step details are covered in Chapter 15.

THE ACIA

The *Asynchronous Communications Interface Adapter* is an input-output device, but of a different nature than the PIAs. The PIA is known as a parallel communicator. If you look at the PIA output lines

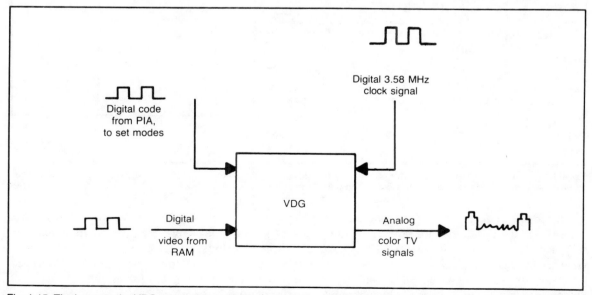

Fig. 4-15. The inputs to the VDG are all digital signals, highs and lows of a square wave. The outputs of the VDG are analog color TV signals that can be viewed on the ordinary TV service scope.

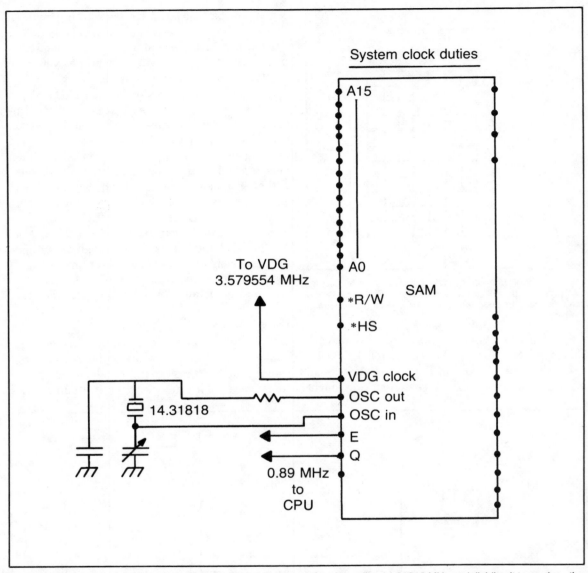

Fig. 4-16. One major job a SAM chip performs is taking the master frequency like 14.31818 MHz and dividing it to produce the other needed frequencies like 3.58 MHz color, and 0.89 MHz system clock.

you'll see two sets of eight lines. Examining one of the sets shows all of them are in parallel. In most microcomputers data is composed of "bytes". A *byte* consists of eight "bits" (Fig. 4-19). Therefore, in order to move data bytes from place to place in the computer, eight data lines each holding one bit, is used. The data moves from place to place on the data bus, which is a set of eight copper traces that run side by side all over the print board. Again look at the PIA (Figs. 4-9 through 4-11). Note the eight line data bus inputs to D0 through D7. Also notice the twin data bus outputs PA0 through PA7 and PB0 through PB7.

The PIA is mostly a parallel device. All eight

bits of a byte enter the PIA via D0-D7 at the same time. All eight bits of a byte can exit the PIA at the same time through PA0-PA7 or PB0-PB7. Inside the computer or to parallel output device this parallel movement of data is ideal. It's fast, efficient and wastes no effort. However, in order to move data that way, there must be eight data lines in a bus. The byte is composed of eight distinct, sepa-

rate bits. Each bit needs its own private line (Fig. 4-20).

Suppose you want to send the data over a telephone. The telephone has only one line, not eight. Or you want to output the data to a printer that can handle one bit at a time, not a whole byte as the data moves in a data bus. A parallel device can't perform the interface for you. It's a *parallel interface*

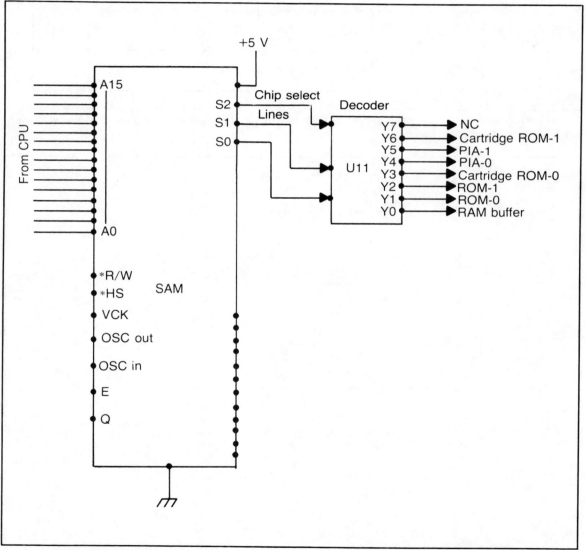

Fig. 14-17. Another important job SAM does is transferring address lines like A15, A14, and A13 to a chip select decoder. The three address lines can choose from among eight chips.

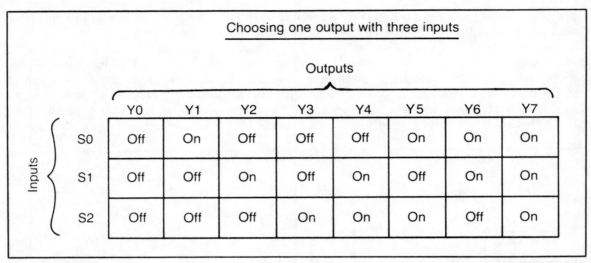

Choosing one output with three inputs

	Y0	Y1	Y2	Y3	Y4	Y5	Y6	Y7
S0	Off	On	Off	Off	Off	On	On	On
S1	Off	Off	On	Off	On	Off	On	On
S2	Off	Off	Off	On	On	On	Off	On

Inputs { (S0, S1, S2) — Outputs { (Y0–Y7)

Fig. 4-18. The three address lines, S0, S1, and S2, can choose from the eight chip select lines, Y0-Y8, by different combinations of offs and ons.

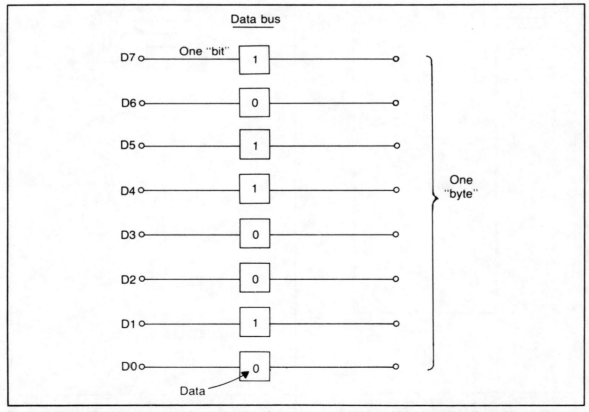

Data bus

D7 — One "bit" — 1
D6 — 0
D5 — 1
D4 — 1
D3 — 0
D2 — 0
D1 — 1
D0 — 0 — Data

One "byte"

Fig. 4-19. The typical home computer has a data bus that can carry eight bits, which is one byte, from chip to chip.

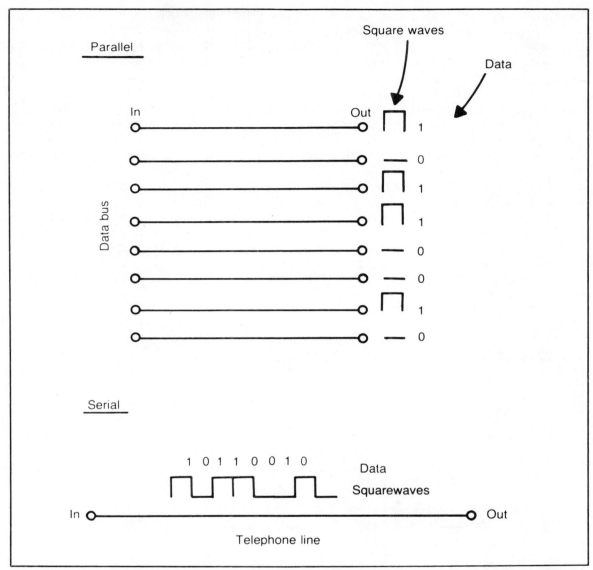

Fig. 4-20. While a data bus has bits riding side by side over eight separate lines, or as it is called in parallel, a telephone line sends the bits over one line, or as it is called in serial fashion.

chip. What you are going to need is a *serial interface.* A serial interface is able to take the eight bits all at once, in parallel fashion, convert the parallel arrangement to serial, and output the bits one at a time (Fig. 4-21).

The ACIA is an input-output chip that is capable of receiving or transmitting a byte of data one bit at a time. For example, the chip can receive eight bits of data from the data bus all at the same time, or as it is called, in parallel fashion. Then the ACIA can take the parallel input and transmit the eight bits to a printer one bit at a time, or as it is called, in serial fashion.

The ACIA can also perform the reverse action.

It can receive eight bits, one at a time, from a device like a telephone modem, and transmit the eight bits, all at the same time, to the data bus in the computer.

How does the ACIA perform these parallel to serial and serial to parallel chores? If you look to Fig. 4-22 there are three byte sized registers shown. The registers are each able to store and move a byte of data. With this capability the registers can do the serial-parallel conversions. First let us examine how the ACIA can output to a line printer.

When a byte of data is sent to the ACIA it enters the lefthand register. All of the eight bits enter D7-D0 of the register at the same time. Once the bits are in the left register, they are then routed to the top register. The top register also has storage circuits labeled D7-D0. The two registers are wired together. The two D7's are connected, the two D6's are connected and so forth. The eight bits are therefore transferred to the top register to the same numbered bit holders.

Once the bits are in the top register, they are shifted out through an exit in D0. The bits shift from D7 to D0 and out through D0. They come out of D0 one at a time or in serial fashion. From there they leave the chip at TX and connect to the line printer.

If a telephone modem is connected to RX, the serial data can be converted to parallel. The serial data enters D7 of the bottom register. The register can also contain one byte. As the bits enter D7 they keep shifting over till the register is full. Once a complete byte has arrived the register is able to move the byte out of the bit holders, so the next byte of data can be stored. All of the bottom register bits are wired to the lefthand register too. The bits are matched up, D7 to D7, D6 to D6 and so on. When the register fills up with the serial data it transfers the data to the lefthand register. The lefthand register then outputs the eight bits to the data bus, all eight at the same time. The result, the data that entered RX in a serial fashion, is transferred to the data bus in parallel.

The 40-pin packages like the CPU, VDG, SAM, PIA, and the 24-pin chip like the ACIA are

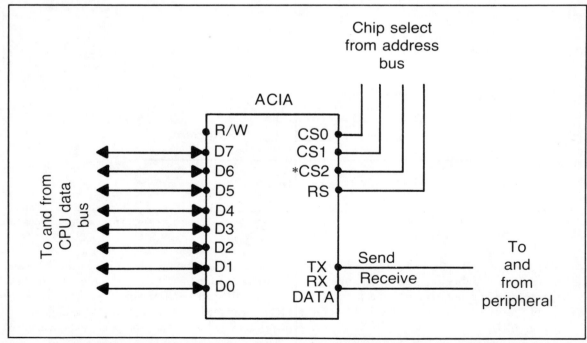

Fig. 4-21. A device like the ACIA is able to transfer data from a one line serial input to an eight line parallel output. Conversely it can transfer data from an eight line input to a one line output.

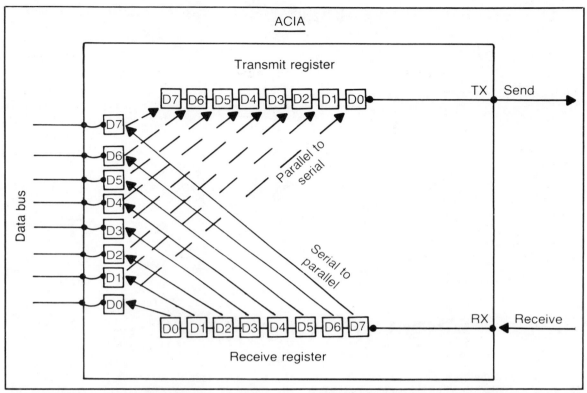

Fig. 4-22. The ACIA performs its job by means of three byte size registers. One register connects to all eight lines in the data bus. The other two registers connect to the one line receive, and the one line send terminals. An internal chip transfer between the registers accomplishes the conversions.

representative of the most complex chips in the computer. During troubleshooting a lot of the activity takes place around them. They have all those pins available to place a logic probe, vom, or scope upon. It is important to learn their theory of operation so you can make input and output tests and then be able to deduce possible reasons why the computer is down. The CPU, VDG, SAM, and PIA all have separate chapters later in the book. The chapters will introduce you to the type of voltages, pulses, and waveshapes you can expect to find on the test points.

Chapter 5

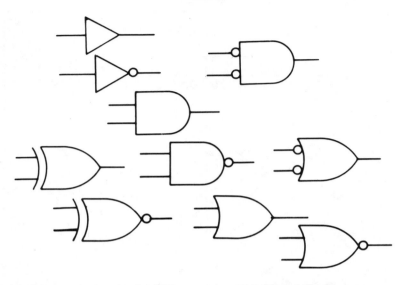

The RAM and ROM Chips

When a home computer is discussed, it is common for it to be described by a "K" number. For instance, someone will say, "It's a 16K type." When a person tells another party that a computer is a 16K, he usually means that the machine has 16,384 bytes of random access memory (RAM). This is the way computers have been described from the very beginning. The early large computers usually were 1K or 2K. Today microcomputers are typically 4K or 16K or more. Let's clear up the computer meaning of K before continuing.

The letter K means thousand. One K would then appear to mean 1000. However, in computerese 1K means 1024 (Fig. 5-1). This is because it is most convenient to work with a computer if all important numbers are powers of 2. The reasons for this will become clearer as you work your way through the understanding of computers. The powers of 2 counted up to near 1000 goes like this: 1, 2, 4, 8, 16, 32, 64, 128, 256, 512, and 1024, which is 1K. If you continue the progression the numbers are 2048 (2K), 4096 (4K), 8192 (8K), 16384 (16K),

32768 (32K), and 65536 (64K). It's a good idea to memorize the numbers up to 64K as you'll be using them during signal tracking and other servicing techniques (Table 5-1).

While computer users call a unit with 16K of RAM a 16K machine, when the sales and advertising people of a manufacturer describes the same computer, they could call it a 24K, 32K, or even a 64K. What are they talking about? In addition to the RAM in a computer there is also another kind of memory called ROM, which stands for read-only memory. There could be 8K, 16K, or more of ROM in a computer. When you add the available ROM to the amount of RAM the larger numbers are arrived upon. Actually, it doesn't matter how a computer K is arrived at as long as you know the difference between the RAM and the ROM. That way you can decide on the relative memory power for yourself.

THE READ-WRITE MEMORY

The term *random-access memory* (RAM) is a holdover description from years ago. It is not really

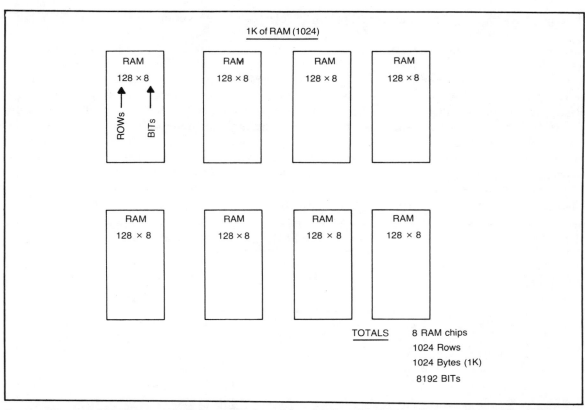

Fig. 5-1. One K of RAM is actually 1,024 bytes of memory. In this RAM chip set there are eight chips, each containing 128 rows of bytes. Since each byte is made up of eight bits, there are 8,192 total bits.

Table 5-1. Each Address Line Can Address Two Addresses.
When the Lines Are Used Together the Number of Bytes That Can Be Addressed Keeps Doubling.

Number of Address Lines	Address Line Numbers	Bytes of Memory They'll Address
1		2
2		4
3		8
4		16
5		32
6		64
7		128
8		256
9		512
10		1024
11		2048
12		4096
13		8192
14		16384
15		32768
16		65536

an accurate description. Most computer people who work with the hardware describe RAMs as read-write memory. Let's pursue this description.

You've all used these kitchen memory boards that you can write on to remember a phone number or item you're out of. The boards have a transparent plastic face. When you lift the plastic the number you wrote disappears and the memory board can be used again for more reminders. The memory board can be used over and over again until it wears out, which can be a long time.

The board has these qualities. It starts out as a blank page. When you want to you can write on it.

Again at your discretion, you can read the information it contains. After you are completely finished with the information, you can lift the plastic sheet and the information is erased. The board is then ready to be used over again.

The RAM, in principle, acts in an analogous way to the kitchen memory board. The RAM chip though is an electronic package. A typical RAM chip comes as a 24- or 16-pin package as shown in Figs. 5-2 and 5-3. The RAMs usually come in a set. For instance the 16K chip set has eight RAM chips (Fig. 5-4). The chips are all identical and form the total RAM of the computer. The set of chips are con-

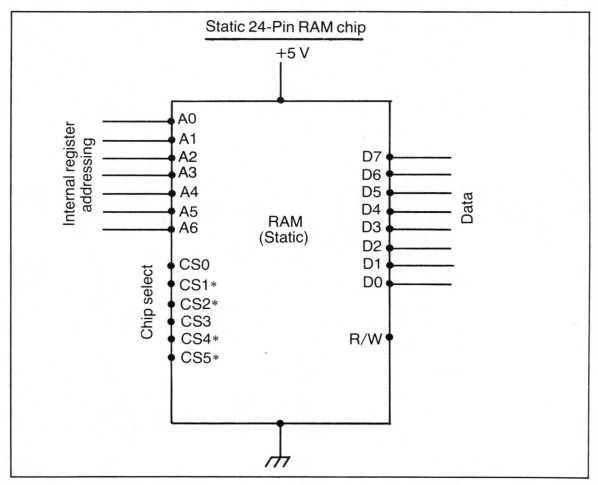

Fig. 5-2. This 24-pin static RAM chip is addressed by the six chip selects and the seven address lines A6-A0. The data bus is connected to D7-D0. The R/W line sets the chip for reading or writing. There is a +5 V to ground power system.

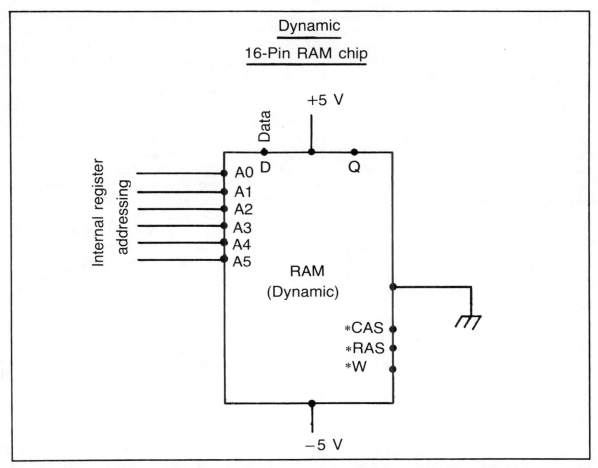

Dynamic

16-Pin RAM chip

+5 V

Data

Internal register addressing

A0 D   Q
A1
A2
A3
A4
A5

RAM
(Dynamic)

*CAS
*RAS
*W

−5 V

Fig. 5-3. This dynamic RAM chip only needs six address lines A5-A0. The chip is selected with the three dynamic inputs *CAS, *RAS and *w. The data uses D and the power is +5 V to ground.

sidered as one if you are going to upgrade the RAM. For example, if you want to change the RAM from a total of 16K to 32K, you must change all the chips. The 16K chips are one type and the 32K chips are an entirely different kind.

The memory part of each chip is called the memory matrix. The matrix is rows upon rows of registers (Fig. 5-5). The registers in the illustration are all identical and are each composed of eight little circuits. Typically the circuits are flip-flops. A flip-flop, which is examined in detail later in the book, has the ability to be conducting at saturation or not to be conducting at all. When it is at saturation it is said to contain a zero. If the flip-flop is not

conducting then it is holding a one. Each of the eight flip-flops can be controlled by one line of the data bus.

If you recall, the lines in the data bus are called D7 through D0. D7 is the MSB (most significant bit) and D0 is the LSB (least significant bit). This pattern follows throughout the computer including all of the RAM (Fig. 5-6). The individual data lines can install 1's and 0's into their respective RAM registers. For instance, if the CPU wants to store eight 1s, it can select a RAM chip, address a register on the chip, connect the eight data lines to the eight flip-flops and output eight 1s. The 1s will make each flip-flop stop conducting. This state of nonconduction of all eight flip-flops gives the register the value of 1111 1111. The value is thus stored in memory and will stay there till it is changed or the computer is turned off. This is how the write part of the read-write is accomplished. It is said that the CPU has written to RAM (Fig. 5-7).

On the other hand, the CPU can also read from RAM. Once the signals 1111 1111 are stored in the register the CPU can obtain that value when it needs to. At the proper instant the CPU can connect the eight data lines to the chip and register that contains the 1111 1111. The value will then output from the register into the data lines. Once in the data lines the value will proceed to the CPU.

The data bus can carry the 1111 1111 to the register in RAM during the write operation, and from the register in RAM during the read operation. The eight lines of the data bus act as a two-way conduit. However, it can only conduct one way at a time. There is a special connection from the CPU that controls the direction the signal can travel. That special line from the CPU connects to every RAM chip. It's called the read/write line and is shown in service notes as R/W (Fig. 5-2). When the R/W line is given a signal of 1 from the CPU it reads data from RAM. If the CPU gives R/W a signal of 0 then the control line R/W allows the CPU to write data to RAM.

It was already mentioned that a typical RAM chip has rows and rows of eight bit registers. Each eight bits makes up one byte. There are some memory chips that have rows and rows of four bit registers. Four bits in computerese is called a nybble. Then there are other larger RAM chips that have 16-bit registers. Sixteen bits in computer parlance is called a word. During repairs you are liable to run into any of them but most of the time you'll be seeing bytes. The memory matrix in the RAM is described by the number of registers × the number of bits. For instance, a small RAM chip could be called 128 × 8. This means there are 128 registers with each register containing eight bits (Fig. 5-5).

If you find yourself checking a 64 × 4 RAM chip, you have a chip with 64 registers, each one able to hold a nybble. Maybe you'll be working on a

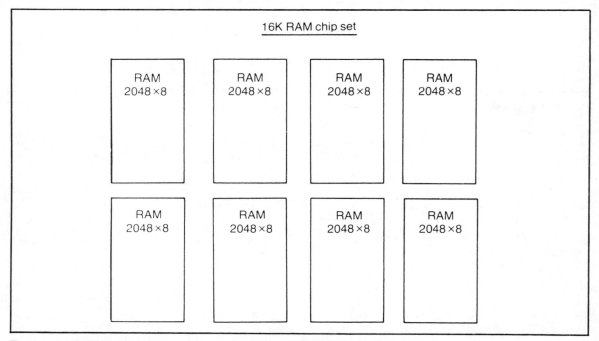

Fig. 5-4. A 16K RAM set could have eight chips, each one containing 2,048 rows of bytes.

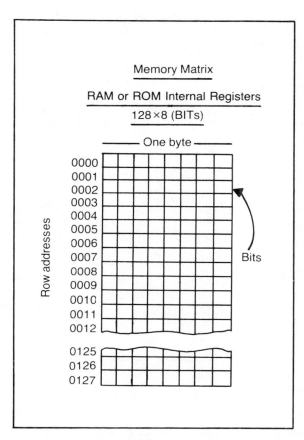

Memory Matrix

RAM or ROM Internal Registers

128×8 (BITs)

─── One byte ───

Row addresses

0000
0001
0002
0003
0004
0005
0006
0007
0008
0009
0010
0011
0012

0125
0126
0127

Bits

Fig. 5-5. Both RAMs and ROMs have a memory matrix that consists of rows and rows of registers. The RAM registers are usually flip-flop circuits that can store a logic state and be changed at will. ROM registers are burned into the chip and cannot have the burned-in state changed.

unit that shows a 1024 × 16 RAM chip. If so you have a large chip that has a memory matrix with 1024 registers and each register capable of holding a full word of 16 bits.

Most home computers use RAM sets that have chips that contain registers that hold a single byte of eight bits. That way, properly addressed, an eight line data bus can make a direct connection upon command to any register in RAM. With the connection the CPU can read and write to any register without complication.

THE READ-ONLY MEMORY

The read-only chips obviously, as their name

indicates, cannot be written to by the CPU. The CPU can only read from the read-only chips contents. If you think of the read-write memory as an erasable kitchen memory board, then the read-only memory can be compared to a printed item like a calendar, cook book, or HOME SWEET HOME picture. These items present prepared information that cannot be erased so the paper can be reused.

The read-only memory is like a RAM chip (Fig. 5-8) except its contents, all those 1s and 0s, are burned into the registers permanently. Instead of using flip-flop circuits that can store a 1 or 0 that can be easily erased or changed like a read-write chip, the read-only registers use diodes, transistors, shorts and opens, that permanently stores information. The read-only memory, known as ROM is manufactured with the 1s and 0s already installed.

In the factory the ROM is built with permanent programs. When you first turn on the computer, the surge of current charges a capacitor. This charging action causes the CPU to make a connection through the data bus with the specific register in ROM. This register and a number of registers following contain a little program that is needed to get the computer operating. Once that program is executing, the computer is ready for action. Also on the ROM chips are lots of other programs burnt in. These programs control the activity in the computer. While the CPU actually does all the work, the ROM tells the CPU what to do and when to do it. The CPU is the heart of the computer but the ROM is the brains.

The ROM is connected to the eight bit data bus just like RAM. The ROM though does not have a R/W line. Since the CPU cannot write data to the ROM, the CPU can only read from the ROM, the R/W line is not needed.

Data between the ROM and the CPU travels in one direction only. The data, the 1s and 0s, the contents of each ROM register, goes from the ROM to the CPU on the data bus lines D7 through D0. You can see those connections on all the RAMs as well as the ROMs. The eight data bus lines are familiar to the servicer. They are eight parallel etch lines on the print board that snake their way from one end of the board to the other. They are a common source of

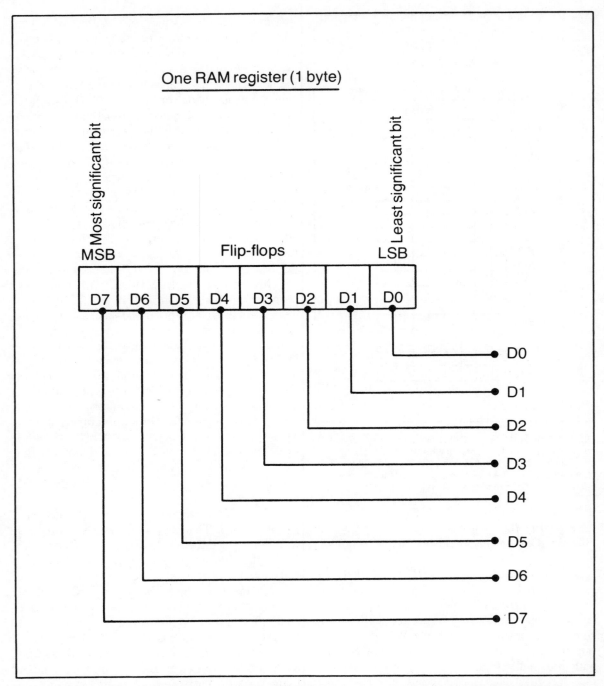

Fig. 5-6. A RAM register is arranged with D7 to the extreme left. D7 here is called the Most Significant Bit (MSB) since its mathematical position makes it the highest number. D0 is in the rightmost position and is the smallest math value and is therefore called the Least Significant Bit (LSB).

shorts and opens as soldering is performed in the close confines of the computer. The data lines convey the contents of RAM memory to and from the CPU, and the contents of ROM to the CPU.

If you look at the sketch of the 24-pin ROM package (Fig. 5-8) D0 through D7 connect at pins 2 through 9. What about the other pins? Pin 12 is +5 V and pin 1 is the ground connection. They power all the components in the chip at the same time. What about the CS and A connections?

The CS pins 10, 11, 13, and 14 are the chip selects. In general, chip selects do exactly as the name implies. There are, in a typical home com-

puter a set of eight RAM chips and two ROM chips making a total of ten. While the CPU is operating it must select one chip after another to get data. The CPU uses the chip select lines to choose a chip. For example, this particular chip could be set up to make a connect with the CPU if it receives the following signals on its chip select lines. Pins 10 and 11 gets 0 and 0. Pins 13 and 14 are sent 1 and 1. When these signals arrive at the CS pins, much like a telephone number is dialed, the ROM is selected and is activated. With four chip select lines, there are 16 possible combinations of 1s and 0s that can be outputted by the CPU as shown in Tables 5-2 and

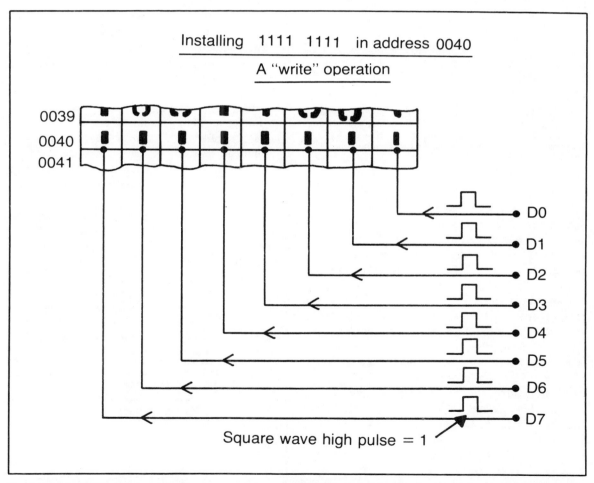

Fig. 5-7. When RAM address 0040 is turned on, and the data bus delivers eight high pulses, the binary number 1111 1111 is installed.

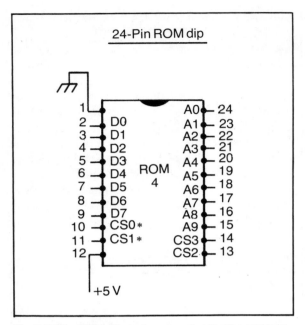

24-Pin ROM dip

```
         A0 — 24
 1       A1 — 23
 2  D0   A2 — 22
 3  D1   A3 — 21
 4  D2   A4 — 20
 5  D3   A5 — 19
 6  D4 ROM A6 — 18
 7  D5  4  A7 — 17
 8  D6   A8 — 16
 9  D7   A9 — 15
10 CS0*  CS3 — 14
11 CS1*  CS2 — 13
12
+5 V
```

Fig. 5-8. The ROM chip looks somewhat like the RAM chip. This 24-pin dual in-line package (DIP), has four chip selects, 10 address lines and the usual eight line access to the data bus. Note there is no R/W line since this is a read only chip. It won't respond if written to.

5-3. Only the one chip combination will activate this chip. However, the four chip CS lines could be hooked to 16 chips and the right combination will select any one of the 16 chips you desire.

The chip select lines are part of the computer's addressing system, that is covered in greater detail in the bus line chapter further on in the book. As you can see in Fig. 5-8, pins 15 through 24 are called A9 through A0. The A stands for address lines. In the home computer there are usually 16 address lines. They also snake their way over the board as etchs and are subject to shorts and opens in exactly the same way the data lines are.

The address lines that are connected to the ROM in this case are ten in number. The ROM has a memory matrix 1024 × 8. The size of the matrix requires only ten address lines (Table 5-1), which is the reason only ten are present. Let's examine the requirements in greater detail.

Suppose the CPU wants to read the data that is contained in the fifth register on the ROM. The first thing the CPU does is select the chip by outputting 0011 to the four chip select lines. This signal activates the ROM. It is ready to do the CPU's bidding.

On the ROM there are 1024 registers, each register containing eight bits. Each register has an address on the ROM. The addresses range from 0 to 1023. This is the same number of addresses as 1 to 1024, except we are counting from zero instead of one. Get used to starting with 0. That is the common method in computers. This gives the fifth register on the ROM an address of 4. Starting at 0 for the first register, the fifth register is 4.(0, 1, 2, 3, 4).

The ten address lines to the chip are capable of making individual connections with every register address from 0 to 1023 on the chip. Each ROM register contains data. When an address line makes contact with a register, the register is activated and outputs its data into the awaiting data bus.

How can ten address lines make contact with 1024 registers? Let's figure it out. Suppose there was only one address line. How many registers could it activate? It could turn on two registers. The line could be +5 V or 0 V. This is the same as calling the line positive or negative, high or low, 1 or 0, or even true or false. All these terminologies are used and they all mean the same thing. The point is, if you had one register that was accessed with a 1 and another by a 0, and both were connected to the same address line, you could turn on one with a 1 and the other with a 0 (Fig. 5-9).

With two address lines you can access four registers. For instance, number 0 register will respond to the signal 00. Number 1 register re-

Table 5-2. The Chip Select (CS) Terminals on Any Chip are Really Address Lines. Typically, They Come from A15, A14, A13, and A12. When a CS Terminal is Labeled CS Only. That Terminal Will Turn on if a High Pulse or 1 Arrives. When the Terminal is * CS It Will Turn on if a Low Pulse or 0 Arrives.

	Chip Select Code	
Name	Turns On Pin	Does Not Turn On Pin
CS	High-1	Low-0
*CS	Low-0	High-1

**Table 5-3. With Four Chip Selects on a Chip. 16 Different Combinations of A15-A12
Addresses Can Be Installed on a Chip. This is Useful When Addresses are Assigned to a Chip.**

Chip Number	Chip Selection				CPU's 1s and 0s
	Chip Select Code				
1	*CS0	*CS1	*CS2	*CS3	0000
2	*CS0	*CS1	*CS2	CS3	0001
3	*CS0	*CS1	CS2	*CS3	0010
4	*CS0	*CS1	CS2	CS3	0011
5	*CS0	CS1	*CS2	*CS3	0100
6	*SC0	CS1	*CS2	CS3	0101
7	*CS0	CS1	CS2	*CS3	0110
8	*CS0	CS1	CS2	CS3	0111
9	CS0	*CS1	*CS2	*CS3	1000
10	CS0	*CS1	*CS2	CS3	1001
11	CS0	*CS1	CS2	*CS3	1010
12	CS0	*CS1	CS2	CS3	1011
13	CS0	CS1	*CS2	*CS3	1100
14	CS0	CS1	*CS2	CS3	1101
15	CS0	CS1	CS2	*CS3	1110
16	CS0	CS1	CS2	CS3	1111

sponds to address 01. Number 2 register answers to the address lines outputting 10. Number 3 register opens for data accessing upon receiving a signal of 11. Those are the four registers 0, 1, 2, and 3 (Fig. 5-10).

Three address lines can pick from eight registers. Four address lines choose from 16 registers. Five address lines can contact 32 registers, six lines can distinguish between 64, seven lines can handle 128 addresses, eight address lines contact

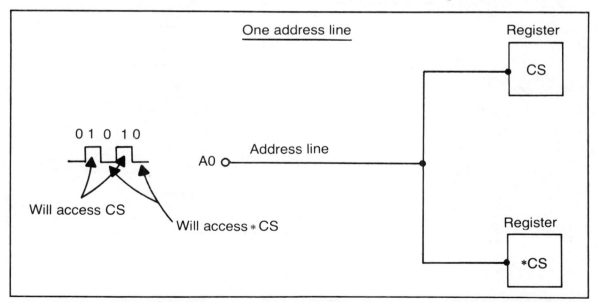

Fig. 5-9. If you had two chips to address, one address line could do the job. With a high pulse you could address *CS and with a low pulse CS could be addressed.

256 registers, and nine lines can turn on 512 individual addresses. Then we come to ten lines A9 through A0 which can address any one of the 1024 registers on the ROM. Each of the registers contains an eight bit byte the CPU needs.

Getting back to the situation where the CPU wants to address the fifth register of the total 1024 registers, the CPU must proffer the correct signal from the ten lines. Remember, each line can send either a 1 or 0 to each connection A9 through A0. If all ten lines send 0's, the total signal is 00 0000 0000. This is a valid address and opens up the first register numbered 0. Should the ten lines produce a total signal 00 0000 0001, then the second register is being addressed which is numbered 1. The third register, numbered 2, is addressed as the ten lines show 00 0000 0010. The fourth register, number 3,

is addressed by the signal 00 0000 0011. The desired fifth register, numbered 4, can be accessed with the ten address lines having a 00 0000 0100 (Fig. 5-11).

ALL THE CONFUSION

All this addressing is very confusing because a lot of activity is happening to two different signals, by two different numbering systems to a group of registers that are counted starting with zero instead of the usual 1.

Let's unravel the skein of facts and clear things up starting with the way things are numbered in computers (there is a good reason for it). As you proceed in computer learning, you'll find that the decimal numbering system you've learned all your life doesn't work too efficiently with computer logic

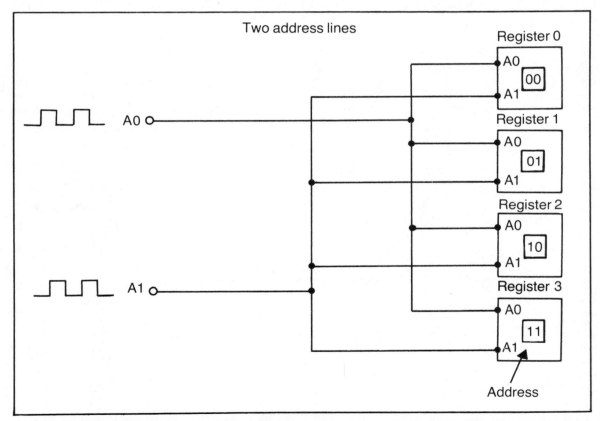

Fig. 5-10. Four registers inside a chip can be addressed with two address lines A0 and A1. Two lows will open up register 0, two highs will activate register 3 and one high and one low will turn on registers 1 and 2 according to the order of the logic states.

70

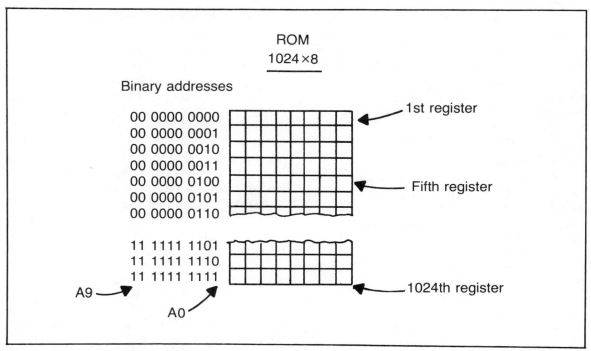

ROM
1024×8

Binary addresses

00 0000 0000		1st register
00 0000 0001		
00 0000 0010		
00 0000 0011		
00 0000 0100		Fifth register
00 0000 0101		
00 0000 0110		
11 1111 1101		
11 1111 1110		
11 1111 1111		

A9

A0

1024th register

Fig. 5-11. The logic state 00 0000 0100 will turn on the fifth register and connect its data lines to the data bus.

circuitry. There are other systems that lend themselves in a much better fashion. You've probably heard them mentioned as *binary, hex* (hexadecimal), and *octal.* Decimal is still used so that makes a total of four numbering systems that could possibly be needed to use a home computer fully.

For servicing, a lot of the testing requires decimal and binary. Binary is an easy count and uses only two numbers, 0 and 1. To count to ten in decimal you've been taught 1, 2, 3, 4, 5, 6, 7, 8, 9, 10. To count to ten in binary the count is 0, 1, 10, 11, 100, 101, 110, 111, 1000, 1001. In decimal you normally start with 1 and end with 10. In binary you start with 0 and end with 1001. This makes decimal 1 equal to binary 0. The two different systems are confusing enough but to make 1 equal to 0 is even more so. As a result the decimal was adjusted so that 0=0 and 1=1. All that was needed was to start counting items in the computer at 0 in decimal instead of counting at 1. Get used to doing that and you'll save complications. Eight data lines are D0-D7. Sixteen address lines are A0-A15. Two

hundred and fifty six registers are addressed 0-255.

Another main confusion area is between data and addresses. If you look at a RAM chip that has 128 registers and each register has 8 bits, you see it is called 128 × 8. Now the 8 bits are attached to the bidirectional data bus. The data is written to the RAM in 8 bits, all 8 bits travel to the RAM at the same time in parallel fashion. When the 8 bits arrive at their destination they are installed in the bit sections of the register.

How do the 8 bits know what register to go to? Immediately before the 8 bits leave the CPU for the RAM register, the CPU outputs an address over the 16 bit address bus. The 16 bits represent an address. In fact, the 16 address lines can address 65,536 separate addresses like the 10 address lines can address 1024 individual addresses. Therefore, the 8 bits in the data bus can be sent to any one of the addresses the address bus addresses.

The confusion is between the sequence of events and the fact that binary bits are used to represent the data and the addresses. It will take time to learn that first the CPU outputs an address and then writes or reads a RAM register. Or the CPU outputs another address and reads a ROM register. Also the addresses are in binary and so is the data the registers contain. All of these items of information will be covered in more detail, just try to realize the confusion highlights.

ROM AND RAM ROWS AND COLUMNS

In the typical home computer memory there are seemingly endless rows of registers. Actually a count of the registers on any chip shows the rows are not endless but can be counted. If you look at a register row count you'll find a mathematical sequence similarity to the common chips. All the row counts total powers of 2. This means the chips have 2, 4, 8, 16, 32, 64, 128, 256, 512, 1024, 4096, 8192, 16384, 32768, or 65536 rows of registers. Each register has 8 cells, each cell capable of holding one binary bit. Eight bits is known as a byte. Every byte has an address. For example, on a chip with 16 rows (Fig. 5-12), the addresses could be numbered 0 through 15, if decimal counting is used. The CPU, which only counts in binary, would address the chip

with the binary numbers 0000 through 1111.

The CPU can address this chip with four address lines. The four address lines can make a connection to any of the rows by outputting the right binary number across the four lines. The four lines connect into a circuit on the chip called the *address decoder*. The address decoder in turn connects to all 16 registers. According to what state each line is in, the decoder will turn on one of the registers. For instance, if A3 is 0, A2 is 1, A1 is 0, and A0 is 1, the lines have 0101 across them. Since 0101 in binary is equal to decimal 5, the address line will activate the 6th register (Fig. 5-13). (Remember this is the 6th register since we start the register count at 0).

Since it has been established that the address lines can open up one of the row addresses by connecting a binary signal to the chip, it is time to see what happens once the row of bits is activated and ready to output its contents. Every row on the typical chip has 8 bits. Each and every bit has its own place in the row. The most significant Bit is D7. The Least Significant Bit is D0. Between MSB and LSB are lesser and lesser bits, D6, D5, D4, D3, D2, and D1. The D stands for data.

The registers are all arranged in rows. The bits in each register are all arranged in columns. There is one column for all the D7s, another column for all the D6s, D5s, and so on. Each column is separate from the one next to it. In this chip we are discussing, a 16 × 8, there are 8 columns and each column has 16 bits, one from each register.

All the D7s are connected together, all the D6s are connected as are the rest of the same positioned bits in each register (Fig. 5-14). Each column is connected to a buffer circuit. A buffer which is discussed later in the book is nothing more than a form of amplifier. A buffer stands between a column and the 8 bit data line. Each column is connected to one of the data lines through a buffer. The 8 columns are connected to the 8 data lines. The D7 column that is attached to all 16 D7 bits, is therefore attached to the D7 data line. The rest of the columns are all connected in the same way. The data lines, as mentioned, run back and forth between the CPU and the chips.

When the CPU upon your command wants

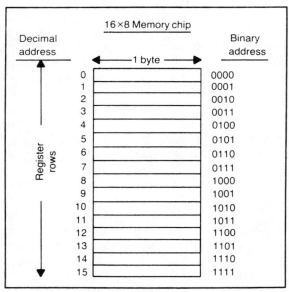

Fig. 5-12. The decimal address of the registers is the one we humans understand easily. The equivalent binary address is the only one the CPU can output.

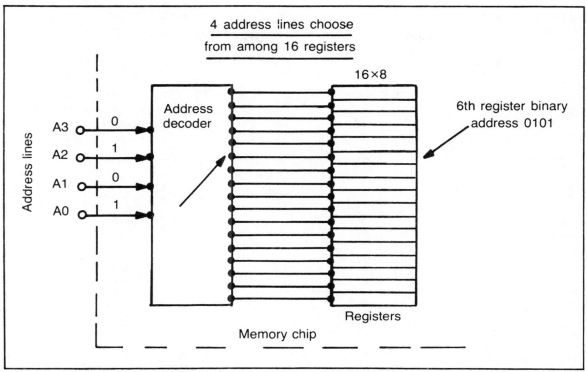

4 address lines choose
from among 16 registers

Address lines

A3 0
A2 1
A1 0
A0 1

Address decoder

16×8

6th register binary address 0101

Memory chip

Registers

Fig. 5-13. If 0101 arrives on the address lines A3-A0 the sixth register will be addressed.

some data, here is what happens. The CPU outputs an address. Suppose that address is 1001. On our example 16 × 8 chip (Figs. 5-12 and 5-13) the address 1001 arrives on the four address lines. The address decoder opens up the tenth register 9.

Let's say address 9 contains the 8 bits, 1011, 0011. Once 9 is activated, its contents 1011 0011, goes to the 8 column buffers (Fig. 5-14). The buffers amplify and otherwise prepare 1011 0011 for presentation. The buffers then output 1011 0011 to the 8 data lines. From there the binary signal goes on to the CPU, where it is said, the CPU has just read the contents of 1001, address 9 on the 16 × 8 memory chip.

If the 16 × 8 chip was a ROM, then the CPU can only read it. Should the chip be a RAM the CPU could write to it in addition to being able to read it. For example, suppose the CPU wants to write the binary message 0111 0011 to address 5 (the sixth register on the chip). The decimal equivalent 5 in

binary is 0101. The CPU promptly outputs 0101 into the four address lines attached to the chip's address decoder. The decoder opens up (Fig. 5-13). Then the CPU outputs 0111 0011 to the 8 data lines. The data travels to the buffers of the chip (Fig. 5-15).

Meanwhile, since the chip is a read-write type, the R/W line must be turned to write. The buffers then allow the signal 0111 0011 into all 8 columns. Since the only address activated is 0101, decimal 5, the signal enters each bit of 5. It can now be said that the CPU has written 0111 0011 to 0101, decimal 5, of the 16 × 8 RAM chip.

WIRED MEMORY

Even though we can't stick a probe into the wiring of a chip, and the only way it can be seen is through the lens of a microscope, we know the wiring is alive and active. RAM memories have wiring in their cells that are able to store and move signal bits. The RAM wiring consists mainly of flip-flop circuits that have no inherent signal of their own, but rather depend on a signal to be sent to them so they can manipulate the signal in the way the CPU instructs. If there are signal bits in RAM and the computer is turned off, the signal disappears and is forever lost.

A ROM, on the other hand, is wired with the signal bits inherent in the wiring. When a ROM is activated it is bristling with bits. They are burnt right into the chip and will always be there, as long as the chip is not defective. Every time you turn on the ROM you can be sure it will be ready to deliver the signal that it has been wired to contain.

How can a ROM be hard wired to deliver the same signal bits over and over again on demand? Let's go back to rows and columns on the 16 × 8 memory matrix on a ROM chip. The address lines

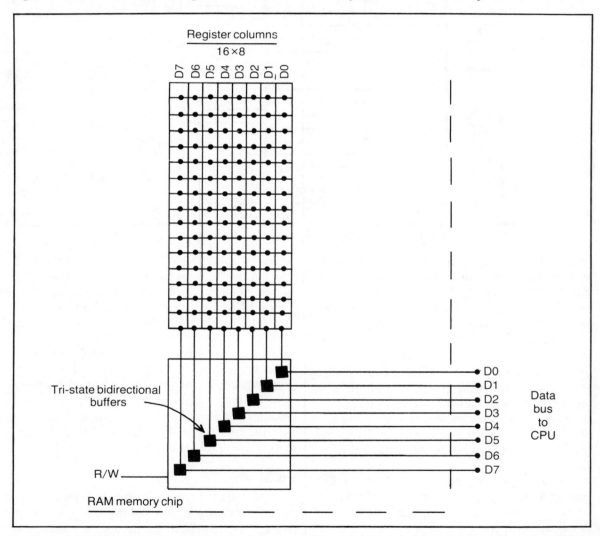

Fig. 5-14. Each column in the register has a D number. They match the data bus D7 to D0. All the D7 s are connected together as is all D6s, D5s and so on. Each column is connected to its respective number in the data bus through a bidirectional buffer circuit.

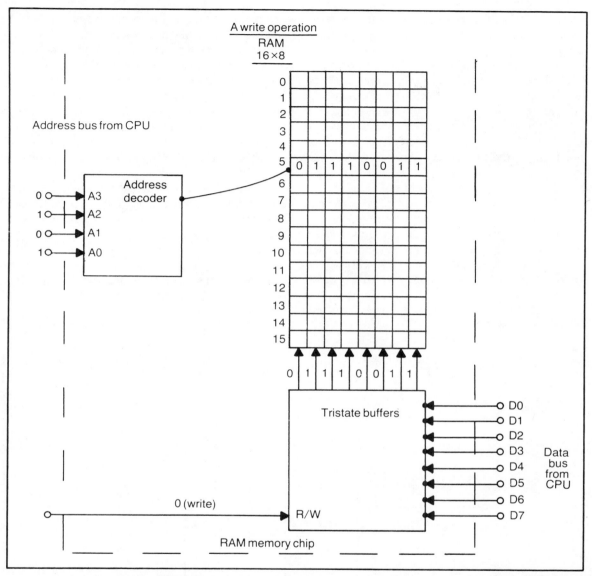

Fig. 5-15. During a write operation to a 16-register RAM, the following happens. First, address lines A3-A0 receives the register address 0101. This activates register 5. Next the R/W line gets a 0 which prepares the register for data from the CPU by adjusting the buffer. Lastly, the data 01110011 arrives on the data bus and goes unimpeded to the fifth register.

attach to the rows of registers and the data lines are connected (through buffers) to the columns of same numbered bits. One of the simplest ways to hard wire the signals in place is by connecting diodes between the rows and columns. Let's go into this scheme in more detail.

Figure 5-13 shows a microscopic section of a 16 × 8 ROM. The addresses, 0000, 0001, 0010 and 0011 are the first four rows on the chip. They are attached to A0, A1, A2 and A3 address bus lines. According to the combination of binary bits on the four address lines, one of the addresses will be opened up. For instance, if A0 has a 0, A1 has a 0, A2 is 1, and A3 is 0, then the third address 0010 will open up.

Between the row addresses and the columns of bits, diodes are installed.There is one diode between each row and every column. For example, row address 0010 has eight diodes attached (Fig. 5-16). The cathodes of the diodes are connected to the row side. The eight anodes of the diodes are connected to the column side. While all eight diodes are attached in common to the row 0010, they are attached separately to the eight columns.

The columns are in turn connected to the data bus. When address 0010 is activated and the eight diodes are connected between that row and the eight columns the diodes will all conduct, cathode to anode. The columns D0 through D7, will each receive the signal 1. The columns will then contain the total signal data 1111 1111. The columns output the data 1111 1111 to the data bus. The signal then proceeds to the CPU.

Suppose you are the manufacturer of this 16 × 8 ROM. You desire address 0010 to output 1001 1100, instead of the 1111 1111 that the diodes produce as they conduct. You must alter some of the diodes to produce the change in signal. An analysis of the change shows you want to alter bits D6, D5, D1 and D0. D7, D4, D3 and D2 should be left alone, since they are already outputting 1, 1, 1, and 1. It's the 1's that should be 0's that need changing.

You proceed to place a voltage high enough to blow out a diode between the following test points. Row 0010 is grounded and high voltage is applied to column bits D6, D5, D1, and D0. This blows open the four diodes between these points. Now when you want a signal from row 0010, the blown diodes output no voltage, which is a signal of 0, and the remaining good diodes output normal voltage, which is a signal of 1. The total signal from address 0010 becomes 1001 1100, which is what you wanted (Fig. 5-17).

While this procedure will work during actual

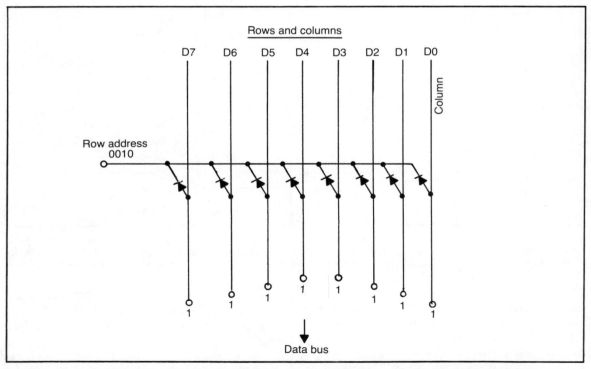

Fig. 5-16. When row 0010 on this ROM is addressed, all eight diodes conduct producing the data 11111111.

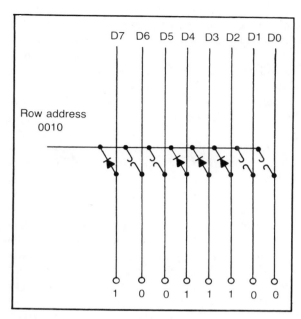

D7 D6 D5 D4 D3 D2 D1 D0

Row address
0010

1   0   0   1   1   1   0   0

Fig. 5-17. If the diodes at D6, D5, D1, and D0 are blown out, when 0010 is addressed, only the intact diodes will conduct producing the data 10011100.

manufacturing, nothing so slow is used, except during some assembly line troubleshooting as specific tests. When a ROM is designed, large printed circuit patterns are made. The junctions that are going to contain a diode or transistor are clearly defined on the pattern. They are the junctions that produce the binary 1s. The inactive junctions are also shown. These are the places that produce the 0's. Once the patterns are completely designed they are reduced photographically to chip size.

The inside of the chip, as mentioned, is not accessible to the servicer. However, all the pin connections of the package, the 16 address bus line etchs, the eight data bus line etchs and a lot of the discrete supporting circuitry are easy to get to and are subject to failure. Even though the chip circuits are microscopic they figure just as importantly in the repair scheme of things and must be considered as you troubleshoot the RAMs and ROMs.

PROMS AND EPROMS

During servicing, you will on occasion run into a computer that uses a special type of ROM called a *PROM* or an *EPROM*. The PROM is a *Programmable ROM*. The EPROM is an *Erasable Programmable ROM*.

A good example of a PROM was shown in the last section. It's a ROM chip before it has the program installed. The chip could be a 128 × 8 with diodes installed, eight to each of the 128 rows, which makes 128 to each of the eight columns. You can program the chip by blowing out any diodes where a 0 is supposed to be, and leaving alone any diodes where a 1 is to reside. Once the program is burnt in, the PROM works just like any other ROM. A good example of a PROM being used for servicing is an exerciser. Lots of times a servicer will be given the job of repairing a large number of the same computers. He could make a PROM that when installed in the computer would render a few valuable exercises on components that indicate trouble.

A typical PROM could have npn transistors installed between rows and columns instead of diodes (Fig. 5-18). The emitters are attached to the rows and the bases to the columns. The collectors are all connected to a common +5 V. With this configuration a fusible link connects each collector to +5 V. To program a bit its fusible link is blown to install a 0, or the link is left intact if you want a 1 in the bit position. Once you blow a link the change is permanent. That bit will contain a 0. The 1s with the link intact still are changeable, since you can make them a 0 by destroying the link with some excess voltage.

The EPROM, on the other hand, can be used over and over again. Instead of using conventional diode type hookups between the rows and columns, *MOSFETs* are used. These *metal oxide silicon field-effect transistors* have a very useful ability ordinary transistors do not. If you apply about 25 volts between the source and drain, a phenomenon called avalanche injection causes the gate to lose its effect and act like an open circuit. It is as if the gate has been blown open. No conduction can take place and a 0 is installed in that bit the MOSFET occupies (Fig. 5-19). If the bit does not receive any voltage it retains its manufactured value which is a 1, since it can conduct.

The MOSFETs, in addition has another useful ability. If you expose it to ultraviolet light for a half hour or so, the avalanche injection effect subsides and the gate can conduct once again. In other words the light erases the program on the EPROM. You can use the EPROM over and over again (Fig. 5-20).

UPGRADING MEMORY

The typical home computer uses a CPU with a register called the program counter. This register usually has a capacity of 16 bits. As shown before 16 bits are able to form 65,536 different combinations of 1s and 0s. The program counter points to the next address in memory where the CPU can get data. Since the PC is able to form 64K different addresses you can fill the computer with devices till you use up the 64K.

For example, a computer with 16K of RAM could also have 24K of ROM and about 8K of other system addresses. This adds up to about 48K total addresses that the CPU can communicate with. However, the CPU is able to handle another 16K worth of addressing. If you look at the memory map which is the layout of what the addresses are, you find the addresses numbered 16384 to 32767 are labeled "not used". This is expansion territory. You can add 16K of devices in the unused areas.

There are many schemes available to take advantage of the gaps in memory maps. In fact, very few computer systems are originally manufactured with every address available filled with devices. There is always a way to upgrade a system as a new need arises.

Most of the time upgrading consists of adding more RAM or ROM. RAM is usually added in the following way. Suppose you have a computer that has 4K of RAM and you want to upgrade it to 16K. When you examine the print board there are eight RAM chips. The parts list describes the chips as 512 × 8 types. This means each chip contains ½K

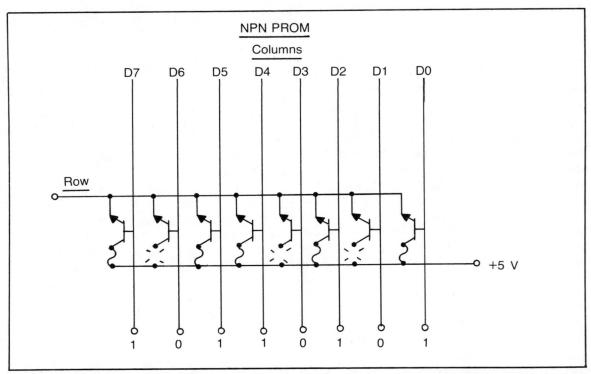

Fig. 5-18. Instead of diodes, npn transistors could be used. A separate +5 V source is needed in this configuration. This arrangement outputs the data 10110101.

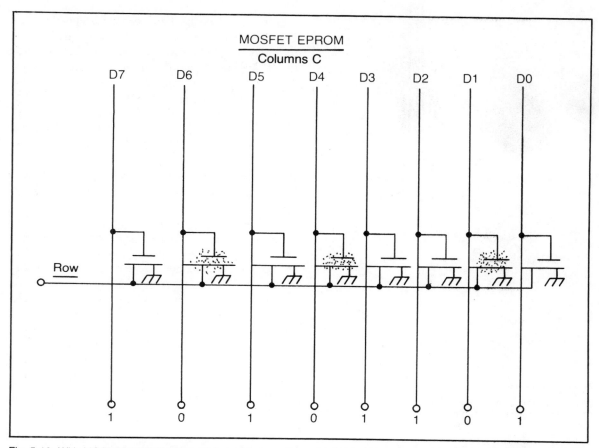

Fig. 5-19. With MOSFET EPROMs a useful phenomena allows the FETs to act like an open circuit and act as a PROM.

bytes. Eight chips times ½K comes to 4K. A look at the memory map shows the 4K of RAM occupies the addresses 0 through 4095. The addresses 4096 through 32767 are labeled Not Used. Those empty addresses are available for more RAM. The program counter is quite able to address the empty addresses even though it is not doing so with the ½K chips installed.

To upgrade the memory from 4K to 16K you purchase eight new RAM chips. They have to be types that will work with the system. These can be obtained from the original manufacturer or a suitable replacement maker. The new eight chips, instead of being ½K are 2K each. Instead of the eight chips totaling 4K of RAM they total 16K.

The conversion consists mainly of removing the eight ½K RAMs and installing the 2K RAMs in their place. The RAM chips are sensitive MOS chips so they must be handled with extreme care to avoid static electric charge rupture. The additional compacting of circuits on the chip increases the ICs distributed capacitance, so part of the conversion could be disconnecting some of the discrete capacitors, like the little bypass ones, on the print board in the RAM circuits. Another problem during conversion could be that the address changes alters some decoding between the large chips. If the changes are needed the manufacturer usually gives you service notes to clue you into a successful conversion.

ROM upgrading works in a similar way. ROM chips are prepared programs. When they are placed

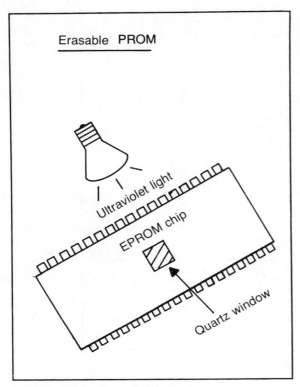

Erasable PROM

Ultraviolet light

EPROM chip

Quartz window

Fig. 5-20. The E in EPROM stands for erase. With an ultraviolet light shining through a quartz window, the EPROM is returned to its original state of all 1s.

into a memory map they perform a specific job. They usually take control of the computer when they are installed. For instance, a ROM chip could turn the home computer into a word processor, a data processor, or a space game. A lot of the ROMs are cartridges and plug into a receptacle on the print board. When the ROM is a cartridge the memory map will show a place for it. It could say, Cartridge ROM 49152-65279. This would be about 16K addresses that are reserved for the cartridge. When the cartridge is plugged in it usually disconnects the built in ROM. Then the cartridge takes over all the control of the computer.

Another type of ROM is one that doesn't fully take control but simply adds to the capability of the built in ROM. For example, a home computer when first purchased will have 4K RAM and a beginner's level programming language. As the user progresses more RAM is desired and a conversion from 4K to 16K is made. Since there is additional memory the user could advance to higher levels of programming. There are ROMs available that will supplement the original ROM and extend the language capability of the computer to the higher levels. The additional ROM is purchased and installed. It could be a cartridge or it could be a 40-pin package that is socketed or soldered into the print board.

Chapter 6

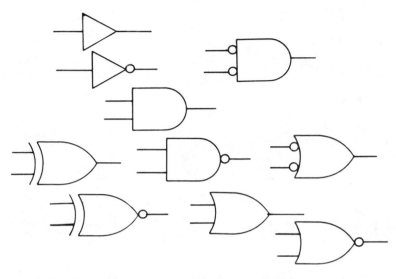

The Rest of the Chips

If you look at the chip location guide, in addition to the main chips in 40- and 24-pin packages, there are many other smaller size packages with fewer pins. There are 12-, 14-, and 16-pin packages (Fig. 6-1). These pins are not usually socketed and thus are not easily replaced as a service test. Fortunately, these chips are not usually as complex as the CPU and its large support chips. These smaller packages are much simpler. The buffers, latches, flip-flops, decoders, and individual logic gates can be tested by routine pin readings. The video mixer, modulator, and power supply regulators can be tested with routine TV service techniques.

INTERNAL WIRING

When you decide to test a chip the first piece of test equipment you reach for is the vom. The vom lets you take voltage readings of the pins on the chip. What these readings mean in terms of chip failure is discussed in later chapters. For now let's examine what is available at the pins. Inside chips are a lot of components and circuits that you cannot

get to with your vom. These internal circuits are connected together and the circuit nodes cannot be reached with a vom probe. There can be literally thousands of these nodes not available for testing. They are microscopically taken out of the normal testing range.

In chips like the CPU or RAM about all you can do during testing is replace the chip or take some input-output tests. There is no routine way you can pinpoint the transistor or other defective microscopic component. There can be one input line, one output line, and a thousand transistors between.

In chips such as a buffer or latch, the internal wiring is not so extensive. A buffer could have a number of FETs wired internally (Fig. 6-2). While you couldn't read an individual electrode, since the nodes, are wired internally and not available at a pin you can read the effect of all the FETs at a pin. This brings the pin readings closer to routine voltage tests. While it is important to realize the reading you are taking represents the total effect of diodes and FETs operating together, you can adjust

81

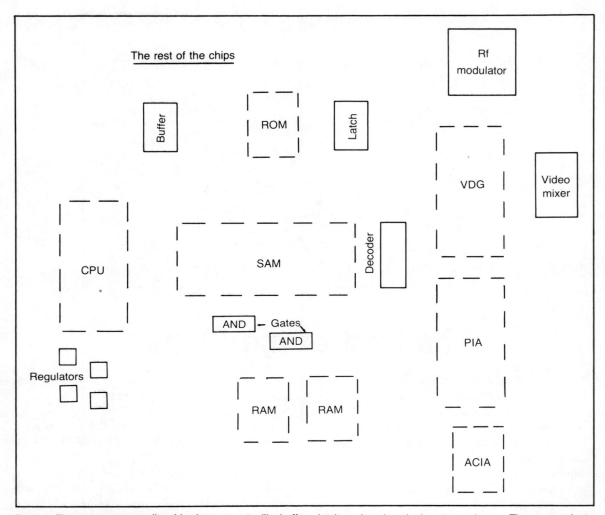

Fig. 6-1. There are many smaller chips in a computer like buffers, latches, decoders, logic gates and so on. They are easier to test than the large 40-pin packages.

your thinking to encompass all the internal wiring as a single circuit. Then you can test the pin as a single entity and come up with a fast analysis.

The single entities, which are in actuality, many internally wired circuits are called buffers, latches, flip-flops, gates, etc. On a chip there can be a lot of these circuits. For instance, there is a chip called a hex buffer. All that is, is six separate buffer circuits, all on one 16 pin package (Fig. 6-3). Each separate buffer has its own pin numbers. If you treat each buffer as a single circuit, you can test each one

by reading its individual pin numbers. Let's examine these various chips, from the point of view that they contain a number of individual accessible circuits. The internal circuits are discussed in later chapters.

BUFFERS

A buffer is a set of internal circuits arranged to accept a 0 or 1 and then transfer the data state through itself. The buffer can't store the 0 or 1, just transfer it. The buffer is used when the data has to

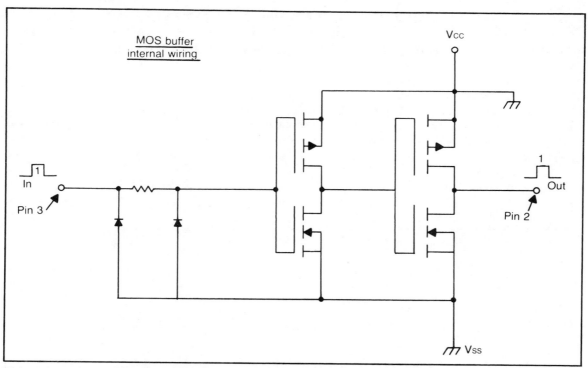

Vcc

In

Pin 3

1

Out

Pin 2

Vss

Fig. 6-2. Even though a buffer has transistors, diodes, and a resistor, the only test nodes available are the input, output, and V$_{CC}$.

be transferred from one logic level to another. For example, when the data has to go from a TTL chip to an MOS chip, a buffer could be used to effect the transfer. Actual details are discussed in Chapter 9.

Buffers can come four, six, or eight gates to a package. The four gate package is called a quad, six gates a hex, and eight gates an octal. Each gate has its own pin numbers. Figure 6-3 shows the little buffers and their pins. There is one pin for an input, at the base of each triangle, and another pin, the output on the point of the triangle. What is not shown are two more connections that go to each gate (Fig. 6-4). They are the voltage VCC and return line (usually grounded) VSS. These two lines are common to all the gates. If you put +5 V on VCC and grounded VSS all the gates would be powered.

This brings up the word *ENABLE*. That term is found all over computers. If you look up enable in the dictionary, one of the synonyms is empower: to make one able to do something. If you empower a

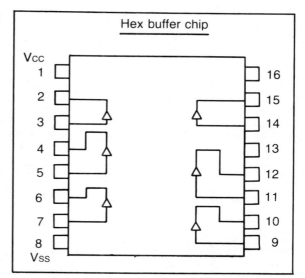

Hex buffer chip

Vcc
1
2
3
4
5
6
7
8
Vss

16
15
14
13
12
11
10
9

Fig. 6-3. A typical chip contains six buffers. You can test each one individually at its inputs and outputs. Vcc and Vss are common to all of them.

83

buffer with +5 V you make the buffer able to transfer a 0 or 1. Should you remove the +5 V power, then the buffer is disabled and not able to transfer the digital data states.

In some buffers there is an enable line or EN (Fig. 6-5). Data can only be transferred through the gate while the gate is enabled. The enable line can turn on the gate in one of two ways. The obvious way is if there is +5 V applied to the gate. When the gate is enabled with the application of +5 V it is said to be a HIGH enable.

On the other hand, the circuit setup might, and often is, arranged so that 0 V is required to enable the buffer. When the gate is enabled with the application of 0 V it is said to be a LOW enable. When the enable is LOW the EN is changed to $\overline{EN}$ or * EN. Note that there is a line over (or an asterisk with) the letters. That designates the LOW condition for the enabling.

This brings up another term servicers must understand to do their job. This is tristating. These buffers, as well as other devices with the enable lines, are said to have tristate capability. There are three states a buffer could be in. One, is transferring a 1. Two, is transferring a 0. Three, is transferring nothing, while the buffer is disabled. The buffer is

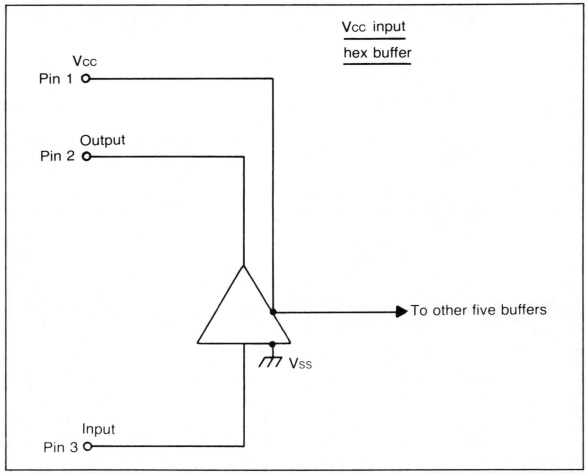

Fig. 6-4. Vcc is connected to each buffer internally in this manner. You can't get to the internal Vcc nodes and can only test the Vcc at its master input on pin 1.

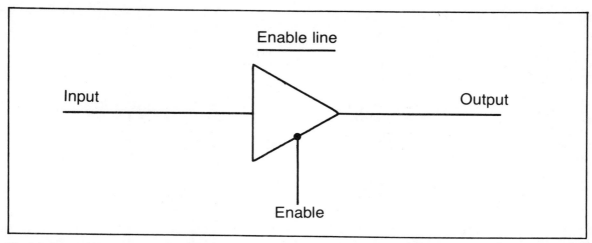

Enable line

Input

Output

Enable

Fig. 6-5. Many buffer types have an enable line that can turn the gate off and on. The buffers that have enable lines are said to be a "tristate" type.

only on while it is enabled. While it is enabled it assumes a state of 1 or 0. When the buffer is disabled it assumes the third state of having a high impedance and being off (Fig. 6-6).

There are lots of logic devices that do not have tristate ability. Yes, these devices can be turned off but their being turned off doesn't have any use in the computer scheme of things. The tristate ability of buffers does have use. The enable line going off and on is part of the data-addressing activity.

During servicing you'll be testing pins and test points for all three states (Fig. 6-7). The vom typically reads +5 V for a High, 0 V for a Low and somewhere in between, like +2 V for the tristate condition. After checking a few circuits the tests will become automatic.

LATCHES

The most striking difference between buffers and latches is, a latch can store a logic state of 0 or 1, while a buffer must pass the state right through itself. The latches come in packages of four, six, or eight devices like the buffers. A latch is also a tristate device like a buffer (Fig. 6-8). The input is on the left-hand side of the square symbol. The output then continues on to the data lines. A third connection to all the latches in the package is the latch ENABLE. Note the asterisk in front of the

word ENABLE. This means the latch will store when the enabling signal is LOW.

Whenever the ENABLE is LOW the latch will store the 1 or 0 in the data line. If a HIGH pulse comes along on the enable line, the latch is opened up and the logic signal is freed. It travels on to the data line. As soon as the HIGH pulse goes LOW, the latch closes up and stores the input signal again. The latch thus stores, releases, and stores again as the enable line goes LOW, HIGH, and LOW again.

The latch ENABLE is usually held LOW which is the store position. Whenever the logic state has to be updated, a momentary high pulse makes the latch flip-flop. That is, it changes from a store to a discharge and then back to a store again. There is a detailed circuit step-by-step description of the flip-flop in Chapter 9.

THE OCTAL D FLIP-FLOP

The latch is a flip-flop circuit. There are also chips called octal D flip-flops. What is the difference? Not very much, they are almost identical. The only difference is in the way the enable line operates.

The ordinary latch is a flip-flop that is said to be sensitive to a dc voltage or to put it another way, the latch is level sensitive. A 1 or 0 will turn the latch from store to discharge. The 1 pulse momentarily

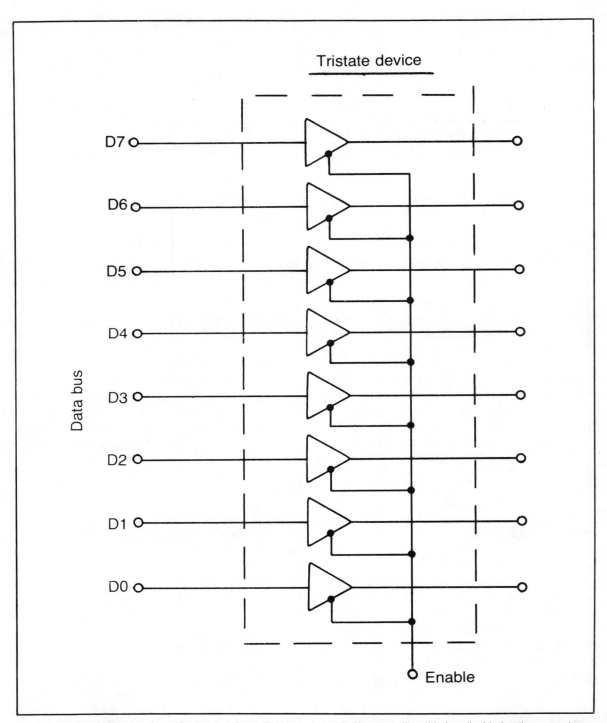

Fig. 6-6. Tristate buffers are found in data bus lines. This set of eight buffers are all enabled or disabled at the same time.

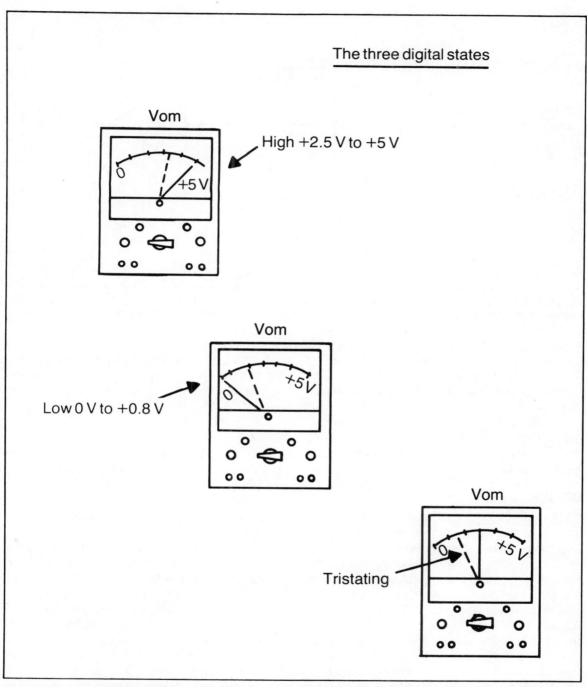

The three digital states

Vom

High +2.5 V to +5 V

Vom

Low 0 V to +0.8 V

Vom

Tristating

Fig. 6-7. The vom will reveal one of three logic states at a test node in the digital circuits. If it reads from about +2.5 V to +5 V there is a HIGH on the node. When the vom reads 0 V to about +0.8 V it represents a LOW. If the reading is somewhere in between, the test point is in a high impedance state which means it is tristating.

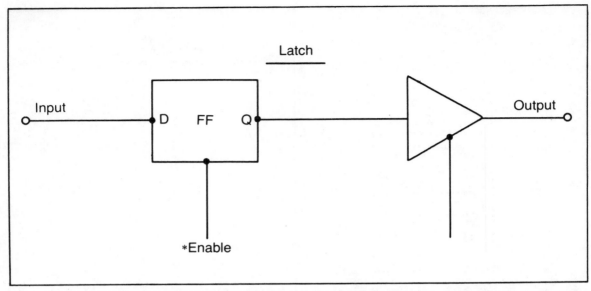

Fig. 6-8. If you hook a flip-flop in front of a buffer, the two devices form a latch. The latch can store a 1 or 0 until it is time for it to be updated. Then the latch is opened, passes its contents to the buffer and receives a new logic state.

unlatches the stored signal to the latch output. The 0 relatches the storage capability.

The other type of flip-flop the octal D, is not sensitive to a dc level. It is only sensitive to an ac input like the computer's clock signal. It is usually called a D flip-flop (Fig. 6-9). It can be triggered by the edge of a pulse. As the pulse causes it to flip-flop, it is said that the clock input moves the data from the D inputs to the Q outputs.

ENCODERS

In Morse code, as you hit the key, you change a letter or a number to a series of dots and dashes. Everybody knows the old SOS call, dididitdah-dahdah dididit (··· --- ···). When you are sending out the international distress call you are encoding the SOS to ··· --- ··· In a computer there is a keyboard. As you type your program in letters and numbers there is a chip or more in the keyboard circuit that encodes the letters and numbers into 1s and 0s (Fig. 6-10). The computer does not understand the alphabet or our decimal numbering system. It only comprehends binary arithmetic, the 1s and 0s. Once your program is encoded then the computer can do something with it. You'll en-

counter encoders in the computer. For the most part, they are taking a single letter or number and coding it into binary output. The binary output can then be used by the computer as pulses or voltage levels.

DECODERS

The decoder name implies that it reverses the encoding. In some cases it does. For instance, in a line printer there will be decoders like this (Fig. 6-11). When you want to print a hard copy of a program you wrote, you have the computer output your program to the printer. The output consists of binary code. The printer receives the code and a decoder chip will make the keys of the printer strike the paper according to the meaning of the code. This is exactly the opposite of the keyboard encoding. However, there are other decoders in the computer that have little or nothing to do with the keyboard encoding. These are address decoders. A servicer uses address decoding often. It is the basis of a lot of the thinking during troubleshooting.

In practice this decoding technique is used to choose RAM chips (as discussed in the chip select section in Chapter 5). If there are eight chips in a

RAM set, each chip contains a decoder. Each decoder is capable of turning on if it receives the correct combination of binary bits. The arrangement follows:

Code	Chip#
0000	0
0001	1
0010	2
0011	3
0100	4
0101	5
0110	6
0111	7

When the MPU outputs the chip select code, the selected decoder pulses and turns on the proper RAM chip. For instance, if 0111 is outputted by the MPU, Chip#7 is addressed.

LOGIC GATES

On the schematic of a computer you'll find a number of symbols that designate gates (Fig. 6-12).

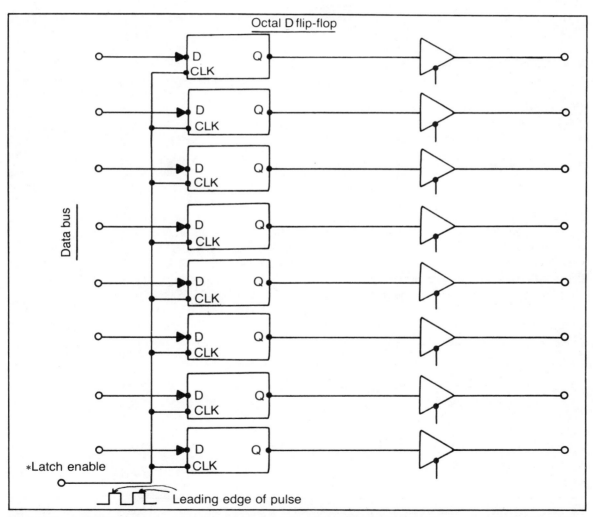

Fig. 6-9. The octal D flip-flop responds only to the leading edge of the clock signal rather than to any dc logic state input.

89

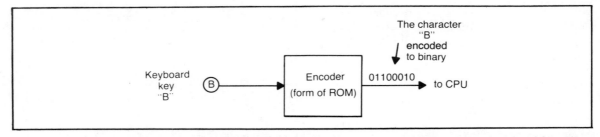

Fig. 6-10. In the keyboard input circuits can be an encoder ROM that will change the keyboard characters to ASCII code.

They are a triangle and two bullet-like shapes. They come with or without tiny circles. They are drawn with one or more input leads. However, they all only have one output lead. Furthermore, when a little circle is present, it is between a lead and the body shape.

When you relate the schematic drawing to the actual hardware you find these gates are on chips (Fig. 6-13). They are in smaller packages, like 12-, 14-, or 16-pin types, but chips just the same. If you had a microscope you would see these gates are made up of transistors, resistors, and diodes just like any other chip. There is a lot of internal wiring that you can't get to, so you must analyze the gates by measuring the inputs and outputs at the accessible pins. Therefore, gates can be thought of as a basic computer element, just as gold is an element even though it's made of atoms. The transistors, the gate is composed of, are relegated to the world of the microscope not the vom probe.

The triangle by itself is not technically a gate. The triangle is a form of amplifier and is used as a buffer. All of these gates are discussed in detail in Chapter 9. The triangle with a tiny circle at its

output (the pointy end is the output) is called an inverter. It is also known as a NOT gate (Fig. 6-14). What the inverter does is simple. It inverts any 1s or 0's that enter. If a 1 comes in the input lead, a 0 exits the output lead. Should a 0 enter the gate a 1 leaves.

There is no storage capability in a gate like there is in a flip-flop. When a logic state enters it is modified and keeps right on going with no hesitation. There is however a third state available in a buffer or an inverter. The tristate is OFF. The tristate is accomplished with additional leads like *enable* which is not shown on the schematic.

The first bullet-shaped symbol is called an AND gate. It never has one input lead. It must have two or more. The AND gate typically takes two input signals and processes them into one output signal. It is called AND because it will only turn on if the two signals are 1 AND 1 (Fig. 6-15). If there are any other combination of 0's and 1's, the AND gate does not respond. When there are three input leads, the AND gate will turn on when 1,1 and 1 is applied. Otherwise the gate remains dormant.

If the AND gate has a little circle at its output

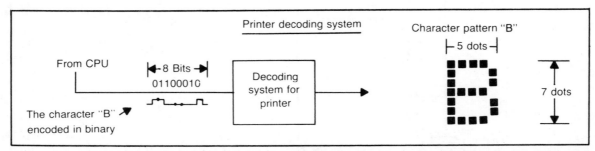

Fig. 6-11. In the printer interface system there is a decoder ROM that accepts binary bits that represent a keyboard character and changes the bits to a 5×7 dot character pattern that is printed on the paper.

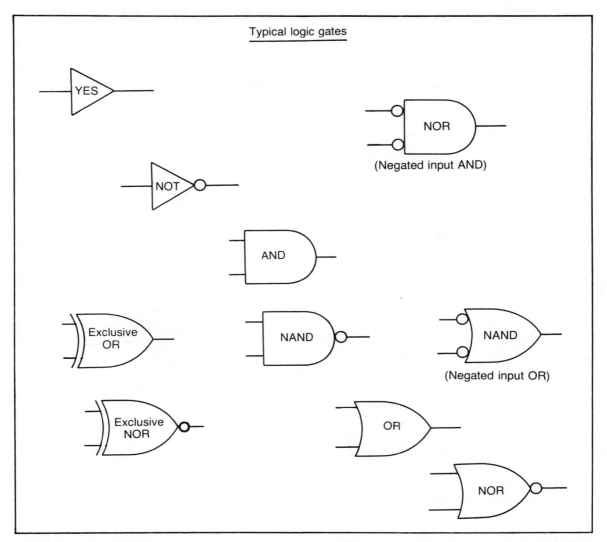

Fig. 6-12. These logic symbols are found on the schematics of home computers. It is essential that you understand what they are and how they work before you try to repair a computer.

lead, the gate is no longer an AND but becomes a NAND. All that means is *Not* AND. It's as if you attached a NOT gate in the output of an AND gate (Fig. 6-16). Whenever you see the little circle it changes the gate symbol. It inverts the output to the opposite state.

The other bullet shape is more streamlined. It designates the OR gate. The OR gate, like the AND gate also has multiple inputs and only one output.

That's the end of the similarity. The OR gate processes states differently. The OR gate will turn on if one *OR* the other of the inputs is a 1. This is unlike the AND gate where only 1 and 1 produces 1 (Fig. 6-17).

This same OR principle follows through on all OR gates. If one or more of the OR gate inputs is a 1 the gate will turn on and output a 1. Even if there are 16 inputs only a single 1 is needed to get the gate on.

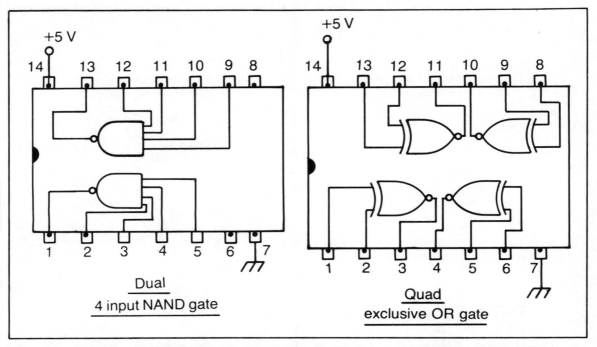

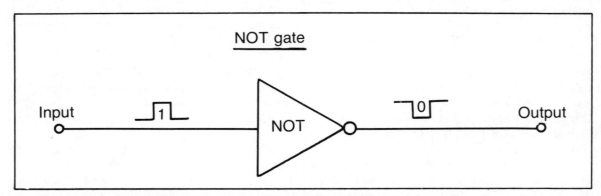

Fig. 6-13. In a chip replacement manual the various ones are described like these gate chips. On the schematics, it is common to show the gates individually with the pin numbers as identification.

When the symbol has a little NOT circle on its pointy output the gate becomes *Not* OR. It's as if an inverter is attached. The gate with the circle is called a NOR gate. If you input a 1, the gate turns on, produces a 1, but then inverts it, so the final output is a 0 (Fig. 6-18).

There is another form of OR gate that is shown on the schematic with the bottom of the bullet having a curved piece pulled away so a space exists between the leads and the gate input. This strange shape is called EXCLUSIVE OR. It is different than the OR gate in this respect. In the OR gate the circuit is arranged so that if any or all of the inputs are in a state of 1, the gate will go on.

In the typical EXCLUSIVE OR gate (Fig. 6-19) there are two inputs. Like the OR gate, if either of

Fig. 6-14. If you check a NOT gate that has a 1 at its input, there should be a 0 at the output.

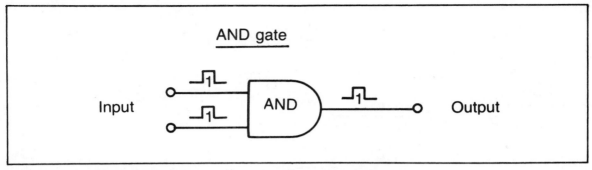

AND gate

Input   AND   Output

Fig. 6-15. The only way an AND gate will pass a 1 to the output is if all inputs are 1s.

the inputs injects a 1, the gate will go on. However, if both of the inputs are 1, the gate will not go on. The gate will only go on if either one *OR* the other of the inputs is 1, not both. It is EXCLUSIVEly an OR. The ordinary OR gate acts like an AND gate when both inputs are 1. Both the AND and the OR gates will turn on when both inputs are 1 while the EXCLUSIVE OR will not.

When the little NOT circle is placed on the point of an EXCLUSIVE OR gate then the gate becomes an EXCLUSIVE NOR (Fig. 6-20). With the inversion, all output 1s are made 0s and output 0s become 1s, in comparison to the EXCLUSIVE OR GATE. All of the gates are covered in detail in Chapter 9.

THE VIDEO MIXER

Another chip you'll find in computers is a video mixer (Fig. 6-21). It is not composed of logic circuits but ordinary black and white or color TV circuits. It is the beginning of the TV part of the computer.

The VDG chip puts out the composite video and sync signal. The video mixer chip receives the signal called Y. The video mixer chip also gets inputs of the three color signals. In addition the chip gets an input of 3.58 MHz from the clock in the computer for a color reference signal. The mixer chip puts them all together and forms the complete color video signal, just like a TV station can make.

MODULATOR

When the computer has a TV monitor as part of its system, the composite signal the mixer produces can simply be amplified and fed through a 72 ohm piece of coaxial cable to the monitor video circuits. If the computer has to use a home TV set as a monitor, then a modulator is needed (Fig. 6-22).

Some computers have modulator chips installed right on the print board. When it is, it is an intercarrier vestigial sideband unit. The modulator receives the composite TV signal from the video

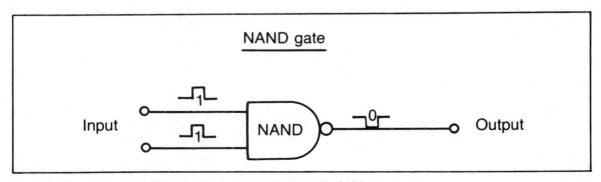

NAND gate

Input   NAND   Output

Fig. 6-16. The only way a NAND gate will pass a 0 to the output is if all inputs are 1s.

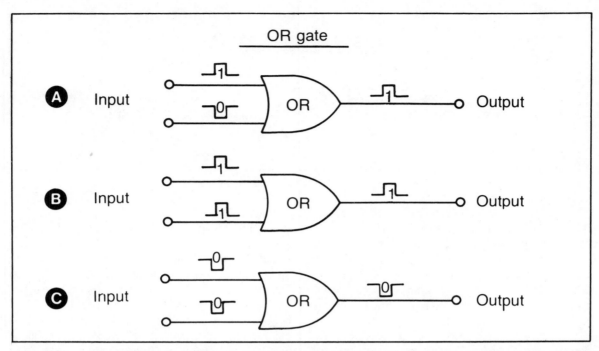

Fig. 6-17. The only way an OR gate will pass a 0 to the output (as shown in C) is if all inputs are 0. In all other cases the OR gate will produce a 1.

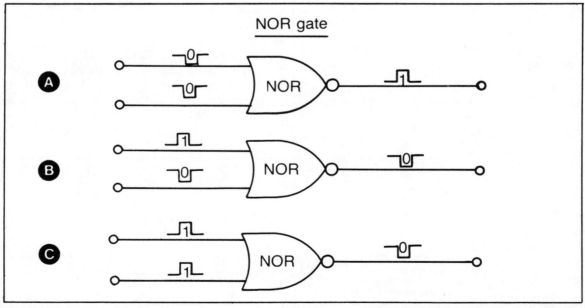

Fig. 6-18. The only way a NOR gate will pass a 1 to the output (as shown in A) is if all inputs are 0. Otherwise the NOR gate outputs a 0.

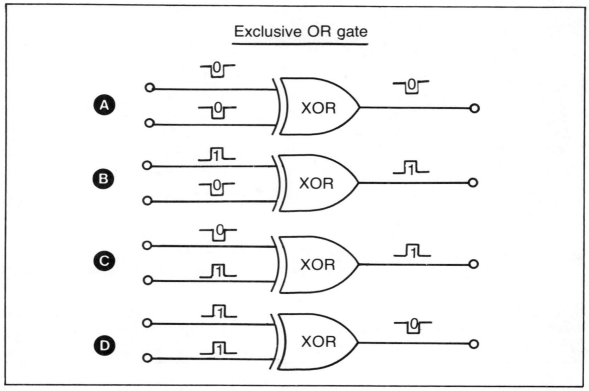

Fig. 6-19. The XOR gate is like an OR gate in all cases except if all inputs are 1. Then (as shown in D) the output is 0.

output transistor and can also get an audio signal as an input. The modulator produces a 4.5 MHz FM and mixes it with the video to produce an output at a selected rf frequency. Typical are channels 3 or 4 at 61.25 MHz for channel 3 or 67.25 MHz for channel 4. The output exits the modulator via a 72 ohm phone jack and can easily be attached to any home TV.

There are a number of home computers that produce the composite TV signal but do not have any rf modulator. These computers are designed to operate on a monitor rather than a home TV. A TV monitor typically has better picture resolution than a home television. For small objects on the display, a monitor will show a clearer image. However, if you want to use your TV you can buy rf modulators for about $50 in a computer store. They are essentially the same as the ones that are in computers and do the same job.

The store-bought modulators might not appear to display as clear a picture as the modulators that are built into the computers. This is because the display in the modulatorless computers are designed to show more objects than the ones with a modulator. The crowding of the objects causes the blurring of the display in these cases. The only way

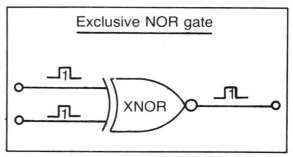

Fig. 6-20. The Exclusive NOR gate is like the NOR gate except if all inputs are 1. Then the output is 1.

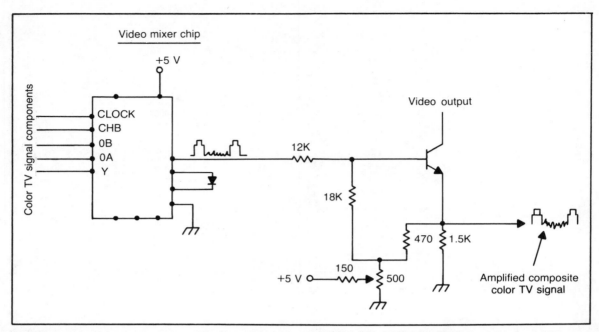

Fig. 6-21. The video mixer circuit is not digital but analog. It is quite like any home TV circuit and is fixed with routine TV repair methods.

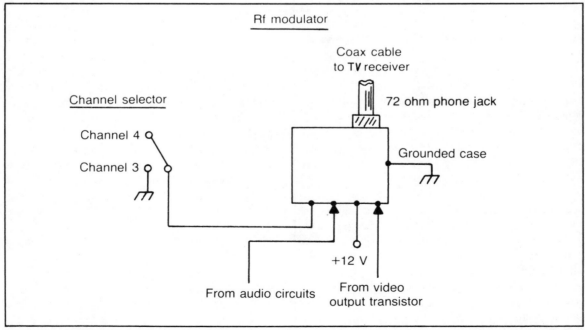

Fig. 6-22. The rf modulator is only needed to produce a channel 3 or 4 frequency so that an ordinary home TV can be used as a computer monitor.

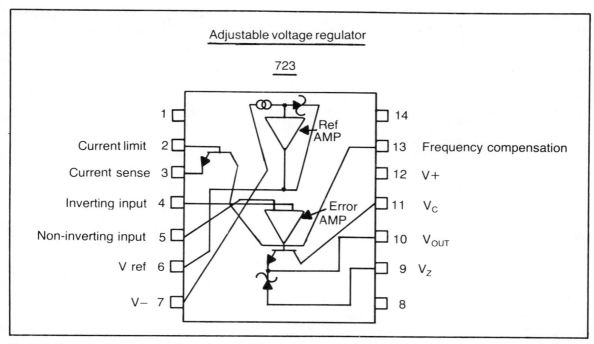

Adjustable voltage regulator

723

1		14
Current limit 2	Ref AMP	13 Frequency compensation
Current sense 3		12 V+
Inverting input 4	Error AMP	11 V_C
Non-inverting input 5		10 V_{OUT}
V ref 6		9 V_Z
V− 7		8

Fig. 6-23. The computer power supply requires a lot of regulation. This 723 voltage regulator chip is commonly used to do the job.

to cure the problem if it bothers you, is to use a monitor the computer calls for.

REGULATORS

There are chips in the power supply. The power supply, of course, does not have anything to do with the 1s and 0s. Like any other supply it has the job of providing the dc voltages to make the computer work. Typical home computer voltages are +5 volts, +12 volts, −5 volts, and −12 volts. Years ago, when there were vacuum tubes in the machines, the supply provided filament voltages too. The solid-state devices eliminated that need.

Solid-state devices though have another need that tubes were not as fussy about. The chips operate best if they have the voltages regulated. In a hand calculator, when the batteries are installed, the steady dc voltage supplied by the batteries provide almost perfect regulation. The current drawn by the chips hardly dents the voltage level. The +5 V that the chips get is steady as it goes. This is good regulation.

When an ac adapter, which is a little power transformer that changes the 120 Vac input to about 14 Vac, is used the regulation suffers. There is a little filter network in calculators that changes the ac to dc and takes out most of the ac ripple. For calculators this power supply means is quite satisfactory but in a computer much better regulation is needed.

A computer also uses an ac adapter which is a large version of the calculator ac adapter. However, the filter network has to do a much better job of regulation. The amount of ripple in the dc has to be practically eliminated, otherwise it could interfere with the computer operation. That's where the regulator chips come in.

An often used regulator is the 723 chip (Fig. 6-23). According to its catalog listing it is called an Adjustable Voltage Regulator. The chip is a 14-pin package. On the chip are two zener diodes, a couple of npn transistors, and a buffer amplifier. The step-by-step operation of the power supply using the 723 is discussed in Chapter 20. The 723 itself has the job of regulating the amount of current that flows through a series-pass power transistor. The 723 gets attached in parallel to the emitter, base, and collector of the transistor. It constantly samples the current flow through the transistor and automatically adjusts the flow with its attachment at the base. If some ripple tends to appear the adjustment cancels the ripple, and allows a steady dc to power the computer components.

There are other types of solid-state regulators in computer power supplies. These are called terminal regulators and do not resemble chips. They only have three pins and look like power transistors. The devices are bipolar transistors and not chips. They are however doing some regulator duty. When they are tested use transistor tests or direct replacement since there are only three leads to desolder.

Chapter 7

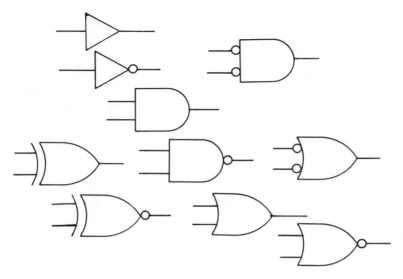

Techniques Needed for Changing Chips

The microscopic components on a chip are both rugged and reliable as well as sensitive and fragile. During computer breakdown, odds are good that the failure is not a chip but some other component or connection. Once the chip has been successfully soldered into place during manufacturing, it has a very high reliability rating. The situation is not at all like the failure rate that vacuum tubes were responsible for.

However, when a computer goes down, a lot of tests, desoldering and resoldering, handling, lead pulling, exposure to voltages, static electricity, dust, humidity, freezing and other deleterious forces are experienced by the chips. Even though a chip is good as you begin a repair, there is always the possibility it will end up damaged as you check out the trouble (Fig. 7-1).

There are some chips that are exceptionally sensitive to heat, voltage, and static electric charges. There are other chips that are not particularly bothered by these forces. The experienced tech knows the different chips and their peculiar characteristics that make them susceptible or not. The

rest of this chapter rounds up all the general techniques as they apply to the different forms of chips. That way, you can be able to change and test them with as much safety as possible.

TTLs, DTLs, AND RTLs

TTL stands for *Transistor-Transistor Logic* (Fig. 7-2), DTL for *Diode-Transistor Logic* (Fig. 7-3), and RTL is *Resistor-Transistor Logic* (Fig. 7-4). You won't see much of DTLs and RTLs anymore. Practically all computer chips of this type are TTLs. The TTL is known as a bipolar digital integrated circuit. The transistors are quite like their conventionally sized ancestors.

These transistors are called bipolar because conduction takes place in two directions at the same time. The electrons travel in one direction while holes travel in the other. This is different than the unipolar transistors, like a FET, that has either electrons or holes on the move but not simultaneously.

Even though you won't see much of RTLs or DTLs, it's a good idea to review them since they

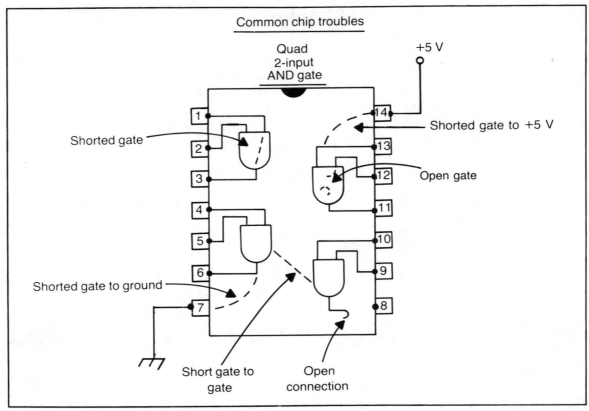

Common chip troubles

Quad
2-input
AND gate

+5 V

1
2 — Shorted gate
3
4
5
6
7 — Shorted gate to ground

14 — Shorted gate to +5 V
13
12 — Open gate
11
10
9
8

Short gate to gate

Open connection

Fig. 7-1 The six common ways a chip fails consist of four types of shorts and two types of opens. If one of the gates on a chip shorts the gate acts like a piece of wire rather than a logic device. When a gate shorts to ground, the leg that is shorted will be stuck low at ground potential. An internal short between two gates is hard to figure and can cause one of many symptoms. If a gate should short to +5 V the leg involved will be stuck high at +5 V. An open connection internal to the chip will assume the state of the circuits it is connected to. An open gate will not operate. Input/output tests at the pins should reveal the condition.

were the predecessors of the common TTLs. The RTL was an inexpensive chip that was easily interfaced with discrete components. However it had low immunity to voltage noises and low fanout ability. Fanout is the characteristic of being able to drive additional parallel logic loads. The number of identical loads the RTL can power are few. The illustration (Fig. 7-4) shows an RTL gate. Notice the resistors in the input base circuit of the npn transistors. That is why they are called resistor-transistor logic. This basic RTL circuit is called a NOR gate.

The DTL (Fig. 7-3) has diodes in the input circuits instead of the resistors. This change of component makes the gate faster, gives a lot of

noise immunity due to diode clipping and increases fanout. Also the DTL permits a large fan-in. The gate inputs are isolated from the previous gates and many parallel inputs can be attached without loading the input. This basic DTL circuit is called a NAND gate.

The basic TTL circuit is also a NAND gate (Fig. 7-2). These different forms of logic gates are discussed in detail in Chapter 9. The TTL first of all is much faster than the RTL and DTL. The circuit operation though is quite like the DTL. The reason the TTL is like the DTL is because there is in use in the TTL a special kind of transistor. The transistor, invented in 1961 by Thompson, has a number of emitters in one transistor. The extra emitters

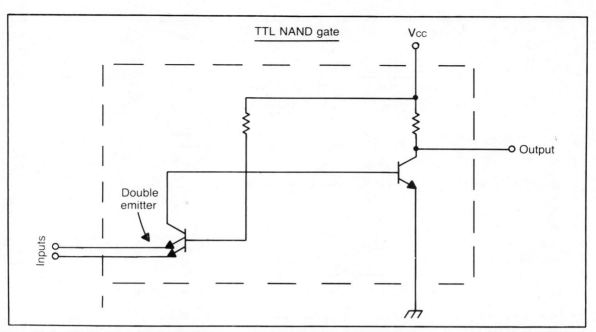

Fig. 7-2. TTL stands for Transistor-Transistor Logic and means the logic is accomplished by inputting the signal directly into two transistor emitters.

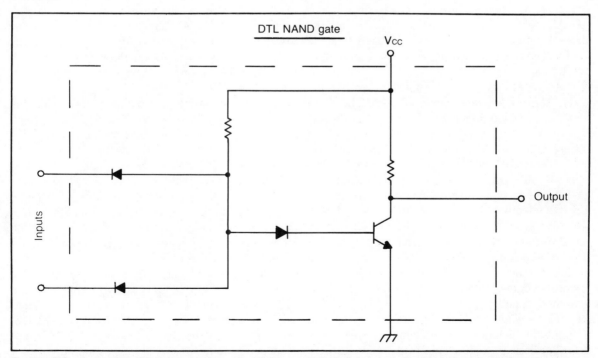

Fig. 7-3. DTL means Diode-Transistor Logic and has its inputs made directly into diodes before the transistor can process it.

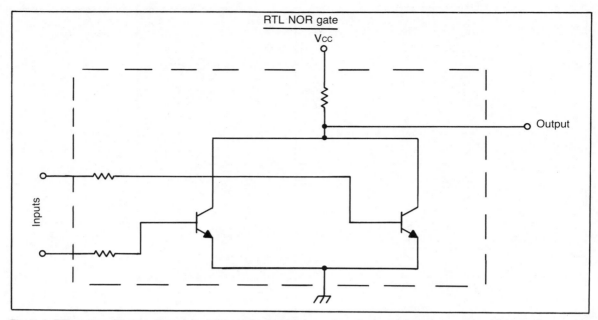

Fig. 7-4. RTL means Resistor-Transistor Logic and refers to the resistor inputs in the base circuits of the transistors.

which are pn junctions, just like diodes do a similar job. All the inputs to the TTL can enter through the multiple emitters and be diode isolated like the DTLs. The circuit operation is almost exactly like the DTLs.

The TTLs are bipolar digital integrated circuits. There is a whole family of them. There are about 160 of them in common use, at this writing. They have been given the series numbering in the 7400s. A list I have in front of me goes from 7400 to 7449. There are lots of missing numbers that will no doubt be filled in as time goes by (Table 7-1).

Actually, a lot of the numbers have the letters LS placed after the 74. For instance 74LS00, 74LS85, 74LS243, and so on (Table 7-2). The L stands for low power. When there is an L in the chip number it means the chip uses 80% less power than a chip without the L designation. However the lower power dissipation is at the expense of slower switching speed.

That's where the S designation comes in. The S stands for Schottky diode clamped. There is a Schottky barrier diode clamp in the base circuits that speeds up the switching action. As a servicer

you'll be replacing chips. If you are changing a 74LS type try to use a 74LS and not a 74 type. While the two chips might be functionally about the same, the exact replacement is always the best way to go. If you do make a change just be aware of it in case it doesn't work out.

There is another improvement to the TTL that has wide use. This is called TRI-STATE. If you'll recall computers are in the business of processing 1s and 0s. A 1 is also known as high, true, on, set, and +5 V. The 0 is also called low, false, off, reset, and 0 V. These are the two logic levels. The tristate is a third condition that TTLs with the TRI-STATE capability can assume. In a tristate condition there is no definable output condition. The TTL is not off, it is just in a high impedance state. The condition is said to be undefined.

In these TTLs there is a special input stage that disables the TTL gate. One example of such a TTL is shown in Fig. 7-5. There are three npn's and a diode in the disable stage. They are Q2, Q3, Q5, and D1. When the disable input is low, Q2 will conduct heavily or as it's called, saturate. As a result Q3 and Q5 will cutoff and the disable circuit

102

Table 7-1. The Family of TTLs Has Been Giving Generic Numbers Beginning With 7400 and Going Up Into Five Digits Beginning With 74.

Number	Price	Number	Price
7400	.19	74136	.50
7401	.19	74141	.65
7402	.19	74142	2.95
7403	.19	74143	2.95
7404	.19	74145	.60
7405	.25	74147	1.75
7406	.29	74148	1.20
7407	.29	74150	1.35
7408	.24	74151	.65
7409	.19	74152	.65
7410	.19	74153	.55
7411	.25	74154	1.40
7412	.30	74155	.75
7413	.35	74156	.65
7414	.55	74157	.55
7416	.25	74159	1.65
7417	.25	74160	.85
7420	.19	74161	.70
7421	.35	74162	.85
7422	.29	74163	.85
7423	.29	74164	.85
7425	.29	74165	.85
7426	.29	74166	1.00
7427	.29	74167	2.95
7428	.45	74170	1.65
7430	.19	74172	5.95
7432	.29	74173	.75
7433	.45	74174	.89
7437	.29	74175	.89
7438	.29	74176	.89
7440	.19	74177	.75
7442	.49	74178	1.15
7443	.65	74179	1.75
7444	.69	74180	.75
7445	.69	74181	2.25
7446	.59	74182	.75
7447	.69	74184	2.00
7448	.69	74185	2.00
7450	.19	74186	18.50
7451	.23	74190	1.15
7453	.23	74191	1.15
7454	.23	74192	.79
7460	.23	74193	.79
7470	.35	74194	.85
7472	.29	74195	.85
7473	.34	74196	.79
7474	.35	74197	.75
7475	.49	74198	1.35
7476	.35	74199	1.35
7480	.59	74221	1.35
7481	1.10	74246	1.35
7482	.95	74247	1.25
7483	.50	74248	1.85
7485	.65	74249	1.95
7486	.35	74251	.75
7489	4.95	74259	2.25
7490	.35	74265	1.35
7491	.40	74273	1.95
7492	.50	74276	1.25
7493	.49	74279	.75
7494	.65	74283	2.00
7495	.55	74284	3.75
7496	.70	74285	3.75
7497	2.75	74290	.95
74100	1.00	74293	.75
74107	.30	74298	.85
74109	.45	74351	2.25
74110	.45	74365	.65
74111	.55	74366	.65
74116	1.55	74367	.65
74120	1.20	74368	.65
74121	.29	74376	2.20
74122	.45	74390	1.75
74123	.55	74393	1.35
74125	.45	74425	3.15
74126	.45	74426	.85
74128	.55	74490	2.55
74132	.45		

Table 7-2. When a TTL Is Endowed With Qualities Such As Low Power and Schottky Diodes, an LS Designation is Added to the Generic Number.

Number	Price	Number	Price	Number	Price
74LS00	.25	74LS164	.95	74LS688	2.40
74LS01	.25	74LS165	.95	74LS689	2.40
74LS02	.25	74LS166	2.40	74LS783	24.95
74LS03	.25	74LS168	1.75		
74LS04	.25	74LS169	1.75		
74LS05	.25	74LS170	1.75		
74LS08	.35	74LS173	.80		
74LS09	.35	74LS174	.95		
74LS10	.25	74LS175	.95		
74LS11	.35	74LS181	2.15		
74LS12	.35	74LS189	9.95		
74LS13	.45	74LS190	1.00		
74LS14	1.00	74LS191	1.00		
74LS15	.35	74LS192	.85		
74LS20	.25	74LS193	.95		
74LS21	.35	74LS194	1.00		
74LS22	.25	74LS195	.95		
74LS26	.35	74LS196	.85		
74LS27	.35	74LS197	.85		
74LS28	.35	74LS221	1.20		
74LS30	.25	74LS240	1.29		
74LS32	.35	74LS241	1.29		
74LS33	.55	74LS242	1.85		
74LS37	.55	74LS243	1.85		
74LS38	.35	74LS244	1.29		
74LS40	.35	74LS245	1.90		
74LS42	.55	74LS247	.75		
74LS47	.75	74LS248	1.25		
74LS48	.75	74LS249	.99		
74LS49	.75	74LS251	1.30		
74LS51	.25	74LS253	.85		
74LS54	.35	74LS257	.85		
74LS55	.35	74LS258	.85		
74LS63	1.25	74LS259	2.85		
74LS73	.40	74LS260	.65		
74LS74	.45	74LS266	.55		
74LS75	.50	74LS273	1.65		
74LS76	.40	74LS275	3.35		
74LS78	.50	74LS279	.55		
74LS83	.75	74LS280	1.98		
74LS85	1.15	74LS283	1.00		
74LS86	.40	74LS290	1.25		
74LS90	.65	74LS293	1.85		
74LS91	.89	74LS295	1.05		
74LS92	.70	74LS298	1.20		
74LS93	.65	74LS324	1.75		
74LS95	.85	74LS352	1.56		
74LS96	.95	74LS353	1.55		
74LS107	.40	74LS363	1.35		
74LS109	.40	74LS364	1.95		
74LS112	.45	74LS365	.95		
74LS113	.45	74LS366	.95		
74LS114	.50	74LS367	.70		
74LS122	.45	74LS368	.70		
74LS123	.95	74LS373	1.75		
74LS124	2.99	74LS374	1.75		
74LS125	.95	74LS377	1.45		
74LS126	.85	74LS378	1.18		
74LS132	.75	74LS379	1.35		
74LS136	.55	74LS385	1.90		
74LS137	.99	74LS386	.65		
74LS138	.75	74LS390	1.90		
74LS139	.75	74LS393	1.90		
74LS145	1.20	74LS395	1.65		
74LS147	2.49	74LS399	1.70		
74LS148	1.35	74LS424	2.95		
74LS151	.75	74LS447	.37		
74LS153	.75	74LS490	1.95		
74LS154	2.35	74LS624	3.99		
74LS155	1.15	74LS668	1.69		
74LS156	.95	74LS669	1.89		
74LS157	.75	74LS670	2.20		
74LS158	.75	74LS674	9.65		
74LS160	.90	74LS682	3.20		
74LS161	.95	74LS683	2.30		
74LS162	.95	74LS684	2.40		
74LS163	.95	74LS685	2.40		

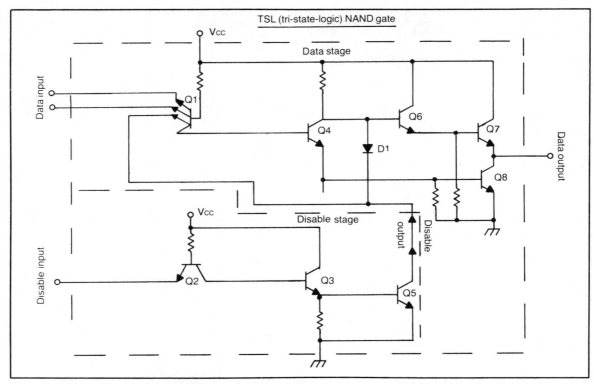

Fig.7-5. This NAND gate is a TSL (tri-state-logic) since the output of the disable stage acts as a switch on the data stage. The two circuits are both in the same gate chip.

has no effect on the rest of the chip. The chip can process the 1s and 0s without interference.

Should the input of the disable circuit go high Q3 and Q5 will conduct and kill the output current at Q4 which makes the output transistors Q7 and Q8 stop conducting. If you test the output you find neither a high nor a low. There will be an undefined state there, somewhere between high and low.

A tristate device typically can be tested at its output with a vom. The output is said to be either in a steady state or floating. The steady state is when the voltage indicates a 1 or a 0. The floating condition happens when the device is in a disabled state. The disabling could be intentional due to the special disable circuit or it could be due to defect in the TTL.

A logical 1 is defined as a voltage equal to or more than 2.3 volts. The logical 0 is defined as a voltage equal to or less than 0.8 volts. During tri-

state floating the noise in the computer creates a voltage in the area of 1.5 volts. Any voltage between 0.9 and 2.2 volts can be considered floating. Learning to analyze the highs, lows, and floating status of signals is one of the most important servicing techniques you'll be using to repair computers (Table 7-3).

MOS CHIPS

In the 1960s, when chips were installed into electronic circuits, they were usually types like the TTL. The TTL uses bipolar transistors as the basic elements. When the servicer thought about the internal workings of these chips, his mind filled with emitters, bases, and collectors in various configurations. The TTLs were packaged in dual in-line packages called *DIP*.

As the 1970s arrived, a second major category of chips surfaced. These were the MOSs. MOS stands for *metal oxide silicon* and they did not use the npn or pnp bipolar transistors. The basic element in these ICs are the FET, the field-effect transistor. The FETs are packaged just like the TTL. The chip is contained in a DIP.

The basic FET is not like an npn or pnp. It acts more like a vacuum tube than a transistor. It is voltage-controlled rather than a current-controlled device. While the current between the emitter and base controls the current flow between emitter and collector in an npn, in the FET it does not. In the FET there is a source, gate, and drain that is roughly analogous to the emitter, base, and collector. However, the source, gate, and drain acts more like the cathode, control grid, and plate of a vacuum tube (Fig. 7-6). A bias voltage between the cathode and control grid of a tube controls the cathode to plate current flow. A bias voltage between the source and gate of a FET controls the current flow between the source and drain.

The FET has a channel of semiconductor material, either n- or p-type silicon. The channel acts like the vacuum in a tube. In the tube there is a cathode at one end of the vacuum and a plate at the other end. The electrons flow through the vacuum from cathode to plate. In a FET the channel could be a length of n-type silicon. If a connection called a source is made at one end of the channel, and

another connection called a drain is made at the other end of the channel, electrons can flow from source to drain. All you need is a + voltage on the drain, a bias voltage on the gate, and the source grounded.

On chips the basic FET is not used. Insulated gate FETs are installed, they are called IGFETs. To control the electron flow a gate can be installed somewhere between the source and drain (Fig. 7-7). The gate is an attachment to the channel too. Only instead of the gate wire being connected directly to the p material a piece of glassy silicon dioxide, which is an insulator, is placed between the wire and the p channel. This stops any dc from passing between the wire and the p channel, but allows ac or signal to pass undisturbed. If this metal oxide separator should somehow rupture, the short kills the FET. Unfortunately, these oxide insulators are prone to rupture. If static electricity (Fig. 7-8), excess heat or humidity, or careless handling occurs, the result can be a dead FET.

There are three types of MOSs in common use in computers. There is first of all the n channel which is called NMOS. It is used a lot in large scale integration (LSI), where there are more than 100 individual gates on a chip. The NMOS uses a positive dc supply. The NMOS is said to be a single channel, one polarity chip. The dc voltage applied

Table 7-3. The Disabled TTL Chip Reads 0.9 to 2.2 Volts. A High State Is Any Voltage Above and a Low State Is Any Voltage Below. The Vom Reads the Voltages Directly, While the Logic Probe Indicates the Existing State With LED Lights.

LOGIC STATE	TEST READINGS	
	VOM READING	LOGIC PROBE LED LIGHTS
HIGH	2.3 V to 5.0 V	HIGH ● LOW ○ PULSE ○
LOW	0 V to 0.8 V	○ ● ○
TRISTATE FLOATING	0.9 V to 2.2 V	○ ○ ○

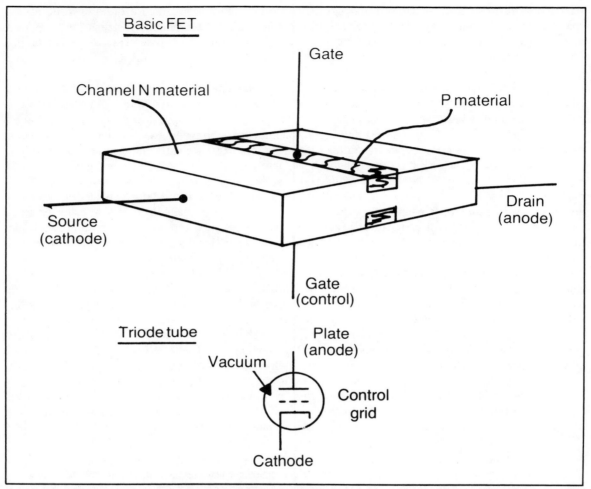

Fig. 7-6. The FET acts almost exactly like a vacuum tube. The semiconductor channel in the FET takes the place of the vacuum in the tube as the electron traveling path. The source acts like a cathode, the drain like the plate and the gate like the control grid.

goes to all the FETs on the chip at the same time. The ground return is also connected to every FET on the chip. The gates, sources and drain though have their own configurations according to the job they are doing on the chip.

When the channel is made of p material, the FET works in a similar way, except holes move from source to drain instead of the negatively charged electrons. A negative dc voltage is needed on the drain to attract the holes. The gate still does the same job except it controls holes instead of

electrons. You can recognize a chip with a p channel because the schematic shows a negative dc supply is connected to the chip. Whatever the polarity, whether holes or electrons are on the move, the sensitivity of the MOS chip to gate oxide rupture remains the same. Great care must be taken while testing and handling MOS chips.

There is a third type of MOS called the CMOS. This is perhaps the commonest type MOS chip in the small scale integration (SSI), less than 10 gates to a chip, and medium scale integration (MSI), 10 to

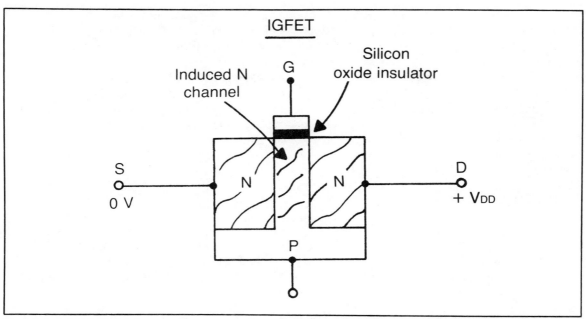

Fig. 7-7. In the FET the electrons or holes pass from the source to the drain. A glassy insulator separates the gate from the channel.

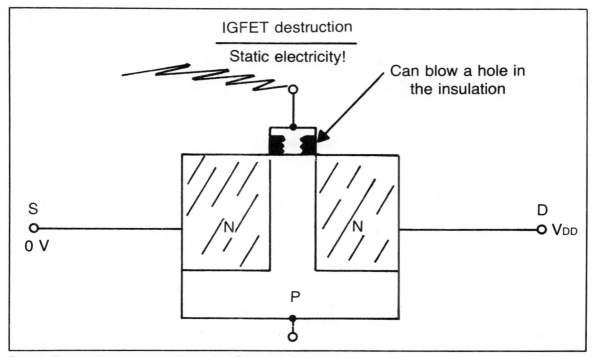

Fig. 7-8. The gate insulator is sensitive and easily ruptured if carelessly handled.

100 gates to a chip. Remember a gate can contain a number of FETs. The CMOS stands for *Complementary MOS*. This means there are FETs on the chip that complement or are the counterpart of each other. There are both p-channel and n-channel FETs on the same chip. How is this done?

Usually the chip starts out with an n substrate (Fig. 7-9). The substrate is a piece of semiconductor material that all the microscopic components of the chip are fabricated upon. If the substrate is n material, PMOS FETs can be built on it. That takes care of a base for the PMOSs. What about the NMOSs?

A pocket of p material is diffused into the n substrate. The pocket of p material becomes a second substrate. NMOS FETs can be fabricated on this second substrate. This layout allows both PMOS and NMOSFETs to reside in the same chip. Typically the supply voltage to a CMOS is of a + nature. Internal wiring takes care of applying the correct voltages to the different type channels. The NMOS is able to propel electrons from source to drain. The PMOS is able to move holes from source to drain. The gates exercise control over the channel currents no matter whether electrons or holes are on the move.

Just as the TTL chips have been designated numbers in the 7400 series, or 74LS00 series, CMOS small package chips have been assigned numbers in the 4000 series. Common off the shelf numbers range from 4000 through 4724. Table 7-4 shows the usually available chips. There are about 90 of them.

In addition to the 4000 series there is also a CMOS 74——— series. A typical CMOS number in this series could be 74C00. The C denotes CMOS. With the 74 classification you can buy a CMOS pin for pin, and exact function that is not an exact replacement but is a designer or hobbyist alternative to the TTL.

THE CHIP IN YOUR HAND

If you pick up a chip and look at it closely, you'll be seeing a dual in-line package or DIP. It obviously is called DIP because there is two rows of tiny feet, with both rows in-line. The chip is a rectangle with a keynotch on one end. The key, like the keyway on a vacuum tube socket, is between the highest number foot and foot number 1. Looking down from the top with the chip standing on its feet, the pins are numbered counter clockwise. Most of the time you'll be testing chips for voltages, states, and resistances, you'll be looking down from the top, so reading pin numbers should become second nature reading counter clockwise. To give you further aid in reading pins, the manufacturer often places a tiny paint dot alongside pin 1.

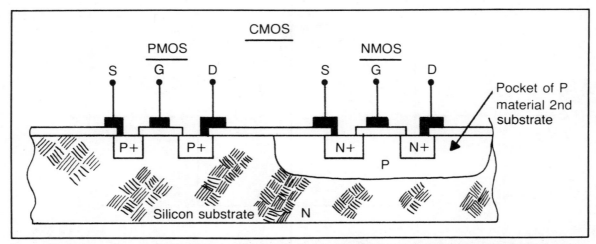

Fig. 7-9. The commonest type of MOS chip is the CMOS which contains both PMOS and NMOS FETs on the same substrate.

Table 7-4. The CMOS Chips Have Generic Numbers in the 4000 Series.
There is also a Line of CMOS Types That Correspond With TTL Types. They Are Identified by a C After the 74. They Begin With 74C00.

4000	.35	4066	.75	4543	2.70	74C161	2.00
4001	.35	4068	.40	4555	.95	74C162	2.00
4002	.25	4069	.35	4556	.95	74C163	2.00
4006	.95	4070	.35	4581	1.95	74C164	2.00
4007	.29	4071	.30	4582	1.95	74C165	2.00
4008	.95	4072	.30	4584	.95	74C173	2.00
4009	.45	4073	.30	4584	.95	74C174	2.25
4010	.45	4075	.30	4702	12.95	74C175	2.25
4011	.35	4076	.95	4724	1.50	74C192	2.25
4012	.25	4078	.30	80C07	.95	74C193	2.25
4013	.45	4081	.30	80C95	.85	74C195	2.25
4014	.95	4082	.30	80C96	.95	74C200	5.75
4015	.95	4085	.95	80C97	.95	74C221	2.25
4016	.45	4086	.95	80C98	1.20	74C373	2.75
4017	1.15	4093	.95	74C00	.35	74C374	2.75
4018	.95	4098	2.49	74C02	.35	74C901	.80
4019	.45	4099	1.95	74C04	.35	74C902	.85
4020	.95	14409	12.95	74C08	.35	74C903	.85
4021	.95	14410	12.95	74C10	.35	74C905	10.95
4022	1.15	14411	11.95	74C14	1.50	74C906	.95
4023	.35	14412	12.95	74C20	.35	74C907	1.00
4024	.75	14419	4.95	74C30	.35	74C908	2.00
4025	.35	4502	.95	74C32	.50	74C909	2.75
4026	1.65	4503	.65	74C42	1.75	74C910	9.95
4027	.65	4508	1.95	74C48	1.20	74C911	10.00
4028	.80	4510	.95	74C73	.65	74C912	10.00
4029	.95	4511	.95	74C74	.85	74C914	1.95
4030	.45	4512	.95	74C76	.80	74C915	2.00
4034	2.95	4514	1.25	74C83	1.95	74C918	2.75
4035	.85	4515	2.25	74C85	1.95	74C920	17.95
4040	.95	4516	1.55	74C86	.95	74C921	15.95
4041	1.25	4518	1.25	74C89	4.50	74C922	5.59
4042	.75	4519	1.25	74C90	1.75	74C923	5.95
4043	.85	4520	1.25	74C93	1.75	74C925	6.75
4044	.85	4522	1.25	74C95	1.75	74C926	7.95
4046	.95	4526	1.25	74C107	1.00	74C927	7.95
4047	.95	4527	1.95	74C150	5.75	74C928	7.95
4049	.55	4528	1.25	74C151	2.25	74C929	19.95
4050	.55	4531	.95	74C154	3.25	74C930	19.95
4051	.95	4532	1.95	74C157	1.75		
4053	.95	4538	1.95	74C160	2.00		
4060	1.45	4539	1.95				

Chips come in SSI, MSI, and LSI levels of circuit numbers. As mentioned, SSI indicates there are less than 10 gates internally connected in the DIP, MSI means there are less than 100 but more than 10, while LSI shows more than 100 gates on the chip. There are chips called VLSI (*Very Large Scale Integration*) and even larger chips. However the LSI is probably the largest you'll see in the typical home computer. Starting in the SSI range, chips are packaged in 8, 14, and 16 pin DIPs. Next DIPs are found 18, 24, 28, and other pin sizes up to 40. The DIPs with more than 40 pins are VSLIs.

Printed on most chips are bits of other information that are useful for testing and replacing chips. You'll see the logo of the manufacturer. There is a date code that is needed to exercise warranties. The warranty code data will be peculiar to the manufacturer. You'll need to know how to read the code. There is also the part number. TTLs will be 7400 series, and CMOSs will be 4000 series or 74C00 numbers.

As you look over the integrated circuit section of a computer's parts list, in addition to the ordinary TTLs and MOSs there are lots of other numbers. There is the MPU, input-output LSIs, RAM and ROM chips, character generators, voltage regulators, and others. We will cover some of them as the book goes on, and others you'll have to figure out for testing and replacing with the help of the manufacturer's service notes. However, if you master the ordinary chips the rest will be easier to cope with.

IC EXTRACTION TECHNIQUE

It probably can't be helped, but a good rule to follow is, never touch an IC with your hand, body, or clothing. TTLs are not as sensitive as MOSs, but I'd use that rule for both. It is quite possible that you are lifting an MOS when you think you have a TTL in tow. The reason for the antiseptic approach is not fear of germs, it is the danger of electrocution by static electricity. The Achilles heel of the MOS is the insulated gates in the multitude of FETs on the chip.

The way to avoid bad handling is with a little gadget called a DIP extractor tool (Fig. 7-10). It's nothing but a tweezer formed of steel. It is built so two little lips can be placed under the two ends of the chip and allows you to pull the chip gingerly out of its socket. Once out the tool allows you to place the chip on a conductive surface. The conductive surface shorts all the pins together and no static potential can build up and kill an FET gate.

The DIP extractor tool will come with a small hole on its top. This is to provide a place to attach a grounding strap. When using the tool for extraction attach the grounding strap to a convenient ground like the computer chassis ground. It goes without saying, do not remove or insert chips while the computer is plugged in to ac, whether it is on or off.

The DIP extractor tool works easily with chips that have 8 to 24 pins. With larger chips it is handy too, but a bit more care must be taken. The longer DIP body will be placed under more strain as you pull it out of its socket by the ends. Therefore, before you lift the chip, make sure you have rocked

it out of the socket. That way there is little or no holding action by the socket. Again once the chip is free, the best place for it is standing on its feet on a conductive surface, so all the pins are shorted together.

The most sensitive of the chips are the RAMs. On some RAM packages you are instructed to ground yourself and keep RAMs in a conductive tube or conductive foam. If you handle the RAMs with the grounded extractor, you are accomplishing the same purposes.

IC INSERTION TECHNIQUE

If a chip is sitting on a conductive surface and you want to install it into an IC socket on a print board, you could use the extractor, if you are surehanded and careful. There are pitfalls though, as the little chip legs are fragile and getting all the feet into the socket hole at the same time is tricky. Therefore it is advisable to use a DIP insertion tool (Fig. 7-11).

At first glance the insertion tool looks complicated. There is a conductive post on top of the tool. That's there so you can attach a grounding strap. The post goes all the way through the tool. The post ends at the two metal holders sticking out of the bottom of the tool. If you pull on the post you can see the way the holders work. The holders are able to

Fig. 7-10. To extract a chip, be sure to use the tweezerlike gadget that is easily purchased. Its use will avoid a lot of complications (courtesy of Michael Gorzeck).

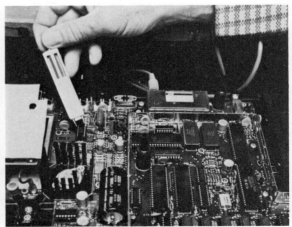

Fig. 7-11. To install a chip, this groundable insertion tool makes the ticklish task easy (courtesy of Michael Gorzeck).

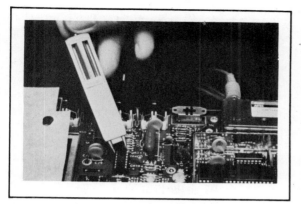

Fig.7-12. It is good technique to always straighten the chip pins one last time before installing the chip permanently into its socket (courtesy of Michael Gorzeck).

grasp a chip and let it go as you pull the post down and up. There is a locking button on the side of the gadget that locks the holders and post so the chip can't accidentally get dropped during the activity.

Lastly, the insertion tool should come with a pin straightener. The pin straightener must be grounded to the post too. All the metal in the insertion tool is grounded to the conductive post. The following is the safe procedure to insert a fragile chip.

The subject chip should be standing on its own feet on a conductive surface. At this juncture the entire pinout is at the voltage level of the surface, which is zero volts or ground. Look closely at the pins. Are any of them bent at all?

If any are, pick up the chip with the grounded extractor tool. Push the chip, legs first into the grounded pin straightener (Fig. 7-12). Rock the chip gently till all the pins have the correct in-line spacing. Then place the chip back on the conductive surface. Do not use the extractor to install the chip in its socket. If you do there is a good possibility of bending the pins out of line.

Pick up the insertion tool. The tool's grounding post is attached to the computer chassis. Pull the post out. The twin holders will retract. Place the tool over the subject chip and release the post slowly. The holders will come down snugly around the chip. The chip will now be held properly and also the metallic holders are grounding all the pins

to the chassis. The chip is as safe as it can be under the circumstances.

Next, place the chip over its socket and put all the pins into their correct holes. Observe the keyway on the chip and socket so the chip is not forced in reversed. The keyway is not like a tube socket where it is impossible to insert a tube in wrong. The chip keyway serves no physical duty. It only points the way.

Once the pins are started in their holes, pull the post up. The holders will release. Push the chip into its socket till it is seated all the way. Remove the extractor tool. If you follow the step-by-step procedure with the idea of keeping the chip pins grounded, you'll see they were grounded for the entire procedure, except for a moment during pin straightening, when the chip was in the air, in the grasp of the extractor. The extractor only holds on to the plastic packaging material. The inserter also holds on to the metal pins. All the time the inserter held the chip, grounding was going on.

While the chip was being rocked in the pin straightener, the chip was grounded, since the metal straightener is grounded. That's the trick to keeping MOS chips intact. During handling keep all the pins grounded together attached to a safe ground area like the computer chassis. If you must move or manipulate the chips by hand, make sure that you are grounded. Attach grounding straps to your wrist watch, belt buckle and so on. Should you have to move chips from one place to another, even across the room, keep the chips in some sort of grounded condition. It is very aggravating to order a chip, have it arrive after a week or two, and then lose it to static electricity as you walk across a carpet on a low humidity day. When a few precautions are taken, even though the safety measures are a bit of trouble, you can avoid the booby trap.

SOLDERING PRECAUTIONS

There comes a time in the life of a troubleshooter when it is necessary to desolder and resolder a sensitive chip. This job has been described as one that is accomplished by an artisan. Perhaps this is true if you want to reproduce the same finished look that is accomplished by a factory production line. However, as much as you take pride in your work, the look of the finished job is no where as important as the fact that the defunct chip is replaced and the computer is working again.

Once the decision is made to desolder a chip, whether it is known bad, just suspected as defective, or must be removed as a test, the exposure to problems becomes a large factor. It is bad enough to have one trouble in a computer and great care must be taken to avoid "inducing" more problems.

The first step to be taken is to reach for the right soldering iron. Only the right one will do. Don't grab the 100/140 watt bench gun. It is too hot! Take out the lowest wattage iron you have. One that will just about melt the solder. Thirty watts is the absolute maximum and if you have an iron with less wattage, better still. The iron should be one specifically designed to be used for chips or sensitive transistors. They are on the market, battery operated and otherwise dc type irons. These can be good to use when replacing MOS chips since there is no 60 Hz line voltage sine waves to contend with. However, you can use conventional low wattage irons if you ground them, like you did your wrist watch, while handling MOS chips.

Controlling the heat is the skill needed to produce good solder connections. Too much heat, even momentarily, or prolonged heat even from a low wattage iron can kill a chip. Too little heat doesn't let the solder attach properly to the connection and a cold solder joint is the result. The surfaces to be soldered must be clean and the tip of the iron nicely tinned all during the operation. That way the good connection is made in the fastest possible time.

Heatsink techniques are mandatory. The best heatsink is to grasp the lead between the connection and the body of the chip. The heat will take the easiest path to dissipation, which is through the fat plier nose rather than the skinny lead to the chip. If you ground the pliers too, you'll get rid of any static buildup at the same time.

The solder tip can be kept clean by wiping it with a paper towel. Naturally, don't let the towel char or burn. The solder should be rosin core 60-40 (tin to lead). It melts at 371 degrees F.

Desoldering a chip is not too difficult espe- cially if you know it is bad and you don't care what happens to it. Even if you do care the technique is easy. The print board must be free at the top and at the bottom where the chip to be worked on is. A good bench lamp with a magnifier is very useful in these tight places. Getting into a position and not feeling awkward or off balance is important. Then the job begins.

A lot of manual dexterity and patience is your next necessity. A small clip lead with lamp cord sized wire can be attached between the connection and the chip. When the heat is applied most of it will flow into the lamp cord. Apply heat to a pin, jiggle the tiny pin with a solder pick and wipe the connection. Keep doing that till the pin is free or the solder in the print board hole is about gone. Then go to the next connection. Work over each individual connection till the chip is free.

If you are sure the chip is bad or the chip won't free up easily, so you must replace the chip in case you destroy it, then you don't have to be so careful. You can apply heat and pry till the chip pops loose. Just be careful of the board and nearby components.

RESOLDERING THE REPLACEMENT

Once the old chip is out clean up the holes in the print board. Use some heat, some wiping and pick out all the excess solder. The new replacement or the old still good chip can then be pushed into the holes. A drop of properly heated solder can then be applied to each connection, checked out for shorts or opens and the job is done.

As you can see, the tough part of the job is the patient extrication of each lead during the desoldering. It is good technique never to have to desolder the same chip twice. Often a particular chip has been the victim of a manufacturer's design mistake. That chip will fail time and again during the life of the computer. You'll not be too thrilled to have to desolder and resolder the same chip over and over again. It's easy to avoid that type of unpleasant chore. Make it a rule in your repertoire of soldering techniques, to always install a socket whenever you have to take out an unsocketed chip. That way you'll never have to resolder that particular chip again.

Chapter 8

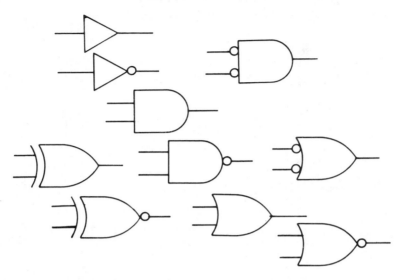

Computer Block Diagram

The chip location guide discussed in Chapter 3 showed where on the print board the different chips were installed. This is a valuable servicing aid and will be instrumental in cluing many repairs to completion. The chip location guide permits a shotgun, direct replacement, tube changing style approach that fixes troubles quickly. However, the shotgun method does not cure more than about half of all troubles. The other half requires knowledge of the computer. Besides knowing where the chips are physically you must also learn where the chips are in the computer scheme of things and how they all operate as a system to do all the home, business, and science jobs of which they are capable.

A SIMPLE COMPUTER

A simple computer needs the following pieces of hardware (Fig. 8-1). First of all, there must be a CPU. This is the heart and the hardest worker in the system. Next the computer needs memory. It has both ROM and RAM. Then the computer has to have some input-output chips. These interface with

the input and output devices. The main input devices are the keyboard and the cassette player. The important output units are the TV display, a line printer, and the cassette recorder. Note the cassette is both input and output, using the player section for the input role and the recorder part to do the output work. With the above mentioned devices a computer can be wired together. Let's go through the system as it takes shape in a block diagram fashion.

THE CPU

The CPU only does five main jobs. It does one job with addresses, one job with instructions, and three jobs with data. We'll examine the addressing duty first (Fig. 8-2).

On the print board you'll see a set of copper etch tracks that run all around from one chip to another. There are a lot of etch tracks on the board, the ones I'm mentioning are a set of 16 parallel lines. This is the address bus. The address bus originates in the CPU. The address bus is attached

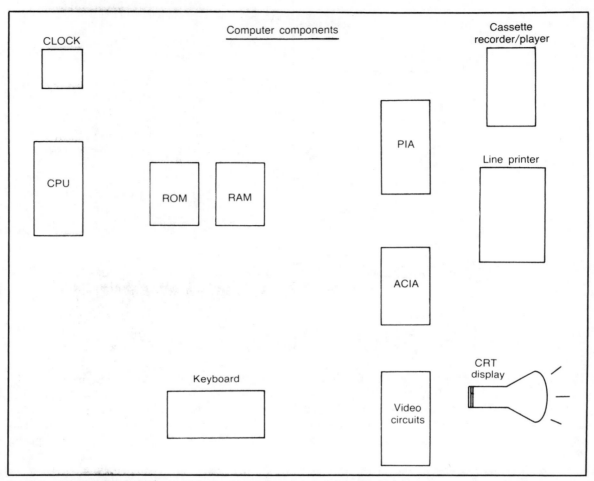

Fig. 8-1. The simple and useful computer should contain these various components.

to the 16-bit registers in the CPU. These 16-bit registers create an address made up of 1s and 0s. There are 65,536 possible combinations of 1s and 0s in 16 bits of a register. This means the registers can create 65,536 different addresses. By sending out one of these addresses the CPU can connect to any address it desires. The destination address is built to answer to its own address and no other, much like what happens when you dial a telephone number. When the CPU forms an address and outputs it over the address bus, that particular address responds by activating its circuit and waiting for an instruction. Therefore, the first job the CPU can do is address one of its possible 65,536 addresses.

The next duty the CPU can do is generate instructions. After a place in the computer has been addressed it stands by for instructions. The instructions which are also a collection of 1s and 0s are electronic tricks the CPU can perform. The instructions are aptly called the Instruction Set of the CPU. One of the instructions is called LOAD. This means "load the 1s and 0s that you are holding into the CPU". When the location that was addressed, and is standing by, receives the LOAD instruction it knows that its contents are to be sent to the CPU.

This brings up the next CPU job. In addition to the 16-track address bus, the CPU has a second bus. The second bus only has 8 tracks and is attached to

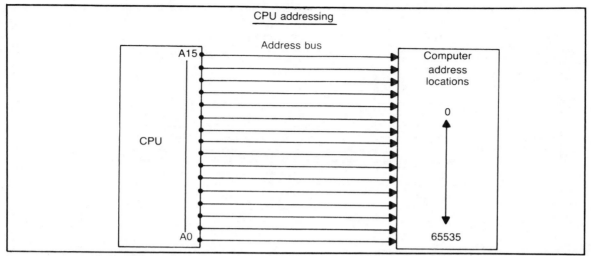

Fig. 8-2. The addressing originates in the CPU. The typical CPU in the home computer can address 65,536 separate locations.

8-bit registers in the CPU. These side-by-side 8-etch tracks are called the data bus. They originate at the CPU too and travel the length and width of the print board from chip to chip. They are there to transport the contents of addresses from the chip to the CPU. The data bus lines are attached to the various chips like the address bus lines but at different pins. This brings us to the third job of the CPU (Fig. 8-3). When the address bus opens up an address, and the instruction says LOAD, the con-

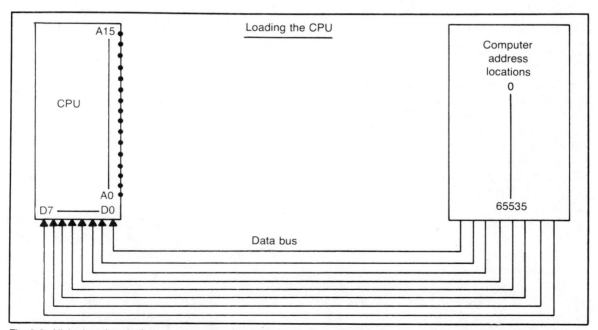

Fig. 8-3. All the locations in the computer are attached to the same lines as the data bus. Once a location is addressed it can LOAD its contents into the CPU via the eight lines of the common data bus.

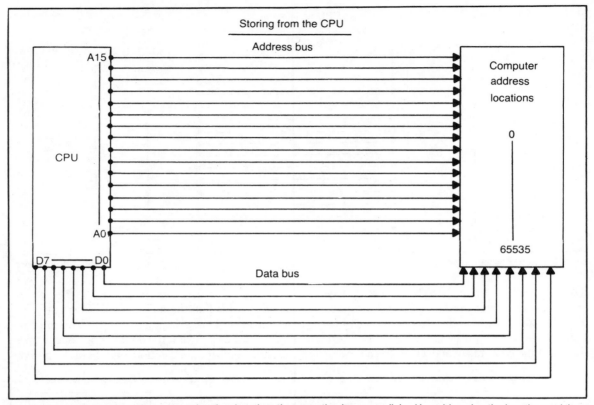

Fig. 8-4. In case it is necessary to store data in a location, the operation is accomplished by addressing the location and then sending the data via the data bus to that address.

tents of the address, more 1s and 0s, are spilled onto the data bus, and speed to the CPU.

The fourth job of the CPU occurs when the contents of the address, which is called data, arrives and is loaded into the 8-bit register in the CPU. Once the data is in the CPU the CPU can operate on the data. It can add to it, subtract from it, change the 1s to 0s, and otherwise manipulate the data. The CPU is thus able to perform a lot of arithmetical and logical operations on the data which is the fourth job it is able to do.

The fifth duty is sending the data back into storage at some address (Fig. 8-4). Once the data has been processed in the CPU, an address is created out of the 64K combinations the address bus can handle. The address activates in readiness. The instruction STORE is given and the finished data is placed into the data bus. The data then speeds to the waiting address and gets its 1s and 0s stored at the address.

RAM

Typical RAMs, read and write memorys, in home computers are made up of rows and rows of 8-bit memory registers. Each row has its very own 16-bit address. The CPU can dial up any individual row it desires.

While the 16-bit address bus can become attached to any register, the 8-bit data bus also gets connected if the register is addressed. However, no data can get into the address bus, the data only travels on the data bus. The greatest confusion in computer understanding happens because the address bus gets mixed up with the data bus. The two buses really have nothing to do with each other. Their connections, although to the same devices, perform entirely different duties. Make a lot of mental effort to keep the addressing and data movement separate (Fig. 8-5).

The RAM is a storage place for data. The data is broken down into 8-bit pieces that will be able to be stored, loaded to the CPU, worked on in the CPU and then be stored again in the RAM. The loading operation is also called reading from the RAM. The storing capability is also called writing to the RAM. That's where the reading and writing name for RAM came from.

The RAM is mostly storage areas for bits that are constantly on the move between the CPU and the RAM chips. There is one section of RAM, for instance 512 bytes, that is called video RAM (Fig. 8-6). This ½K byte area does more than store bytes of data. The video RAM is also connected to the TV part of the computer. Any bytes that go to the video RAM are immediately transferred to the video display circuits and appear on the TV screen.

The TV display is a carefully designed area (Fig. 8-7). If 512 bytes of RAM is assigned for video duty, 512 little blocks of picture tube area is laid out to accommodate and display the contents of video RAM. For example, if the TV display has 512 blocks they could be in 16 rows of 32 columns each. As you type on the keyboard, each letter or number gets put into video RAM in sequence. The letters or numbers then appear on the TV screen 32 characters to a line and can fill 16 lines. This procedure is discussed in detail in the video chapters. The video RAM plays an important role.

ROM

The ROM, read only memory, is attached to the address and data bus lines in the same way as

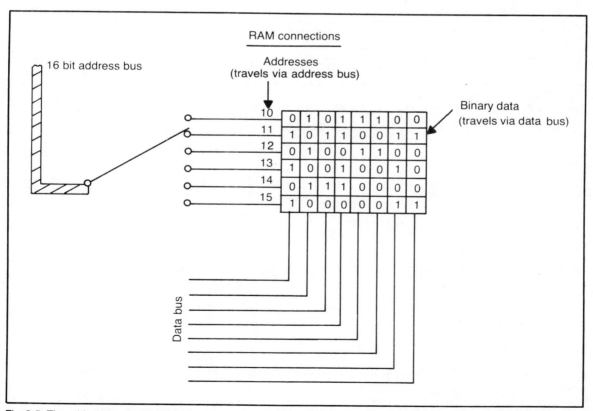

Fig. 8-5. The address bus is able to switch electronically from location to location. The data bus gets connected to whichever location is addressed.

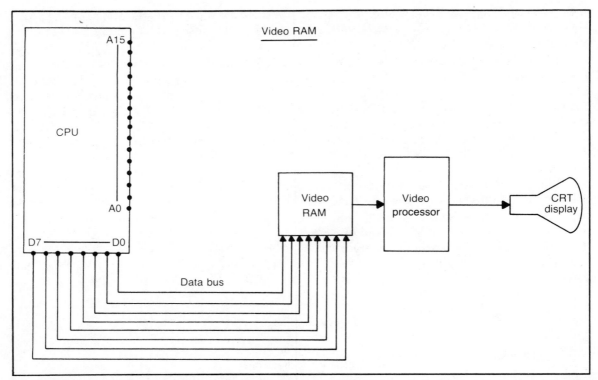

Fig. 8-6. The part of RAM that is called video RAM is connected to the video circuits as well as the data bus. A copy of the video RAM contents is sent to the video circuits for display as well as being stored.

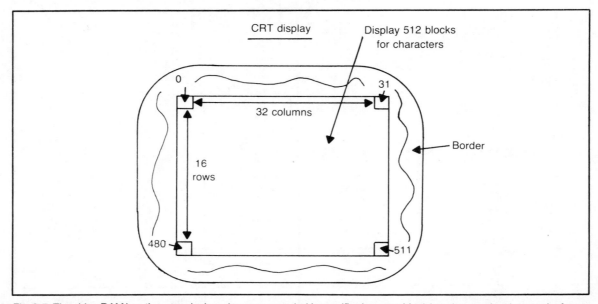

Fig. 8-7. The video RAM locations are designed to correspond with specific character block locations on the picture tube face.

the RAM chips are. The ROM is also made up of rows and rows of 8 bit memory registers each with its own 16-bit address. The ROM, though, has entirely different circuitry in the registers. In each of the eight cells of a register is a transistor or diode that is either able to conduct or is blown open. If it can conduct it represents a 1. When it's open it is the electronic representation of a binary 0.

The RAM registers, on the other hand, have little circuits in each bit that is capable of holding a 1 or 0 while the computer is energized. If the computer goes off the RAMs lose all the 1s and 0s they are storing. The ROM keeps the information all the time whether the computer is on or not. The ROMs 1s and 0s are burnt into the registers permanently.

The ROM is in charge of the operation of the computer. Most home computers are basically alike. They all have similar CPUs, RAMs, and the other devices. Only the ROMs are different. If the computer is mainly a game unit, the ROM will contain a program that is burnt in to play the game. When the computer is working as a word processor, the ROM is full of word processing instructions. Should the computer be used to detect burglaries, the ROM contains all the instructions and data to do the job. You can get RAM to act like ROM by filling RAM with a program.

A ROM gives the computer instructions on what to do. If the ROM should go bad, the CPU would blindly turn on and start addressing in a wild and haphazard fashion. The CPU would then continue and begin executing any instructions in any way. The results would be garbage on the TV display and burps from the sound system if the computer did start.

The ROM normally starts the computer working as you turn it on. The CPU is built so that it jumps to the start address of the ROM as soon as it is energized. This is about the extent of the CPU knowing what to do. The CPU needs instructions to do practically anything else. Once the start address is reached the ROM takes over the operation.

INPUT-OUTPUT CHIPS

The CPU, RAM, and ROM wired together with the address and data bus lines and other supporting hardware, can do all the work inside the computer. The RAM can store the instructions and

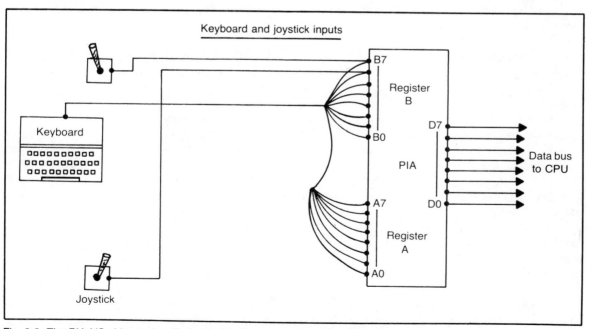

Fig. 8-8. The PIA I/O chip can handle inputs like the keyboard and joysticks among others.

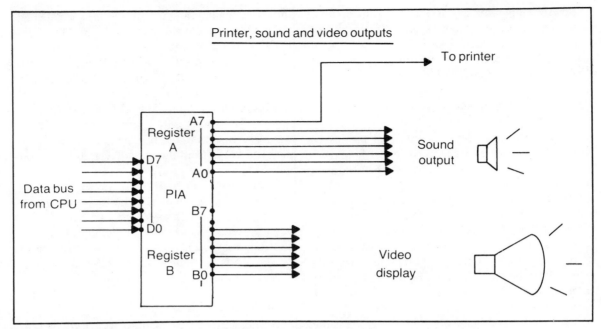

Fig. 8-9. The PIA I/O chip is also able to handle outputs like the video display, sound, and printer.

data, the CPU can address the system, work on the instructions and data, and the ROM can oversee the operation and make sure the CPU is working in a logical and not haphazard fashion. All that's missing from a complete system is some way to get input to work on, and another way to output the results. That's the job of chips like a PIA or ACIA.

The PIA has four 8-bit addresses. There is one 8-bit register that connects to the data bus line just like the RAM and ROM does. There are two 8-bit registers that can connect to devices like the keyboard, cassette, or joysticks. There are eight miscellaneous bits that take care of various other duties.

The PIA can use the two registers that connect to the I/O devices as either input or output lines. For example, one PIA can use these two registers to take the inputs from a keyboard or a joystick (Fig. 8-8). A second PIA can use these identical registers to output to the printer, to a sound circuit and to the video display generator (Fig. 8-9).

An ACIA is another chip that can connect the computer to I/O devices. It is also connected to the eight data bus lines. It has two addresses in the memory. These addresses are also 8-bit registers. The ACIA has been used to communicate with teletypewriters. It is not as common in a home computer as a PIA.

THE COMPUTER IN ACTION

You sit down at your home computer (Fig. 8-10). The keyboard is beneath your fingertips. The TV display is at eye level. The printer, cassette, and joysticks are arranged neatly. You turn on the TV and the printer. The cassette is under control of the computer and will become available when you turn on the computer itself. The computer is always the last on and first off so the activation of the other pieces cannot interfere with computer workings.

The TV starts lighting its face. Meanwhile in the computer, the master clock, a crystal controlled oscillator, starts running. All the pulses needed by the computer are derived from the clock frequency. The clock cycles for every move that is made in the computer. During one of the beginning cycles the CPU is built to address the start address in the ROM. That is about the extent of what the CPU can do on its own (Fig. 8-11).

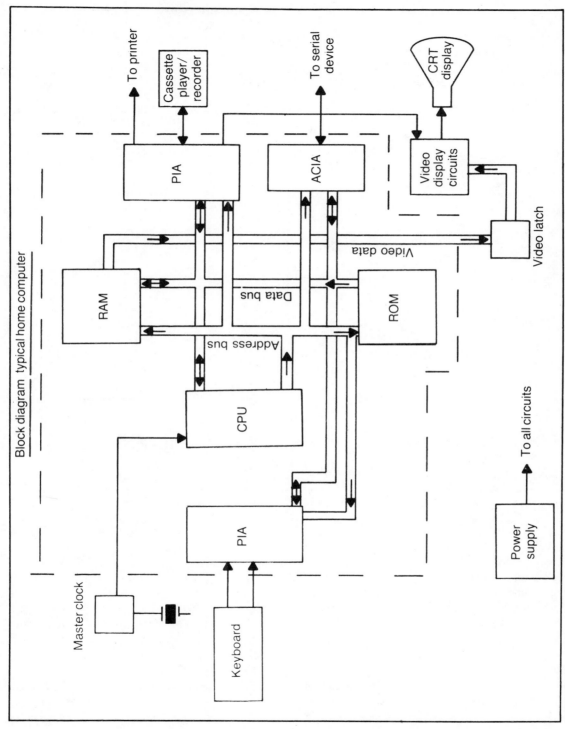

Block diagram typical home computer

Fig. 8-10. When the master clock turns on, the computer starts working. All the activity from initialization to the CRT display takes place in time to the beating of the clock.

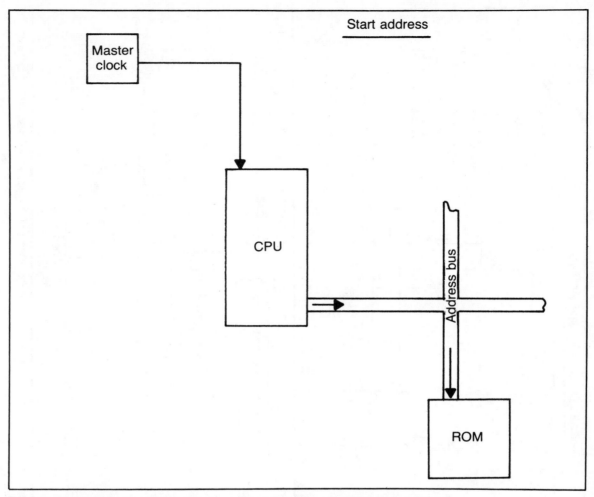

Fig. 8-11. The first thing the CPU does upon startup, is to address the ROM for instructions.

In the starting addresses in the ROM is a permanent program. This program is called the *operating system*, or often it is called the *monitor*. Either name, its job is simple and short. It gets the computer underway and oversees the operation. The computer gets ready for action by setting all the registers, like you do with your trip mileage indicator in your car when you start on a journey. The monitor does this to all pertinent registers. Setting the registers is called *initialization*. The monitor takes control of the computer and acts like a traffic cop to make sure the information tends to travel logically and not haphazardly. Once the TV is lit up, the computer registers are initialized, and the monitor is overseeing the operation then you can begin computing.

The next move is to begin typing. The computer as it stands right there is helpless. The clock is running, the CPU is ready, the ROM with its monitor program is in control and the RAM is empty and waiting to be filled. You decide to write a letter. All well and good but you need a word processing program.

Let's say you are a programmer and have one that you have written. The program is on tape. You plug the cassette into your player. The program is going to have to be put into RAM (Fig. 8-12). You type the commands the instruction manual gives, the cassette player starts operating and the 1s and 0s from the tape pass through the PIA, onto the data bus, to the CPU and then are stored in RAM. This type of operation takes about four minutes due to the slow cassette playing.

Now you have a program stored in RAM. All of it under the auspices of the operating system program; A program in charge of a second program. The second program is the word processor. The computer can now print a letter that you type into it.

Back at the keyboard you begin to type. As you hit letters you are shorting out rows to columns. A typical keyboard has 7 rows and 8 columns. This gives 56 possible combinations of rows and columns. Suppose you strike "t" without a shift (Fig. 8-13). That means you hit row 3 and column 5. The

columns are being scanned continually near clock frequency. The strobing picks up the intersection of row 3 and column 5 much faster than you can hit keys. The intersection shows a short while all the other keys denote opens. Each intersection, when shorted produces its own signal. This signal comes in one of the PIA's registers according to which intersection is shorted. This signal is then applied to a ROM that produces a seven-bit code representation of the keyboard letter that was struck. (The eighth ms bit is always 0.) This code is called ASCII and uses strings of 7 binary digits just like the old Morse code uses strings of dots and dashes (Tables 8-1, 8-2, and 8-3). There is an ASCII string of bits for every letter, number, and symbol used by typewriters. Once the key you strike is coded the bits proceed on the data bus to the CPU.

The first thing you must type into the com-

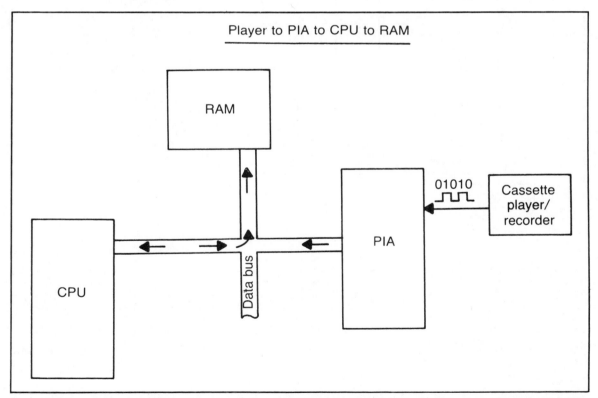

Fig. 8-12. The home computer can be programmed quickly by playing a cassette tape into RAM. The CPU addresses the player through the PIA. The player then sends the program to the CPU, back the other way through the PIA. The CPU then stores the program in RAM.

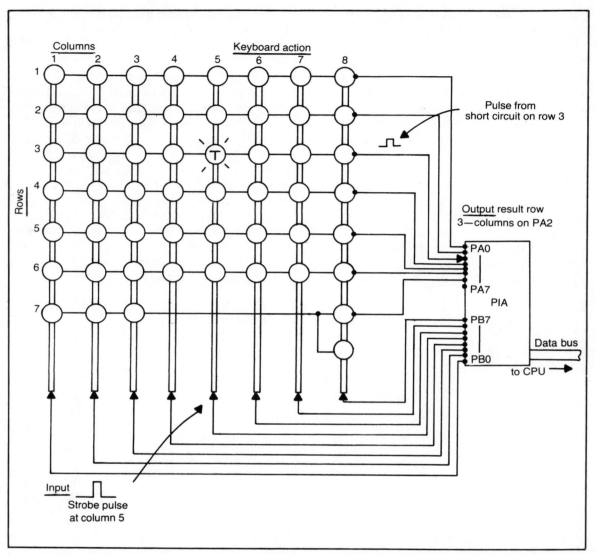

Fig. 8-13. The columns in this keyboard receive a strobe pulse via the PIA from the CPU. The strobe pulse scans the columns for any short circuits. Most of the time all the columns are open. If you strike a key, like T, a short circuit is created on row 3. The strobe pulse detects the short as it pulses column 5. The row 3-column 5 information is sent to a special internal ROM that codes the row-column information into the ASCII seven bit code letter. These seven bits are then sent to the video RAM addresses for storage and also display.

puter is a command to the control program to run the word processor program. The kind of program the operating system consists of determines what command you use. Let's assume the operating system will get the word processor going with the command RUN. You type RUN and press the car-

riage return on the keyboard. This enters the command RUN. In fact lots of the keyboards have the name ENTER on the carriage return.

The word processor is stored in RAM. The program instructions consists of 1s and 0s stored in sets of 8 digits in the RAM rows of registers.

CHARACTER	DECIMAL CODE	MODIFIED ASCII BINARY CODE
A	65	01000001
B	66	01000010
C	67	01000011
D	68	01000100
E	69	01000101
F	70	01000110
G	71	01000111
H	72	01001000
I	73	01001001
J	74	01001010
K	75	01001011
L	76	01001100
M	77	01001101
N	78	01001110
O	79	01001111
P	80	01010000
Q	81	01010001
R	82	01010010
S	83	01010011
T	84	01010100
U	85	01010101
V	86	01010110
W	87	01010111
X	88	01011000
Y	89	01011001
Z	90	01011010

When the command RUN is entered the CPU sends out the address of the first program instruction. That opens the first address of the word processor and a copy of the contents of that address travels that data bus back to the CPU. The CPU then begins processing the program. When the computer finishes with the contents of the first address it outputs over the address bus the second address. This opens the second address and its contents enter the data bus and heads to the CPU. The computer is built to address one address after another in automatic fashion unless it gets an instruction to JUMP or BRANCH to some other address that is not in numerical order.

Once you get the word processor program running it works with the operating system and you to produce the letter you want to write. As the program proceeds it draws you into the action. The program will display a menu of choices and stop. The menu stays on the TV screen. You can choose from a group of options. The menu could look like this one:

1 ERASE TEXT
2 TYPE TEXT
3 PRINT HARD COPY
4 SET STANDARDS
5 SAVE ON TAPE
6 LOAD TO TAPE

To write your letter you press 2. The program then produces a blank screen and a cursor to show you where the next key you hit will be displayed on the screen. You can now compose your letter on the TV screen. You begin hitting keys and the letter takes shape.

As you hit keys, each strike causes the keyboard to produce one of the 56 possible row to column shorts. The impulse enters the computer through the PIA. That particular short gets the coder in a ROM to output the ASCII bits. The bits enter the CPU on the data bus. The bits are then addressed to the video RAM (Fig. 8-14). The bits are stored in the video RAM. The storage of the bits in the video RAM automatically outputs them to a

Table 8-2. The Lower Case Letters are 01100001-01111010, Which is 97-122.

CHARACTER	DECIMAL CODE	MODIFIED ASCII BINARY CODE
a	97	01100001
b	98	01100010
c	99	01100011
d	100	01100100
e	101	01100101
f	102	01100110
g	103	01100111
h	104	01101000
i	105	01101001
j	106	01101010
k	107	01101011
l	108	01101100
m	109	01101101
n	110	01101110
o	111	01101111
p	112	01110000
q	113	01110001
r	114	01110010
s	115	01110011
t	116	01110100
u	117	01110101
v	118	01110110
w	119	01110111
x	120	01111000
y	121	01111001
z	122	01111010

Table 8-3. The Rest of the Characters and Numbers are 00100000-01000000, in Decimal This is 32-64.

CHARACTER	DECIMAL CODE	MODIFIED ASCII BINARY CODE
(SPACE)	32	00100000
!	33	00100001
"	34	00100010
#	35	00100011
$	36	00100100
%	37	00100101
&	38	00100110
'	39	00100111
(	40	00101000
)	41	00101001
*	42	00101010
+	43	00101011
,	44	00101100
-	45	00101101
.	46	00101110
/	47	00101111
0	48	00110000
1	49	00110001
2	50	00110010
3	51	00110011
4	52	00110100
5	53	00110101
6	54	00110110
7	55	00110111
8	56	00111000
9	57	00111001
:	58	00111010
;	59	00111011
<	60	00111100
=	61	00111101
>	62	00111110
?	63	00111111
@	64	01000000

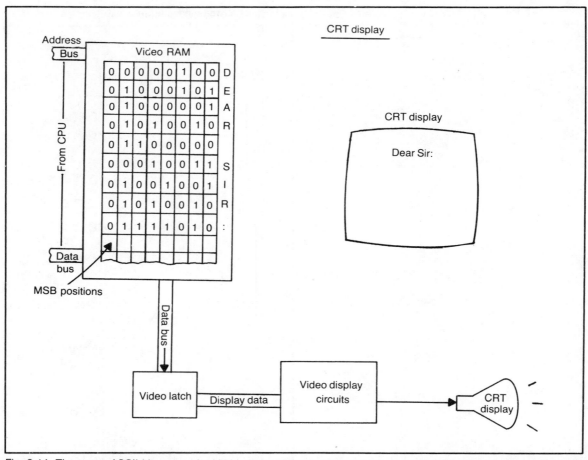

Fig. 8-14. The seven ASCII bits are embedded into the eight-bit registers in the seven LSB positions. Note all the MSB positions are 0s. The ASCII code bits pass through the video circuits. In the video circuits is a character generator that converts the ASCII code into video information that forms the character in its assigned character block on the TV screen. Note each character takes up one byte of RAM.

video latch. The latch proceeds to output the bits to the VDG, the video display generator. Once there the bits are then decoded back into video signals and get displayed on the TV in the block that corresponds with the address it is stored in the video RAM. It all happens so fast, you see the letter take shape as fast as you hit the keys.

The video RAM is only used to print the letter on the TV screen. Also the video RAM only has a limited number of memory registers. Just enough to fill up the TV screen, one register for every display block. The typical small computer could have 512 addresses in video RAM to correspond with 512

blocks on the TV screen that will light up and display a character. What happens is you have more than 512 characters, including spaces and periods, in the letter? Also how can you print a hard copy?

A copy of the contents of the video RAM has to be stored in another place in RAM. The program will cause a copy of the characters in video RAM to be stored elsewhere in RAM everytime the carriage return is pressed. The storage is an exact copy of the video RAM and is stored in the order that you type the letter.

When you have finished your composing and you like what is displayed on the TV, you press a key to get the menu back. This time you press 3. The printer springs to life and the letter takes shape on the paper. When you hit 3, the addressing, instead of staying on the TV display, jumped to the section of the program that contained the printer's instructions. Once the address jump was made, the CPU started receiving copies of the printing instructions from the RAM addresses (Fig. 8-15). The CPU then began outputting a copy of the letter, out the PIA and to the printer interface. From the interface the letter went to a little bit of buffer RAM in the printer itself, where it is stored while the printer produces one character at a time. The printer can usually hold about one sentence of the letter at a time.

ADDRESSES IN THE BLOCK DIAGRAM

The block diagram of a home computer is laid out by the addresses of the chips (Fig. 8-16). The only chip without an address is the CPU. It does all the addressing, it is not addressed. The address bus originates in the 16-bit registers of the CPU. The

main register for addressing is called the Program Counter (Fig. 8-17). It always comes up with the next address to be used in the program execution.

This example computer has a 16-bit program counter, which means the register is capable of having 65,536 different combinations of 1s and 0s. They are counted starting with zero so the possible addresses are 0 through 65,535.

Addresses 0 through 1023 are RAM but these addresses are reserved for the computer. This part of RAM is said to be general housekeeping memory locations. These locations are usually left alone and not addressed except for special advanced purposes in certain programs.

Addresses 1024 to 1535 are 512 RAM locations that are used for video RAM. As mentioned, any characters the CPU addresses here will proceed without hesitation to a PIA and on into the video display.

Addresses 1536 all the way up to 32,767 are the rest of the RAM. This is all available to the programmer and with proper manipulation you can

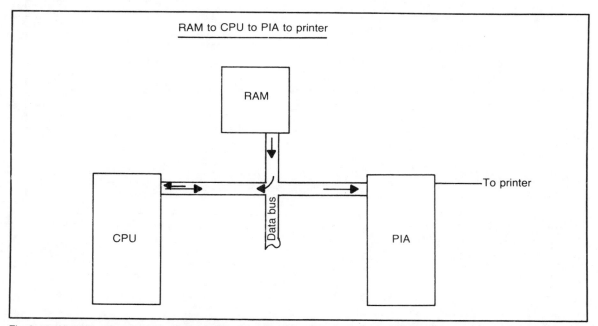

Fig. 8-15. When it is time to print a hard copy, the RAM sends the ASCII characters to the CPU. From there the characters go to the PIA and then out to the printer. The printer can have a small amount of its own RAM to hold about one line's worth of characters. Then a character generator in the printer circuit converts the ASCII to dots that are printed in a character block like they are on the CRT.

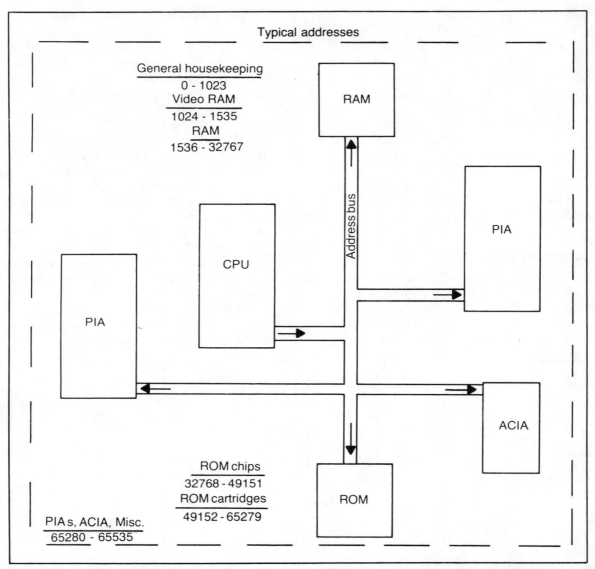

Fig. 8-16. Typical addresses in a home computer has RAM at the lower addresses, ROM at medium number addresses, and the I/O near the highest addresses.

store programs, data, graphics, and lots of other items. This is the area where the programmer does most of his work. The CPU addresses this RAM storage place and constantly loads up with the contents of the addresses and stores data into the locations.

Addresses 32,768 to 49, 151 are 16,384 or 16K

of ROM addresses. In this machine 16K of ROM is installed. The CPU can address these ROM locations just like it can address RAM spots. However, the CPU cannot store any data here. The locations are already permanently filled with instructions and data. The CPU can load the data all it wants but can't store. The data bus is a one way street when these

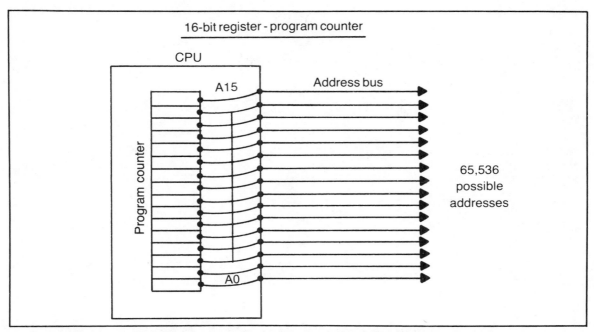

Fig. 8-17. The addresses originate in a 16-bit register in the CPU, called the program counter or PC.

addresses are outputted. The data can only travel from the ROM to the CPU and not the other way, like the RAM is capable of doing.

Addresses 49,152 to 65,279 are also ROM addresses. These addresses though come equipped with a cartridge receptacle. The cartridges are plugged in. The cartridges contain ROM chips. When you plug them in they usually disconnect the ROM chips that are wired on the print board, internal to the computer. The cartridge ROM takes over control of the computer. The internal ROM just stands by. The cartridges contain special programs games such as word processors.

The final addresses on the memory map are 65,280 to 65,535. These are locations that are used by the PIAs and perhaps other input-output type chips that do not require too many addresses. The PIAs only need 4 addresses each. Another chip like the SAM uses 32 addresses. Then there could be additional special items that need an address. The 256 addresses are plenty of locations to handle these chip functions.

In this particular computer there are no addresses needed to accommodate the keyboard, the cassette, the VDG, or other I/O devices. This is because bits in the PIAs take care of these devices. It is said that this keyboard is not memory mapped due to the PIA being in between. There are lots of computers though that include the keyboard in the memory map. When it is, you must consider the keyboard as part of the computer and not as an I/O device.

Chapter 9

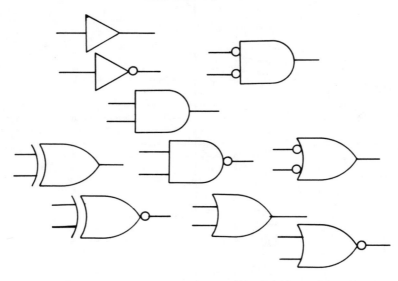

Servicing Logic Gates

When you type on the computer keyboard you strike letters, numbers, and symbols that you've been using all your life. As soon as these characters enter the circuits they get changed to streams of square waves. They stay in the form of electrical highs and lows for the rest of their journey in the computer (Fig. 9-1). They are not reformed into characters again till they get displayed on the TV screen or get printed on paper.

Manipulating continuous streams of square waves from place to place is the job of the computer chips. The chips contain *digital logic circuits*. Digital logic signals are square waves. Square waves are a special breed of electronics. It is not like the familiar analog electronics. The old analog type of electronics works on signals like rf, i-f, video, and audio. Analog signals are amplified, detected, and are shown on color TV screens as moving pictures and heard from speakers as audio. Analog signals are manipulated with components like transformers, potentiometers, filters, impedance matchers, and other routine components. Analog chips are called linears since they mainly amplify analog signals.

Analog and digital systems both use transistors, diodes, resistors, and capacitors. They are both electronic systems, but they work on entirely different kinds of signals. The digital signal consists of the high and low states of the square wave. The circuits needed to process these states are called logical YES, NOT, AND, OR, NAND, NOR, EXCLUSIVE or, EXCLUSIVE NOR, and flip-flop. These logic circuits are carefully arranged in the computer to take all those 0s and 1s in hand and make them do the fantastic tasks of which a computer is capable. Anyone who wants to do more than just change chips in a computer, must become familiar with these logic circuits and how they process the 0s and 1s.

THE THREE LOGICAL STATES

The square wave has two states (Fig. 9-2). It is either in a state of 1 while it is high, or in a state of 0 when it is low. What is the third state? That's easy—when it is gone no level is present at a test point. It was shown in a previous chapter that a special input circuit can be installed on a chip that

132

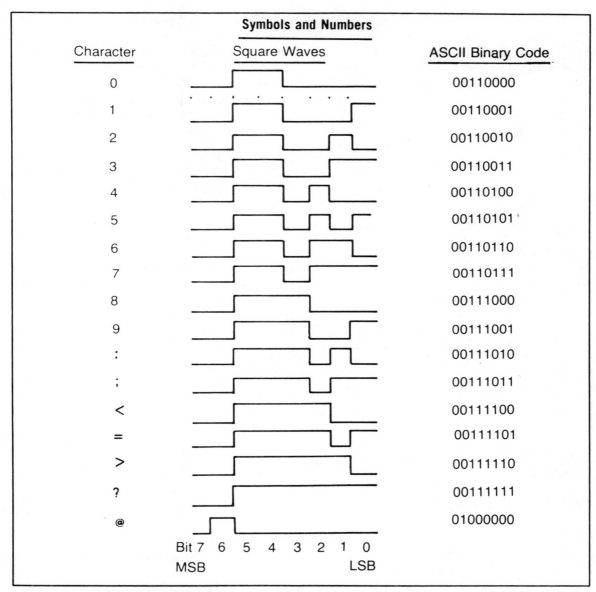

Character	Square Waves	ASCII Binary Code
Symbols and Numbers		
0		00110000
1		00110001
2		00110010
3		00110011
4		00110100
5		00110101
6		00110110
7		00110111
8		00111000
9		00111001
:		00111010
;		00111011
<		00111100
=		00111101
>		00111110
?		00111111
@		01000000

Bit 7 6 5 4 3 2 1 0
MSB   LSB

Fig. 9-1. Every character on the keyboard has its own computer code. The code is universal and is called ASCII. The code is formed in eight bits with the MSB always a low. The remaining seven bits can assume 128 different combinations of highs and lows which is more than enough to code all the characters on the keyboard and more.

turns the chip off or on, and not allow any signal, high or low, to pass through the chip. Why have the third state?

During the processing of the highs and lows, it is useful, to have a number of digital gates to be attached to a single bus line. If every gate is in a state of high or low then all the gate outputs would be coupled to the bus line at the same time. The various outputs would interfere with each other. Consternation would reign.

For instance, suppose three inverters, the NOT gates, were attached to one bus line (Fig. 9-3). If they were all on all the time, they would all inject signals into the common bus line. This causes trouble. However, with a third state, in the form of an off-on switch, that can be activated by a third connection to the inverter, two of the gates can be turned off while the remaining gate can be on and couple its signal without interference. The tristate control is a necessary part of a lot of gates. You'll see test points called TSC which stands for Three State Control.

In addition to tristating there is, of course, the other two logical states 0 and 1. In TTL chips, if you take your vom and measure a terminal you are liable to find dc voltages between 0 V and 5 V (Fig. 9-4). The usual definitions for the different voltage levels are:

2.4 V or higher—logical 1
0.8 V or lower—logical 0
0.7 V to 2.3 V—tristating

The tristating condition is called by some digital technicians, "floating". Floating is thought of as the tristate condition between a logical 1 and a logical 0. There are a lot of tristate devices in a computer. The CPU, RAMs, ROMS, circuits in the data and address lines, and others can be tristate devices. When a test point is found in a floating condition, one of two things is occurring. First of all, the condition could be normal, and the pin is unselected by the computer. Secondly, the condition could be abnormal and the pin is disabled because of component failure. Either way, floating should be recognized and understood so you can troubleshoot effectively.

Most of the time, as you trace through the computer for trouble, you'll be seeking a clue. A clue is a pin with the wrong voltage state on it. The pins, according to factory notes, or your own knowledge and experience, should possess a certain state. There are only four signal conditions to worry about. Three of the four conditions are logical

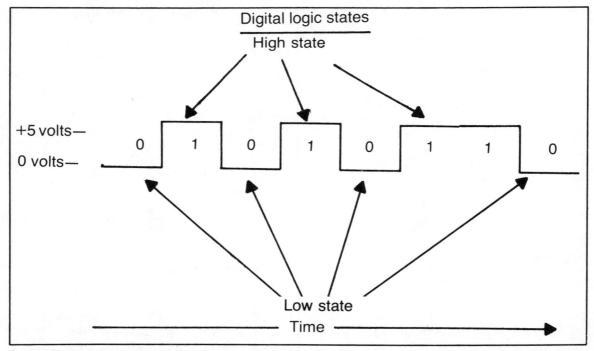

Fig. 9-2. The square wave is typically a voltage traveling through time that changes from +5 V to 0 V and back. The voltage changes happen almost instantaneously while the highs and lows take a little time. This produces the square effect. While the high is present the wave is considered to be in a state of 1. During a low the state is described as 0.

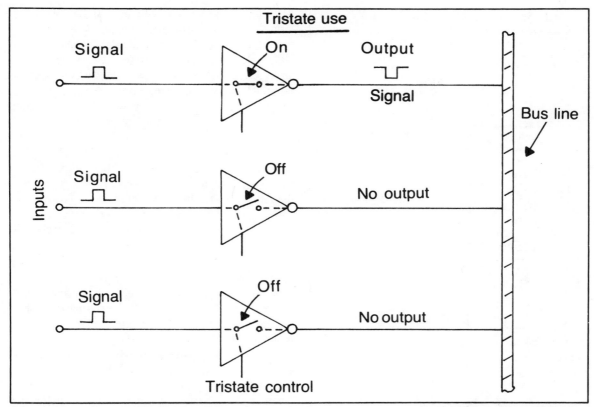

Fig.9-3. The third logical state, when the chip is purposely turned off, called tristate, is useful to keep gates off when they are not needed during an operation. This permits many gates to be tied to the same lines without interfering with each other.

1, logical 0, and tristating. The fourth signal condition is a pulse train that the oscillator clock produces. We'll cover that in the Clock chapter (Chapter 13).

The handiest piece of test equipment to check logical states is the good old vom. You can go from test point to test point and look at the amount of voltage present quickly and easily. You stay on the

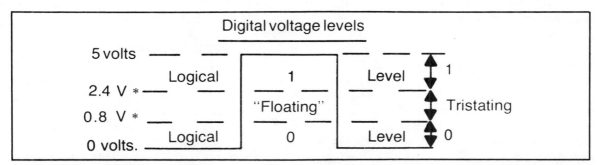

Fig. 9-4. The three states can be detected with a vom. For example, in a TTL chip, a voltage between 2.4 V and 5 V can be a high. Zero V to 0.8 V is a low. Any voltage between 0.9 V and 2.3 V could be a tristate condition.

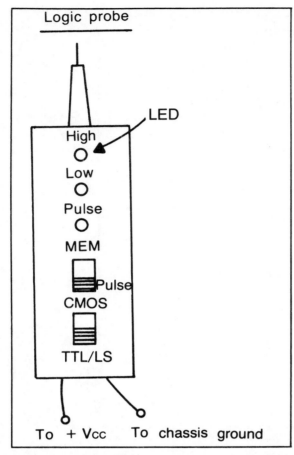

Logic probe

LED

High
○
Low
○
Pulse
○
MEM

Pulse
CMOS

TTL/LS

To + Vcc   To chassis ground

Fig. 9-5. The digital logic probe is a handy substitute for the vom. It shows LED lights for highs and lows. The absence of any light could mean the test point is tristating and in a high impedance condition.

little practice before it becomes as handy as the vom. You do have to attach a clip lead to the computer power supply to energize the probe. Also you must set a switch position to test TTL after testing an MOS, and vice versa. This can cause a delay if you don't know if the chip under test is a TTL or MOS. The probe will test for the presence of pulse trains which makes it handy in your tool box.

If you are a scope oriented technician, the scope can be useful during checkouts. However, many techs repair computers without ever using a scope, except on rare occasions. This sort of thing though is up to individual preferences. To sum up, states can be tested adequately with the voltmeter in the vom and with the ordinary logic probe all digital techs have in their tool box.

THE YES GATE

If you look at Fig. 9-6 you'll see a triangle with two leads protruding. This is the schematic symbol for the YES gate. The lead on the flat side is the input. The lead coming out of the point is the output. The YES gate is also called a *driver*. The driver is included in the logic elements. Yet the strange thing is, the driver is not a true purveyor of 1s and 0s and is not really a logical component. In fact, the driver is an amplifier and is actually a linear or analog device. However, it is needed in the digital scheme of things so it can be included among the other purely logical chips.

Let's see what these drivers do in the computer. The schematic shows a CPU (Fig. 9-7). There are eight leads emerging from the pins of the CPU. This is the data bus. It carries a 1 or 0 on each etch trace. The data is headed for storage in a RAM address. Notice you can tell the data is on its way out, since the CPU side leads are attached to the flat side inputs of the drivers. The output pointy end leads are going to the RAM. There is a third tristate control lead that can turn off all eight drivers at the same time if the need arises.

These drivers are also called buffers. Buffers are usually needed between the CPU and the other computer circuits. CPUs are able to do a lot, but they can't get much current output to its pins. In fact, there is not anywhere enough current from the

same scale and test TTLs, MOSs, of all size pin packages and feel secure that your readings are accurate. Almost any vom, cheap or expensive will do fine. The vom is completely independent of outside electric needs which eliminates line voltage or even tying into the computer's power supply. You'll find a lot of experienced computer techs using nothing but a vom to test states.

There is a second kind of test equipment that also will test states and do a good job. That is the *digital logic probe* (Fig. 9-5). The probe is handy and denotes states by means of tiny LED lights. It is a more exotic test means than the vom and requires a

CPU to drive the bus lines so they can maintain correct logic levels. The buffers are there as current amplifiers. They are designed to take the miniscule CPU output current and amplify it to prescribed levels. Amplification is not a logic job. It is an analog type duty. However, it is needed here and drivers are installed.

While the amplification job was not a logic one, the rest of what the buffers do is. That third lead on the side of the drivers is the tristate entrance to the buffers. A logical 1 or 0 here can turn the buffer on and off like a switch. Remember, this part of the data bus stores data in RAM. When the CPU calls for loading data from RAM the signal is going the other way (Fig. 9-8). To avoid interference, these buffers can be turned off while data is flowing from RAM to CPU, then these buffers can be turned back on if data must once again be sent from the RAM back to the CPU.

The main logic job the drivers do is the YES function. All YES means in logic is, whatever state signal enters the driver gate, that same signal state will exit that gate. If a state of 0, enters the YES gate, a state of 0 leaves. Should a 1 enter the gate, a 1 leaves the gate. The input must agree with the output. The driver does not alter the logical state of the signal.

The gate is a chip or part of a chip. A typical TTL chip used in computers as a YES gate is the 74LS367. It is a *hex 3-state bus driver*. All that means is, there are six driver gates on the chip. It is used as a buffer on a data bus. Also the chip is a tristate type.

All the gates are made up of a number of transistors internally wired. There is no way to get to the internal transistors, so servicers forget them and treat the gates as single components. Therefore the individual driver gates are considered as components with an input pin and an output pin. Then the tristate types also have the disable input.

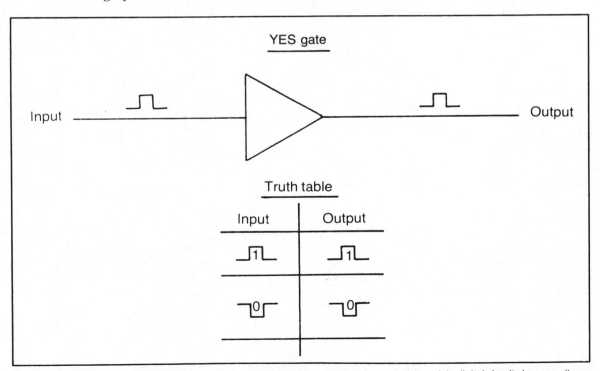

Fig. 9-6. The YES gate is really an analog device rather than a digital type. It is needed though in digital circuits because it can match different digital devices together and it has tristate capability. Whatever state enters a YES gate also leaves the YES gate. That's why it is called YES.

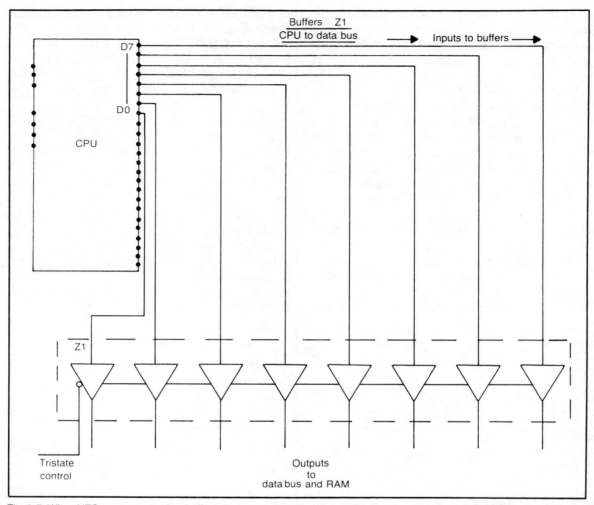

Fig. 9-7. When YES gates are used as buffers, they can be attached in series in the data bus to match the CPU to the memory. The tristate control gives the bus an off-on switch.

Another piece of service information that comes with a logic chip, is called a *truth table*. The "truth table" name, comes from the fact that 1s and 0s are also called true and false. The truth table really is an input-output chart for the chip. For example, the YES gate has the same output as the input. Therefore its chart looks like this:

Input	Output
0	0
1	1

That truth table is very simple. They do get much more complicated. For instance, if the buffer is a tristate type, the chart gets a bit more complex.

Tristate	Input	Output
1-off	0 or 1	floating
0-on	0	0
0-on	1	1

From an equivalent circuit point of view you can think of a buffer as an npn transistor (Fig. 9-9).

138

As the sketch shows the +5 V powers the buffer through the collector resistor. The logic signal input is into the emitter. That way the same signal appears at the collector since there is no signal inversion like there would be if the square wave had been injected into the base. There is more current available at the collector with the same signal that entered the buffer. If a logic 1 enters the emitter a logic 1 exits the collector, fulfilling the truth table of a YES gate.

INVERTERS

At first glance, the schematic symbol of an inverter looks like a YES gate (Fig. 9-10). A closer look though, shows one change. There is still only one input and one output lead. The symbol is still

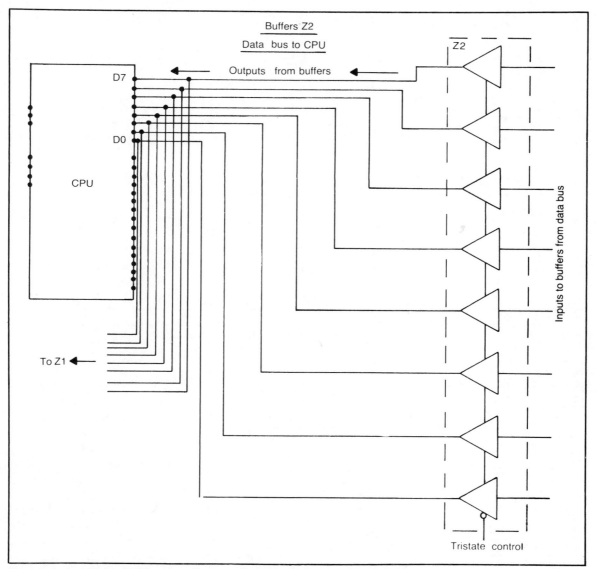

Fig. 9-8. A second set of YES gates with tristate control makes the data bus a two way path.

139

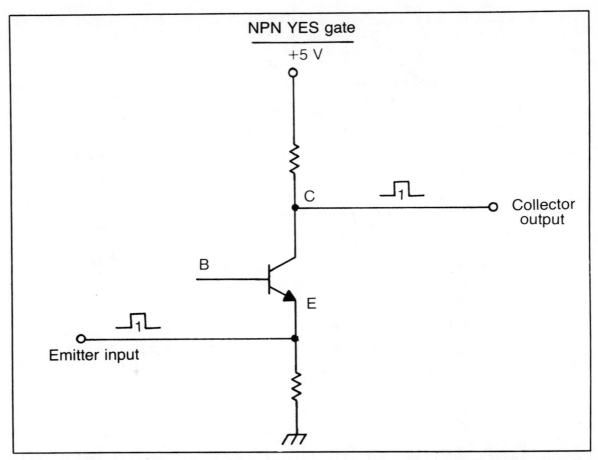

Fig. 9-9. You could think of a YES gate as an npn transistor with an emitter input and a collector output. Whatever signal state goes in also comes out. The voltage can also be adjusted to match the following circuits.

the same triangle. The only difference is on the point of the triangle where the output lead emerges. There is a tiny circle on the point that the output lead attaches to.That little ring is called the NOT circle. It makes the gate a NOT gate. What that means is, whatever state enters the gate, the opposite state leaves the gate. If a 0 enters the NOT gate a 1 exits. Should a 1 go into the gate, the 1 is changed to a 0 in the gate and a 0 comes out. The truth table for the NOT gate looks like the following:

Input	Output
0	1
1	0

While the internal wiring of a NOT gate consists of bipolar TTL or FET MOS circuits, we can simplify troubleshooting the gates, if we think of the circuits as a single npn transistor configuration (Fig. 9-11). V_{cc} on the collector can be +5 V and the emitter is returned to ground. As mentioned earlier, any voltage on the collector above 2.7 V represents a logical 1. A voltage below 0.8 V means a logical 0 is present.

When a 0 or practically no voltage is applied to the base, the base is practically at ground like the emitter and the npn is cut off. With no current flow in the npn there is no voltage drop on the collector, and the voltage there is pulled up to +5 V, which is a

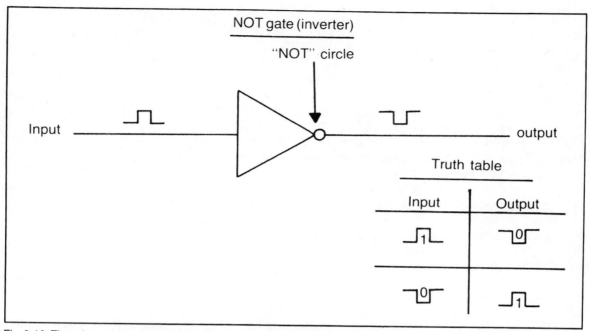

Fig. 9-10. The schematic symbol of the NOT gate looks like the YES gate except for the little "not" circle on the output point.

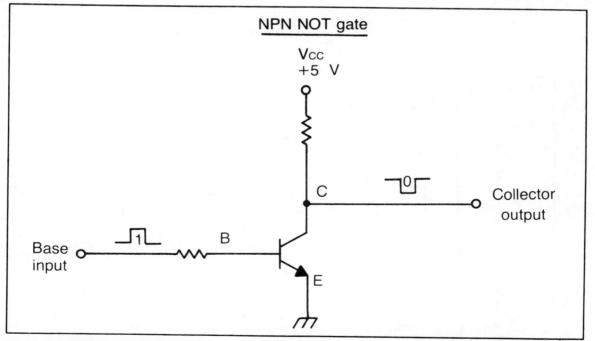

Fig. 9-11. The NOT gate can be thought of as an npn transistor with the square wave input into the base and the output from the collector. Whatever state enters the stage gets turned upside down and exits as the opposite state.

141

logical 1. The npn acts as an inverter, the 0 on the base input becomes a 1 on the collector output.

On the other hand, if a logical 1, or about +3 V is applied to the base input, the transistor will go into saturation. With maximum current flowing from emitter to collector, a large voltage drop will occur on the pull up resistor, collector to V_{cc}. The collector, as a result, drops to near zero volts. This low voltage on the collector output represents a logical 0. Thus the input 1 inverts to an output 0 as it passes through the npn doing duty as an inverter.

In computerese, this inversion of the logical state is the opposite or the *complement*. NOT gates always output the complement of the input. During testing, the fact that the output logic level is always the opposite of its input, provides a quick way to checkout an inverter.

The word NOT is used a lot in computers. As you read the schematic during troubleshooting, you'll see terminals with a straight line drawn across the top of the name. This means NOT (Fig. 9-12). This is the NOT line. It means an inverted quantity. Sometimes instead of the line over the pin designation, there will be an asterisk. This is also a NOT sign. The asterisk is used as a convenience because a lot of computer printers are not capable of showing the line. However, they are all capable of printing the asterisk.

In use, if a terminal called RESET is supposed to be held low (at 0 volts) then it is printed on the schematic without a NOT line. That was you know by the lack of the NOT line to expect to find 0 volts on the test point. When you want to reset the computer you press the reset button. A high is sent to RESET and the pin responds since the high changes the state of the terminal which is normally held low.

When the terminal is called $\overline{\text{RESET}}$ or *RESET (Fig. 9-12) then you know it is being held high not low. When you press the reset button, this terminal will receive a low. The pin responds since the low changes the state of the terminal which is normally held high if it is called $\overline{\text{RESET}}$. There will be more about this as the various chip pinouts are examined.

The inverter is one of the simplest logic elements because it only has one input and one output. It is important as it is one of the basic building blocks of other logic gates we'll be discussing in this chapter. These other gates all have more than one input to produce a single output.

LOGICAL AND

During the tracing of logic signals you'll find on the schematic chips that are drawn to look like a bell lying on its side (Fig. 9-13A). There are two leads sticking out of the flat input side and one lead coming out of the rounded output end. Note there are no little NOT circles at the connections. If there were any NOT circles, then the symbol would not be an AND but some other type of gate.

Inside the AND gate, as well as the other gates, there are a lot of components. There could be all sorts of transistors, resistors, diodes, and so on. In fact a gate can be formed by configuring a lot of other gates on a chip and wiring them to tailor a particular gate (Fig. 9-13B). The little bell on the

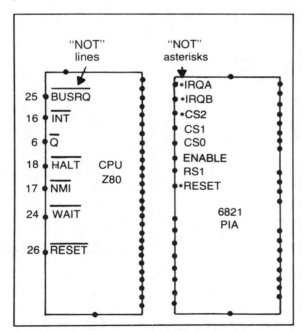

Fig. 9-12. The logical term NOT is used in other ways in digital circuits. NOT signs can take the form of a line over a name or an asterisk accompanying a name. Usually the NOT sign (with a name on a terminal) means that terminal is held turned off in a high state and can be turned on if a low is applied. The NOT sign indicates a low is needed to activate the terminal.

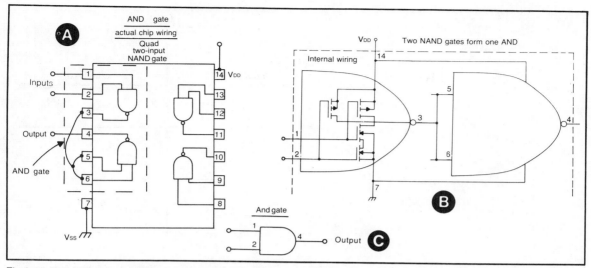

Fig.9-13. The AND schematic symbol looks like a bell lying on its side. There are two input leads and one output (A). An AND gate can be formed by wiring up a couple of NAND gates that are on a quad chip (B). Inside the NAND gates that are wired to form an AND gate, and four FETs with their drains powered by V$_{DD}$.

schematic could actually be dozens of separate components. Figure 9-13C shows a typical gate and the actual "internal circuit."

From a servicing point of view, all you want to do is think of the gate in the fastest accurate way possible. Then you can trace the signal and pinpoint the source of a trouble. The schematic shows the gates in the simplest possible terms so that's the way to go.

An AND gate has two or more inputs and a single output. If you comprehend the AND gate, you can take your vom or logic probe, test the inputs and know what the output should be. Then when you test the output, if it agrees with the logic, the gate is operating properly. If the output has the wrong state, then the gate is suspected as defective.

The logical inputs and possible outputs are shown on the truth table (Fig. 9-14). If an AND gate has two inputs, then there are four possible combinations of 1s and 0s that could be injected into the gate. These are the following:

Inputs
0-0
0-1
1-0
1-1

If there are three inputs, then there are eight possible combinations that can be applied to the gate. These are the following:

Inputs
0-0-0
0-0-1
0-1-0
0-1-1
1-0-0
1-0-1
1-1-0
1-1-1

When the AND gate has four inputs, there are 16 possible combinations. Five inputs makes 32 combinations of possible logic states and so on.

An AND gate though, no matter how many inputs there are, will always output a logical 0, except if all the inputs are a logical 1. All the inputs are a logical 1, in only a single case of all the possibilities. That means, if you are reading the state of an AND gate, the output will be 1 only when all the inputs are 1. If even a single input is 0, the output will be 0. Let's see what's happening inside of an AND gate to find out why.

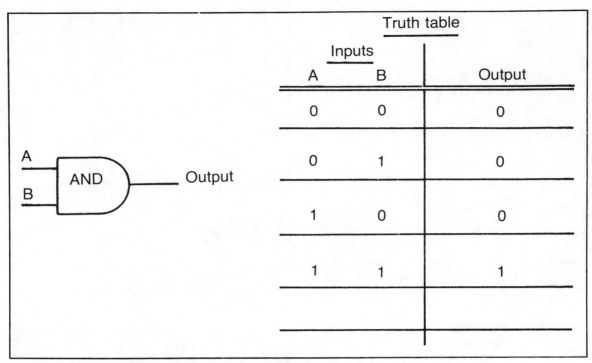

	Inputs		Truth table	
A	B		Output	
0	0		0	
0	1		0	
1	0		0	
1	1		1	

Fig. 9-14. The AND gate's output is usually low except if both inputs are high.

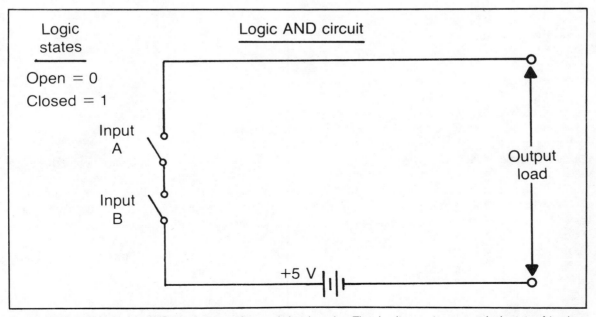

Fig. 9-15. You can think of an AND gate in terms of two switches in series. The circuit cannot assume a logic state of 1 unless both switches are closed.

144

You can think of an AND gate as a series circuit containing two or more switches (Fig. 9-15). Each switch is an input. If the switch is open the input is a 0. When the switch is closed the input is a 1. In actuality the switch is composed of bipolar transistor circuits in a TTL and FET circuits in a MOS.

With the switches in series, the only way the output can be energized, is if all the switches are closed in the logical 1 position. If any of the switches are open, in the 0 position, the output cannot be energized. the output being energized designates a logical 1. With the output open it will read logical 0. The truth table for two inputs (A and B) is shown in Fig. 9-14. In the fourth row, where A AND B are both 1, then and only then, is the output 1.

LOGICAL OR

The logical OR schematic symbol (Fig. 9-16) looks more like an artillery shell on its side, instead of a bell like the AND symbol. If you consider the AND gate as switches in series, then you can think of the OR gate as switches in parallel (Fig. 9-17).

Figure 9-16 shows two input leads on the curved bottom of the shell, while the output connection is made on the pointy end of the symbol. In your mind's eye think of the inside of the gate symbol as having two parallel switch circuits, each switch being an input and a single tied together output (Fig. 9-18).

The OR function is the counterpart of the AND function in the following way. There is only one combination of logical states that makes the AND output 1. That is, if all inputs are 1. There is only one combination of logical states that makes an OR output 0. That is, if all inputs are 0. I'll admit that is not a strong counterpart relationship, but that is the only way the two gates are related. AND and OR are two different logic elements in the computer.

The input possibilities for all gates are the same. What happens to the inputs in the gate causes the different outputs. This is how the OR gate works. If two 0s, or lows as they are called, are applied to the two inputs, then the internal circuit remains open as neither switch gets closed. The output will read low. However, if either one OR

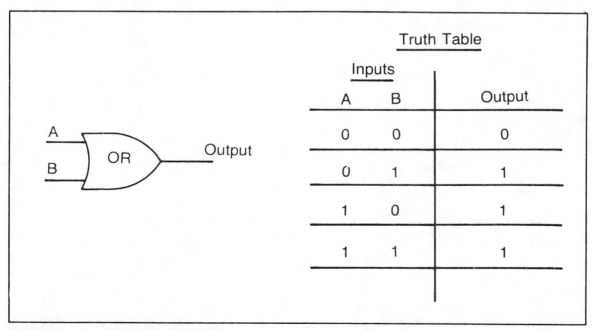

Fig. 9-16. The OR gate symbol looks like an artillery shell lying on its side. The OR gate's output is usually high except if both inputs are low.

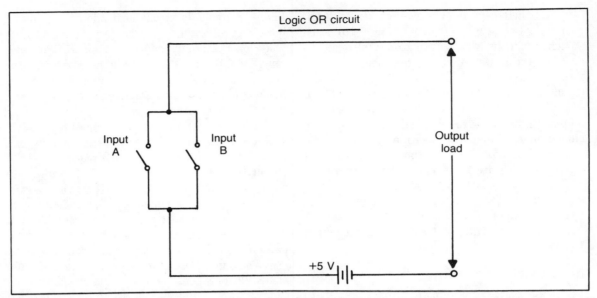

Fig. 9-17. You can think of an OR gate as two switches in parallel. The circuit assumes a logic state of 1 as long as one or both of the switches are closed.

both of the inputs has a high, then a high will be at the output.

Truth tables, over the years, have used different designations (Table 9-1). You are liable to run into any of the different kinds as you peruse service notes from different publishers and manufacturers. The commonest type are the tables that use the binary numbers 1 and 0. These numbers are most familiar to programmers since they use binary codes when they work with the machine language of the computer. You can actually write a program using only 1s and 0s. This is the way the programs parade through the machines. All the other programs you've heard of, such as assembly language, BASIC, COBOL, FORTRAN, PASCAL, and so forth must be coded into 1s and 0s before the computer can actually run a program.

When engineers design or technicians work on a computer they typically change the 1 to high or simply H, and the 0 to low or L. On most logic probes, you will not find 1 or 0, but high and low. Also while taking voltage readings, any voltage above 2.7 V is high, and voltage below 0.7 V is low. There are lots of truth tables that read with Hs and Ls instead of 1 and 0. The high and low designations

are more hardware oriented than 1 and 0. The 1 and 0 tends to be used more by software people, although this is not a hard and fast rule.

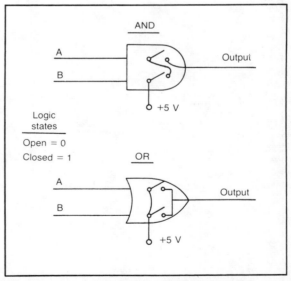

Fig. 9-18. The +5 V is able to connect to the AND output, only when both electronic switches are closed. The +5 V is able to connect to the OR output as long as one or both of the internal switches are closed.

146

Logic State Descriptions	
⊓	⊔
High	Low
1	0
Yes	No
True	False
+5V	0V

Other table forms use yes and no for 1 and 0. Still others use true and false, which is how the name truth table came to be. Some very technical ways to describe the logical functions is to use Boolean algebra and Venn diagrams. These techniques have very little to do with servicing computers. However, for those of you who want to learn these math forms there are many fine books on the subject.

What does the OR gate do in the computer? It causes a high output on the OR gate when one or more highs arrive at the input. During servicing, when you test an OR gate, you can predict its output by testing the inputs. If all the inputs are low, then a low should be at the output. If a high is there the gate could be shorted (Fig. 9-19C). When the inputs have one or more highs, then a high must be at the output, unless the gate is open (Fig. 9-19D).

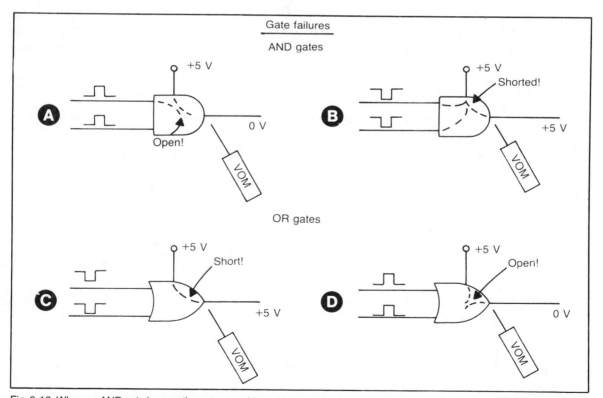

Fig. 9-19. When an AND gate is open the output could read 0 V even though both inputs are highs (A). If an AND gate is shorted the output might read +5 V even though both inputs are low (B). Should an OR gate be shorted the output can read +5 V while two lows are entering the inputs (C). When an OR gate is open the output could read 0 V while the inputs are high (D).

EXCLUSIVE OR

The EXCLUSIVE OR gate symbol (Fig. 9-20) looks almost exactly like the OR symbol, except for the space between the input leads and the bottom of the body of the symbol. A closer look reveals that at the input end, the leads are attached to a curve and there is a space between the curve and the rest of the symbol. If you think of the symbol as an artillery shell, then you can think of the input leads as the ramrod used to push the shell into the big gun. The output lead is at the same place, on the pointy end of the shell appearing symbol.

Let's examine the OR truth table again to see the difference the exclusiveness makes. If you are signal tracing a two-input OR gate there are four and only four possible input combinations you'll encounter. They are the same four combinations, that will be on any gate's two leads. The outputs are different though.

On the OR gate outputs, the state will be always 1, except if two 0s are input. If you logically think about these results, they do not really follow the definition of OR. The OR definition is, if one *or* the other of the inputs is 1 then the output is 1. This is true for the inputs 0-0, 0-1, and 1-0. For 0-0, neither input is 1, so the output is 0. For 0-1, one of the inputs is 1, so the output is 1. For 1-0, again one of the inputs is 1, so the output is 1. However, for the last possibility 1-1, both of the outputs are 1, not one *or* the other, yet the output is still illogically 1. That is the nature of the OR gate, logical or not.

The EXCLUSIVE OR gate, is the variation on the OR gate that does follow the logic. When the four possibilities are considered, they are like the OR gate, except for the last possibility 1-1. When 1-1 appears at the EXCLUSIVE OR input, the output is 0. The EXCLUSIVE OR gate only outputs a 1 if one or the other of the inputs is 1, not both. That one input possibility 1-1, with its 0 output is the difference between OR and EXCLUSIVE OR.

The EXCLUSIVE OR name is abbreviated XOR. The XOR, OR, AND, and NOT logical functions are really all the logic a computer does. If you learn what the four functions do, and what the outputs of the gates do with the various inputs, troubleshooting the computer will become appreciably easier (Fig. 9-21). The functions that are covered in the rest of the chapter are only combinations of these four gate types already discussed.

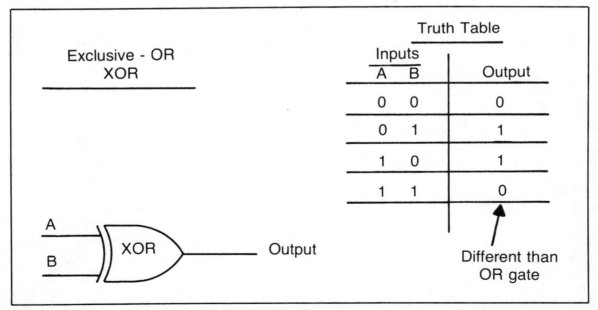

Fig. 9-20. The XOR gate is like the OR gate, except when two highs are applied to the inputs. The output produces a low.

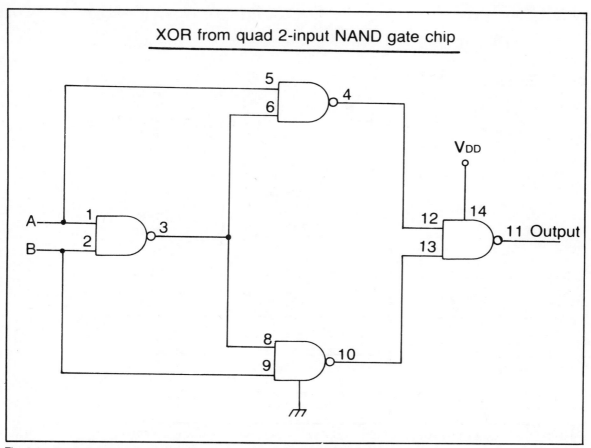

XOR from quad 2-input NAND gate chip

Fig. 9-21. The handy quad 2-input NAND gate can be easily wired to form an XOR gate.

THE NAND GATE

Early in this chapter, it was shown how a YES gate was turned into a NOT gate, when the YES symbol received a little NOT circle between the pointy output end, and the output lead. In the same manner an AND gate is transformed into a NAND gate by putting a NOT circle at the gate's output lead. This makes such a schematic component, a NOT AND gate (Fig. 9-22). The truth table shows what happens inside the gate. The inputs are first of all ANDed. Then once they get ANDed, they are changed to NOT AND. This is shortened to NAND and the inputs are said to be NANDed (Fig. 9-23).

A basic sample NAND gate can be shown by placing two npn transistors in series (Fig. 9-24). There are two inputs, one into each base. There is

one collector output. If you apply 0-0 to the inputs, the transistors can't conduct and the collector will read high since there is no conduction and the collector will read high since there is no conduction and the collector gets pulled up to Vcc. The high, of course, means a logical 1. Therefore, a 0-0 input produces a 1 output, exactly the opposite of an AND or fulfilling the requirement of NAND.

If a low is applied to one input and a high to the other input, conduction still can't take place because the npns are in series. Since there still is no conduction the output is still held high and the output still is called logical 1.

However, if a 1 pulse is applied to both bases, then the npns conduct in unison and the conduction pulls down the collector voltage as the collector

149

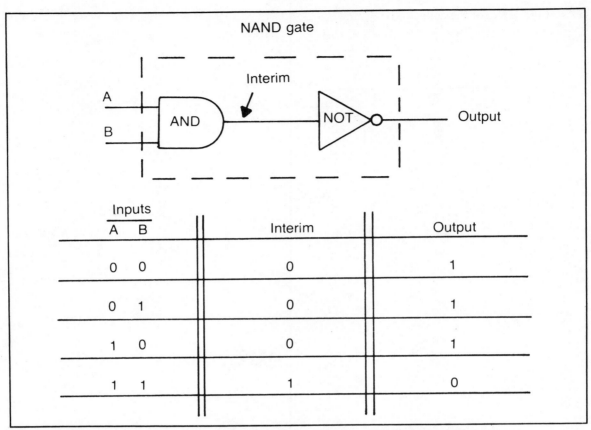

Fig. 9-22. The NAND gate is really a NOT AND gate. The interim output is identical to the AND output.

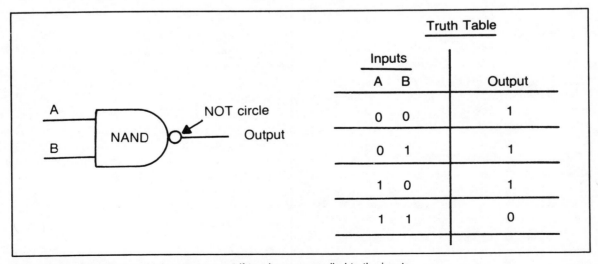

Fig. 9-23. The NAND has a high output except if two lows are applied to the inputs.

resistor drops V_{CC} or the collector below the 0.8 V level. This makes the two 1s on the bases produce a 0 on the collector.

If the inputs to the transistors were into the emitters, instead of the bases, the output would be ANDed instead of NANDed. The NOT function electronically is produced by inputting the bases instead of the emitters. The actual internal circuitry of a NAND gate is much more complex than our sample npn setup, although our sample is a legitimate NAND gate. What does a NAND do in the computer? Let's examine an application.

Consider the case, of a chip that has an Enable terminal that is held high (Fig. 9-25). While the Enable is high the chip is not active. If a low appears at Enable the chip turns on.

The Enable terminal can be controlled with a NAND gate. The output line of the NAND gate gets attached to Enable of the chip. The input lines of the NAND gate receive the controlling signals. The signals get NANDed. If 0-0 enters the NAND gate, the gate will output a 1. This high does not change the state of the Enable terminal and the chip remains inactive. Should 0-1 or 1-0 get NANDed, the gate output is still 1 and the chip is still inactive. However, if 1-1 arrives at the NAND inputs, then

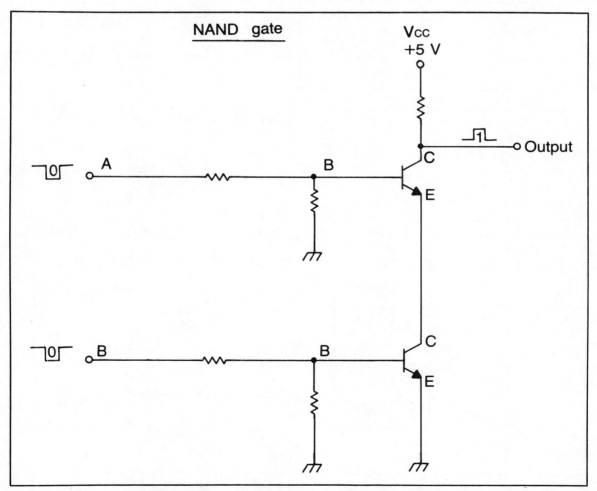

Fig. 9-24. You can think of a NAND gate as two npn transistors in cascade with the inputs at the two bases.

151

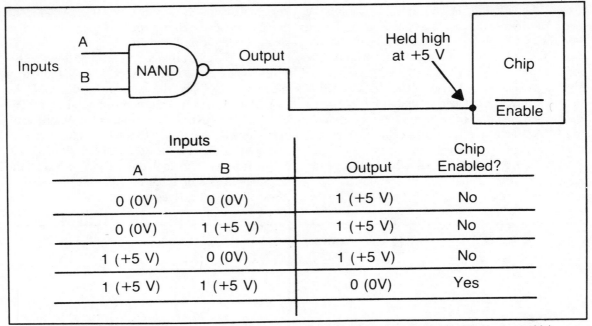

Fig. 9-25. A NAND gate can be used to enable a chip that has the terminal held high, if both of its inputs are high.

Inputs		Output	Chip Enabled?
A	B		
0 (0V)	0 (0V)	1 (+5 V)	No
0 (0V)	1 (+5 V)	1 (+5 V)	No
1 (+5 V)	0 (0V)	1 (+5 V)	No
1 (+5 V)	1 (+5 V)	0 (0V)	Yes

the gate goes low, which enables the chip and it becomes active.

Get used to the word "enable". Enable is a computerese word that describes turning on a chip (Fig. 9-26). The enabling signal can be a low that turns on a terminal being held high, or it can be a high that turns on a terminal being held low. Either way, when you enable a terminal, you are turning it on. To turn it off you have to disable the terminal.

THE NOR GATE

Like its NAND counterpart, the NOR gate is

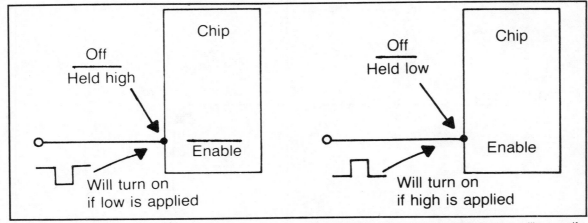

Fig. 9-26. An enable terminal that is held high will turn on if a low is applied. An enable terminal that is held low will turn on if a high is applied.

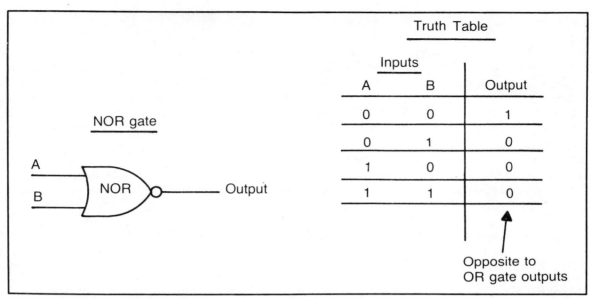

Truth Table

Inputs		
A	B	Output
0	0	1
0	1	0
1	0	0
1	1	0

Opposite to
OR gate outputs

NOR gate

Fig. 9-27. The possible outputs of a NOR gate are the opposite of an OR gate.

really a NOT OR gate. Anyway, NOT OR is contracted to NOR (Fig. 9-27). A NOR gate can be constructed, as an example, around a single npn transistor (Fig. 9-28). For instance, the npn transistor could have a pull up resistor in the collector, and two diodes in the bases. The emitter is tied to ground as is the base bias resistor.

This NOR gate is held in a constant off state

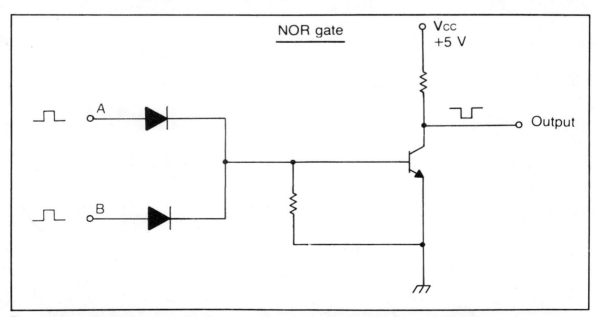

NOR gate

Vcc
+5 V

Output

A

B

Fig. 9-28. The NOR gate can be thought of as an npn transistor with dual diode inputs at the base.

which means there is a high at the collector as V_{cc} appears at the collector due to the npn being off. Should a 1 arrive at either diode input, the diode turns on and goes into saturation. The collector's sudden current flow drops the collector voltage to logical 0.

To sum up the NOR action, the gate outputs a logical 1 as long as both inputs are at 0. If one or the other of the inputs receives a 1, then the gate will output a 0. This output activity is the complement of the OR gate or NOT OR. The NOR gate appears on schematics looking like an OR gate, except for a little NOT circle perched on the output point. The two input leads do not have circles.

During servicing you can check out the NOR gate by checking the voltage of the inputs and the output. If the inputs are both low the output should be high. Should either one or both of the inputs be high, the NOR gate should be outputting a low. If you find an output low, with two input lows being applied, the gate could be defective (Fig. 9-29). Should you read an input high and the output is also high, that is an indication that the gate is opened or shorted.

The NOR gates, like all the other common gate types are typically found as a section of a chip package. In the example (Fig. 9-30) is a 74LS02, which is a Quad 2-Input NOR gate. It is a dual in-line package with 14 pins. There are three pins assigned to each individual NOR gate, 2-inputs and a single output. The Quad arrangement uses up 12 pins. The other two pins, numbers 14 and 7 are V_{cc} and ground. They are common to all four gates.

To test the voltages on the chip, the pins,

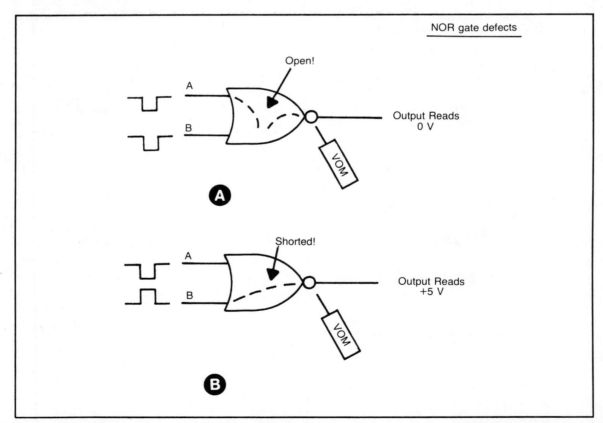

Fig. 9-29. If a NOR gate should open up, two input lows will not produce a high. The output could read 0 V. (A). When a NOR gate shorts, the usual low output produced by a high and low input will not be there, A +5 V could be present (B).

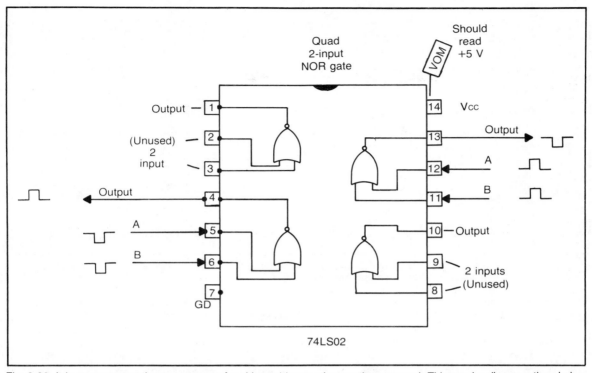

Fig. 9-30. It is common practice to use part of a chip and leave other sections unused. This can be disconcerting during troubleshooting.

though tiny and fragile, are available to the vom test leads. Vcc is typically +5 V, and ground is usually 0 V. The active input pins will have lows or highs as the schematic indicates. The active output pins should have lows or highs according to what their truth table dictates. When the wrong logical state is at one of these test nodes, the seat of trouble could be near.

In lots of chips in computers, there will be unused gates. This is because the chips are so inexpensive, even when they are fairly complex, it is often cheaper, during manufacturing, to use a portion of a readily available complex chip, than to hunt around for the exact chip that only has the needed parts on it. The computer then ends up with a bunch of extra gates and components that play no part in the machine. The only problem with this common approach is that during testing the troubleshooter gets confused. These extra parts are like little dead end paths. Try to recognize them to

avoid wasting time. These extra parts also must be attached to the voltages in the computer. If they are not they could cause false indications. Just keep an eye out for them during troubleshooting.

EXCLUSIVE NOR

The EXCLUSIVE NOR symbol (Fig. 9-31) is an EXCLUSIVE OR symbol with a NOT circle on its output point. Its output is thus EXCLUSIVE OR NOT. The truth table shows the opposite kind of output that the EXCLUSIVE OR shows.

The EXCLUSIVE NOR gate, when used, is often not a gate in its own right, but is the end circuit of a number of other gates put together. For instance, you could construct an EXCLUSIVE NOR gate from two 7400 chips (Fig. 9-32). The 7400 is a 14 pin DIP package called a QUAD NAND gate. There are two inputs to each of four NAND gates on the 7400. By judiciously attaching the NAND gates together you can obtain an EXCLUSIVE NOR

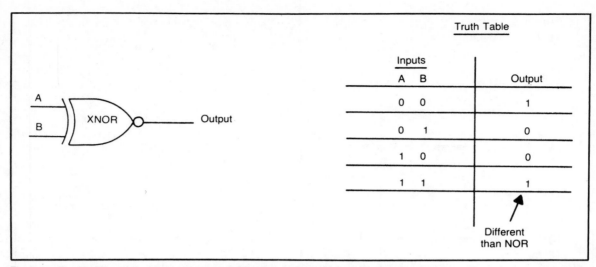

Fig. 9-31. The XNOR gate is different than the NOR only when two highs are applied to the inputs. The output becomes high unlike the NOR gate that would be low under the same conditions.

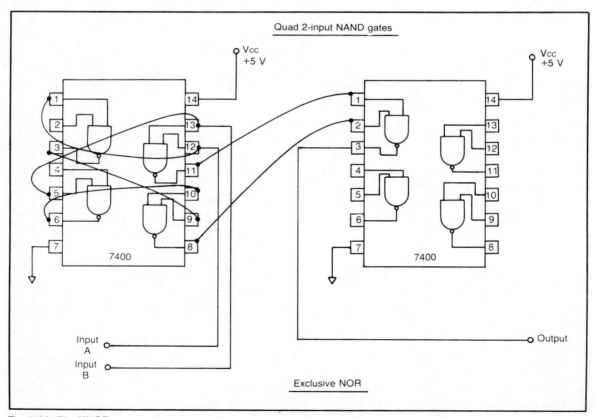

Fig. 9-32. The XNOR gate can be produced by wiring two quad 2-input NAND gates together.

GATE. The completed gate will require four NAND gates from one chip and one NAND gate from the other chip. The remaining three NAND gates are unused.

The 7400 has 7 pins in-line on a side. Pins 14 and 7 are Vcc and ground respectively. Vcc gets +5 V and ground is 0 V. Pins 3, 6, 8, and 11 are the four outputs. Pins 1, 2, 4, 5, 9, 10, and 12, 13 are all the dual inputs. If you make the connections as shown on the sketch, you will have an EXCLUSIVE NOR with two inputs at A and B and an output. Furthermore, if you make different connections as shown in the other sketches, you can make the QUAD NAND gates act as EXCLUSIVE OR, NOR, AND OR, or an INVERTER (Fig. 9-33).

During troubleshooting this EXCLUSIVE NOR gate could be checked out in the following sequence. First off, Vcc should be tested for +5 V. The +5 V should be present no matter what the logic signals are doing. If Vcc is not correct or missing that's an indication of trouble. This test is exactly like any power supply check except that it is more exact. If Vcc is off by more than 5% that could mean there is a problem in the supply or some short is sinking too much current or some open is not sinking enough current. When Vcc and ground are correct the next step is logic tracing.

There are two chips involved. Avoid confusion that might result due to the duplication of pin numbers. On the first chip pins 12, 1, and 2 are tied together to be input A. Pins 13, 4, and 5 form the input B. Pin 3 on the second chip is the first final

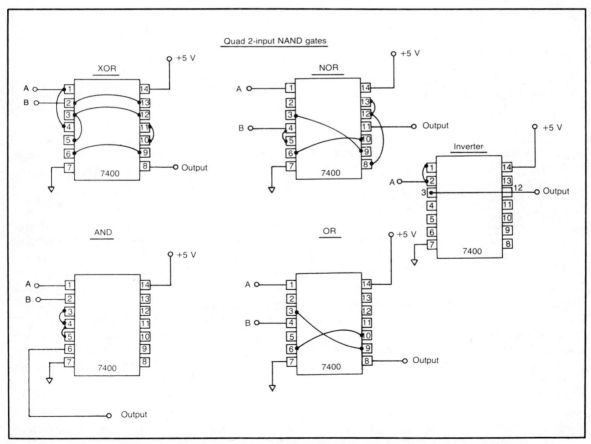

Fig. 9-33. As you can see the quad 2-input NAND gates are able to be wired into all the common logic gates.

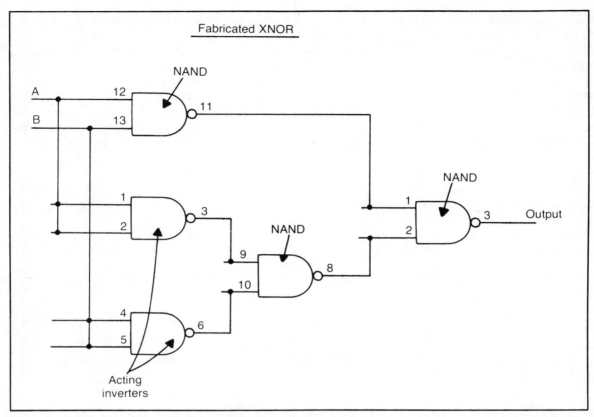

Fig. 9-34. The computer schematic can depict an XNOR function as five NAND gates without even mentioning the overall logic effect.

single output. The inputs are processed from input, through five NAND gates, where they are finally EXCLUSIVE NORed.

Let's trace through the gate and see what happens to an input of 1-1 (Fig. 9-34). When the two highs enter the NAND gate at Pins 12 and 13, they get NANDed and exit Pin 11 as a low. This low is applied to Pin 1 of the output NAND on the second chip.

When the two input highs simultaneously enter the shorted together pins 1, 2 and 4, 5 they get inverted. With their dual inputs shorted to a single input, the two NAND gates are made into IN-VERTERs. The two input highs are inverted into lows at Pins 3 and 6. These two lows are applied to Pins 9 and 10. These lows are NANDed to a single

high. This high is applied to Pin 2 of the output NAND.

With an input of 0-1 the output NAND produces a high at Pin 3 the final EXCLUSIVE NOR output. The net result of the total circuit is, the 1-1 input is EXCLUSIVE NORed to 1 just like the truth table ordered. If you trace out the other possible inputs 0-0, 0-1, and 1-0 you can complete the two input EXCLUSIVE NOR truth table.

During actual signal tracing the testing of each part of the overall EXCLUSIVE NOR gate, is treated as an individual. The inverter parts are examined with the idea that the inverter's outputs are the opposite of the inverter inputs (Fig. 9-34). The NANDs are treated for the verification that their outputs are always high except if both inputs are high. Then the output is low. The only time the truth table for EXCLUSIVE NOR is used, is when the final output is checked against the beginning input.

GATE TESTING

The chips are made as circuits within circuits within circuits. Deep down inside are the actual bipolar transistors, FETs, and other components that actually do the computing. These internal circuits have no nodes that are available to you and your test probes. The internal wiring of a circuit like the EXCLUSIVE NOR is forever sealed in its microscopic space. As a servicer you might as well not consider them hardly at all.

The gates are at the next level and do have nodes that you can get to for your various tests. In fact, the gate level is really the level where most of your voltage testing will take place. There are inputs, outputs, and V_{cc} pins readily available. The more you know about what happens to the 1s and 0s as they progress through the gate level the quicker you will spot incorrect logical states and pinpoint troubles.

The highest level of circuitry is the chip level. When the chip is considered as a single component and is replaced as a test much like a vacuum tube is tested by a direct replacement, you are in the overview mode. That is the area we have been operating in, in this book up to this chapter. A lot of the troubleshooting that takes place in the field is in this overview mode. As a matter of fact, servicers have taken this mode of servicing one step further. They are swapping entire boards, rather than even replacing chips. This is an effective servicing procedure, especially in business operations where every minute the computer is down is very expensive. However, for home computers, board swapping almost means swapping the entire computer, and downtime is not usually too critical.

The mode of servicing that home computers will probably use will be like TV repair. The repairs will be mostly a carry-in type. The servicers will approach the repair by changing indicated chips. Once the socketed chips are deemed ok, then the servicer will attack test nodes with the vom or logic probe and look for incorrect logical states. Highs where there should be lows, lows where there should be highs and floating states in the wrong places. As you can see, knowing the way the gates process the highs and lows is a must.

Chapter 10

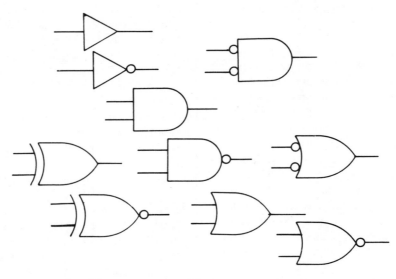

Digital Registers

In addition to logic gates, there is another entire category of TTL and MOS devices. They are called *registers*. They are used in jobs such as shift registers, RAM, ROM, latches, and flip-flops. The main difference between a gate and a register is, a register can store the 1s and 0s, and a gate cannot (Fig. 10-1). As soon as a logic state arrives at the input of a gate, it gets quick passage to the output. It can't stay in the gate, it is forced in and out. A register, on the other hand, is a place of storage. If a 1 or 0 arrives, it can stay as long as you want it to, just so the electricity stays on.

A typical storage device that can hold one bit, is called a flip-flop. If a number of flip-flops are wired side by side, they form a register. Typical registers can hold 4, 8, or 16 bits. Let's see how a flip-flop can store a bit.

THE R-S FLIP-FLOP

When a flip-flop is powered up, it is clear. This clear state is by its very nature, a logical 0. The standard symbol for an R-S flip-flop is a square with two input leads, S and R, and two output leads, Q and Q* (Fig. 10-2A). The symbol is also shown with additional leads when necessary, like the C lead (Fig. 10-2B). The flip-flops can be made up of a couple of gates. While the gates themselves cannot store a logic state a pair of cross-coupled gates can.

With the flip-flop being powered, if you check the Q output there will be a low there (Fig.10-3A). Should you test Q* though there will be a high. The flip-flop under these conditions is storing a low. If you apply a high to the input S, and a low to the input R, the circuit will flip-flop and the Q output will now read a high (Fig. 10-3B).

The input name S stands for *set* (Fig. 10-4). The alternate input name R means *reset*. The flip-flop is called set when it is storing a bit 1. It is termed reset when it has a bit 0. You can add the word "set" to your collection of terms like high, true, and on. The word "reset" becomes the same as low, false, off, and clear.

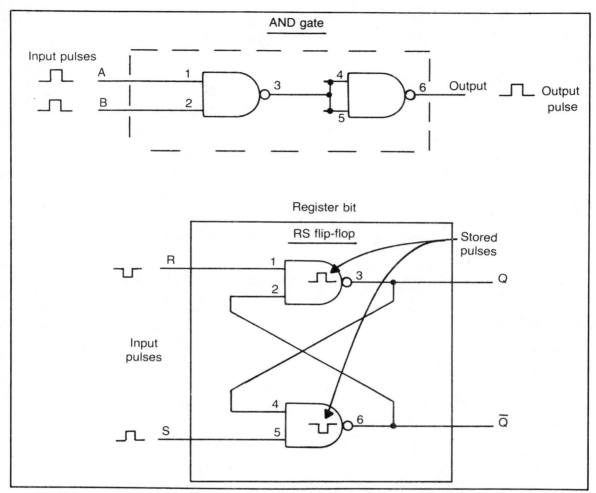

Fig. 10-1. The main difference between a gate and a register is that a register can store a logic state and a gate cannot. In the AND gate composed of two NAND gates, the input pulses enter and pass immediately to the output. In the register bit also composed of two NAND gates, the input pulses enter and are stored in the internal circuits.

THE BASIC FLIP-FLOP CIRCUIT

There are a number of variations of flip-flop. In addition to the R-S, there is the T that toggles by the injection of a clock pulse. Then there is the J-K, a variation of the R-S, and the D which can only act upon a clock input. The flip-flop can be formed with inverters, AND gates, NOR gates, and other cross-coupling arrangements. Figure 10-5 shows some AND and NOR gates forming a flip-flop. All the circuits are microscopic.

The basic flip-flop can be built around two pnp transistors with inputs into the two bases (Fig. 10-6). Since the inputs are into the bases, the individual circuits are inverters. Their bases are cross-coupled into the other collectors. The emitter base bits is designed, so that on power up, one pnp goes into saturation and the other is cut off. There is feedback from the collectors to the bases. This holds the pnps in a state. Only a high pulse to

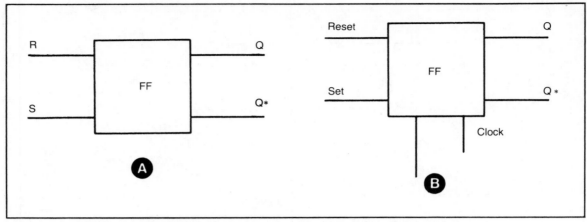

Fig. 10-2. The typical symbol for a flip-flop circuit on a chip is a square with four or more leads.

the base of the cut off transistor or a low pulse to the saturating transistor will change the stored state. If a pulse does arrive and change the state, the flip-flop will hold the new state till another pulse arrives to change the state again.

THE COUNTER

One important job registers do is count. If you add two AND gates to a flip-flop the circuit can count. It can count in binary, 0, 1. It's called a *binary counter*. Besides counting, with the help of the AND

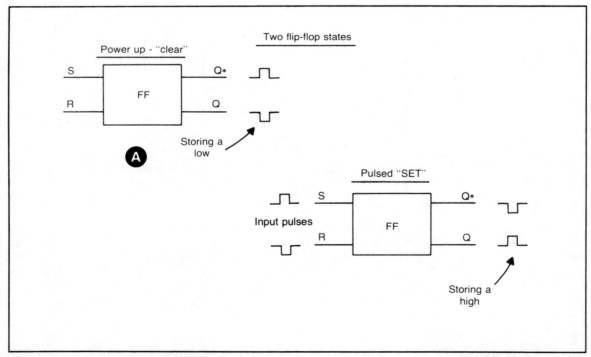

Fig. 10-3. When a flip-flop is storing a low, Q will be low and Q* will be high (A). If a flip-flop is storing a high, Q will be high and Q* will be low (B).

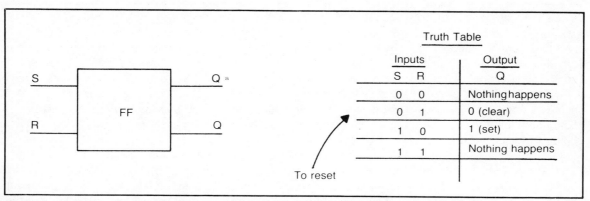

Fig. 10-4. The flip-flop shown develops two useful states out of the four possible input conditions.

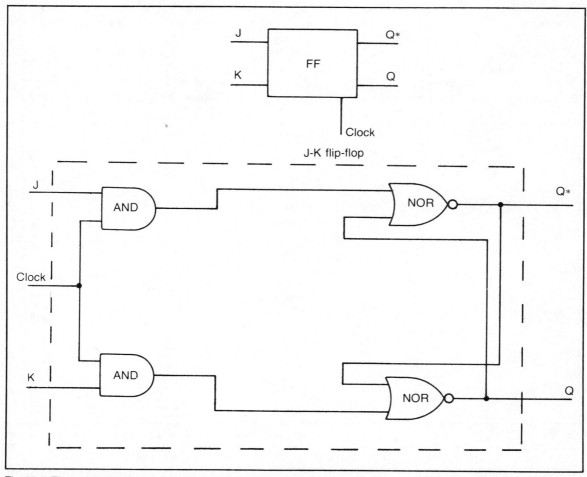

Fig. 10-5. The various flip-flops can be fabricated with groups of logic gates. Here is a J-K flip-flop composed of two input AND gates and two NOR gates.

gates the output has an arithmetical carry (Fig. 10-7).

The binary counter can, as it is powered up, develop an initial output state of 0. The 0 state comes about as the two cross-coupled circuits develop the following states. The set-Q* side becomes 1 and the reset-Q side assumes 0. With Q being held low the entire flip-flop is thought of as being 0. Q* is automatically held high when Q is low.

At that time, if a 1 pulse is applied to the set-Q* input, the pulse causes the two sides to flip-flop. Q* goes low and Q goes high. With Q now being held high, the entire flip-flop is thought of as being 1. Therefore the binary counter does the following. It receives pulses at its input. Each incoming pulse changes the state of the counter. If the counter is in a 0 state, the pulse sets it into a 1. Should the counter be in a 1 state, the pulse resets it into a 0.

Since a single flip-flop can only count 0, 1, as the counter resets, or is thrown back into a 0 state, a

pulse leaves Q. This is an arithmetic carry and can be applied to the next flip-flop in a register.

The AND gates are used to direct the incoming pulses to either set or reset input terminals. The top AND gate has two of its own inputs. One is coming from Q and the other from the incoming count pulse. The bottom AND gate inputs are attached to Q* and the same incoming count pulse. The top AND gate's output goes to set, while the bottom AND gate output connects to reset.

The AND gate that has two 1s in its input will be enabled and apply a 1 to its flip-flop connection. The AND gate that has a 1 and a 0 will be disabled and will output a 0 to its connection. Both AND gates get high pulses at the same time through their common count pulse input. If Q* is high and Q is low, Q* with its 1 at the bottom AND gate enables the gate and a 1 is applied to reset. The circuit thus flip-flops.

As the next pulse arrives Q* is now low and Q is high. This places two 1s on the top gate. The gate

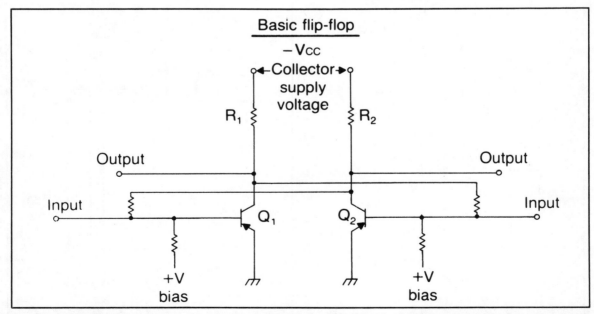

Fig. 10-6. The basic flip-flop can be built around two pnp transistors. When the circuit is first turned on, the normal imbalance due to the matched components really not being matched perfectly, causes one transistor to go into saturation and the other transistor to cutoff, If Q1 cuts off and Q2 is saturated the total circuit is said to be in a low or 0 state. Should Q1 be saturating and Q2 be off the register bit is storing a 1. The states can be changed by flip-flopping the stages. A high pulse to the base of the off transistor, or a low pulse to the base of the on transistor changes the stored state. The off transistor turns on and the on transistor turns off.

is enabled and a 1 is applied to set. The circuit again flip-flops.

COUNTING HIGHER THAN 1

A single flip-flop can't count any higher than 1. If you want to get into a higher count you can attach a second counter to the first one (Fig. 10-8). Then you can count to 11 in binary, which is equal to 3 in decimal. If you connect a third counter the count can go to 111 in binary which is 7 in decimal. A fourth counter will take you up to 1111 which is 15 in decimal.

With two counters, the carry pulse from the original counter to the second one, causes the second counter to change states. If the second counter held a 0, the circuit will flip-flop to a 1. If a 1 had

been there the circuit will go to a 0 and a carry will be available for a third flip-flop circuit.

With three counters, the carry pulse from the second counter to the third counter will cause the third one to flip-flop. If there are four counters, the third one has the ability to send a carry pulse and make the fourth counter change states. This can go on and on.

During servicing, you'll find it very useful to be able to count from 0 to 15 in binary. That's because a four bit register can count from 0 to 1111, which is 0 to 15. By knowing the binary count and its corresponding circuits, and to visualize the streams of data passing through the circuit, among other things.

Figure 10-9 shows a four-bit counter and how it

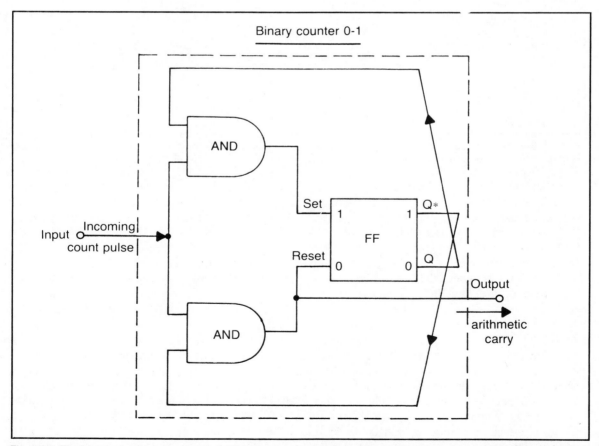

Fig. 10-7. The binary counter can count 0, 1. The output pulse can be applied to the next stage as an arithmetic carry.

165

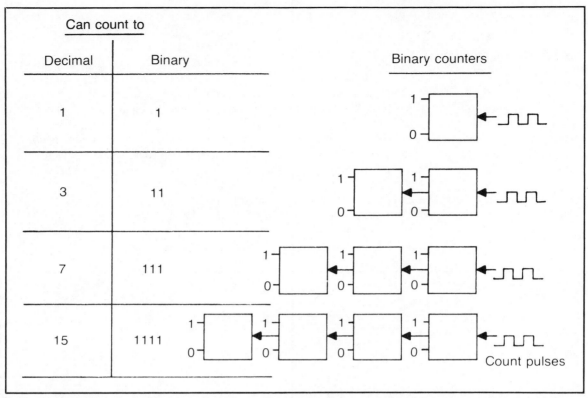

Can count to		Binary counters
Decimal	Binary	
1	1	
3	11	
7	111	
15	1111	

Fig. 10-8. Two counters can count 0, 1, 10, 11. Three counters can count 0, 1, 10, 11, 100, 101, 110, 111. Four counters can count 0, 1, 10, 11, 100, 101, 110, 111, 1000, 1001, 1010, 1011, 1100, 1101, 1110, 1111.

counts sixteen times, from 0 to 1111. The first fact to realize is, there are four binary digits to one decimal number. The decimal 0 is described in a four-bit counter as 0000. Decimal 15 is 1111, decimal 9 is 1001 and so on. This 4/1 ratio between binary digits and decimal is a code. Its importance will be shown throughout the rest of the book.

The four flip-flops in Fig. 10-9 are all connected together to count. Each flip-flop has its output connected to the one on its left. That way the carry is transferred from counter to counter right to left. The count pulses enter the four bit register at the extreme right-hand bit. The four bits can all assume either a 0 or 1 state and thus can count from 0 to 1111. In computerese, four bits is called a *nybble*.

The counting operation is straightforward. The nybble counter is initialized at 0000. As the highs in the pulses enter the input of the first counter the circuit flip-flops to a 1. The counter becomes 0001. The next pulse reverses the first counter to a 0. However, as the reset takes place, a carry of 1 is injected into the second counter. Now the nybble reads 0010. The pulses keep coming. Each pulse either sets or resets the first counter. On each reset a 1 is carried to the second counter. The first and second counters can take the count from 0000 to 0001 to 0010 and 0011. In decimal that is 0, 1, 2, and 3.

As the fifth pulse enters the nybble counter, the second counter outputs a 1 to the third counter. The count becomes 0100. The sixth pulse makes it 0101, the seventh pulse 0110 and the eighth pulse 0111. The count continues pulse after pulse, 1000, 1001, 1010, 1011, 1100, 1101, 1110, and finally 1111. The following pulse resets all the bits to 0000.

When these bits have to be described, they are

done so in a very special way. There are four bits to the nybble. The leftmost bit is called the *most significant bit.* In computerese it's the *MSB*. It is the most significant of all since it carries the most mathematical weight. A 1 in the MSB position makes a larger value than a 1 in the next bit position. A 1000 codes into a decimal 8, while a 0100 is coded to a 4. Eight is obviously larger than 4.

The rightmost bit in the nybble is, with the same type of reasoning, dubbed the least significant bit, abbreviated *LSB*. The LSB can only produce the very lowest binary numbers 0 and 1. When the LSB is coded into decimal the binary numbers are the same as the decimal 0 and 1. This is the only bit position where the values of binary and decimal are identical.

The description of the bit position is an important factor in servicing computers. Practically every circuit in the computer needs bit position descriptions at one time or another.

HEXADECIMAL

The four bits in a nybble is the basic digit of a computer. With the four bits you can count from 0 to 15. The digits 0 to 9 are the basic digits that we know. As we look at the two numbering systems it is obvious that one system that uses 0000 (0) to 1111 (15), and another system that uses 0 to 9, are not easily compatible (Table 10-1). There are six more basic digits in a nybble count than in a decimal count. The computer counts naturally with nybbles and it has been determined, over the years, to leave it that way. Many other numbering schemes have been tried, but the nybble as a digit appears to be, on balance, the best way to go. As a result, a special decimal numbering system is in use. This system, called *hexadecimal*, hex for short, is the way nybbles are coded into digits, in a way us humans can understand (Table 10-2).

With hex, the 4:1 binary to decimal ratio is preserved. Hex means six, and hexadecimal means,

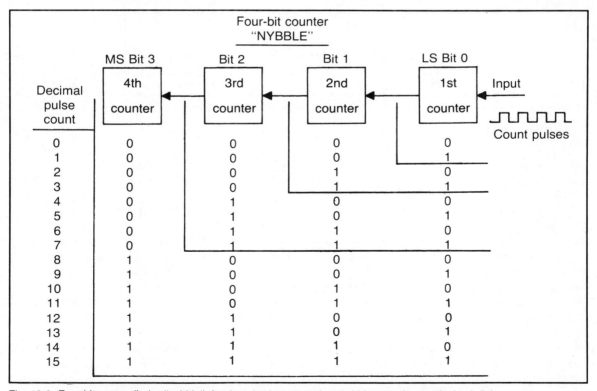

Fig. 10-9. Four bits are called a "nybble". It takes the four digits in a nybble to code one decimal digit.

Decimal Basic Digits	Nybble Basic Digits
0	0000
1	0001
2	0010
3	0011
4	0100
5	0101
6	0110
7	0111
8	1000
9	1001
	1010
	1011
	1100
	1101
	1110
	1111

Not Compatible

decimal plus six more digits. The digits are the letters A, B, C, D, E, and F. This lets you count single digits from 0 to 15. The count goes 0, 1, 2, 3, 4, 5, 6, 7, 8, 9, A, B, C, D, E, F. Each hex digit can be coded into a 4 bit nybble.

If you count past 1111 which is F in hex, the next number is 10, then 11, 12, 13, 14, 15, 16, 17, 18, 19, 1A, 1B, 1C, 1D, 1E, 1F and then 20. Interestingly, 10 in hex equals 16 in ordinary decimal. Twenty in hex equals 32 in decimal. Also one nybble only can count to F. To count any higher you need another four bits. For instance, the hex number 10 needs two nybbles, 0001, 0000 (Fig. 10-10). If the count was made on two nybble counters, the right nybble is the least significant nybble. The left nybble is the most significant nybble. As the count goes from 0 to F, the LS nybble has its states changing while the MS nybble sits and waits

with its states at 0000. As the count passes from F to 10, the LS nybble resets itself to 0000, sends a carry pulse to the MS nybble and the MS nybble begins counting. Ten in hex is 0001 0000 in the two nybble counters.

With the two nybble counters working together, they become an eight bit counter. Two nybbles are a *byte*. The byte is the most used data size in today's home computers. The registers in RAM, ROM, and other chips are mostly byte size.

As a servicer, you must have a clear idea of the relationship between the 1s and 0s of binary and their coded hex equivalent. It would be useful to memorize the code of 0000 through 1111 and the hex equivalent. If you can look at a string of eight bits and know, just like an old elementary school multiplication table, what the hex of the bits equals, your servicing will go faster. For example, if you

Table 10-2. A Special "Decimal" Numbering System Called "Hexadecimal" Had To Be Devised To Make Our Human Numbering System Match The Computer's Binary. The Letters A, B, C, D, E, and F Were Added To 0, 1, 2, 3, 4, 5, 6, 7, 8, and 9.

Hex-Binary Code Table	
Decimal	Hex / Binary
0	0 / 0000
1	1 / 0001
2	2 / 0010
3	3 / 0011
4	4 / 0100
5	5 / 0101
6	6 / 0110
7	7 / 0111
8	8 / 1000
9	9 / 1001
10	A / 1010
11	B / 1011
12	C / 1100
13	D / 1101
14	E / 1110
15	F / 1111

want to poke 1100 0111 into a memory register for a service test, knowing that 1100 is C, and 0111 is 7, allows you to poke C7 into memory without looking up the code in a table (Fig. 10-11).

The home computer has a confusing group of methods that must be used to get bits into the registers. The registers can only hold logic states. Yet, most home computers do not permit you to install bits directly into the registers. The computer usually has a form of hex loader that installs the bits. The loader is a code machine. If you install hex into the coder, through the keyboard, the coder will in turn install bits into the registers. During servicing there are lots of tests in the form of binary programs that you can use to pinpoint troubles. The bits of the programs are usually put into the computer in hex.

SHIFT REGISTERS

Besides counting by bits, a set of flip-flops, doing register duty can shift the bits to the left or to the right. What good can shifting the bits from side to side do? First of all, it is a multiplication or division operation. Let's take a byte size register and set the LSB (Table 10-3). This gives us a register with 0000 0001. In decimal this is 1. Now shift the bit 1 to the next most significant bit, or one to the left. This gives us 0000 0010. In decimal this is 2. Now shift the bit 1 to the next higher bit. The register contains 0000 0100. In decimal the register reads 4. Shift one more and the register is 0000 1000, which is 8. 0001 0000 is 16, 0010 0000 is 32, 0100 0000 is 64, and 1000 0000 means 128. As you can see, shifting the bits higher multiples the decimal equivalent by 2 for each bit moved. If you reverse the shifting, and go lower, you'll divide by 2 for each move lower. This is one way computers multiply and divide. This is an important function of the shift register.

Shifting bits in a register is also a valuable aid when converting a stream of data from parallel to serial, and vice versa. A stream of data can be serial or parallel. When you input data from a tape recorder to your computer the bits are entered one at a time. This is serial operation. When an eight-bit memory cell sends data over an eight trace data bus

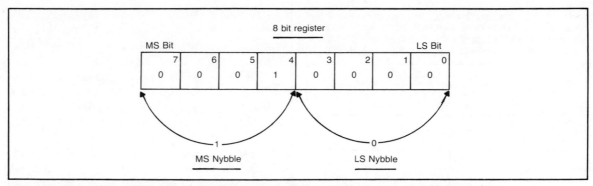

Fig. 10-10. The number 10 in hex is formed by producing a 1 in the MS nybble and a 0 in the LS nybble.

to an eight-bit register in the CPU, all eight bits move at the same time, not one at a time. This is parallel operation.

The shift register is able to convert the serial bit movement to parallel (Fig.10-12). The shift register is able to receive each serial bit in turn, store it till it gets sets of eight bits, and then send the byte on its way, in a parallel form.

In order to be a shift register, the set of flip-flops must have a second set of storage circuits, like flip-flops, installed between each bit holder. In a byte-size register, this means seven more flip-flop type circuits that link the register cells to one another (Fig. 10-13). Then the shift procedure can begin.

Let's shift the binary code 0010 0010, which is

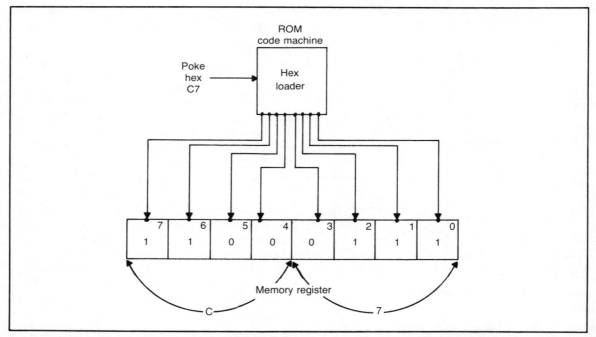

Fig. 10-11. Most home computers are not capable of installing 1s and 0s directly into memory. They have some sort of ROM code machine to do the job. Typical is a hex loader. For example, in order to get 11000111 into memory, you would have to code it into hex C7 and poke it into the hex loader. The code machine would then install the bits into the memory.

Table 10-3. Multiplication by 2 is Accomplished Naturally in a Shift Register by Shifting the Bits One Place to the Left.

Register Multiplication

MSB							LSB	
7	6	5	4	3	2	1	0	Decimal
0	0	0	0	0	0	0	1	1
0	0	0	0	0	0	1	0	2
0	0	0	0	0	1	0	0	4
0	0	0	0	1	0	0	0	8
0	0	0	1	0	0	0	0	16
0	0	1	0	0	0	0	0	32
0	1	0	0	0	0	0	0	64
1	0	0	0	0	0	0	0	128

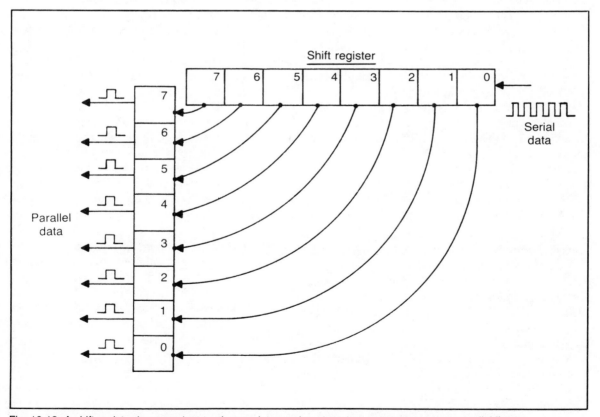

Fig. 10-12. A shift register is convenient to change data moving along in a serial manner into parallel lines.

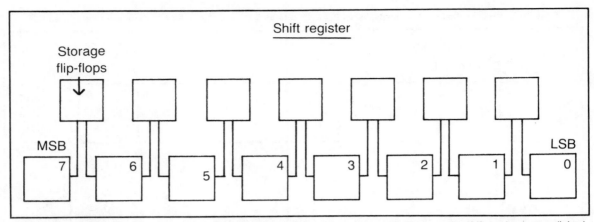

Fig. 10-13. The shift register needs another storage flip-flop between each register bit. That way the shift can be accomplished. During the shift the first thing that is done is, whatever states are in the bit holders are transferred to the storage flip-flops. Next the register bits are all cleared. Lastly the stored bits are reinstalled into the register but shifted one bit to the right or left, whichever is desired.

22 in hex, one bit higher. The first thing the register does is put a copy of the 1 bits into the storage area between the register cells going higher. The next step is to change all the register cells to 0s. The last step is to place any 1s that were stored between the cells, into the next higher cell. There is no reason to do anything with the 0s since all the cells were made to contain 0s in a previous step. This gives us the new register code 0100 0100, which converts to hex 44. By shifting the bit one cell higher we have successfully multiplied the hex number 22 by 2. If we decided to shift the bits back to the lower cells a division by 2 would take place.

CLEARING AND COMPLEMENTING

Two more jobs a register can do are called clearing and complementing. This brings up the definitions of set and reset, and set and clear once again. The two terms mean the following: A register usually starts operating in a state of logical 0. The computer man refers to the register in this state as being *clear*. When a 1 is installed into the register instead of the residing 0, the register is said to be *set*. Then if the 1 is replaced with a 0, the register is said to be *reset*. Therefore going from clear to set to reset to set would be 0 to 1 to 0 to 1, in the same register bit.

The words clear and reset are just about inter-

changeable. The only thing is, it is awkward to refer to the beginning 0 in a register as being a state of reset. It seems to make more sense if a register starts off being clear rather than being reset. However you will see the beginning state referred to as reset. At any rate, reset and clear both refer to the state of 0. Set means the register bit is in a state of 1 (Fig. 10-14).

A register therefore has the capability of being cleared. This means all the bits in the register are reset to 0s. The register also has the capability of being set. This means all the bits in the register are set to 1s. These two capabilities are very important during the operation of the computer.

Another related job a register can do is complement itself (Fig. 10-15). When a register bit gets complemented it is changed to its other state. If a register bit is in a state of 0 and it is complemented it is changed to a 1. When a bit is a 1 and it is complemented it is changed to a 0. If an eight bit register gets complemented, all the 0s are changed to 1s and all the 1s are changed to 0s. The complementing of register bits is also a very important duty of a register.

INCREMENTING AND DECREMENTING

Another pair of jobs a register can do is increment and decrement itself. Most of the time the

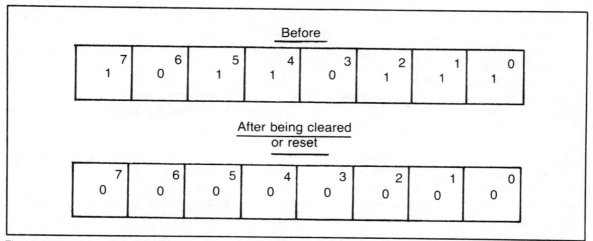

Fig. 10-14. When a register is instructed to clear or reset all the bits are replaced with 0s no matter what was there beforehand.

incrementing or decrementing is done one at a time. There is a register in the CPU called the program counter (Fig. 10-16). This important register has 16 bits and is attached to the address bus. The 16 bits of the address bus connects to the address the program counter puts on. Whatever address the PC puts on the bus the CPU gets connected to.

The PC is designed to increment itself by one after every address cycle. It does increment automatically unless instructed otherwise by a program. As long as the PC simply performs its incre-

menting the PC puts out one consecutive address after another, which is a very convenient job for it to do.

The incrementing is simply adding a 1 to the LSB of the register. If there is a 0 in the LSB it is replaced by the 1. When there is a 1 in the LSB it is replaced by a 0 and the 1 is shifted to the next left bit, where the same action occurs. As each new 1 is shifted into the LSB the total register binary number is incremented by 1.

Decrementing is the reverse of incrementing. During the decrement job, the total binary number

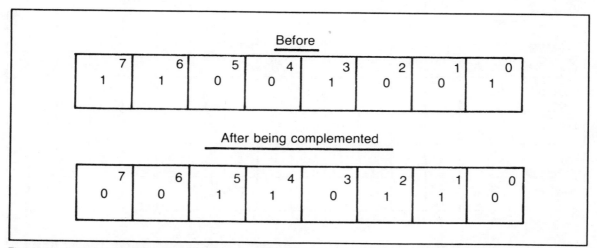

Fig. 10-15. If a register is instructed to complement, all the 0s are changed to 1s and the 1s to 0s.

in a register is reduced by 1. In the CPU is another 16-bit register called the index register. One of the techniques of indexing has to do with decrementing the index register after each addressing cycle. The decrementing is accomplished by removing 1 from the LSB after each cycle. As the 1 is removed the entire register binary number is reduced by 1.

Incrementing and decrementing registers by 1 is a common practice during computing. However it is not the only way the registers will operate. Instead of changing the registers by 1 they could be changed by 10, 11, or other binary values. There are many different variations of incrementing or decrementing a clever programmer can arrange. Anyway the incrementing and decrementing are very important jobs registers can do.

ANDING AND ORING

Another logic job registers are involved in is the ANDing and ORing of the said registers. The registers cannot perform the ANDing and ORing by themselves. The use of logic gates are needed.

If you want to AND an eight-bit memory location with an eight-bit register in the CPU it is done bit by bit (Fig. 10-17). The bits are numbered 7-0 in each register. The first thing you do is take bit 7 from the memory byte and bit 7 from the CPU register. The two bits are then applied to the two inputs of an AND gate. The bit 7's outputs are then stored in bit 7 of a third register. Next the two bit 6s are applied to another AND gate's inputs. The bit 6's output are placed into bit 6 of the third register. In turn bits 5, 4, 3, 2, 1, and 0 of the registers are ANDed.

The ORing of two registers are accomplished in a similar manner. The same position bits are injected into an OR gate and the results stored in the similar positions. ANDing and ORing registers are important duties during computer operations. There will be a lot more detail about these operations in the next chapter on CPUs.

All the different register operations are interrelated. The adding, subtracting, multiplication, and division are all performed by manipulating the

							Program counter incrementing by 1									First address	
MSB															↓ LSB	
	15 0	14 0	13 0	12 0	11 0	10 0	9 0	8 0	7 0	6 0	5 0	4 0	3 0	2 0	1 0	0 0
2nd	0	0	0	0	0	0	0	0	0	0	0	0	0	0	0	1
3rd	0	0	0	0	0	0	0	0	0	0	0	0	0	0	1	0
4th	0	0	0	0	0	0	0	0	0	0	0	0	0	0	1	1
5th	0	0	0	0	0	0	0	0	0	0	0	0	0	1	0	0
6th	0	0	0	0	0	0	0	0	0	0	0	0	0	1	0	1
7th	0	0	0	0	0	0	0	0	0	0	0	0	0	1	1	0
8th	0	0	0	0	0	0	0	0	0	0	0	0	0	1	1	1

Next addresses ↑

Fig. 10-16. A register like the program counter, is capable of incrementing automatically. The job is accomplished by counting.

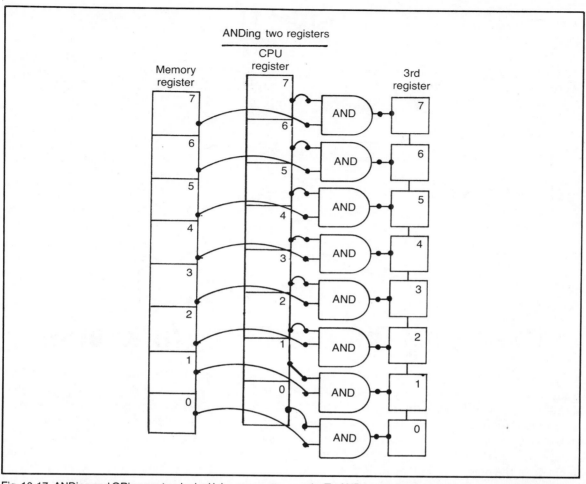

Fig. 10-17. ANDing and ORing are two logical jobs a computer can do. To AND two registers together the corresponding bits in each register are passed through an AND gate and stored in the corresponding bit of a third register.

binary digits. Adding is really nothing more than incrementing the registers one at a time. This is the hard way for us humans but the computer finds the task quite easy with its blinding speed and inability to feel boredom. The computer subtracts with an addition trick called 2's complement. Two's complement is interesting to learn but is not needed to repair computers. If you'd like to learn it there are plenty of books around for you to check it out.

In most home computers multiplication is accomplished the hard way again with incrementing the registers. Division in the same way is a varia-

tion of computer subtraction. There are some computers that actually have special multiplication and division circuits but these considerations are really not the province of the servicer.

Register operations in the home computer can be summed up in the following jobs: First there is the ability to shift. A variation of shifting is called rotating. Then there is incrementing and decrementing. After those are the jobs of clearing, setting, and complementing. Then there is the arithmetic jobs and the logic duties of ANDing and ORing. That's really about all registers can do.

175

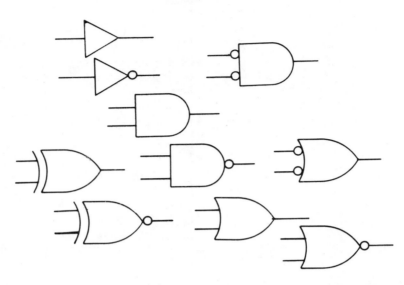

Chapter 11

Checking Out the CPU Workhorse

As you look down at the computer print board, ready to test pins on the CPU, you find that it is socketed right in the midst of the activity. Typically it's a 40-pin DIP (Fig. 11-1). There is a notch on one end of the large chip (Fig. 11-2). If the notch is at 12 o'clock, pin 1 starts counterclockwise and continues to pin 40 at the other side of the notch. It's a good idea to remember that pins 20 and 21 are at the other end of the chip, with 20 in the same line as 1 and 21 on the same side as 40. This remembrance saves time during testing of pin after pin.

The next item of importance to locate is Vcc and ground (Fig. 11-3). These pins will vary according to the CPU under test. For instance, a Z80 uses pin 11 for Vcc and 29 for ground. A 6809E uses pin 7 for Vcc and pin 1 for ground. During testing you will probably check Vcc again and again. If you know where it is right off you won't have to keep looking it up.

There are 24 other pins that are easily checked (Table 11-1). They consist of 16 pins attached to the address bus and 8 pins connected to the data bus. That makes 26 of the 40 pins on a CPU easily

located and tested with a vom or logic probe. When you do check them out, if they are ok, this is what should be on the typical pins with the power on.

When you touch down on Vcc the vom needle should read +5 V. Ground, of course, should be 0 V. As you probe the address and data pins, they should read an unsteady dc voltage somewhere between 2.4 V and 4.0 V. The logic probe gives the same readings except they are in a different form. Vcc on the logic probe shines a high on one LED. Ground shines a low. The address pins all turn on the high LED, but also turns on the pulse LED. The data pins show only a pulse, under these conditions.

As you look over the pin assignments of the CPU, more likely than not, there will be a number of the pins with no connection. The CPUs have all types of capabilities, but there are very few home computers that milk every single use out of one. As a result there are pins with no connections. For instance the 6809E could have 5 pins inoperative, the Z80 could have 3 pins not connected, and the 6502 might have 4 pins you do not have to concern yourself with. Suppose there are 5 pins with an nc on their pinout. Out of the 14 remaining pins you are to test, only 9 remain.

Examining the 9 pins reveals an interesting test fact. Five of the 9 have asterisks in front of the pin name. Crosschecking the same CPU in a different manufacturer's schematic, finds the same pins with a line over the name, which has the same

Z-80

2.5 Mhz

Z80-CPU	6.00
Z80-CTC	5.95
Z80-DART	15.25
Z80-DMA	17.50
Z80-PIO	6.00
Z80-SIO/O	18.50
Z80-SIO/1	18.50
Z80-SIO/2	18.50
Z80-SIO/9	16.95

4.0 Mhz

Z80-A-CPU	6.00
Z80-CTC	8.65
Z80A-DART	18.75
Z80A-DMA	27.50
Z80A-PIO	6.00
Z80A-SIO/O	22.50
Z80A-SIO/1, O	22.50
Z80A-SIO½2	22.50
Z80A-SIO/9	19.95

6.0 Mhz

Z80B-CPU	17.95
Z80B-CTC	15.50
Z80B-PIO	15.50

ZILOG

Z6132	34.95
Z8	39.95

8000 SERIES

8035	7.25
8039	7.95
INS8060	17.95
INS8073	29.95
8080	3.95
8085	7.95
8085A-2	11.95
8086	59.95
8087	Call
8088	39.95
8089	89.95
8155	7.95
8156	8.95
8185	29.95
8185-2	39.95
8741	39.95
8748	29.95
8755	32.00

6800

68000	call
6800	4.95
6802	10.95
6808	13.90
6809E	19.95
6809	19.95
6810	2.95
6820	4.95
6821	4.95
6828	14.95
6840	12.95
6843	34.95
6844	25.95
6845	16.95
6847	12.25
6850	3.45
6852	5.75
6860	10.95
6862	11.95
6875	6.95
6880	2.95
6883	24.95
68047	24.95
68488	19.95
68B00	10.95
68B02	22.25
68B09E	29.95
68B09	29.95
68B10	7.95
68B21	12.95
68B45	35.95
68B50	12.95

6800 = 1 MHZ

68B00 = 2 MHZ

6500 SERIES

1 MHZ

6502	6.95
6504	6.95
6505	8.95
6507	9.95
6520	4.35
6522	8.75
6532	11.25
6545	22.50
6551	11.85

2 MHZ

6502A	9.95
6522A	11.70
6532A	12.40
6545A	28.50
6551A	12.95

3 MHZ

6502B	14.95

Fig. 11-1. These price lists show most of the 40-pin CPU chips that are readily available and are being used in home computers.

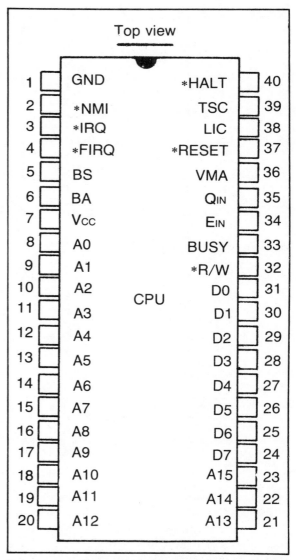

Fig. 11-2. Most CPUs look like this from the top view. To test the individual pins a schematic should be used since the functions of the pins are not universal.

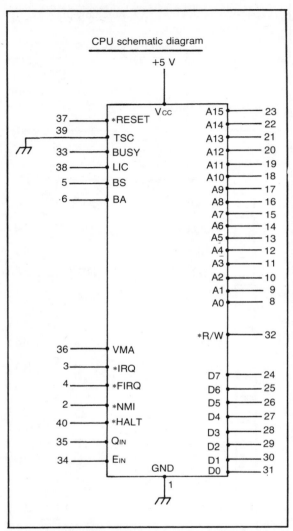

CPU schematic diagram

+5 V

Vcc

37 ——	*RESET	A15 —— 23
39	TSC	A14 —— 22
33 ——	BUSY	A13 —— 21
38 ——	LIC	A12 —— 20
5 ——	BS	A11 —— 19
6 ——	BA	A10 —— 18
		A9 —— 17
		A8 —— 16
		A7 —— 15
		A6 —— 14
		A5 —— 13
		A4 —— 12
		A3 —— 11
		A2 —— 10
		A1 —— 9
		A0 —— 8
		*R/W —— 32
36 ——	VMA	
3 ——	*IRQ	D7 —— 24
4 ——	*FIRQ	D6 —— 25
2 ——	*NMI	D5 —— 26
40 ——	*HALT	D4 —— 27
35 ——	Qɪɴ	D3 —— 28
34 ——	Eɪɴ	D2 —— 29
		D1 —— 30
	GND	D0 —— 31

1

Fig. 11-3. The supply voltage and ground pins are prominently displayed on the schematic version of large CPU chips. The address and data lines are usually grouped together. The remaining control lines are placed haphazardly in open spaces.

meaning as the asterisk. The asterisk or line means NOT. Without going into a longwinded computer design explanation, the asterisk to a servicer means the following: With a few exceptions, when the asterisk is in the pin naming, it means the pin is held high. The vom will read 5 V. While the pin is held high the job that pin is supposed to do is held off.

When it is time for that job to be performed, a low enters the pin and enables the section of the CPU the pin is controlling. During servicing, most of the time when you see a pin with an asterisk or line, it should read high on both the vom and the logic probe. On our example pinout, pins 3, 4, 2, 40, and 37 all should read high. If they don't, then a clue to the trouble is indicated.

This leaves 4 pins to be tested out of the original 40. Pin 39 is grounded so it should read low. Pins 35 and 34 are the clock input. If you read them on the vom they will show about 2.4 V each. In this case they are two inputs at the same frequency but with different phase angles. The logic probe will show them as blinking LED pulses, neither high or low. The scope will display them as a clock input at the clock frequency.

The last pin to be tested, 32, is the *R/W line. R/W means read and write. The 16 address lines go from the CPU to all addresses in the memory. The address lines only go to the memory. They do not return. The address lines are one way lines. All they do is open up an address.

The 8 data lines, on the other hand, are a two way street. Once an address is opened, the CPU can either read, which means load from, or write, which means store into the address. The data must be able to travel from the address to the CPU, or the other way, from the CPU to the address.

The R/W line directs the data traffic on the bidirectional data bus. When the R function is in charge, the bus will allow data to go from the address to the CPU. If the W function is in control, the bus will only let data flow from the CPU to the address.

The normal stand by state for the R/W line on this schematic is high. When the line is high it is in the read state. The write state is being held high. A vom reading should read high if all is well as *R/W. Should it read low or below high that could indicate trouble nearby.

INSIDE THE CPU

The servicer can check out the CPU by probing the pins plugged into the socket. Once an inconsistency between what is supposed to be on the pins,

Table 11-1. If This Type of Service Checkout Chart was Available From Manufacturers, Service Moves Would be Considerably Easier. This Chart Shows What Voltages and Logic States Should be Present on a 6809E CPU, at Startup, When the Computer is Operating Ok. With This Chart the 40 Pins can be Tested. If any of the Operating Conditions as Shown are not Being Met, That is a Valid Clue. This Indicates the Circuit Around the Suspect Pin Could Contain the Trouble.

Pin Number	VOM Reading	Logic Probe		
		High (1)	Low (0)	Pulse
Vcc 7	+5 V	✓		
GND 1	0 V		✓	
8				✓
9				✓
10				✓
11				✓
12		✓		✓
13				✓
14	2.4 V - 4.0 V	✓		✓
15		✓		✓
16		✓		✓
17		✓		✓
18		✓		✓
19				✓
20				✓
21		✓		✓
22				✓
23		✓		✓
24				✓
25				✓
26				✓
27				✓
28				✓
29				✓
30				✓
31				✓
*Reset 37	+5 V	✓		
*Irq 3	+5 V	✓		✓
*Firq 4	+5 V	✓		
*Nmi 2	+5 V	✓		
*Halt 40	+5 V	✓		
Qin 35	+2.4 V			Blinking
Ein 34	+2.4 V			Blinking
*R/W 32	+5 V			✓

(Left-side labels: Pins 8–23 — *16 Address Lines A0-A15*; Pins 24–31 — *8 Data Lines D7-D0*; Pins 35, 34 — *Clock*)

and what is actually there is found, a question arises. What is causing the wrong voltage or missing waveshape? In order to intelligently try to answer that question, some idea of what's going on inside the CPU is required. By having some CPU understanding you'll be able to figure out if the trouble is in the CPU itself or in the supporting circuitry. If the CPU is defective it can be changed. Should the trouble be originating elsewhere the tracing can be continued.

The ALU

The CPU of today is the result of more than 30 years of evolution. The first kernel of the CPU was originated years ago, and is known as the *Arithmetic*

Logic Unit, abbreviated *ALU*. The ALU as its name implies is able to perform arithmetic and logic functions. Typically an ALU can have two inputs and one output. Consider the two inputs as eight bits each and the output as one byte too. The ALU can do the following things to the two inputs (Fig. 11-4).

1 The ALU can add input A to input B. The eight bits of A are added to the byte of B. The result is a byte output.

2 The ALU can perform subtraction, multiplication and division on the two inputs. These functions are often just clever manipulations of the addition ability, but the result is correct. The result is a one byte output.

3 The ALU is able to complement one of the

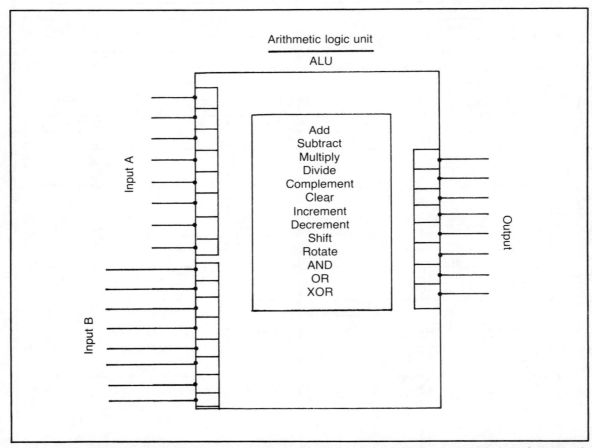

Fig. 11-4. The ALU is the very core of the computer. It does the jobs that are listed. These few jobs and the help of a memory is what computing is all about.

inputs. That means one of the eight bit inputs has all its 0s turned into 1s and its 1s made into 0s. This byte complementing is used in the arithmetic manipulation as well as other needs.

4 The ALU can clear one of the inputs. What that means is, the ALU can take the input byte and make all eight bits become 0s.

5 The ALU is able to increment or decrement one of the input bytes by 1. That means it can add 1 to the byte total or subtract 1.

6 The ALU can become a shift register and shift all the bits of one input either to the left or the right. When the shift left takes place the total value of the byte is multiplied by 2. If a shift right takes place the value of the byte is divided by 2.

7 With the shifting ability, the ALU is also able to do a job called rotate. Rotating is like shifting but with one difference. When you shift a byte, one of the bits is lost. A shift right loses the LSB. A shift left loses the MSB. They are shifted right out of the register and lost. When you rotate a byte, the lost bit is brought around to the other end of the register, and installed there. If you rotate right the LSB is brought around and becomes the new MSB. When you rotate left the MSB is brought around and becomes the LSB.

8 The ALU can compute logical inputs. If two byte size inputs are to be ANDed, they are done so bit by bit. The two MSBs are ANDed and the result becomes the new MSB. Each set of bits are also ANDed all of them simultaneously, in parallel fashion to form a total AND output byte. Whenever the ANDed bits are both 1s the output bit is also 1. Any other combination of bits are ANDed into a 0.

9 The ALU can also OR the two input bytes in the same manner. Whenever one of two input bits is a 1 the output bit is a 1. The only way two ORed bits can produce an output 0 is if both input bits are 0. The total result of all the bits being ORed is an ORed output byte.

10 The ALU can also XOR a pair of input bytes. If the two bits being XORed are both 0s or both 1s their output bit will be 0. If one bit is a 0 and the other bit is a 1 then the XOR bit result will be a 1. The total result of the two bytes being XORed in the ALU is an XORed byte.

Those are the jobs the ALU in the CPU are able to do. At first glance these 10 general operations do not seem to be unusually powerful. Yet they are the roots of the computer's ability to make the world perform with greater efficiency.

The Accumulator

The ALU by itself is helpless. It is completely wired inside the CPU. There are no pins on the DIP that lead to the ALU. In order to get data to the ALU and then receive an ALU output, the data must pass through some data registers. In an 8-bit CPU these registers are built with 8 bits each. That's the reason a CPU is called an 8 bit type, or a 16 bit type, because of the size of these registers that surround the ALU (Fig. 11-5).

Typically there can be seven of these registers. With seven of these ALU companion registers there would be three called multiplexers, two called storage registers and two are accumulator types. All have 8-bit registers. They receive their inputs and send their outputs in parallel fashion over 8-bit buses.

The three multiplexers are used to transfer a byte of data into and out of the ALU. There is one multiplexer at each ALU input and the third one at the ALU output. The multiplexers make sure that the data enters and exits the ALU in an orderly manner.

The multiplexers are in turn fed from, and have outputs to, the remaining four registers. Two of the four registers are little more than storage registers. They can receive data from the cassette, joysticks, or other I/O devices via the data bus and hold the data till it's time to have the ALU work on the data.

The remaining two registers are accumulator types. An accumulator, besides being able to store data can also add. It has an electronic adder built into its register circuitry. By being able to add gives it a lot more power than the other registers in the area.

While the ALU and the multiplexers are wired internally with no way for the servicer to probe them through a DIP pin, the accumulators and the I/O storage registers are attached to the internal data bus in the CPU. The internal data bus exits the

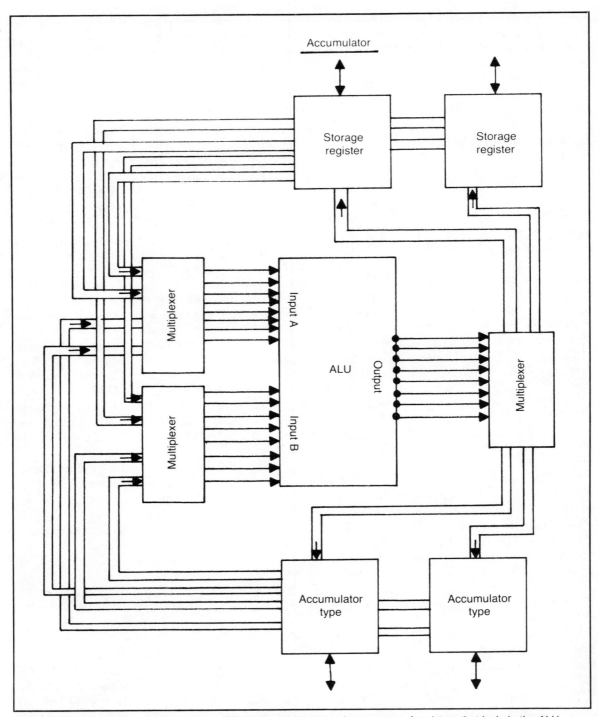

Fig. 11-5. The so called accumulator in the CPU is loosely thought of as a group of registers that include the ALU.

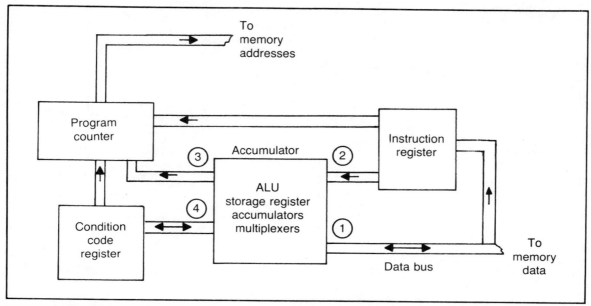

Fig. 11-6. The accumulator (1) receives and gives back data to the data bus, (2) gets instructions from the instruction register, (3) sends data to the program counter and (4) sends data to the condition code register.

CPU at the data bus 8 pins, which you can read with a probe. When there is activity on the pins the ALU is in operation. Impaired activity on a data bus pin could be indicating trouble in these circuits.

Considering the ALU, multiplexers, storage registers, and accumulator types as a single block in the CPU it can be called the accumulator (Fig. 11-6). There are typically four input-outputs. One is the data bus that is two directional. When the data bus is loading the accumulator from memory, that is one direction. If the data bus is storing the memory with data from the accumulator, the traffic is going in the other direction.

Number two is an input only internal bus line from a register called the *instruction register*. Three is an output bus from the accumulator to the program counter. Four is an input-output bus called the CCR, the condition code register. Let's see what these CPU registers are doing in the scheme of things.

The CCR

The condition code register sits between the ALU and the program register. The CCR gets set from the ALU and in turn gives the program counter instructions.

The CCR is typically an 8-bit register (Fig. 11-7). The bits in the CCR are called "flags". The flags can get set or reset. If a flag is set, its bit is 1. When a flag is reset, it is cleared to a 0. Flags can get set or reset for a lot of reasons. We'll examine six common flags in a CCR that occupies 6 of the 8 bits.

First of all a flag bit could be called Z. Z means zero. The Z flag can get set by the ALU if all the bits in the accumulator become zero. This means that when an accumulator register reaches the value 0000 0000, the Z bit becomes 1. This flag alert then can cause something to happen. For instance, it could stop the operation if the 0000 0000 signaled the end of a computation.

Another flag bit could be called N. N stands for negative. The flag N would be set if the accumulator reaches a negative number. How can we tell if the accumulator has a negative number? The MSB of a binary result is 0 if the number is positive. The MSB is set to 1 if the number is negative. For example, 00001111 is +15 in decimal. 10001111 is

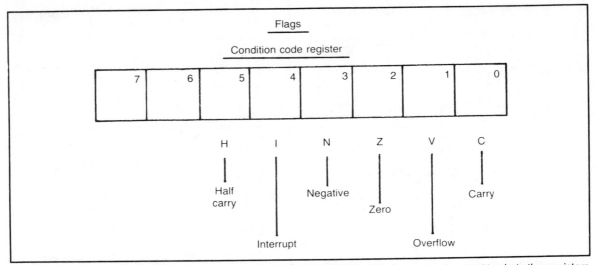

Fig. 11-7. The CCR is an 8-bit register that contains the flags of the computer. The flags get set or reset to alert other registers when trouble or special circumstances arrive during operation.

−15 in decimal. When the accumulator gets a 1 in its MSB then the N flag gets set to 1. This signals the ALU to conduct its operation accordingly.

Another common flag bit is called C. C stands for carry. This has to do with the arithmetic in the accumulator. If during addition in the accumulator, an arithmetical carry must be made out of the MSB because there are just too many numbers for the register to hold, then the carry is put in the C flag. The C flag is normally clear till it gets set by a carry.

A fourth flag is called H. H means half-carry. The C flag gets set if the MSB spills over. The H flag gets set if there is a carry halfway through the 8 bits or from the fourth to the fifth bit. The H flag is normally clear until a carry takes place from the LS nybble to the MS nybble in the byte of the accumulator.

The fifth flag is called I. I stands for interrupt. The interrupt flag gets set when a program that is in operation must stop the program for an important reason. The interrupt flag is normally cleared. If the flag gets set the program goes into a special interrupt sequence and conducts the interrupt business. When the computer is built with all 8 bits able to throw flags, instead of only 6 of the 8 bits being used, there are usually three interrupts instead of one.

The sixth flag is called V. V stands for overflow. This is somewhat like the carry flag setting. The carry flag gets set if the addition overflows the register. The V flag gets set if addition overflows the register too. However, the V flag gets set only if the overflow is during a very special type of addition.

Most computers can't really subtract, they subtract by using a special kind of addition called two's complement. It's really not that hard to do. It turns out that in binary, if you add the two's complement of a number to a second number, the result will be subtraction, not addition. The two's complement is computed easily. First get the one's complement of the number, then add 0000 0001.

For example, suppose you had a binary number 0110 0100. The one's complement is obtained by changing all the 0s to 1s and all the 1s to 0s. That would make the one's complement 1001 1011. To then get the two's complement add 0000 0001.

```
  1001 1011   1's complement
+ 0000 0001
  1001 1100   2's complement
```

Once the ALU arrives at a 2's complement figure it can add it to the desired register and the result is the subtraction of two numbers. Anyway, when a 2's complement addition is made and there is an overflow, the V flag gets set to 1.

The CCR is wired internally between the accumulator and the program counter. The flags get set and reset from the operation of the ALU and the accumulators. The CCR can signal the program counter when some of its flags like the N and Z get set and reset. The program counter has no reason to signal the CCR, so the bus between them is one way, CCR to PC. Between the CCR and the ALU group the signals must go both ways, so that bus is bidirectional.

The PC

The program counter is not an 8-bit register like the ones we have been discussing. The PC has 16 bits (Fig. 11-8). The PC does not handle data like the other registers. The PC has three inputs and one output (Fig. 11-6). The output of the PC is an address. The PC is connected to the 16 address pins of the CPU chip. As the CPU chugs along running a program, the PC outputs the next address to be opened up.

Since the PC has 16 bits it can form a possible 65,536 addresses. That means it can handle a program with 65,536 steps. Each 8-bit memory register can hold the data for one program step. The 16-bit PC can free the contents of any one of 65,536 addresses at each program step.

The addresses the PC outputs are created by the three PC inputs. Under ordinary circumstances, a program is stored in a computer starting with address 0000 0000 0000 0000. Each 8-bit step of the program is installed in subsequent memory registers with their 16-bit addresses. A ten step program would be stored in the first ten addresses 0000 0000 0000 0000 through 0000 0000 0000 1001. When you get the program running a computer is built to automatically start at the beginning address and continue on from address to address till all the addresses have been able to send a copy of their contents out over the data bus.

The PC takes care of this addressing chore. The PC at the beginning of its operation gets its bits initialized to all 0s. Then as the program is run, the PC in time with the beat of the clock, outputs address after address over the address bus. As each

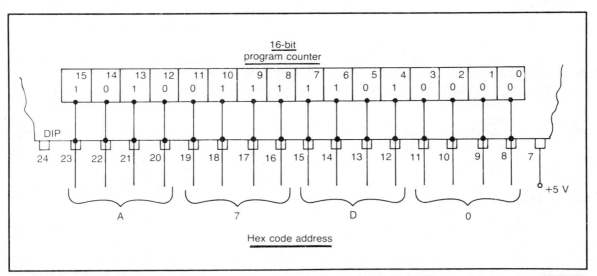

Fig. 11-8. The program counter is a 16-bit register that is attached to the address bus. Whatever address appears in the PC becomes the next address to be activated. The 16 bits are coded into four hex digits that forms one of the 65,536 individual addresses in the typical home computer. Incidentally, the address in the illustration is the same one that was read by the logic probe in Table 11-1. If you match up the pins 23-8 in this illustration with pins 23-8 in Table 11-1 you'll see the highs are the 1s and the nonreadings are the 0s. The address formed is one of the start up addresses in ROM of the computer on which I ran the test.

addressing frees the data contents of the memory cell, the data gets processed and the computer job gets done.

The PC doesn't need any particular input to start at zero and address memory registers that are in sequence. It will do that automatically without any assistance. The inputs are needed when the PC must be stopped sequencing and form an address that is not in order.

The condition code register is one of the PC's inputs. While the PC is perking along going from address to address in order, a Z flag could suddenly be set. The program could have an instruction "if a Z flag is set JUMP to address 0011 1100 1110 0011." This would input a change of address to the PC. The PC would then output the change over the address bus. Instead of the next available address in line getting opened, the new address would be accessed. The PC would then continue incrementing by one at the new address site.

An N flag could then get set. Another instruction could say "if an N flag is set RETURN to original program." This would be input to the PC. The PC would then form the original address where the PC had left off.

The accumulator complex, with all its surrounding registers, is another PC input source that can change the normal sequencing the PC does automatically. Around the accumulator are registers called *index register*, *stack pointer* and others. They work with the accumulator to create special addresses. These addresses are important when running a program. The index register and the stack pointer are both 16-bit registers like the PC.

In a typical computer the index register and stack pointer's outputs are connected directly to the address bus. They are in parallel with the PC. At certain times in a program, instead of the PC installing an address on the address bus, the PC is made to hold, while the index register or the stack pointer puts an address on the bus line. This is effectively the same as if the index register's bits were transferred to the PC and the PC in turn outputted the address. Any way, the index register and the stack pointer are considered a PC input

where they can change the sequencing of the PC to address some other memory byte, rather than the one in numerical order.

A third PC input bypasses the accumulator-CCR circuits entirely. This input is one that comes directly from another circuit area called the *instruction register*. We'll discuss that section shortly. When the PC input comes from the instruction register, the input is a program address that is immediately installed in the PC replacing the number the PC had been working on.

The PC, index register, and stack pointer are all connected in parallel to the 16 address pins of the CPU. These registers are thus available to be probed by a vom, logic probe, or scope.

The IR

The instruction register is connected to the 8 data bus pins of the CPU. As the program counter accesses a memory location, the byte that is stored there sends a copy of itself out over the 8-bit data bus. The byte enters the CPU at the data pins and is stored in the instruction register (Fig. 11-9).

The IR then decodes the byte. The byte can either be an 8-bit instruction or an 8-bit piece of data. The instructions can refer to either addresses or data. There are typically about two dozen general instructions for a home computer. The bytes are composed of eight bits. In eight bits there are 256 possible combinations of 1 s and 0 s. That means 256 different instructions can be coded into 8 bits.

The decoder in the IR is built to respond to the various arrangements of bits in a byte. For example, if the IR of a 6800 CPU receives 1000 0110 over the data bus, its circuit causes the contents of a memory location to be loaded into the A accumulator.

The 1000 0110 instruction is part of an instruction set the CPU has built in the instruction decoder. There are typically about six dozen actual byte sized instructions a decoder can get the computer to act upon. The six dozen though are made up of about two dozen general instructions. Half of the two dozen are the arithmetic-logic manipulations and the ALU does, as discussed earlier.

The remaining dozen instructions are broken

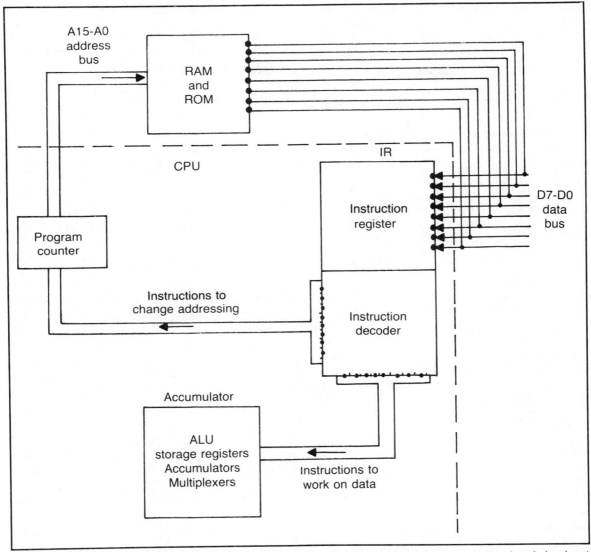

Fig. 11-9. The Instruction Register in the CPU receives its input from the data bus. The incoming data is then decoded and sent to the accumulator to be manipulated or the program counter to change the sequence of the addressing.

into two groups. One is a group of instructions that can move data over the data bus from register to register, from register to an output device, or from an input device to a register. The remaining instructions are orders for the program counter. Let's see how the IR can move data over the data bus.

1 When a program is stored into memory and the computer begins running the program, chances are good, as the computer accesses memory location after location, the instruction LOAD will be at one of the addresses. The instruction is encoded in 8 bits. The instruction could be one of 16 different LOAD instructions, according to what transmitter is being loaded into what receiver. A different set of

bits is used for each of the 16 LOAD instructions.

The LOAD instruction means a CPU register is to get a byte of data from some transmitter. The transmitter could be, RAM or ROM. The receiver register could be an accumulator, the index register, or the stack pointer.

The LOAD instruction also must contain the address of the byte of data that is to be transferred from the transmitter to the receiver. For example, the LOAD instruction will need the following information if it is to transfer a copy of the contents of RAM location 25 to the accumulator.

☐ The LOAD instruction.
☐ The accumulator is the receiver.
☐ RAM location 25 is the transmitter.

All of this information is contained in the program in the form of bytes. When the CPU accesses the memory location that is holding this particular LOAD instruction, the bytes are outputted to the data bus and go straight to the IR in the CPU. There the bytes are decoded and the CPU follows the instruction. It accesses RAM address 25 by using the address bus. A copy of the contents of 25 is outputted over the data bus. The copy enters the IR. The IR then sends the copy to the accumulator. The LOAD instruction has been executed.

2 The STORE instruction is like LOAD except data travels the other way on the data bus. A STORE instruction sends a copy of the contents of the CPU registers to RAM. The register transmitters are the accumulator, index register, and the stack pointer. Assuming a program is being run, the STORE instruction is as likely to appear as often as the LOAD instruction. When the program causes the CPU to access an address and a STORE instruction is inputted to the data bus, the instruction could contain the following information.

☐ The STORE instruction.
☐ The accumulator is the transmitter.
☐ RAM location 35 is the receiver.

The instruction arrives at the IR. The IR decodes the instruction. The CPU then opens up RAM location 35 with the address bus. A copy of the contents of the accumulator is sent out over the data bus.

As you know, there are 65,536 possible addresses for the byte from the accumulator to go to. Normally though all of the addresses are held inactive. When a particular instruction is being executed, the IR decoder only opens up the address where the byte from the accumulator is to be stored.

There are also a number of CPU registers that act as a transmitter or in the case of a LOAD instruction as a receiver. These registers are also held inactive. However, while the instruction is in operation, the pertinent register is activated by the IR decoder. Therefore, during the instruction sequence the decoder gets the transmitter and receiver operational. All the other addresses and registers stay on hold.

If RAM location 35 is the receiver specified in the program instruction, then it and the accumulator are both activated. A copy of the contents of the accumulator then travels over the data bus to the activated address 35. The contents of the accumulator is thus transferred to RAM 35 with a STORE instruction.

3 A third data transfer instruction a CPU comprehends is called TRANSFER. This is like LOAD and STORE except it is between the registers in the CPU. The data never leaves the CPU. It simply gets transferred from place to place. The registers in the CPU that can TRANSFER are the accumulators, the condition code register, the index register, and the stack pointer.

When one register transfers its contents to another register, it is only transferring a copy. The contents of the register that receives the data though, has its contents altered. For instance, if the contents of accumulator A is transferred to accumulator B, the contents of A remains the same since only a copy of the contents was transferred. The contents of B get altered as the 1s and 0s from A get mixed with whatever was in B.

If you are dealing with a CPU that has two accumulators, a condition code register, an index register, and a stack pointer, the following TRANSFERs are possible (Fig. 11-10).

☐ TRANSFER Accumulator A to Accumulator B

☐ TRANSFER Accumulator B to Accumulator A

☐ TRANSFER Accumulator A to Condition Code Register

☐ TRANSFER Condition Code Register to Accumulator A

☐ TRANSFER Index Register to Stack Pointer

☐ TRANSFER Stack Pointer to Index Register

There are other possibilities like accumulator B to CCR, and so on. However, the six instructions listed will handle the programming chores adequately. To install more decoding circuits into the IR would be an unneeded expense for the manufacturers.

Notice that the IR is not mentioned in any of the instructions. As a matter of fact, lots of skilled programmers hardly know the IR is there. The IR is not thought of during programming. The IR though is the register that is connected to the 8 pins of the data line. During servicing the IR has a place in the data line troubleshooting. The servicer must be aware of the IR even if the programmer ignores the IR.

4 A fourth data transfer instruction type has to do with transmitting data to an external device like a cassette or a line printer, or receiving data from a device like the cassette or the keyboard. There are chips in the computer, as discussed earlier in the book, like Uarts and PIAs. These chips are called I/O ports. The I/O ports are connected directly to all the I/O devices. The CPU does not have to communicate directly with the I/O devices. The I/O ports do that. The CPU only has to deal with data streams to and from the I/O ports.

The I/O ports are given addresses in the memory map just like the RAMs and ROMs. As a result the CPU is not able to discern any difference between an I/O port address and a RAM or ROM address. When it is necessary for the CPU to read an input device like the keyboard, the CPU sends a LOAD instruction over the data bus to an I/O register address activated by the address bus. The I/O address is attached to the keyboard. The keyboard is read in that indirect fashion.

When it is necessary for the CPU to write to an output device like the printer, the CPU sends a STORE instruction to the I/O port address that is attached to the printer. The data stream goes out over the data bus, arrives at the I/O port and is promptly forwarded to the printer.

This data transfer instruction type is identical to the type used to load and store data between the CPU and memory. The difference is not in the instructions. The difference is that memory destinations are replaced with I/O ports.

The third group of instructions does not deal with the data at all. These instructions do not go near the ALU, accumulators, index register or the stack pointer. Some of them though check out the status of the CCR. This group of instructions has the job of directly affecting the bits in the program counter. As discussed, the program counter is attached to the 16 lines in the address bus. The program counter is usually initialized to 0000 0000 0000 0000 at the beginning of a program run. The program bytes are stored in memory starting with address 0000 0000 0000 0000. Once a program starts running the program counter increments itself by 1 after every program step. Since it is connected to the address bus, the addresses in the memory starting with 0000 0000 0000 0000 are activated and the program proceeds as each memory byte is sent to the IR one at a time.

The program will continue, byte after byte, coming from memory register after register. That is, unless one of the instructions that enter the IR is able to go directly to the program counter from the instruction decoder and change the automatic numerical incrementing in the PC.

There are two kinds of instructions that are able to go directly from the IR decoder to the PC. One is called "unconditional" and the other is

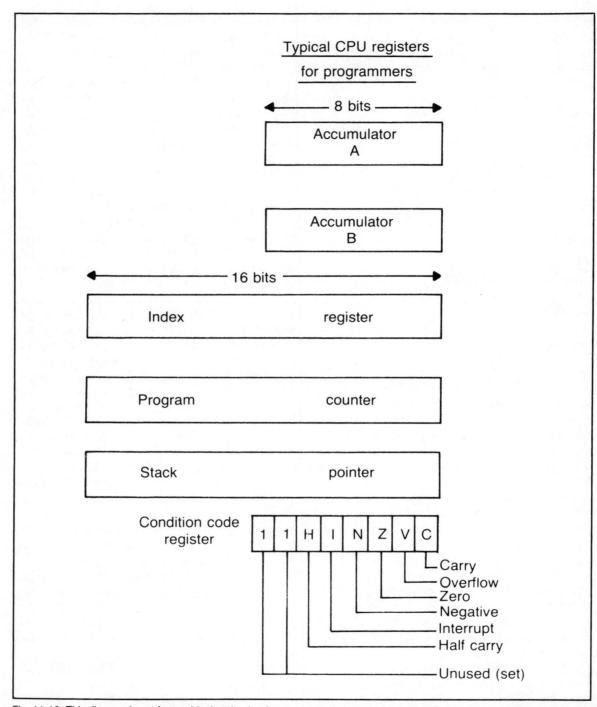

Fig. 11-10. This diagram is not for troubleshooting but for programming. It only describes what registers a CPU has, which is valuable information a programmer often needs.

named "conditional". The unconditional instruction simply goes from decoder to PC and changes the next address from the regular increment to a special one specified in the instruction. The conditional instruction, before going to the PC, must check with the CCR to see if it is allowed to change the regular incrementing of the PC. The permission to change the PC addressing is granted or not according to which flags are set or reset.

1 The main unconditional instruction is named JUMP. When the decoder gets a JUMP instruction, it can say in binary digits, JUMP to memory location decimal 239. The decoder will send the instruction to the PC. No matter what address is coming up next in the PC, the instruction forces the PC to cancel the next address and instead output the address 239 in binary. Decimal 239 in binary is 0000 0000 1110 1111. There are no ifs, ands, or buts, the JUMP instruction is usually unconditional. I say usually because in some computers the JUMP instruction might have a condition attached to it.

2 The main conditional instruction is named BRANCH. There are a lot of BRANCH instructions in an instruction set. This is because the BRANCH instruction must check with the CCR to see if conditions are arranged for it to change the PC's automatic incrementing. The BRANCH instruction will be executed or ignored according to flag settings. The branching could go on if bit N in the CCR is set or reset. That means if the accumulator is showing a positive or negative number. The branch could take place if bit Z is set or reset. Those settings could provide conditions where the accumulator equaled 0000 0000 or did not equal zero. Other ways a branch could occur is if C was set or reset or V was set or reset. There are not usually branch instructions for the H bit or the interrupts.

3 There are some variations and combining in some other of the JUMP and BRANCH instructions. There is one branch instruction named BRANCH ALWAYS. This is an unconditional instruction much like JUMP. There are some JUMP instructions in some computers that have conditions attached to it. That makes these instructions quite like a BRANCH. For the most part though JUMP

indicates an unconditional new PC address, and BRANCH usually means a change of PC addressing only if the flags are set or reset properly.

The flag settings in the CCR are not changed or affected in any way by the branch type instructions. The connection between the CCR and the PC is one way, from the CCR to the PC. The PC can only receive signal from the CCR. The PC can't send a signal to the CCR.

4 There is one more type of program counter changing instruction that deals with subroutines. A subroutine is a program that is installed somewhere in the memory that is secondary to the main program. For instance, a math program might have to get the logarithm of a number every now and then. The routine to compute such a number can be installed in some unused RAM section. Then when the log is needed a JUMP TO SUBROUTINE or BRANCH TO SUBROUTINE instruction can be used. When that kind of instruction arrives at the IR, it is sent to the PC and the PC addresses the memory location where the subroutine is residing. The general name for this instruction is CALL. The CALL instruction commands the PC to jump to the start address of a subroutine.

Once the subroutine has been run, another instruction is installed, as the last instruction in the subroutine. This type of instruction is called RETURN. The RETURN instruction after it is decoded in the IR is also sent directly to the PC. It gives the PC the return address, and the PC outputs the address. Operation then is returned to the main program.

From computer to computer these general instructions are varied, altered and even completely changed. If you are programming the computer, then you must learn all the details and nuances of the instruction set and dare not write a program from a general point of view. For repairing a computer the instruction set is useful in understanding what is happening, so you can puzzle out what broke down. Knowing what the instructions will do is also useful in analyzing the digital inputs and outputs that are found on the 40 pins of the CPU. However, it is not necessary for the servicer to understand how to use the instruction set in programming, to repair the computer. Of course, the more you know about all aspects of the computer the better off you'll be working on them.

THE INSTRUCTION SET LAYERS

While it is not a necessity for the repairman to know how to program the computer it is important to know what an instruction set is and how it performs its job in the computer. There are times when some parts of a program are working and other lines in a program are not. If you can visualize what duties of the instruction set are operative, and what jobs are down, the diagnosis of the trouble tends to be more accurate. Also there are tests the manufacturer will have in the service notes that are in the form of programs. As you type these little programs into the machine and run them, the results are interpreted intelligently if you know why you are making these tests.

The instruction set for most home computers is a group of 8-bit numbers. Since there are 8 bits in each instruction, there are 256 possible combinations of bits and 256 possible instructions. The possibilities range from 0000 0000 to 1111 1111. (The space between the 4th and 5th digits are only there as a convenience for this book's purposes. The actual instructions are 00000000 to 11111111.)

These numbers are called the *machine language*. These are the numbers the CPU understands. The CPU will not respond unless the input to the instruction register is in binary (Fig. 11-11). The CPU is nothing more than a gigantic conglomeration of logic devices. Just as the logic gates and various register types will only perform according to their truth tables, the CPU will only perform when its truth table inputs, the instruction set, arrives at the IR. Even though the CPU and the instruction set are far more complicated than a gate and a truth table, they both operate in a similar manner.

A typical program in machine language could look like the following to the IR:

1010 0011
0111 1100
0101 0000

1000 1000
1111 0011
1100 1010
0100 1101
0001 1001
0111 1100
0011 0111

These are the program bits that are stored in RAM or ROM in sequential addresses. When the order is given to run the program the address bus starts and addresses the first memory register. A copy of the contents of the register, which is 1010 0011, is sent to the IR. The IR decodes the 1010 0011 and causes the instruction to be executed. After the instruction is completed, the address bus addresses the second memory register in line, and the second instruction is fetched over the data bus. This continues till the entire program has been fetched and executed. The CPU does a predictable job and never makes a mistake with the 8-bit instructions, unless the CPU is defective.

The machine language is the bottom layer of the instruction set. The groups of 8 bits are actually the medium by which the computing electronics can take place. If a programmer wanted to, he could replace the typewriter keyboard with a front panel that has 8 data switches. Then he could key the bits into the memory by switch. There are many computer designers and home hobbyists who do use front panels. In years past, the front panel was the only inexpensive way to go (Fig. 11-12).

As you can see though, using a front panel to install bit-by-bit is the hard way to install a program. Today there are many practical inexpensive input mediums like the cassette and the keyboard. With the keyboard, the binary bit input is done away with altogether. The standard of the industry is to replace the 8-bit input with a two hex input. It was discussed earlier that four bits can be coded into one hex character. Eight bits are coded into two hex characters. If 0000 0000 to 1111 1111 is made up of 256 combinations, then hex 00 to hex FF is also made up of 256 combinations. The ten step machine language program can be coded into the following ten step hex program.

Machine Language	Hex
1010 0011	A 3
0111 1100	7 C
0101 0000	5 0
1000 1000	4 4
1111 0011	F 3
1100 1010	C A
0100 1101	4 D
0001 1001	1 9
0111 1100	7 C
0011 0111	3 7

Now that we have a hex code to replace the cumbersome, difficult to work with binary, all well and good. However, the machine can only use binary. The hex code is meaningless to the chips in the computer. What happens to the hex if it is typed into the computer?

The hex is the next layer of the instruction set.

Between the bottom layer, the machine language, and the next layer up, the hex code, a program is installed. This program is stored in memory. It is part of a larger program called the operating system or the monitor. The section that is concerned with the hex is called a *hex loader*. As the hex is typed into the computer, the program section called hex loader accepts the hexadecimal digits. The hex loader codes the hex digits into 4 binary digits each and stores them into memory. Then the CPU is able to use them (Fig. 11-13).

If the binary digits are called "machine language", then the hex digits can be called "object code." There is some confusion between the two names. You'll find the bits are sometimes called object code and the hex is called machine language. The definitions are not completely standardized by everyone. The above definition is as good as any

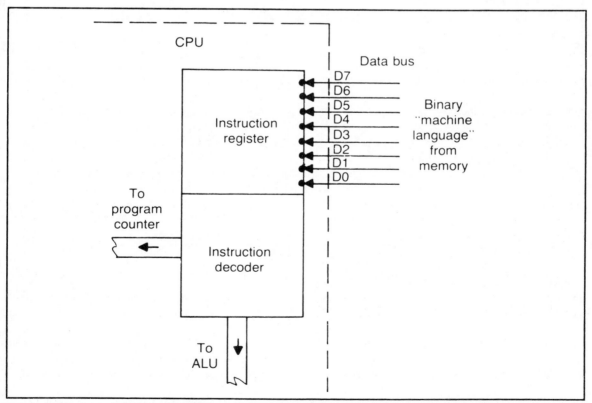

Fig. 11-11. The Instruction Register, buried deep in the computer can only work with "machine language", the high and low pulses of voltage.

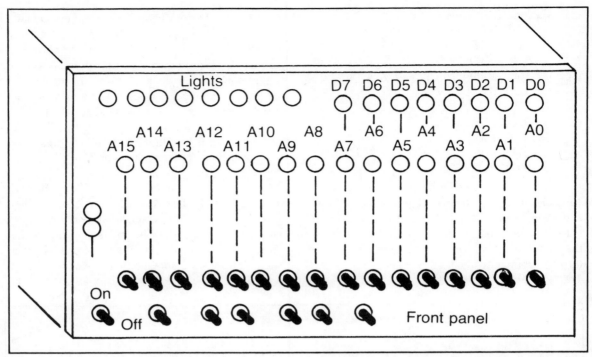

Fig. 11-12. The very basic input device is the "front panel." With it you can insert the 1s and 0s of addresses and data directly into the computer.

others. I use machine language for bits and object code for hex. The important thing is to know their place in the layers of the instruction set.

In a lot of the home computers, you cannot type a program written in binary into the memory in a direct fashion. The program has to be written in hex and then it can be poked into memory. As the hex is poked in, the hex is converted to binary which actually goes into the memory registers.

The top layer of computing language is called high level language. This high level language is designed for easy programming. Home computers usually have a high level language capability. The commonest language is known as BASIC (Beginners All Purpose Symbolic Instruction Code).

When a program is installed into memory in a high level language the following happens. The instruction is first sent to an interpreter which is in the form of a program stored in RAM or ROM. The instruction is forced to go through the interpreter. The interpreter can then code the instruction from the high level language into binary. The binary bits are then sent to the memory. The binary can then be fetched by the CPU to perform the instruction.

This encoding and decoding from language to language might seem to be cumbersome. However, for a home computer, the entire process is almost instantaneous and the complexity means practically nothing to the electronic circuits. The important thing is to make computer operation by the human involved as easy as possible.

ASSEMBLING A PROGRAM

The experienced computer repairman often must take the instruction set of the CPU under test and devise a test program to check out or exercise some area in and around the CPU. If you look at the sample list of instructions in the set they are composed of hex numbers. The numbers range from 00 to FF (Table 11-2).

After the hex number is another code of letters. After 00 is NEG, after 2E is BGT, and after FF

194

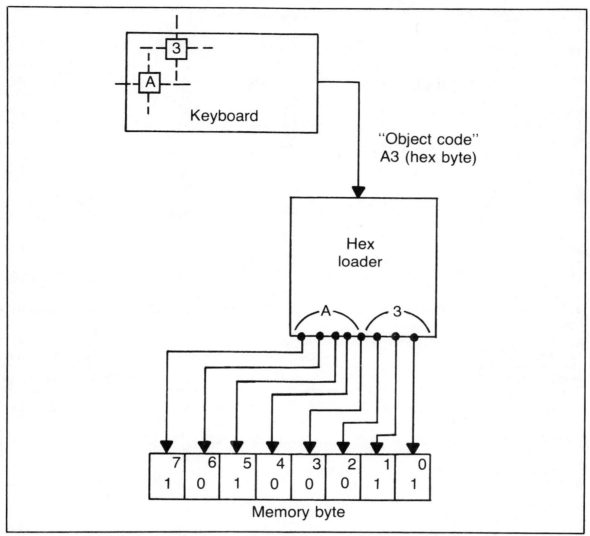

Fig. 11-13. The hex characters that are coded into binary are called "object code." Object code can be inserted into the computer through the keyboard in most home computers.

is STU. These letters are called *mnemonics*. These mnemonics are descriptions in three or four letters of what the instruction does. The NEG stands for negate, BGT indicates branch if greater than zero and STU means store the U register. The letters are chosen to be abbreviations of the jobs. These abbreviations are easier to memorize than the hex digits. The idea is, write the program in mnemonics instead of hex. The writing will be much easier

since the mnemonics stick in your head after you use them a few times. The hex numbers do not handle that easily. Also if you work on one type CPU in the morning and another kind in the afternoon, the mnemonics will be somewhat the same. The hex numbers will be definitely different.

While the manufacturers do include a set of mnemonics with their instruction set listing, and there is a mnemonic to match up with each hex number, the CPU has no mnemonic capability. The mnemonics are there as a handy reference but have absolutely no meaning to the computer. If you write a program in mnemonics you must convert the mnemonics to hex before it can be installed into the computer to be turned into binary.

Why bother? When you write a program in mnemonics it can be read by you and others. A program written in hex appears meaningless until it is decoded into English step by step with the aid of a listing of the instruction set. It is more convenient to write a program in mnemonics than in hex.

If you write a test program in mnemonics you can turn it into a hex program in one of two ways. One, you can assemble the program by hand. Two, you can get hold of an assembler, which is a program that turns the mnemonic program into hex, with the aid of the computer. The mnemonic program is called an *assembly language program*. To write an assembly program requires a lot of familiarity with instruction sets.

HAND ASSEMBLY

The instruction set shows a list of hex numbers that range from 00 to FF. Each hex two digit number represents a byte. The byte is the standard in home computers. All memory locations are one byte wide. All instructions are one byte wide. All data units are one byte wide. If more than one byte of information must be stored in memory, then additional memory locations have to be used, but the information is still arranged into individual one byte units. The data bus is composed of 8 lines that are connected to all the memory locations on one end and the internal CPU data bus and IR on the other. These are all one byte matches. When you write an 8 bit or its equivalent hex program, each program step is one byte.

Some instructions can perform their job with a single program byte. When it does a single memory register is accessed and the instruction is transmitted to the CPU and executed. Other instructions can't do their job with a single byte. These instruc-

Table 11-2. The Instruction Set of a CPU is Really a Set of Binary Numbers. Each Number is Eight Digits Which Codes into Two Hex Digits. The Hex Digits, the Object Code, is Called the Op Code. If you Want to Write an Assembly Language Program, Each Op Code has to be Changed to the Equivalent "Source Code." To Write the Source Code Instead of the Object Code, Each Op Code Number Must be Replaced, Taking into Consideration, a Mnemonic, An Addressing Mode, the Number of Cycles the Operation Takes, and the Number of Bytes Needed in Memory. Nobody Said it's Easy.

OP Code HEX	"Source Code" Mnemonic	Addressing Mode	Cycles	Bytes
00	NEG	Direct	6	2
03	COM		6	2
04	LSR		6	2
06	ROR		6	2
07	ASR		6	2
2E	BGT	Relative	3	2
2F	BLE	Relative	3	2
30	LEAX	Indexed	4	2
31	LEAY		4	2
32	LEAS		4	2
FB	ADDB	Extended	5	3
FC	LDD		6	3
FD	STD		6	3
FE	LDU		6	3
FF	STU		6	3

tions need two to five bytes. The instruction stores one byte in each memory location.

Why does an instruction that is listed as a single byte need more hex numbers? How can an instruction be five bytes long? It's because the instruction part is only one byte long. The rest of the instruction sequence is data that the instruction works on. In an instruction sequence, the first byte is the instruction that is called the *op code*. The rest of the bytes are called the *operand*. The op code operates on the operand. If you look at the hex digits randomly there is no way you can tell the difference between the instructions (op code) and the data (operands). The computer though has no problem in using them. The only requirement the CPU insists upon is that the bytes must be stored in sequential-memory registers.

The op code is always an instruction from the instruction set. The operand can be one of a number of forms of data. It can be an address where data is stored, it can be a register name, or it can be straight data like math numbers or the like. The op code and operands all must be put into one byte hex forms before the computer can understand it. That is what hand assembly is: taking an assembly program and with pencil and paper coding it into a long string of program steps in hex form. The hex can then be typed into the computer where the hex loader codes it into binary and stores it sequentially in RAM. As you can imagine, this is a tedious, error prone way to assemble hex from an assembly program. That's where assemblers come in.

ASSEMBLERS

Looking again at Table 11-2, after the hex number are four columns. There is the mnemonics, the addressing modes, the CPU cycles, and the number of bytes needed by the instruction. Those four columns are all taken care of automatically by the hex number. To put it another way, when you load the hex byte into the CPU, you are in effect telling the CPU, the mnemonic, and the addressing mode how many clock cycles will be needed to execute the instruction, and the number of bytes in memory the instruction occupies.

When you write an assembly program, each line of the program has to take into consideration those four columns. That way each program line can be coded into a number of hex bytes. When you use an assembler instead of using hand assembly, the assembler will transform the program lines into the hex object program. The assembly language program that is written is called a *source program*. This is in contrast to the object program in hex and the machine language program written in binary. The source program is a compilation of mnemonics in English for the op codes and hex, decimal, binary, and symbols for operands.

The assembler is a program that is able to take the jumble of op codes and operands in all those different forms and assemble them into a string of hex bytes the hex loader will take from there. The assembler is a program just like the high level language interpreter, and the hex loader. Like those other coders, in order to use an assembler, the rules of the assembler program must be followed. There are many different kinds of assemblers since there are many different CPUs. Each instruction set requires a different assembler program. In fact, there are different assemblers for the same CPU. However, once you master the use of one assembler, switching to another one is not that hard.

Fortunately, it is not necessary to be an assembly program expert to be able to repair home computers. The preceding information is presented to acquaint you with the overall system that you are dealing with during a repair. Of course, the more you know about computing, the faster and surer a troubleshooting job will proceed. If you are interested in learning how to program with the use of instruction sets, there are a lot of good books around that will get you started.

Chapter 12

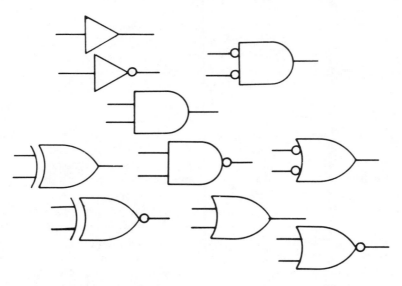

The Memory Map

The typical home computer that processes 8-bit data, uses 16-bit addresses to do the job. While the data bus has eight separate lines the address bus has 16 individual copper traces travelling around the print board from chip to chip. The address bus originates in the CPU. It goes to all the RAM, ROM, and I/O addresses. There are a possible 65,536 addresses. A directory of all the addresses outside the CPU is called a *memory map* (Fig. 12-1).

THE CPU ADDRESSING CIRCUITS

Inside the CPU, attached to the pins labeled A15 to A0 is the internal address bus. Connected to the address bus are three registers that deal directly with addressing. All three registers are 16-bit or 2-byte types. They are the program counter, the index register, and the stack pointer.

The program counter (Fig. 12-2), as it starts to operate is initialized or set to 0000 0000 0000 0000. This setting points to the address in memory 0000 0000 0000 0000. The program counter manages to point to the address electroni-

cally by outputting 0 V to each of the 16 address bus lines. If you read the initial address with the vom you'd get 16 lows at the CPU pins A15 to A0.

In hex this address is 0000. In decimal the initial address is zero. With the program counter acting as the transmitter and the hex address 0000 being the receiver, a copy of the contents of hex 0000 is sent out over the data bus. When this happens the program counter is made to automatically increment by 1.

This makes the program counter register become 0000 0000 0000 0001. The hex address that is now pointed to is 0001. In decimal the same address is one. With the transmitter now pointing to one, the receiver is the second memory location. The first location is now no longer the receiver and deactivates. The second location then sends its data out on the data bus. This makes the program counter increment to 0000 0000 0000 0010. In hex that address is 0002. The decimal address is two.

The program counter keeps on placing its reg-

Memory Map

Decimal Address	Hex Address	Resident of Address
0 to 1023	0000 to 03FF	Housekeeper
1024 to 1535	0400 to 05FF	Video RAM
1536 to 16383	0600 to 3FFF	RAM
16384 to 32767	4000 to 7FFF	Expansion RAM
32768 to 40959	8000 to 9FFF	Expansion ROM
40960 to 49151	A000 to BFFF	Operating ROM
49152 to 65279	C000 to FEFF	Cartridge ROM
65280 to 65535	FF00 to FFFF	I/O devices

Fig. 12-1. A typical home computer with an 8-bit processor has a 16-bit address bus that can address 65,536 individual locations. Typical residents at these addresses are the computer's housekeeper, RAM, ROM, and I/O devices.

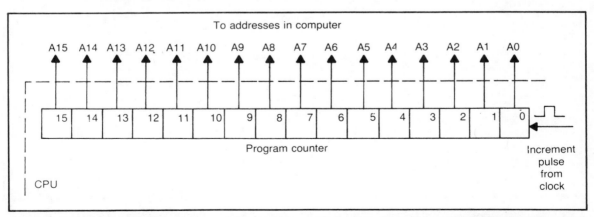

Fig. 12-2. The program counter addresses all the computer residents. It starts at address 0000000000000000 and will steadfastly increment to address 1111111111111111 unless given an instruction to do otherwise.

ister contents onto the address bus. Everytime it activates an address it increments by one. Left alone, it would start counting at decimal 0 and continue right up to address 65,535. In hex that count is 0000 to FFFF. In bits it is 0000 0000 0000 0000 to 1111 1111 1111 1111. As each address was pointed to the 8-bit contents would be outputted to the 8 data bus lines.

RELATIVE ADDRESSING

The program counter provides the consecutive pointing service as long as an instruction doesn't come along and change the count. There are a number of instructions that do nothing but change the value of the program counter. These instructions are called JUMP, BRANCH, CALL, and RETURN. These instructions are found in the instruc-

tion sets. When these instructions enter the IR and get decoded, they are immediately sent to the program counter. At the program counter they alter the current address. The JUMP instruction makes the program counter's number change from the next consecutive address to an entirely different address. The new address is in the next bytes of data after the JUMP instruction byte (Fig. 12-3).

The BRANCH instruction is like the JUMP and also changes the program counter's address. For instance, a BRANCH instruction could be a two byte instruction (Fig. 12-4). The first byte is the instruction to branch. The next byte in memory is a trailer offset attached to the first byte. It contains a number that is added or subtracted to the contents of the program counter. The result of the adding or subtracting produces a new number in the PC. In-

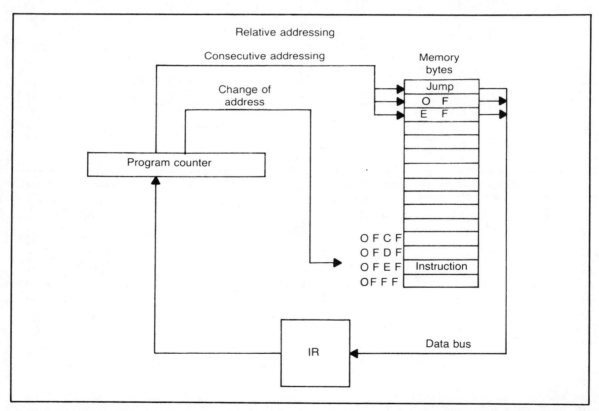

Fig. 12-3. The JUMP type instruction is followed in the memory bytes by a change of address. The address is then put on the data bus and sent to the program counter via the instruction register. The program counter stops incrementing, puts the change of address on the address bus, and the new address is activated.

200

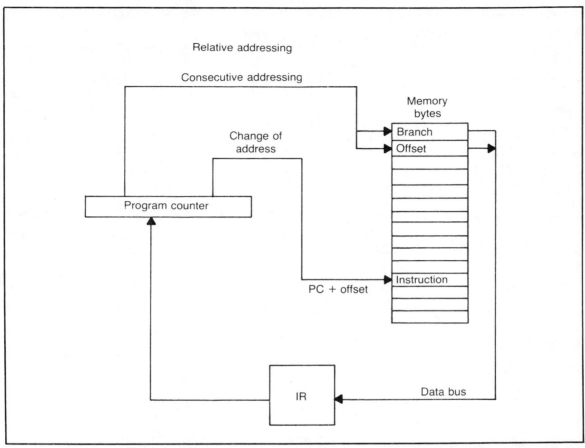

Fig. 12-4. The BRANCH type of instruction is followed by a trailer offset number. The offset can be added (or subtracted) to the program counter address. The addition produces a change of address instead of the automatic incrementing. The program counter branches to the new address.

stead of the PC simply incrementing by 1, it branches to the new address formed by the addition of the trailer.

With the relative type of addressing, a program that is running is able to jump or branch to any location on the memory map. As the program counter is addressing the memory map in numerical order, it will suddenly receive a new address from a JUMP instruction or an offset number from a BRANCH instruction. The PC will then address the new number instead of the next number.

INDEX REGISTER ADDRESSING

Another CPU register that is attached to the address bus is the index register. It is in parallel to the program counter and is almost a twin. It holds 16 bits and is used to output an address to the memory map. The index register can only output an address when the CPU activates it. During the time the index register is active the program counter is on hold. Both of them are not permitted to be on at the same time, or they will interfere with each other. If they should fail by shorting together internally, the addressing by the CPU will go wild and garbage will appear on the screen, if an interrupt doesn't shut down the operation altogether.

As a program is being run the PC could address a memory location that contains an instruction that is in the indexed mode (Fig. 12-5). The indexed addressed instruction is a two byte type. The first byte is the instruction in hex. This byte enters the IR and the decoding turns off the PC and activates the index register. The next byte, which is a trailer for the index instruction, contains a hex number. This number is an offset, that is added to the contents of the index register to form a new address. This is quite like the BRANCH instruction except the index register is used instead of the program counter.

The program counter actually counts out the steps of the program. The index register is used during one of the program steps. The index register is used during the trailer bytes for a program step.

The index register really does a different job than the program counter. They both cause an address to be placed on the address bus, but at different stages in the running of the program.

While a program is being run, the program counter points to the next location in memory that is the next step in the program. The index register only points to a location where data is being held that is needed for the step being run. Once the data is placed on the data bus, the program counter takes over again and continues addressing the memory map in its consecutive fashion.

THE STACK

There is another register, in parallel with the

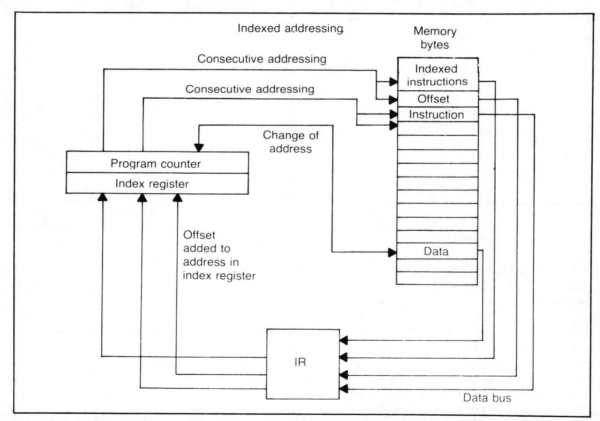

Fig. 12-5. Another way the CPU can address a location on the memory map is with its index register. Between normal program counter address moves, the index register can be activated and output an address of its own. The address is formed by adding an offset, that follows an indexed instruction in the memory, to the number in the index register. The indexed address is then activated. After the indexed address the program counter resumes addressing control and continues its consecutive addressing.

202

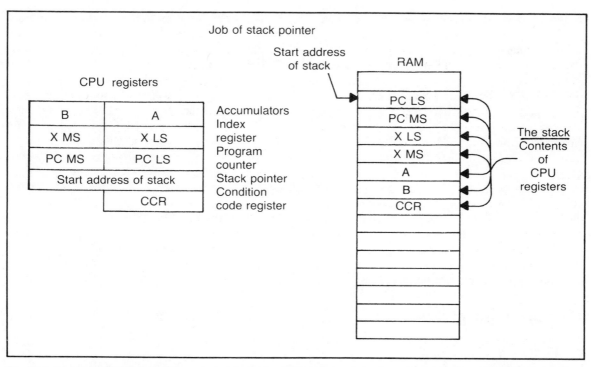

Job of stack pointer

CPU registers

B	A
X MS	X LS
PC MS	PC LS
Start address of stack	
	CCR

Accumulators
Index register
Program counter
Stack pointer
Condition code register

Start address of stack

RAM

| PC LS |
| PC MS |
| X LS |
| X MS |
| A |
| B |
| CCR |

The stack
Contents of CPU registers

Fig. 12-6. If an instruction like JUMP is executed the address bus switches from one area of the memory map to another. As a result all the CPU registers will get changed as the new locations are accessed. At the end of the JUMP the address bus will switch back to the original locations. The original numbers in the CPU registers are no longer there. However, nothing is amiss because the values of all the registers were saved in a place in RAM called The Stack. Upon RETURN to the original program the stack is loaded back into the CPU registers, where they were before the JUMP instruction.

PC and index register, that is attached to the internal address bus. It is called the *stack pointer*. It points to an area in RAM called the stack. The stack is a number of bytes of memory in sequential order. The stack does one job. The stack is a storage place where the numbers contained in the CPU registers can be held for safekeeping. Why have a stack? Why does a record of the CPU register's numbers have to be kept? Suppose a program is being run. The program started at memory location hex 0000 and reaches hex 002F. In 002F there is a JUMP instruction to a small program starting at location 00C7. The program counter is changed to 00C7 and begins running at that memory place. The PC continues running there. After 00C7 it addresses 00C8, then 00C9 and so on till a RETURN instruction is received. Then the PC changes back to where it was originally. How does the PC know what memory

location to go back to? The stack pointer register knows where. When the CPU received the JUMP instruction, it immediately set up a place in RAM for a stack. In the stack, in sequential bytes, the CPU stored the following:

☐ Contents of the LS byte of the PC.
☐ Contents of the MS byte of the PC.
☐ Contents of the LS byte of the index register.
☐ Contents of the MS byte of the index register.
☐ Contents of accumulator A.
☐ Contents of accumulator B.
☐ Contents of the condition code register.

The stack pointer register then received the starting address of the memory stack. When the PC returned from the JUMP and the running of the small subroutine, the stack pointer register indicated where to get the original contents of all the registers from the stack storage in RAM. The PC and the other registers can continue their work at the place they were before the JUMP to subroutine.

ADDRESSING WITH OTHER REGISTERS

Besides the PC, index register, and stack pointer, there are other registers in a CPU that attach to the address bus. First of all, there can be a register or more right in the internal address bus, in the CPU. This register is called the address bus register. Secondly, the accumulator can be used as a temporarily holding register and output to the address bus. These registers permit you to address the memory map with many other program modes. The more addressing modes a CPU can exhibit the more versatile it is. The more versatile, the more program manipulation can be performed.

THE MEMORY MAP ITSELF

The memory map shown in Fig. 12-1 is the one for a typical home computer. The addresses are shown in decimal and hex. Actually the machine can't directly use either of these number systems. The computer uses 16-bits with the 65,536 different arrangements of bits sent out over the address bus to activate a memory location.

In decimal the numbers from 0 to 1023 represent memory locations that are used for special purposes. On a map you'll see descriptions of the locations called "internal use", "keyboard alpha lock", and so on. For the servicer, these locations can be described as "housekeeping", and let it go as that. For programmers some of these locations have importance but not usually for servicing.

Locations 1024 to 1535 are showed as video RAM. These locations are set aside from the rest of the RAM and is used for video display purposes. In the operating system is a small program that operates video RAM.

When you strike a key on the keyboard, the symbol is automatically displayed on the TV screen. This is courtesy of the video RAM arrangement. Notice there are 512 locations in video RAM. On this TV screen of this computer, 512 keyboard symbols can be displayed, including spaces. There is one symbol block on the TV screen for every video RAM location. When you strike a key, the key character is transformed into bits and sent to the video RAM. Location 1024 is addressed first and is the upper hand block. As the keyboard is continually hit, the video RAM fills up sequentially, and fills the TV screen in normal left to right writing fashion. The lower right-hand TV character block is filled when video RAM location 1535 receives its data bits.

The locations in this map, 1536 to 32767, are for RAM storage. This gives exactly 31231 RAM locations out of the total 32767 locations, for the user's needs. This is typical for a 32K system.

Beginning at location 32768 through 65279 there are 32511 addresses that can be used for ROMs. All of this ROM area plus the available 32K RAM makes for a very handy computer. A lot can be done with it.

At the bottom of the address list are 255 locations from 65280 to 65535 that are used for input-output ports. This is usually plenty of addresses. I/O chips like the PIAs and ACIAs need only a few addresses each. The memory map can be manipulated by different ROMs in different ways. The housekeeping locations are usually fixed, as is the video RAM. The long stretch of RAM and the locations reserved for ROM though can be switched around in many different ways.

Chapter 13

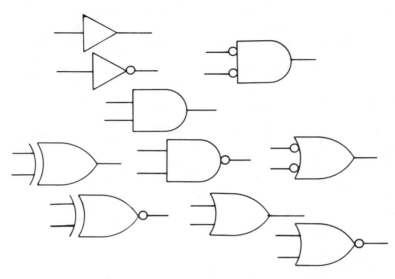

The Clock

Every TV transmitter has an rf oscillator. This circuit produces the basic frequency of the station. It is the frequency that the video, audio, and other frequencies are installed upon. It is the frequency that you tune to when you want a particular TV show. The rf signal is known as the carrier wave.

Every computer also has an oscillator circuit that produces an rf signal. Like the TV transmitter signal the rf begins as a sine wave and is the basic frequency of the machine. That's where the similarity ends. While the TV station deals in analog signal manipulation, the computer works on manipulating digital signals. Therefore, the sinewave signal, as soon as it leaves the oscillator area, is changed to a square wave. The frequency remains the same. Only the waveshape is changed. The sine wave signal is useless in digital circuits. Square waves have to be used to do the jobs.

A CLOCK CIRCUIT

The clock circuit in a home computer is typically a crystal-controlled oscillator. The frequen-cies differ somewhat according to manufacturers. In the TRS-80 early models, some frequencies were 10.6445 MHz. Their Color Computer is 14.31818 MHz. The Heathkit H-89A runs at 12.288 MHz. The circuits are conventional (Fig. 13-1).

The TRS-80 Color Computer uses the following configuration (Fig. 13-2). The master frequency originates in a crystal that is cut to ring at 14.31818 MHz. The crystal is tied into pins 5 and 6 of the SAM chip. These pins attach the crystal to an internal oscillator circuit that is series resonant. C51 and C4 fix the frequency of the oscillator. C4 is a trimmer capacitor that will adjust the frequency slightly.

THE FREQUENCIES

The 14.31818 MHz is the master frequency. It is the basis for all the frequencies in the computer. In this computer there are a number of frequencies. The timing diagram (Fig. 13-3) shows all the frequencies in the computer. The 14.31818 MHz master frequency is drawn with 16 highs and 16 lows. The perfect square wave with the perpendicular

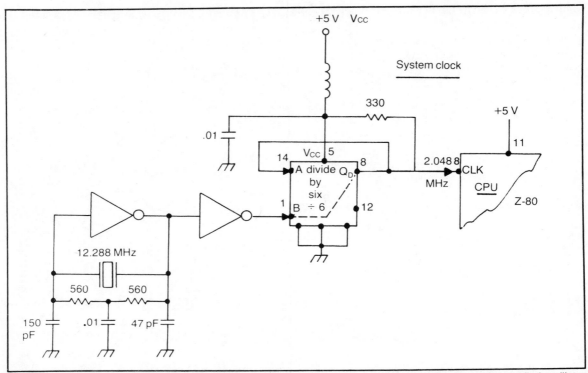

Fig. 13-1. The Heathkit H-89A computer uses a System Clock circuit based around a conventional crystal-controlled oscillator that rings at 12.288 MHz.

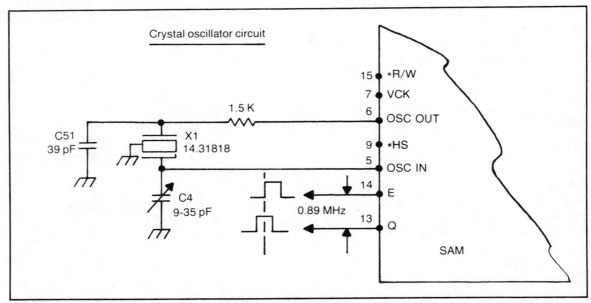

Fig. 13-2. The TRS-80 Color Computer has its oscillator circuit wired into a large SAM chip.

sides indicates the frequency goes from low to high to low in no time at all. This clearly is not possible. The actual waveshape slopes to the right as it goes from low to high and to the left as it comes down from high to low (Fig. 13-4). Low to high is called the rising edge, while high to low is called the falling edge. These edges are important since they trigger off a lot of the activity in the digital circuits.

In the timing diagram, beneath the 16 square waves is a row of 8 square waves. The 8 highs, at the same time as the 16 highs come about because the 14.31818 is divided by 2. The frequency to produce the 8 waves is 7.15909 MHz.

Beneath the 8 waveshapes, is a frequency that produces 4 square waves in the same time period. This frequency is the result of 14.31818 divided by 4. A TV servicer will recognize this frequency 3.579545 MHz, as a TV color oscillator frequency.

This is indeed exactly what it is and is one of the reasons this computer can produce a color display. In this color computer the 3.579545 MHz is called the video clock frequency. C4, the trimmer capacitor is used to set the video clock on frequency. The video clock is exactly 14.31818 divided by four and must be the most accurate frequency in the computer, or else the color picture will not be displayed properly.

The next frequency shown is 1.789772 MHz. There are 2 highs in the same time period. The frequency is derived from 14.31818 divided by eight. The final division of the master frequency is by 16. This produces the working frequency of the computer that is listed in the instruction manual. 14.31818 divided by 16 is 0.89 MHz.

The CPU receives an input of 0.89 MHz at pins 35 and 34, Q_{in} and E_{in}. Q and E are both 0.89 MHz

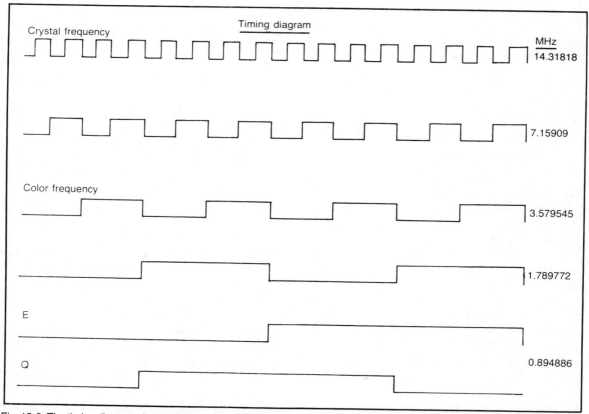

Fig. 13-3. The timing diagram shows all the working frequencies that are derived from the original crystal-generated frequency.

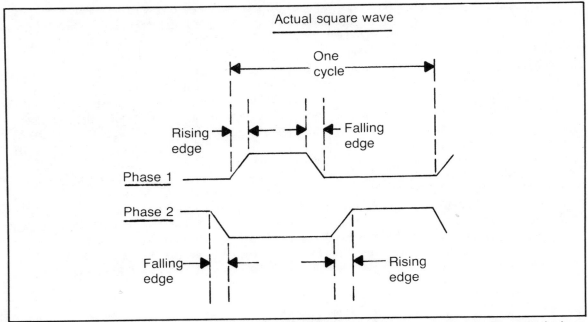

Fig. 13-4. An actual square wave is not really square. The wave has a rising edge as the voltage rises. The wave also has a falling edge as the voltage falls. These edges are triggers to set off digital activity.

each but the Q signal leads the E signal by 90 degrees. The phase shift is accomplished in the SAM chip which generates all the computer's timing.

WHAT THE CLOCK DOES

The CPU is the main part of any computer. It is full of digital gates and registers. The digital circuits are able to address any location on the memory map and load data from the location or store data in locations that are able to store. The CPU is also able to perform arithmetic and logic operations on the data. The clock is an indispensible part of all these operations.

In a typical CPU there are two clock inputs (Fig. 13-5). They are the working frequencies. They are both the same frequencies but 90 degrees out of phase with each other. Phase 1 is there to time the addressing by the program counter and the other addressing registers. Phase 2 is given the job of timing the data movement from the memory locations that get addressed (Fig. 13-6).

Since the two square waves are 90 degrees out

of step, phase 1 will always be high when phase 2 is low. Also phase 1 will also be low while phase 2 is high. This arrangement works out fine for the timed interplay between addressing and data movement.

As discussed, the program counter always has the address of the next instruction. When phase 1 enters the CPU it is wired to the program counter. When it arrives it enters the PC circuit. The rising edge of phase 1 triggers the PC. The address in the PC is then placed on the address bus. As time goes by, phase 1 becomes high and continues high until the falling edge of phase 1 arrives. The falling edge then triggers the program counter. The PC then increments its register. The rising and falling edges of phase 1 thus caused the PC to output the current address and increment to the next address.

Meanwhile, down at phase 2 the following is happening. As phase 1 is having a falling edge, phase 2 is exhibiting a rising edge. This enables the addressed chip and places data on the data bus. If the operation is a LOAD, the memory location will output its contents to the data bus. The data will head for the instruction register in the CPU.

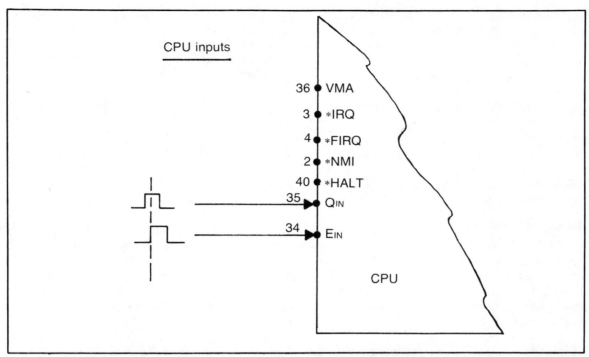

CPU inputs

36 ● VMA
3 ● *IRQ
4 ● *FIRQ
2 ● *NMI
40 ● *HALT
35 → Q_{IN}
34 → E_{IN}

CPU

Fig. 13-5. A CPU is driven by two clock inputs. They are the same frequencies but 90 degrees out of phase with each other. Note the leading edge of E occurs at the same time as the middle of the high plateau of Q.

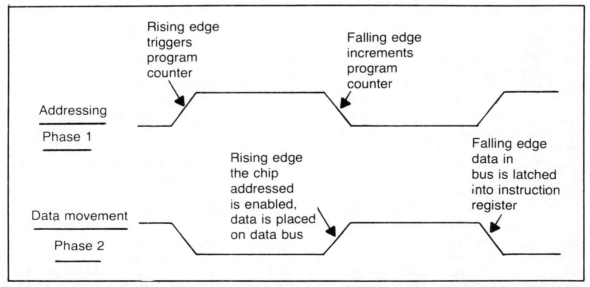

Rising edge triggers program counter

Falling edge increments program counter

Addressing

Phase 1

Falling edge data in bus is latched into instruction register

Rising edge the chip addressed is enabled, data is placed on data bus

Data movement

Phase 2

Fig. 13-6. The rising edge of Phase 1 triggers the program counter into placing its contents onto the address bus. The falling edge of Phase 1 increments the program counter in readiness for the next addressing. Meanwhile the rising edge of Phase 2 triggers the register that was addressed to place its contents on the data bus. The falling edge of Phase 2 then latches the data into the CPU's instruction register.

209

Phase 2 will then continue in time and reach its falling edge. If the operation is a LOAD the falling edge will latch the data into the instruction register. During a STORE operation the falling edge will install the data into the addressed memory location. Phase 2 therefore causes data to be placed on the data bus during its rising edge and locks the data into its destination during the falling edge. These edges in phase 1 and 2 are constant and cause the computer to continually address locations and then cause data to move back and forth on the data bus. This is the important activity of the CPU and what computing is all about.

THE CLOCK SIGNAL IN ACTION

Let's examine carefully the part the clock signal, phase 1 and phase 2, plays, during the running of a program. During a program there could be seven memory locations addressed during some three program lines. The following is a list of seven addresses in binary and their contents:

Address In Binary	Register Contains
0000000000000000	10000110
0000000000000001	00100101
0000000000000010	11010110
0000000000000011	00110101
0000000000000100	10110111
0000000000000101	01000000
0000000000000110	00000010

The 16-bit address contains 8 bits in its memory register. The 8 bits could be an instruction from the CPU's instruction set. If it is an instruction, when it arrives at the instruction register, it makes the CPU perform an operation.

The 8 bits could be another address. If it is an address, the instruction preceding it will alert the CPU that this 8 bits is an address or half of an address. When the 8 bits is all of the address then the CPU will add 00000000 in front of it to fill the address out to 16 bits so the PC can hold it. When the 8 bits is only half an address then the rest of the address will be in the next byte to arrive at the CPU. Either way the instruction sets up the CPU to handle it.

The contents of the location could simply be some data to be worked on. When the data is in the location in rotation in the program, the data gets worked on immediately. The details of these seven memory locations being worked on follows.

1 The clock is running and the rising edge of phase 1 enters the CPU. This triggers the program counter. The PC starts the operation by placing 0000000000000000 on the address bus. This forms a circuit between the CPU and the address 0000 00000000.

2 Phase 1 peaks out and its falling edge sets off the PC into incrementing to 0000000000000001.

3 Meanwhile, as phase 1 goes low, phase 2 develops a rising edge. This rise actuates the chip the address is located on and the data is placed on the data bus. In other words the rising edge of phase 2 caused the memory location to place its contents on the data bus. In the location are the 8 bits, 10000110. This is an instruction from the Set.

The instruction travels the 8-bit data path from the location to the instruction register in the CPU. The falling edge of phase 2 latches the 8 bits into the instruction register. The IR decodes the instruction. The bits 10000110 activates the CPU. The instruction says, "Get the A accumulator ready. The next byte that will arrive on the data bus is pure data. This data is to be LOADed into the A accumulator."

4 The 16 bits 0000000000000001 in the PC are placed on the address bus as the next rising edge of phase 1 arrives. This eliminates the circuit to 0000000000000000 and forms a new address circuit to 0000000000000001.

5 Then as phase 1 tops out, the falling edge causes the PC to increment to 0000000000000010.

6 The rising edge of phase 2, which arrives about the same time as the falling edge of phase 1, causes the memory location 0000000000000001 to output its 8 bits onto the data bus.

7 Phase 2 tops out and the falling edge latches the data bus contents into the IR in the CPU. The CPU was waiting for this data because it was alerted by the earlier instruction. The IR loads the 8 bits into the A accumulator as it was instructed to

do. The A accumulator then reads 00100101 which is a copy of location 0000000000000001 contents.

The preceding 7 steps shows the activity of one machine language program line. The first part of the line is the instruction or op code as it is called. The second part of the line is the trailer part and is called the operand. The line reads 10000110 00100101 in machine language. If you decoded the line into hex it reads 86 25. Should you use an assembler the same line reads LDA A #$25. The assembled line says "load accumulator A with the next byte in the program." The symbol # means data is in the next byte and the symbol $ means hex. The program line needed two phase 1 cycles and two phase 2 cycles to complete the fetch and execution of the two bytes in the line.

8 As the third clock cycle enters the CPU the rising edge of phase 1 places the contents of the PC 0000000000000010, on the address bus. This disables the circuit to 0000000000000001 and enables 0000000000000010.

9 Phase 1 then peaks out and the falling edge increments the PC to 0000000000000011.

10 At about the same time, the rising edge of phase 2 triggers 0000000000000010 to place a copy of its contents on the data bus. 11010110 travels the data bus.

11 The falling edge of phase 2 makes the data bus contents latch into the IR. It gets decoded. The CPU reads 11010110 as the instruction "load accumulator B with the contents of an address. The address is contained in the next byte." The CPU then prepares for the next byte which is an address, not a piece of data like the previous instruction indicated.

12 The next rising edge of phase 1 places 0000000000000011 which is in the PC on the address bus. This disables the connection to 0000-000000000010 end enables 000000000000-0011.

13 The falling edge of phase 1 then increments the PC to 0000000000000100.

14 The rising edge of phase 2 then places the contents of the addressed register on the data bus. The contents are 00110101.

15 The falling edge of phase 2 latches the address from the memory storage into the CPU. Since the instruction stated the register contents is an address and not just data, the CPU knows to place the address in the LS byte of the internal address bus of the CPU. The MS byte in the bus is 00000000 so when the rest of the address is formed the address bus reads 0000000000110101. In hex this is 0035.

16 The rising edge of phase 1 now does not affect the PC. There is an address in the internal address bus of the CPU, so the edge places this address on the address bus. This address, hex 0035, is enabled. The falling edge of phase 1 does not increment the PC in these cases. The falling edge is not involved in this addressing procedure. It simply passes. The falling edge only triggers the PC after the PC places an address on the bus. If another register is doing the addressing the PC does not get incremented.

17 Phase 2 then makes an appearance. Its rising edge causes the contents of hex address 0035 to be placed on the data bus.

18 The falling edge of phase 2 loads the address into accumulator B. There were three clock cycles, each total cycle containing a phase 1 and a phase 2, needed to fetch and execute this program line. The program line has 11010110 as the op code and 00110101 as the operand. In hex that is D6 35.

As the preceding two program lines were executed, the R/W connection was held high. This is because the two lines were both *read instructions*. They addressed a memory location, read the contents and loaded the contents into the CPU. The CPU knows to do this if the R/W line is high. The R/W line is held low during a write operation, where the CPU has to store data in a memory location.

The next three memory locations in the seven line program contains 10110111 as the op code with 01000000 and 00000010 as operands. In hex they are B7 40 02. If you look at the instruction set, the B7 op code, means, STORE the contents of the A accumulator at the address formed by the two bytes in the operand. If the two bytes are placed together on the internal address bus, with the first byte being the MS and the second byte the LS the address,

01000000000010 is formed. The data in the A accumulator could then be sent to the address and latched in there. Let's go through the step by step procedure to finish up the program.

19 The rising edge of phase 1 arrives to do its job and triggers the PC. The PC contents of 000000000100 is placed on the address bus.

20 The falling edge of phase 1 then increments the PC to 0000000000000101.

21 The rising edge of phase 2 makes the contents of 0000000000000100, which is the op code 1011011, output onto the data bus.

22 The falling edge of phase 2 latches the op code into the IR where it is decoded and gets the CPU ready to work on the two byte operand that will be arriving on the data bus.

23 The PC contents are then placed on the address bus. The address is 000000000000101. The new address disconnects 0000000000000100 and connects this new address.

24 The rising edge of phase 2 causes the memory location to output the operand 01000000 to the data bus.

25 The falling edge of phase 2 latches the operand into a temporary register. Since the CPU has to get the second operand before it can combine it with the first to form the 16-bit address, the CPU has to temporarily hold the first operand. Sort of like a scratch pad is used if the operation was being performed with pencil and paper. Most of the time, one of the accumulators are used for this scratch pad work, but other registers can also be used. Anyway, the first operand is placed into temporary storage.

26 The rising edge of phase 1 then triggers the next PC address into the address bus. It is 0000000000000110.

27 The falling edge then increments the PC to 0000000000000111.

28 The address is enabled and the rising edge of phase 2 outputs the second operand 00000010 onto the data bus.

29 The falling edge of phase 2 latches the operand into the IR. The IR then takes the second operand and placed it into the internal address bus as the LS byte. The CPU takes the first operand out of temporary storage and puts it into the MS byte of

the address bus. The two operands form the address 0100000000000010.

30 The rising edge of phase 1 then places the formed address on the address bus. Up till now, the R/W line had been held high. The clock was busy loading the CPU with the op code and the two operands. Now, according to the op code a memory location was going to be written to and a piece of data from the A accumulator was to be stored. The CPU makes the R/W line go low so the writing can take place.

31 The formed address opens the memory location. With R/W now low, the A accumulator gets its contents ready for transport. Back in steps 4 through 7 we loaded the A accumulator with 00100101. The CPU then sends the 8 bits 00100101 out over the data bus. The data latches into the readied location. The program has been run.

TESTING THE CLOCK

When the computer does not produce any output at all, the clock could have stopped. A quick go no-go test will show if the clock is running or not. The best place to make the test, is not near the crystal but on the other side of any buffer in the circuit. If the test is made near the crystal, the test probe could load down the oscillator circuit and kill the frequency, if it is indeed running.

For a quick test you can use an inexpensive scope with a high impedance probe. If the oscillator is running, the scope will display an envelope containing the frequency, even if you can't see what frequency is displayed, because your scope can't get that high. The appearance of the envelope means the oscillator is running (Fig. 13-7A). The frequency is also probably ok because the crystal won't work easily unless the oscillating frequency is near the frequency at which the crystal is cut to run. Theoretically, a crystal could operate at an entirely different frequency, if there is a flaw in its cut and the supporting components change in value to run at the incorrect frequency. This possibility is somewhere between rare and impossible.

Another quick way to see if the clock is running is with a logic probe. With the probe connected, touch down on the address and data bus pins or the phase 1 and 2 CPU inputs. There should be constant activity on these pins which will light the LED that indicates a pulse is present (Fig. 13-7B). The vom also will show you there is activity present. The meter will read a floating value and be slightly unstable. Some of the pins could even cause the meter needle to wobble (Fig. 13-7C). Whichever

test piece you use, the idea of the test is to determine whether or not the clock is ticking away.

There are occasions when it is necessary to actually check the frequency of the clock. This can be done with a frequency counter. It is useful to have a frequency counter that does the job with a pickup-loop probe rather than a probe that must be connected. Either one will do but the induction-loop

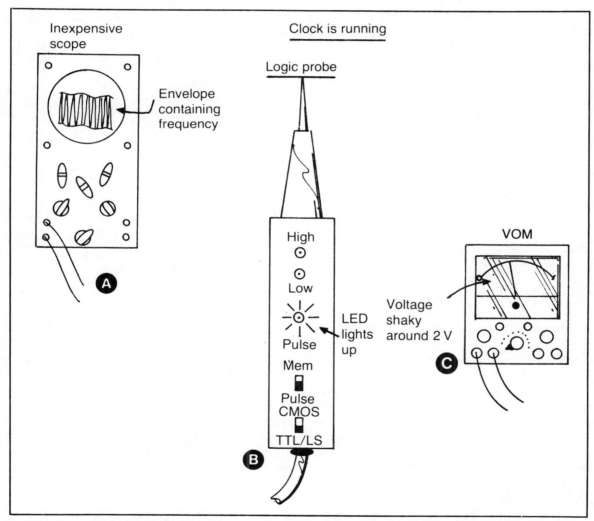

Fig. 13-7. You can find out if the clock is running with an inexpensive service scope. Touchdown on a clock test point at a spot that won't load the circuit. If an envelope containing a frequency appears the clock is running and probably good (A). The logic probe affords a quick way to see if the clock is running. When it is, the probe will light its pulse LED. Good test points are any spots that normally show a pulse like the address or data bus connections or clock inputs and outputs (B). The vom can indicate a running clock to the experienced technician. The meter needle will get into a tristate range and possibly wobble a bit (C).

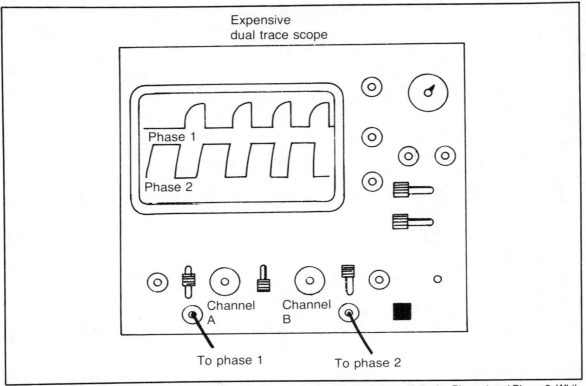

Fig. 13-8. To really get fine details on the clock signals an expensive dual trace scope will display Phase 1 and Phase 2. While this scope is indispensable in computer design or manufacturing line troubleshooting, it is rarely if ever needed in ordinary repair work.

probe is faster and safer. The pickup-loop probe can be placed right near the crystal and pickup the frequency from a capacitor or coil in the circuit. If the frequency is off the crystal is probably defective.

If you really want to check out the clock signal then you must use a dual-trace scope with a high-frequency response. You must take stable pictures of phase 1 and phase 2 and compare them on the scope face with respect to frequency and phase. This pattern is called a timing diagram.

For the CPU in Fig. 13-8 the two phases are called phase 1 and phase 2. The scope is attached to these two clock pins. Phase 1 is attached to channel A of the scope and, phase 2 is attached to channel B. The two traces are then locked into the correct frequencies. A pair of traces should then be on the scope like in the illustration. Notice the peaks in the top trace coincide with the valleys in the bottom trace.

If the top trace is phase 1 and the bottom trace is phase 2, the action is as follows. The rising edge of phase 1 will trigger the program counter to place the current address on the address bus. The falling edge will then cause the program counter to increment.

As the falling edge of phase 1 reaches its bottom, the rising edge of phase 2 triggers the addressed memory location to output its contents onto the data bus. The falling edge of phase 2 then latches the contents of the data bus into the instruction register. This is the main clock action and you can view it on the scope. If the traces are not correct then that could indicate troubles in the computer.

Chapter 14

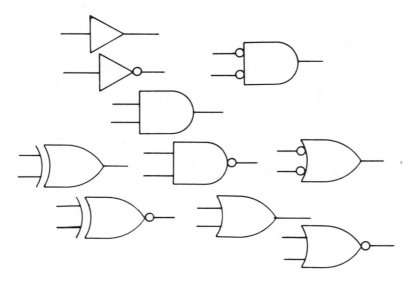

The Address and Data Buses

If you think of the address bus lines as the pathways from the CPU to all the addresses, then the data bus lines are more pathways to and from the CPU and all the addresses. Notice the "to and from" with regards to the data bus. Remember the data bus is a two way street and the address bus is one way (Fig. 14-1). Addresses are only outputted from the CPU. Data is also outputted during a write operation, but in addition inputted during a read.

CONNECTING DATA LINES

In the typical home computer the data pathway has 8 lines to be able to transport one byte or 8 bits. The data path starts in the CPU and emerges out of the data pins. They are usually names D7, D6, D5, D4, D3, D2, D1, and D0. These numbers are the same throughout the computer. There is a D7 through D0 connection on every RAM, ROM, PIA, and all other chips that are connected to the data bus (Fig. 14-2).

The data lines are connected to every address in a chip (Fig. 14-3). The addresses represent a byte-sized register on a chip. The data lines are connected line by line to each byte. The connections are parallel. When an address is enabled, all the data in the address byte goes onto the data bus immediately. The 8 bits of any byte addressed travels down the pathway 8 abreast, not one at a time.

Most of the time the addresses are not active. The registers just sit there waiting to be addressed. The only time a register connected to the data bus is active is when it is addressed.

When a RAM register is addressed by a LOAD instruction, a copy of the data in that register is sent out over the data bus to the CPU. If the register is addressed by a STORE instruction then the data in the CPU is sent out over the data bus to the RAM register. When a ROM is addressed with a LOAD instruction a copy of the data in the ROM address is sent onto the CPU. The STORE instruction sends nothing over the data bus to the ROM. The ROM contains permanent data in its register and ignores STORE instructions. Even though the data bus is a

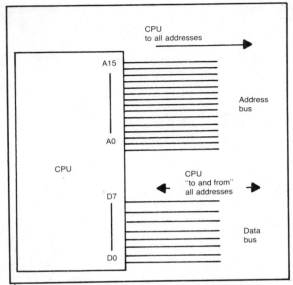

Fig. 14-1. The address bus can carry address bits "to" every address row in the computer. The data bus can carry instruction and data bits "to and from" every data column in the computer.

two way street, it need only be a one way street as far as the ROM is concerned, one way from the ROM to the CPU.

DIGITAL COMPONENTS IN THE DATA BUS

The data path lines are connected from the CPU to RAM, ROM, PIA and what have you. When a bit travels the bus it continues without hesitation from one end of the line to the other. However, there are some digital components in the lines to process the bits.

First of all, the amount of current that comes out of the CPU is small. The bits have a lot of copper to traverse and a lot of destinations. The amount of current must be amplified somewhat in order to insure the bit will arrive at its destination strong enough to do work. Secondly, the bits are traveling on a two way bus. The bus direction not being used must be turned off while the current is coming from the other direction. These two jobs can be accomplished by installing tristate buffers in series with the data lines.

There are 8 data lines. The bits travel in two directions. There must be one buffer to handle the

CPU to memory direction and a second buffer to handle the memory to CPU bit flow, in each data line. This means 16 buffers are used, two for each line.

Figure 14-4 shows the buffering can be accomplished with four chips. They are three tristate hex buffers and parts of a quad 2-input NAND gate. Since 16 buffers are needed and the three hex buffers total 18 units, 16 of the 18 can be used.

Each of the 8 data path lines are cut and a pair of buffers, wired in parallel, pointing in opposite directions, are inserted at the cut. That way, any bits traveling in either direction will get buffered.

All of the CPU to memory direction buffers have their tristate controls tied together. All of the memory to CPU direction buffers have their tristate controls tied together. That way, if one tristate signal is applied, it will turn off the entire direction it is applied to. Either the CPU to memory direction can be shut down or the opposite direction

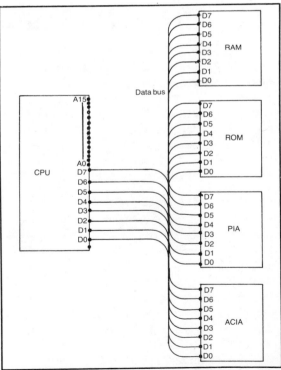

Fig. 14-2. The data bus is connected the same way to every chip that it operates within the computer.

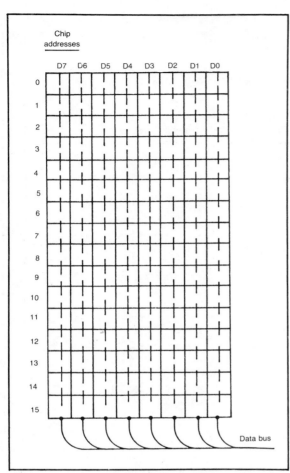

Fig. 14-3. The 8 data bus lines connect to every address in a chip.

can be turned off. During operation one or the other, but not both directions, is on.

The quad 2-input NAND gate decides which direction should be on. The NAND gate uses two sections for control of the tristate ability of the buffers. One NAND gate outputs to all the tristate controls of the CPU to memory buffers. The second NAND gate outputs to all the memory to CPU buffers. The second NAND gate has its two inputs tied to the first gates output. This gives the first gate complete off-on control over all 16 buffers.

If the first gate has a high output, this turns on the CPU to memory buffers. With the first gate high the second goes low, which turns off the memory to CPU buffers. Should the first gate go low, then the CPU to memory buffers are disabled. At the same time the second gate goes high which enables the memory to CPU buffers. The two rows of buffers go off and on according to the output of the first buffer. This output is a result of its input being NANDed.

The two NAND inputs are connected to source +5 V and the R/W line. The source +5 V is present at all times. The R/W line here is 0 V during read and +5 V while in the write mode. When in write at +5 V the two NAND inputs are both high. The gate fires and the two highs are NANDed. The NAND output is low. With the first gate outputting a low, the second gate outputs a high. This disables the memory to CPU buffers. At the same time the CPU to memory buffers are enabled. The data lines are able to carry bits from the CPU to the memory which is a write operation.

If the R/W line is 0 V then the input to the NAND gate is low. With one low input and one high input, the NAND assumes a high output. With the high output the second NAND gate goes low and turns on the memory to CPU buffers. At the same time the high first NAND output turns off the CPU to memory buffers. The data bus is now able to transport bits from the memory to the CPU which is a read operation.

Tristate buffering components are mostly the type of digital components the data bus uses. If you are tracing digital signals from the data pins of the CPU to their memory locations, it is necessary to understand the changes that take place as the signal passes from component to component. The vom and logic probe will reveal the type of signal that is present at the test points. It is important to know that if two signals get NANDed, their single output is the opposite of them getting ANDed. It is also important to know that the signal leaving a buffer is in the same logical state as it was when it entered. Deviations from the norm of logical states could be indications that a component is defective.

THE COMPONENTS IN THE ADDRESS LINES

The 16-bit pathways of the address bus are usually numbered A15, A14, A13, A12, A11, A10, A9, A8, A7, A6, A5, A4, A3, A2, A1, and A0. The

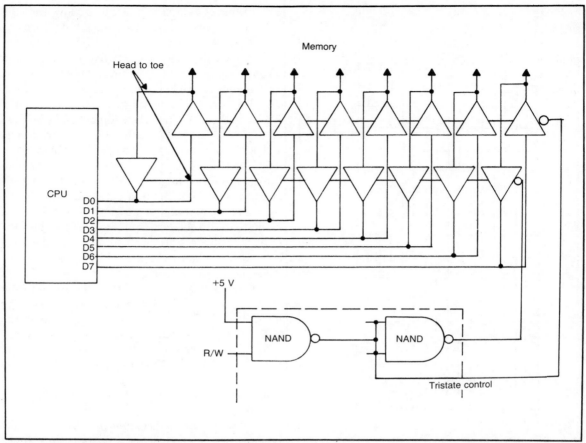

Fig. 14-4. Tristate buffers connected head to toe in the data bus turns off the direction not being used, while keeping on the direction the data is traveling.

address lines are usually buffered like the data lines and for the same reasons. The buffers amplify the amount of current so there is enough logical level height to trigger off the correct address. The buffers are also tristate, so the address lines can be disabled upon command.

In the data bus, the tristate control was needed to turn off one direction when bit traffic was coming from the other direction. In the address bus, bits only travel from CPU to memory and not back (Fig. 14-5). The reason for the tristate control is not traffic direction. The control is needed when the address bus will be in the way during external data transfer. During routine work the address bus is usually on most of the time.

An address bus buffer is identical to a data bus buffer. They are wired in each line and permit bits to travel from CPU to memory but not the other way. The 16 buffers have all their tristate control lines connected together. When there is a low on the tristate control, the buffers are enabled and conduct their amplification. Should the tristate line be pulled high, the buffers turn off and the address lines float at high impedance.

In this circuit there is one NOT gate that controls the tristate. The input of the NOT gate is attached to +5 V through a pullup resistor. This places a +5 V on the input of the NOT gate. With +5 V on the input the output of the NOT gate is low. This low enables the entire bank of address buffers.

218

As long as the NOT gate outputs a low the address bus operates normally.

If the NOT gate should get a low input then it would develop a high output. This would disable the address bus. As a test of the address bus, you could short out the +5 V on the NOT input and be able to disable the address bus as the NOT output goes high.

ASSIGNING ADDRESSES

In the ordinary 8-bit computer, all the addresses are registers that hold 8 bits. If you think of a register as a row of 8 holding circuits, then you can visualize the computer memory map as row after row of registers. Each register has 8 circuits named D7 through D0. The circuits are laid out in columns. All the D7s are one column, all the D6s are the

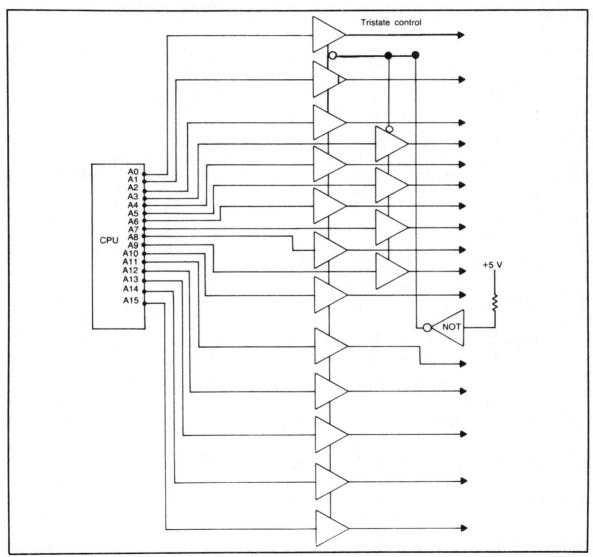

Fig. 14-5. In the address bus bits travel from the CPU to memory but not back. The tristate is rarely needed since the address bus is on most of the time.

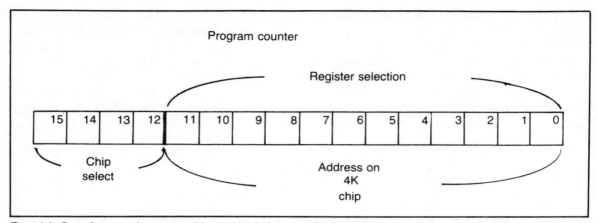

Program counter

Register selection

| 15 | 14 | 13 | 12 | 11 | 10 | 9 | 8 | 7 | 6 | 5 | 4 | 3 | 2 | 1 | 0 |

Chip
select

Address on
4K
chip

Fig. 14-6. One of many schemes to address chips is by using the four MS bits to select the desired chip. For addresses 0-32,765 in decimal, bits 14, 13, and 12 could be used to select among eight chips, Bit 15 is cleared to 0 for the addressing. The other 12 bits 11-0 can then be used to address the 4,096 in each chip.

next column and so forth. There are 8 columns of circuits. Each register contributes its bit holders to form the overall columns in the memory map.

Assigning the connections for the data bus is a simple matter. Each data pathway is attached to its column. D7 from the CPU is connected to every single D7 in the memory map. The same goes for D6 and so on. There are actually only 8 types of connections for the data bus, the D7s, D6s, D5s, D4s, D3s, D2s, D1s, and the D0s. All the connections are wired to be in an inactive stage. A register is activated only when it is addressed by the CPU.

The address assignments are an entirely different matter. In the 8-bit computer the program counter which is the main addresser has 16 bits. It has been shown that there are 65,536 different possible combinations of 1s and 0s in 16 bits. That means the program counter can place on the address bus 65,536 different addresses. If there are 65,536 register rows in a memory, the CPU can make a connection to each one individually, by placing its binary number on the address bus. Each register, as mentioned, is inactive until it is addressed. When the register is addressed it is able to place its contents on the data bus.

Chip Select. An 8-bit processor can *work* with 32K worth of RAM easily. A set of 32K RAM can come on 8 chips. The chips are 4096 × 8. That means there are 4096, 8-bit registers on each chip.

Eight of these chips total 32,768 registers in the total chip set. This is 32,768 addresses, one for each individual register. Typically, the RAM is placed into the memory map at the bottom starting with 0. The decimal addresses of this chip set starts at 0 and goes up to 32,767. Don't forget 0 is one of the addresses. In hex the addresses are 0000 to 7FFF. In binary the addresses are 000000-0000000000 to 0111111111111111.

The four most significant bits in the binary address are used for the chip selects (Fig. 14-6). The 8 chips are numbered 0, 1, 2, 3, 4, 5, 6, and 7. If the program counter places the following binary numbers on the address bus, the first address in each chip will be addressed.

BINARY Address	Chip #	HEX Address
0000000000000000	0	0000
0001000000000000	1	1000
0010000000000000	2	2000
0011000000000000	3	3000
0100000000000000	4	4000
0101000000000000	5	5000
0110000000000000	6	6000
0111000000000000	7	7000

In this case bits 14, 13, and 12 were assigned the chip select duty. The three assigned bits are able to form 8 separate combinations of logic states. On the chip itself there could be three connections for the chip select. They can be called S3, S2, and S1. On the schematic each S number is drawn with a line over top or not. If there is a line over the S then the connection will be enabled if a 0 is applied. If there is no line then the connection is enabled if a 1 is applied. Each chip has a different combination of Ss with lines. Only the correct combination will enable that chip. As long as the correct combination is not present the chip will sit there inactive. The program counter selects a chip by placing appropriate bits into A14, A13, and A12.

Register Selection. Once the chip has been selected the next step for the addressing is to select the register that contains the contents that is needed. These chips are 4096 registers long. To choose one register out of the 4K a group of bits has to be chosen that will have 4096 possible combinations of 1s and 0s. That group is 12. Twelve binary digits can form 4086 combinations. Twelve bits can form addresses from 000000000000 to 1111-11111111. In hex that is 000 to FFF.

All of the internal registers in the 8 chips are identical. They also all have the same addresses, only the chips are different. Therefore, once the most significant four bits of the address are formed for the chip select, then the 12 least significant bits can be added to the four MS bits and the complete address formed. When this is sent out over the address bus, the chip is selected and then the register in the chip is chosen.

All of the rest of the addresses in the computer are arranged in a similar manner. There will be more about addressing of the I/O ports and other entities in later chapters.

TESTING ADDRESS AND DATA BUSES

In the factory, when computers are made, the address and data bus lines develop a lot of problems. Most of the troubles are due to the heavy use of solder during manufacturing. The solder gets all over and forms balls, threads and all sorts of odd shapes. It drapes itself over the top and bottom of the board and creates havoc. Since the address and data bus lines run from one end of the board to the other, they develop all kinds of solder shorts. They get solder between traces, from trace to ground and in all the little cracks and crevices around components and sockets.

Fortunately, the quality control section of the company gives a lot of attention to the problem and solves most of it in the factory. They have all sorts of test jigs and procedures to root out all the short circuits and do get most of it. As a result the address and data bus lines are not as much of a problem as they once were. However, since they are so extensive they do account for a large percentage of troubles. They not only develop shorts, they do account for lots of open circuits and the bus logic components are subject to failure.

The bus lines are really the wiring of the computer logic. If you use house wiring as an analogy the buses are like the wiring in the walls. The tristate buffers are somewhat like the circuit breakers in the switch box. How is a wiring breakdown checked out by an electrician? He rings out the circuits one by one. To test the buses in a computer a form of ringing out the lines can be used. However, some care must be taken as you push current from an ohmmeter through the lines. Some of the components in chips are not capable of handling the 1.5 volts the typical vom puts out during the resistance tests. The way around this problem is to use a low voltage tester as described in Fig. 14-7. The tester is a form of a continuity tester. Instead of forcing 1.5 volts through the resistance being tested, the device will light the bulb with only a ¼ of a volt being inserted. This voltage does the job on gates and is so low it will not even cause a silicon junction to turn on.

Static Tests. A common trouble in computers, as well as all electronic gear, is bad connections and breaks in wiring. If an address or data pathway in a bus should develop one of these opens, the computer would operate a lot of the time. However, when that particular trace was needed to access an address or pass some data, an error develops in the program. Some parts of a program would work while other parts would not.

With this type of trouble, a trace by trace checkout of the address and data bus lines, with the

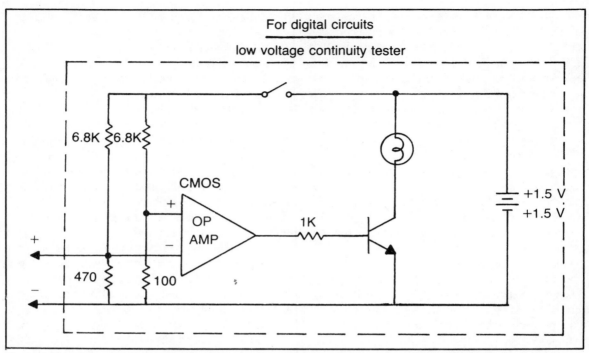

For digital circuits

low voltage continuity tester

6.8K 6.8K

CMOS

OP AMP

+

−

1K

470 100

+

−

+1.5 V
+1.5 V

Fig. 14-7. This shows a commonly used continuity tester that digital technicians make for themselves with a few parts. Only ¼ of a volt can reach the sensitive microscopic components on a chip, rather than 1.5-3 volts that the usual continuity tester or vom would apply.

power off, is indicated as the first troubleshooting test. A continuity test is the best way to start. With the low voltage continuity tester, the lines are checked one by one. The job should be done from the top. It might be necessary to remove some of the socketed chips to get a good resistance test. If any open connections are found they should be reconnected with care.

Once the 16 address lines and the 8 data lines are cleared for opens, you can run some resistance tests for shorts. This method is not foolproof like finding an open trace, but it is worth the effort. Measure the resistance to ground of all the address and data lines. The resistances should be all alike, with maybe a slight variation. If you find any of the traces quite different in resistance than the others this is a clue that needs further investigation. Look over the schematic and see if that particular trace has a good reason for being different in resistance to ground, than the others. If not, you could have found a short that is causing the trouble.

In addition to the reading of trace to ground, check the resistance between traces. The resistance should be high, if not check out that indication as a possible trace to trace short (Table 14-1).

Dynamic Tests. While resistance tests are useful and will catch a large percentage of bus line troubles, it won't get them all. There are components in the lines, like buffers, gates and latches that will not reveal their failure with simple power off resistance tests. These need other procedures. The computer must be turned on and checked by running simple test programs.

Each address and data pathway can be tested individually. All the bus lines really do is address a memory location and either write to that location or read from it. A simple program that will test these capabilities can be written quickly and tailor made for a particular computer. The following is one that can be used, as it is, or modified slightly to work on particular computers.

The address bus has 16 lines. Each trace is

capable of transporting a 1 or 0. A trace is deemed ok if you can send a 1 successfully from the CPU to a memory location on that trace. Therefore if you output an address on the bus that has all 0s except for the trace you want to test, which will be a 1, and the address is accessed, then that trace is good. If that address can't be accessed then the trace being tested is not transporting the 1 and could be the trouble you are seeking.

To perform the test, take out the memory map and see what chips are at the destinations you are going to try to access with the little program. For example, the memory locations you are going to try to access are the following. The MS bit travels on A15, the LS bit on A0 with with rest in between.

Address in Binary	Hex
0000000000000001	0001
0000000000000010	0002
0000000000000100	0004
0000000000001000	0008
0000000000010000	0010
0000000000100000	0020
0000000001000000	0040
0000000010000000	0080
0000000100000000	0100

Address in Binary	Hex
0000001000000000	0200
0000010000000000	0400
0000100000000000	0800
0001000000000000	1000
0010000000000000	2000
0100000000000000	4000
1000000000000000	8000

If you check the addresses against the memory map, there will be a few that are not RAM. For instance, hex 0080 is the address of some housekeeping functions, 0100 are stored vectors, 0200 is used by the internal workings, and 8000 is the address on a ROM. All the rest of the addresses are RAM. The RAM addresses can be read or written to. The rest of the addresses can be read but it is best not to write to them. The test will proceed like the following.

In most home computers, BASIC is the resident language. With a lot of BASICs the commands Poke and Peek can be used. Poke lets you store a byte in a memory location. Peek lets you read what is in a memory location. These two commands let you poke a byte into memory using the test address.

Table 14-1. One Of The First Bench Type Tests That Is Made On An Ailing Computer Is Continuity Tests. These Are The Go No-Go Checks And Results.

Service Chart		
SYMPTOM-CONSTANT PROGRAM ERRORS		
RESISTANCE TEST	GO	NO-GO
POINT TO POINT	ALL POINTS CONTINUOUS	OPEN TRACE
TRACE TO GROUND	ALL RESISTANCES FAIRLY HIGH AND ALIKE	A TRACE READS SHORT TO GROUND
TRACE TO TRACE	ALL POINTS ARE HIGH RESISTANCE	SHORT BETWEEN TRACES

For instance, you could poke byte 00001000 (hex 08) into address 0000000000000100 (hex 0004). The command could look like POKE hex 0004, hex 08 (Fig. 14-8). This would send a 1 traveling through A2 on the address bus. Then you could command to read the address to see if hex 08 ever got to the address hex 0004.

The read command could be PRINT the contents of hex 0004. If the computer then displays hex 08, that means the address bus operated normally with the address hex 0004. Since addressing hex 0004 is a test of the pathway A2, A2 is considered intact.

Each pathway from A15 to A0 can be tested by sending a 1 over it and 0s over the other lines. When the 1 does not arrive at the RAM address it could be because the pathway under test is shorted or open. A close point by point examination is then needed to find the defect.

At the non-RAM locations, instead of writing to the addresses, just take a reading. There is already some sort of data in those addresses. The Peek function will give you a reading of the data that resides in those spots. If the data is meaningful, then the pathways you are Peeking across are probably good. If a reading is garbage you might have located a defective address line.

The data bus can be dynamically checked out in a similar manner. Devise another group of binary numbers like the address test group. Since the data bus only has 8 pathways, 8 numbers like the following will do.

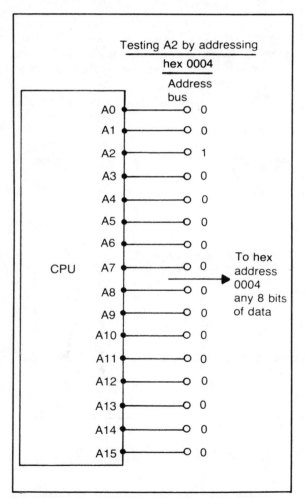

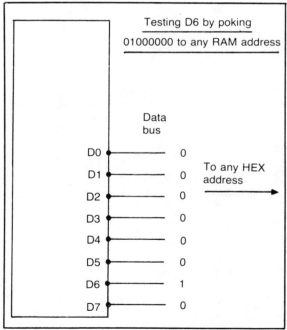

Fig. 14-8. Each address line can be tested individually by addressing places that are reached with a binary number containing one high and all the rest lows. This addressing tests line A2.

Fig. 14-9. Each data line can be tested individually by sending data to any address. The test data contains one high and all the rest lows. This data test checks line D6.

Binary Number	Hex
00000001	01
00000010	02
00000100	04
00001000	08
00010000	10
00100000	20
01000000	40
10000000	80

The MS bit sends a binary number through D7 of the data bus. The LS bit sends a number through D0. If a 1 can travel its own pathway, then that line is clear. If a 1 cannot make it the line could be defective. Any set of RAM locations can be used by the test. Just Poke the bytes into locations and Peek to see if they got there. As long as the bytes arrived intact, the pathways are ok. If one of the bytes did not arrive, then the indicated pathway is suspect. For example, if 01000000 did not arrive at its location then D6 pathway could have a short, open, defective buffer, bypass capacitor, or other component (Fig. 14-9).

Chapter 15

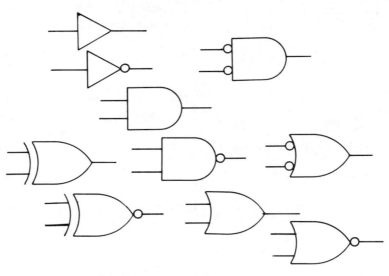

The SAM Chip

In the TRS-80 Color Computer is a chip called SAM (Fig. 15-1). The initials stand for *Synchronous Address Multiplexer* which is only one of the jobs the chip does. SAM is a good example of the newer 40-pin chips that are arriving on the scene. The SAM combines a lot of digital logic circuits and makes the manufacturing and service of the computer simpler. Where there were a lot of small buffers, gates, and registers, the one 40-pin chip replaces them all.

The SAM does three general jobs. One, with the aid of an external crystal, the SAM generates all of the timing signals for the computer. Two, SAM does all of the device selection (Fig. 15-2). Thirdly, it generates video address lines and multiplexes them with the address coming out of CPU (Fig. 15-3). That's where the SAM name comes from. The SAM is a controller for the dynamic RAM.

THE SAM SCHEMATIC

Looking down at the pins on the schematic, the 16 address lines A15 through A0 are the signal inputs. If you check these lines with a logic probe there should be a lot of general activity there. A good scope and frequency counter will show the activity and the frequency of the clock.

The schematic shows the R/W line below the address lines (Fig. 15-4). It too is an input from the CPU. The connections below the R/W line are for the clock. The clock is resident with the SAM chip. The clock circuit is part internal to SAM and part external. The clock output is E and Q. They connect to E_{in} and Q_{in} on the CPU. The CPU is able to use the rising and falling edges of the SAM generated square waves to fire up the program counter and other registers. The program counter in the CPU is producing the address activity input to the SAM.

There are three chip select lines coming out of SAM, S0, S1, and S2 (Fig. 15-1). They enter a 74LS138 decoder chip. The three chip select lines have 8 possible combinations of 1s and 0s between them. Therefore, the three chip select lines can choose one of eight chips. The SAM can therefore choose to put in action RAM, two internal ROMs,

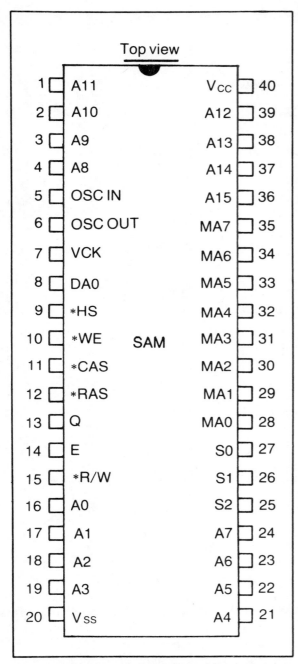

Top view

	SAM	
1 ▢ A11		Vcc ▢ 40
2 ▢ A10		A12 ▢ 39
3 ▢ A9		A13 ▢ 38
4 ▢ A8		A14 ▢ 37
5 ▢ OSC IN		A15 ▢ 36
6 ▢ OSC OUT		MA7 ▢ 35
7 ▢ VCK		MA6 ▢ 34
8 ▢ DA0		MA5 ▢ 33
9 ▢ *HS		MA4 ▢ 32
10 ▢ *WE		MA3 ▢ 31
11 ▢ *CAS		MA2 ▢ 30
12 ▢ *RAS		MA1 ▢ 29
13 ▢ Q		MA0 ▢ 28
14 ▢ E		S0 ▢ 27
15 ▢ *R/W		S1 ▢ 26
16 ▢ A0		S2 ▢ 25
17 ▢ A1		A7 ▢ 24
18 ▢ A2		A6 ▢ 23
19 ▢ A3		A5 ▢ 22
20 ▢ Vss		A4 ▢ 21

Fig. 15-1. Most of the 40-pin chips look alike from the top view. It would be helpful to a servicer, if a sketch like this SAM chip showing the actual physical pin layout, was available in service notes. It saves the servicer having to relate the schematic drawing's pins to the actual physical pins.

two cartridge ROMs and two PIAs. Follow the eight decoder output lines and you'll see the selection.

The lines MA7 through MA0 are multiplexed address lines that choose addresses in the dynamic RAM. RAS and CAS are strobe lines that constantly scan the row address and column address lines of the dynamic RAM. DA0 is a clock signal that comes from the VDG chip, which is discussed later in the book. Vcc and ground, of course, is the +5 volt power to energize the entire chip.

THE SAM BLOCK DIAGRAM

There is a 16-bit register in the chip to do all the controlling of the signals as they enter, work their way around, and then exit. Each of the 16 bits are able to assume one of the two logical states to do the controlling. The register is installed in the memory map of this computer at addresses in hex of FFC0 to FFDF. There are 32 memory locations for the 16 bits. There is a reason for this (Fig. 15-5).

There are two addresses for each of the 16 bits. One address is an odd number and the other is even. In order to set a bit in the register, the odd number is written to. When you want to clear the bit, the even number is written to.

This is an unusual way to use the ability of the computer to address a location. Normally, locations on the memory map are addressed so the contents of the location can be placed on the data bus. Both the address and data buses are attached to a location. In SAM there is no connection to the data bus. There is no data in SAM that has to be transported via the data bus to the CPU.

In SAM there is one 16-bit register (Fig. 15-6). The register is used to control six different circuits on the SAM chip. The setting or clearing of the 16 bits puts the circuits into their correct operating mode. For example, in SAM is part of the clock circuitry. The rest of the clock circuit is external to SAM.

The external circuit contains the crystal. The crystal is cut to oscillate at 14.31818 MHz. The sine wave signal is applied to SAM at pins 5 and 6, osc in and osc out. Inside SAM (Fig. 15-7) is a General Timing circuit and a generator-rate controller cir-

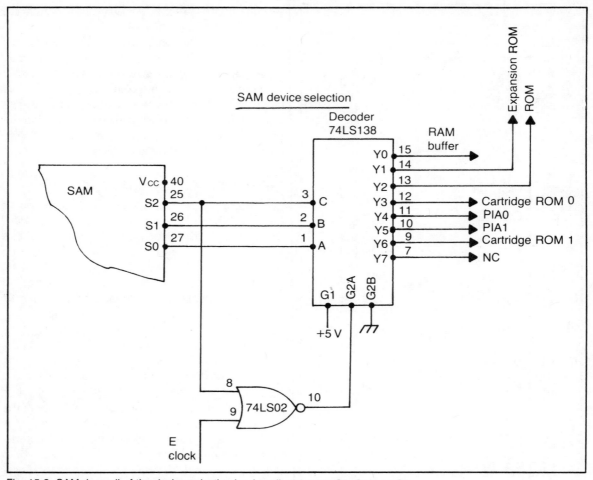

Fig. 15-2. SAM does all of the device selection by decoding outputs S2, S1, and S0.

cuit. In these circuits the crystal's signal is shaped into a square wave and divided in frequency. If the 14.31818 is divided by 16, the generated frequency is 0.89 MHz. This is the frequency the Color Computer operates on.

However, this versatile chip is made to be used in a lot of computer types, not just the Color Computer. The circuit, not only has the ability to divide by 16, it can also divide by 8. This will produce a frequency of 1.78 MHz which another manufacturer might find useful. In order to change SAM's control frequency, two bits 0 and 1 (MPU Clock Rate) in the control register are attached to the timing circuits. The bits are designed in the

following way. If both bits are cleared, then the SAM will generate 0.89 MHz. Should the 1 bit be cleared and the 0 bit be set, then 1.78 MHz is the SAM output.

Each one of the bits has two hex addresses. The 1 bit has FFD9 and FFD8. The 0 bit has FFD7 and FFD6. The bits are odd numbers and even numbers. If you place FFD9 on the address bus you will set the 1 bit. Should you access FFD8 you will clear the 1 bit. By correctly addressing the odd and even bits you can set or clear any of the 16 bits in the control register.

In the Color Computer there are three other SAM circuits that are controlled by the register.

Alongside the frequency control bits are two memory size bits. The computer is built to contain 4K of RAM. However, the computer can be expanded to 16K and even to 32K. One of the expansion moves is to set or clear the two memory size bits. These two bits each have two addresses that are used to set or clear a bit. Like the previous bits, accessing the odd numbered address sets it, while accessing the even numbered address clears it. By addressing the two memory size bits the RAM can be changed from 4K to 16K to 32K and the larger number of addresses will be addressed correctly.

Another group of bits in the control register are used to arrange addresses for the video RAM. Video RAM is a section of the dynamic RAM that is set aside for the video display. As you strike the keyboard the key is sent to video RAM. There are 7 bits in this group. They are shown from FFC6 to FFD3. If all the bits are cleared, the computer will normally start addressing at hex 0000. The video

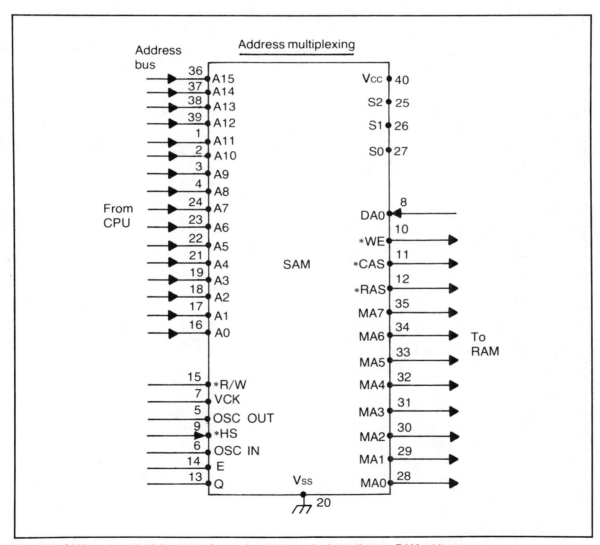

Fig. 15-3. SAM receives the full address bus and multiplexes the lower lines to RAM addresses.

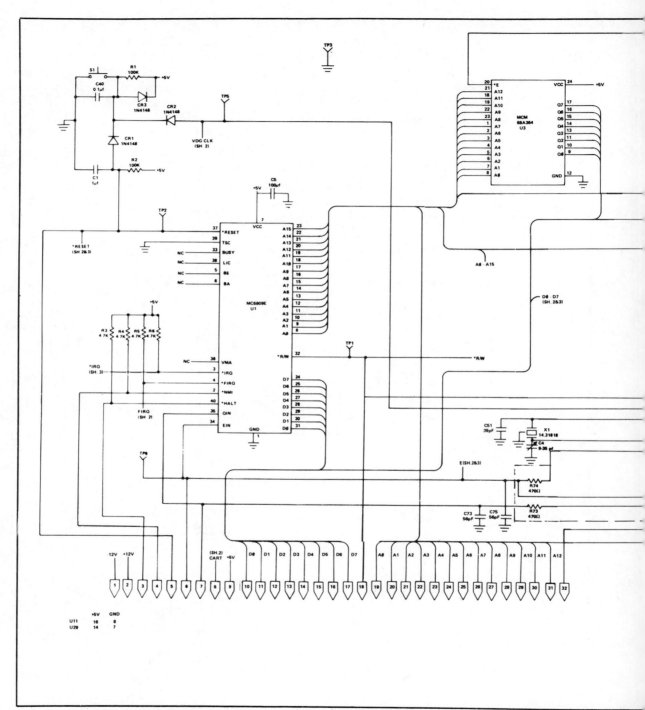

Fig. 15-4. The SAM chip is found operating in the TRS-80 Color Computer. This is the schematic diagram (courtesy of Radio Shack, a division of Tandy Corporation).

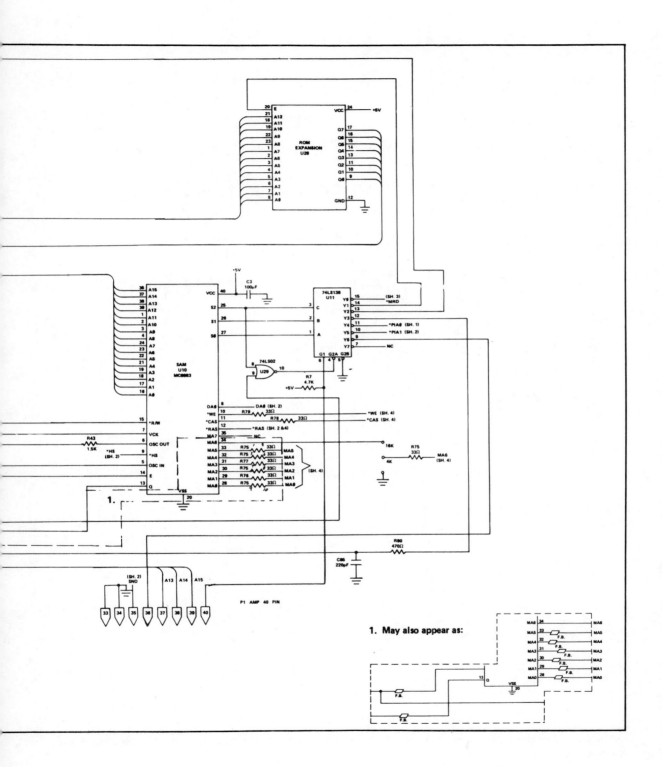

1. May also appear as:

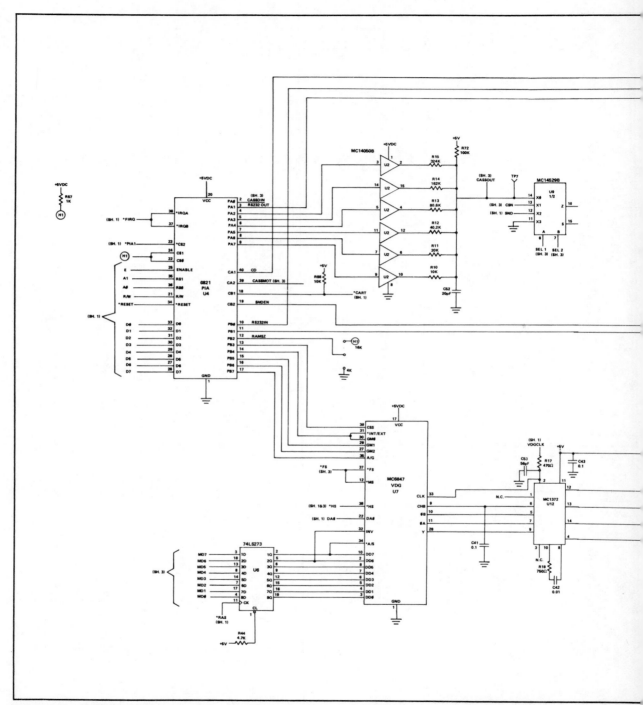

Fig. 15-4. The SAM chip is found operating in the TRS-80 Color Computer. This is the schematic diagram (courtesy of Radio Shack, a division of Tandy Corporation). (Continued from page 231.)

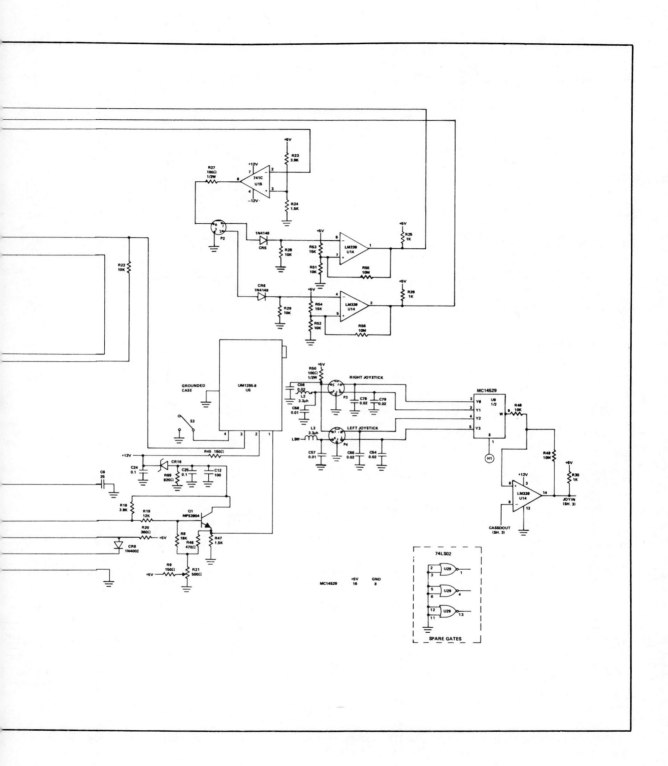

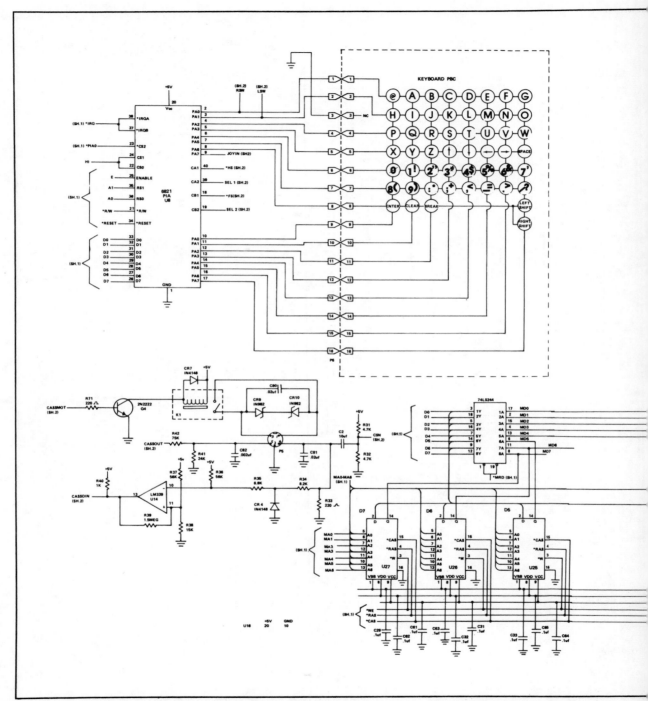

Fig. 15-4. The SAM chip is found operating in the TRS-80 Color Computer. This is the schematic diagram (courtesy of Radio Shack, a division of Tandy Corporation). (Continued from page 233.)

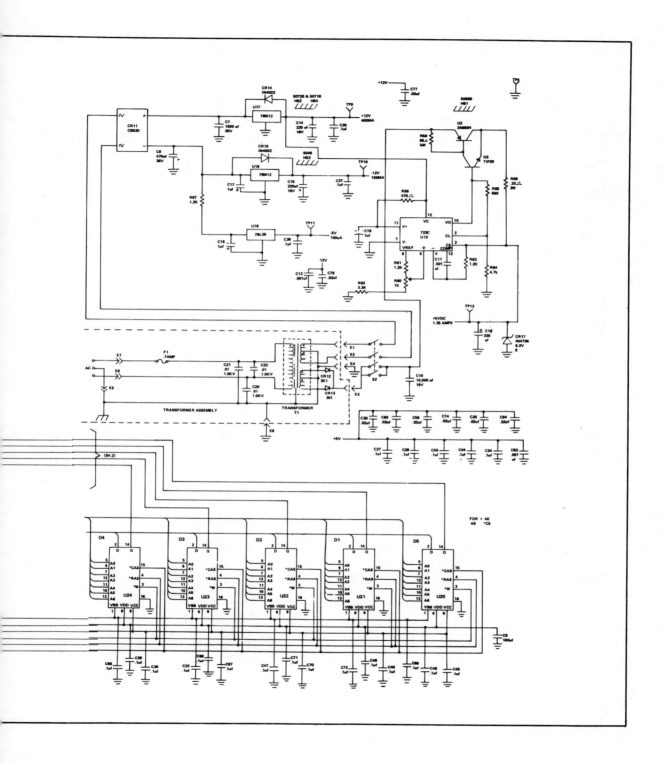

235

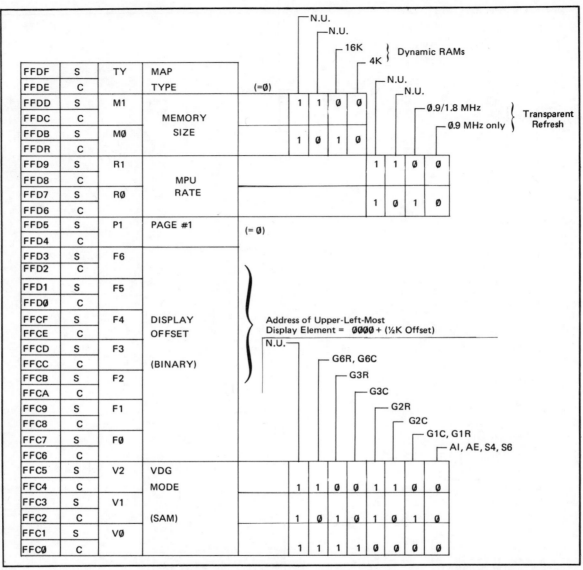

Fig. 15-5. The memory map of the SAM chip shows addresses in hex of FFCO to FFDF (courtesy of Radio Shack, a division of Tandy Corporation).

RAM is assigned at 0400. Therefore bit 2 of the 0-6 bits is set by addressing its odd numbered address. The 7 bits are then added to the starting address and the result is 0400. This address is the upper left most display block on the picture tube. As each key is struck a character takes its place on the TV face. There will be more about this in the video chapters.

The last group of bits in the register this computer uses are 3 bits to arrange the display mode. The addresses FFC0 to FFC5 are the six addresses that set and clear the 3 bits. There are 14 display modes available in this computer. These 3 bits can be set and cleared in 8 combinations. The 3 bits are mixed with bits in the PIA and between them all the

236

Hex address To clear	Hex address To set	SAM 15-bit control register	
FFDE	FFDF	0	To choose map type (1 bit)
FFDC	FFDD	1	To choose memory size (2 bits) 4K or 16K
FFDA	FFDB	0	
FFD8	FFD9	1	To choose MPU clock rate (2 bits)
FFD6	FFD7	0	
FFD4	FFD5	0	Page switch (1 bit)
FFD2	FFD3	6	
FFD0	FFD1	5	Offset to address video RAM by adding in (7 bits) multiplexer
FFCE	FFCF	4	
FFCC	FFCD	3	
FFCA	FFCB	2	
FFC8	FFC9	1	
FFC6	FFC7	0	
FFC4	FFC5	2	To choose VDG mode
FFC2	FFC3	1	(3 bits)
FFC0	FFC1	0	

Fig. 15-6. In SAM there is one 16-bit register that controls all its internal circuitry. The register is divided into six separate control sections.

14 display modes can be used. There is more about the display modes in the chapter on VDGs.

There are two unused bits in the 16-bit register. They are not needed in this computer. Both of them are kept clear at all times. They are kept clear by having the CPU address the even addresses at start up. Incidentally, in these large 40-pin chips it is common practice not to use every available capability. The chips are designed for general use for a lot of manufacturers and not for a single dedicated use. Some manufacturers use some of the chip's capabilities while others use different ones.

SYSTEM TIMING

The E square wave signal that is used by the CPU to work the program counter, is also used by SAM in a number of ways. The fact that the program counter addressing and the SAM multiplex addressing both use the same E signal, keeps the two circuits in perfect sync. This is necessary so no

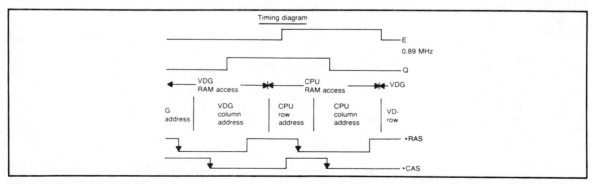

Fig. 15-7. SAM produces all the timing for the computer. The operating frequency is 0.89 MHz which is the crystal frequency 14.31818 divided by 16. E is the frequency actually derived. Q is the same frequency but 90 degrees out of phase. *ras and *cas are two strobe frequencies that are used to strobe the row addresses and column addresses of the dynamic RAM.

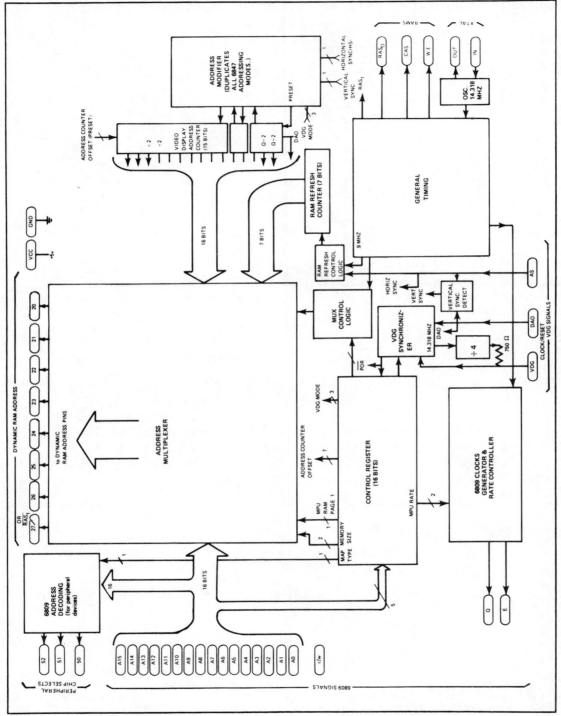

Fig.15-8. The SAM block diagram shows the complications and machinations the digital signal goes through from the time the address lines enter the input until they leave the outputs (courtesy of Radio Shack, a division of Tandy Corporation).

conflict develops between the two chips. The CPU addresses the storage RAM during the rise and fall of the E signal pulse. The SAM addresses the video RAM during the fall and rise of the low part of the E signal.

With the aid of the timing diagram (Fig. 15-7) schematic (Fig. 15-4) and SAM block diagram (Fig. 15-8) let's piece together the way the SAM handles the complex addressing and how the data gets past the computer into the display circuits.

When the E signal rises the program counter outputs an address. The A15-A0 bits enter the SAM pins. The SAM control register is preset in a VDG mode, with the correct memory size, at the correct clock rate, with the video address offset correct and the unused bits cleared.

The 16-bit address enters the Address Multiplexer in the SAM chip. In the multiplexer the least significant 7 bits are separated from the rest of the address and sent out pins 34-28 which are MA6-MA0. The multiplexed addresses MA6-MA0 are sent directly to RAM.

Meanwhile, in the General Timing section of SAM two strobe signals, *row address strobe* (ras), and *column address strobe* (cas) are being generated. They can be seen in the timing diagram (Fig. 15-7). There are two ras and two cas types. One pair is for

the CPU addressing and the other pair for the video addressing. These signals leave the SAM and go to each of the RAM chips. The row address and column address signals are strobed into RAM to form the rest of the address, the most significant bits that were removed in the multiplexer earlier. This forms the complete address so RAM can be accessed.

When the E clock goes low, instead of the multiplexer causing the storage RAM address to be selected it takes the address counter offset and adds those 7 bits to the MS part of the address and the video RAM is addressed. The E clock continues addressing RAM during the high portion and video RAM during the low portion of its pulses.

The data in the CPU meanwhile, takes no part in the addressing activity. The data is placed on the data bus at the proper times and when the data is to be stored goes to the activated address. In the data bus is a tristate buffer. The data can pass through the buffer when the buffer is selected by the address decoder. The 74LS138 that is the chip select out of the SAM pins S2, S1, and S0. The pin mrd at Y0 can select the buffer.

When mrd turns on the buffer (Fig. 15-9) data lines D7-D0 pass the data into the buffer. The data goes through the buffer, is amplified and processed.

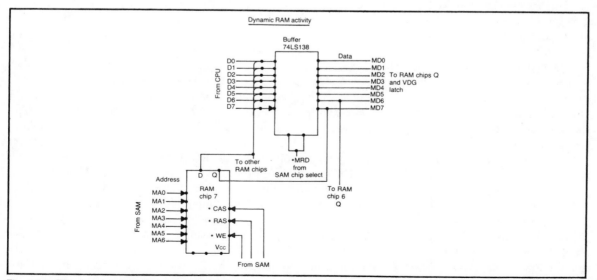

Fig. 15-9. The dynamic RAM has all its chips receive *ras and *cas to strobe the chips looking for active addresses.

The data exits the buffer as MD7-MD0 and goes directly to the VDG latch, a 74LS273. Once in the latch, the data can be processed for the video display. This will be discussed in the video chapters.

DEVICE SELECTION

The pins 25, 26, and 27 on the SAM output the signal for the device selection. The pins insert S2,S1, and S0 into the decoder 74LS138. There are three pins on the bottom of the decoder for +5 V, ground, and a clock select signal. The clock select comes from the output of a NOR gate. The NOR gate has its inputs from the E clock and S2. If both inputs are low at the same time the decoder will be inactive, otherwise it will be active.

While active the decoder can choose between eight outputs. In this computer only seven are used and the eighth is not connected. When active the decoder, according to the 8 inputs can choose from a choice of mrd, two ROMs, two PIAs, or two cartridge pins.

CHECKING OUT THE SAM CHIP

As a servicer it is not necessary to fully realize the operation of a chip like SAM as a design engineer does. Of course the more you know the more expert you'll be, but your job is to locate the defect and restore operation, not redesign the activity. In general, the operation as described in this chapter should enable you to check and restore the computer to operation.

Once the SAM area is under scrutiny, the best way to start is a pin by pin checkout with a logic probe or vom (Table 15-1). The logic probe gives more information, since it shows pulsing along with the logic state. The vom reveals the logic state as +5 V for high and 0 V as low.

With the aid of the schematic the first pins to test are 40, the +5 V source, and 20, which is ground. They should read high and low respectively. If the +5 V is missing the power supply is not working or C3 the 100 pF bypass is shorted. Should the ground connection be high or dead that indicates an open internal ground in the chip. Pin 20 should glow a low if the ground is intact and the chip energized.

Once the power is deemed good the next pins to test should be the address bus. On the SAM A15-A12 are pins 36-39. A11-A8 use pins 1-4. A7-A4 use 24-21 and A3-A0 are on 19-16. On all the address pins there should be a pulse. If any of them does not show a pulse, that pin is not active and indicates trouble, either in that address pathway or one of the components.

In addition to the pulse on a pin, there will be a high or no LED light. If there is a high that means there is an active 1 on the pin. If only a pulse is present with no glowing high or low, that means a low is present. Some logic probes might show a low glow to indicate a 0 in this instance but mine doesn't.

Early in the book, it was mentioned, that when the computer is first turned on, the CPU is built to address the ROM that is in control of operations. That is the only addressing the computer is able to do on its own. After the CPU does this initial addressing, the ROM then takes over. It does all the housekeeping jobs and gets all the registers started at their beginning numbers. When the ROM completes these program steps it goes into a waiting pattern and stays there until you start striking the keyboard. The address of the waiting pattern simply is repeated over and over again on the address bus until work is begun.

With the logic probe you can read the address on the bus. By going from pin to pin and recording the logic state on A15-A0 you should read a ROM address. If a pin reads pulse-high on the probe that is a 1. Should it read pulse only or pulse-low that means a 0 is on that pin. In my computer, the SAM chip holds this pattern and pins A15-A0 reads 1010011111010000. In hex this is A7D0. Looking up this address on the memory map, I find that it is on the BASIC ROM that is in control. The point of the entire exercise is to see if the SAM address line input is correct. If it is, it is indicated that the CPU to SAM input lines are ok, just as the power supply was ok when +5 V and ground were intact.

The osc in and osc out can be checked with the logic probe in the usual manner. If you touch down on pins 5 and 6 with the logic probe and you are using an ordinary TV set as a monitor, chances are

Table 15-1. This Service Checkout Chart Shows What Logic Probe Readings
Should Be Present When the Computer is Started and is Operating Normally. During Troubleshooting,
the Pins are Probed and Compared With What Should Be There. Any Discrepancy is a Clue That Could Indicate Trouble.

Pin Number		Sam Service Checkout Chart Logic Probe		
		High (1)	Low (0)	Pulse
Vcc 40		✓		
GND 20			✓	
A15 36		✓		✓
37				✓
38		✓		✓
39				✓
1				✓
2		✓		✓
3		✓		✓
4		✓		✓
24		✓		✓
23		✓		✓
22				✓
21		✓		✓
19				✓
18				✓
17				✓
A0 16				✓
OSC IN 6				
OSC OUT 5				
*R/W 15		✓		✓
E 14				✓
Q 13				✓
S2 2			✓	✓
S1 26		✓		✓
S0 27			✓	✓
MA7 35				✓
MA6 34				✓
MA5 33			✓	✓
MA4 32			✓	✓
MA3 31				✓
MA2 30				✓
MA1 29				✓
MA0 28				✓
*CAS 11				✓
*RAS 12				✓
*WE 10		✓	←	✓
*HS 9		✓	←	✓
DA0 8		✓	✓	✓
VCK 7				✓

16 Address Lines A0-A15

you will cause a bit of TV interference to happen, A slight amount of herringbone TVI will appear in the display. This is because the oscillator frequency, up above 10 MHz will generate a lot of spurious frequencies as it is loaded down by the logic probe. The probe itself though, doesn't respond to the oscillator. The probe won't light at all as it touches pin 5 and 6.

In order to see the oscillator waveshape a good scope must be used. However, the oscillator will either be on or not most of the time. A go no-go test is all that is needed. Just see if the oscillator is running, and the checkout 99% of the time will be all you need.

The next pin to check is 15, the R/W line. Normally it is held high and does have a clock pulse present. The probe should show pulse-high if the R/W line is working properly. If it doesn't read pulse-high there could be a problem on the line. The line travels from the CPU to all the places the address and data bus does, so a problem in the line could be anywhere in the computer.

When pins 5 and 6 were tested, if you did use an expensive scope, a sine wave would have been seen going into SAM. Inside SAM the sine wave was changed to a square wave and a second square wave produced 90 degrees out of phase with the first wave. These are E and Q. They exit SAM at pins 13 and 14. They go back to the CPU where they go to work triggering the addressing and data processing. At 13 and 14 there should be a pulse only reading on the probe. If there isn't any pulse and the osc in and osc out are ok then a problem in the general timing and clock generator area of SAM is indicated. This could mean a new SAM chip is needed.

At pins 25, 26, and 27 are the chip select signals. The three signals can produce 8 different combinations of 1s and 0s. When you touch down on the three Ss there should be a pulse as the computer is waiting for the keyboard information. In addition the chip select should be there. In my checkout, while the address bus was waiting at A7D0 the chip select S2-S0 read 010. This must be the chip select for the BASIC ROM that was being addressed. This is one of the outputs the SAM produces as a result of the input A7D0. As long as

the chip select input is present with pulses and one of the 8 possible selects, the chip select decoder section of SAM is ok. If the chip select output is not correct in any way, that could be an indication that a new SAM chip might be needed.

Pins 28-35 are used by the multiplexed addresses for their exit from SAM. Here again a pulse must be present on each line if the MA7-MA0 bus is taking signal from SAM correctly. There could be logic states also as the multiplexed address chooses locations in RAM. If the address inputs are all good and these RAM location selections are missing pulses, that indicates the address multiplexer in SAM is defective. If it is, a new SAM chip has to be installed.

Pins 11 and 12 are two more outputs that have to do with the multiplexed addressing. They should both show pulses or else they are not operating. They are SAM outputs and are strobing the dynamic RAM. They are ras (the row address strobe) and cas (the column address strobe) frequency. They follow the E signal and a pulse should be on the probe. If all else is well and cas or ras does not have a pulse, the SAM could be defective.

The last few pins are 10, 9, 8, and 7. They are all frequency driven pins and should all have pulses too. Pin 10 works with ras and cas. It is called we and is connected in the general timing section. It will cause spurious oscillations and some weak TVI too. That's how you can tell it is ok in some computers with regular TV monitors. Pin 9 (hs) is the horizontal sync control. Testing it is identical to Pin 10, TVI, and all. Lastly, are pins 7, 8, DA0, and Vcc, DA0 also must show a pulse. In addition it will also show a high, low or even both. It is a signal from the VDG chip that aids in the syncing of the oscillator. Both hs and DA0 must show a pulse if they are present.

There is no easily obtained test equipment that will test a chip like SAM. Chances are you will not stock an extra SAM so you can test it by direct replacement. In addition you cannot gain access to the internal wiring. Therefore the only way to test SAM fast, is to have a schematic and block diagram of the internal circuits and take input and output readings. Then by deduction you can tell if SAM is doing the job or not.

Chapter 16

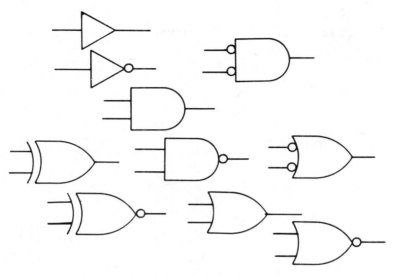

The PIAs

The *peripheral interface adapter* is packaged as a 40-pin chip (Fig. 16-1). It has the job of interfacing the CPU with all the external devices the computer has to deal with, such as inputs like the keyboard, joysticks, and cassette and outputs like the video display, cassette, and printer.

As far as the CPU is concerned, it needs to interface with devices like RAM and ROM. They operate at the identical speed, frequencies, currents, and voltages. The CPU can simply attach buffered pathway buses to RAM and ROM and begin operations. Unfortunately, the peripheral devices do not usually have the same characteristics as RAM and ROM. The CPU cannot just hook into the external devices.

That's where the PIA and other I/O chips come into use. The PIA is built to receive the CPU streams of data and couple the data to the peripherals that are receivers, like the display and printer. Also the PIA is able to receive data from peripherals like the keyboard and joysticks and send it to the CPU. The PIA takes care of all the mismatching and smoothes the way.

ADDRESSING PIAS SIX REGISTERS

The MC6821 PIA is typical of the large chips that contain the latches, buffers and other logic circuits that make up a PIA (Fig. 16-2). The activity is based around six registers. They are all one byte wide. There are two sides to the chip, A and B. Each side has three registers. The sides, from a servicers point of view are twins. There is a peripheral data register, PDR, a data direction register, DDR, and a control register, CR on each side.

There are only four addresses to contact the six registers. The PDR and DDR operate together. As a result the PDR and DDR together only get one address. The CR gets its own private address. The four addresses therefore, are typically arranged as follows.

Address	Registers
FF00	PDRA-DDRA
FF01	CRA
FF02	PDRB-DDRB
FF03	CRB

The even number addresses are usually the I/O registers and the odd numbers are the control

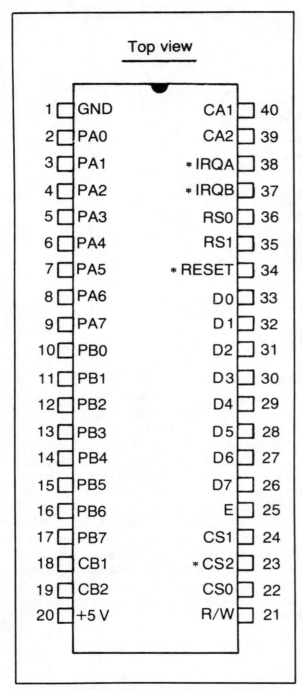

Top view

1	GND	CA1	40
2	PA0	CA2	39
3	PA1	*IRQA	38
4	PA2	*IRQB	37
5	PA3	RS0	36
6	PA4	RS1	35
7	PA5	*RESET	34
8	PA6	D0	33
9	PA7	D1	32
10	PB0	D2	31
11	PB1	D3	30
12	PB2	D4	29
13	PB3	D5	28
14	PB4	D6	27
15	PB5	D7	26
16	PB6	E	25
17	PB7	CS1	24
18	CB1	*CS2	23
19	CB2	CS0	22
20	+5 V	R/W	21

Fig. 16-1. The top view of the 40-pin PIA chip clearly shows the data bus D7-D0 pins and the peripheral output pins PA7-PA0 and PB7-PB0.

registers. There is no electronic reason for this odd-even numbering, it's just the way it is done for easy remembering.

The registers are the same size as the RAM registers and are contacted in the same way, just as if they were RAM. The addresses are still 16-bits wide. The 16-bit address can activate one of the four addresses in normal fashion. The PIA is right in the memory map, and is attached to the address bus in a normal fashion.

The 8-bit registers are all attached to the 8 bit-data bus. The register that is addressed can either send data to the CPU or receive data in accordance with the dictates of an R/W line that is attached to the chip. As far as the CPU is concerned, the six registers of PIA look and act like compatible RAM.

CHOOSING BETWEEN PDR AND DDR

As a servicer you probably won't have to actually choose between PDR and DDR with their one even address. The DDR usually gets taken care of automatically during power up, and all you have to deal with are the PDRs as if the DDR doesn't exist. However, you should know what happened so you can logically deduce some troubles.

The PIA chip is selected by addressing its three chip select pins. They are CS0, CS1, and *CS2. When 1s are applied to CS0 and CS1, and a 0 is sent to CS2 the PIA chip is selected. During this initial addressing the DDR is addressed. The PDR is not addressed. The DDR must configure its bits for the PDR. That is why the DDR is there. It has only one job (Fig. 16-3).

In the PDR register there are eight bits. When a bit in the DDR gets cleared with a 0 or set with a 1, then that corresponding bit in the PDR will act as an input or output port. It will be able to receive a data bit from the CPU and output the bit to an external device. It will also be able to receive a bit from an external device and send it to the CPU.

Upon start up, one of the things the operating system does is contact the DDR. The eight bits of the DDR are connected to the eight bits of the PDR, bit for bit. The operating system configures the DDR bits, which automatically makes the PDR bits into inputs and outputs.

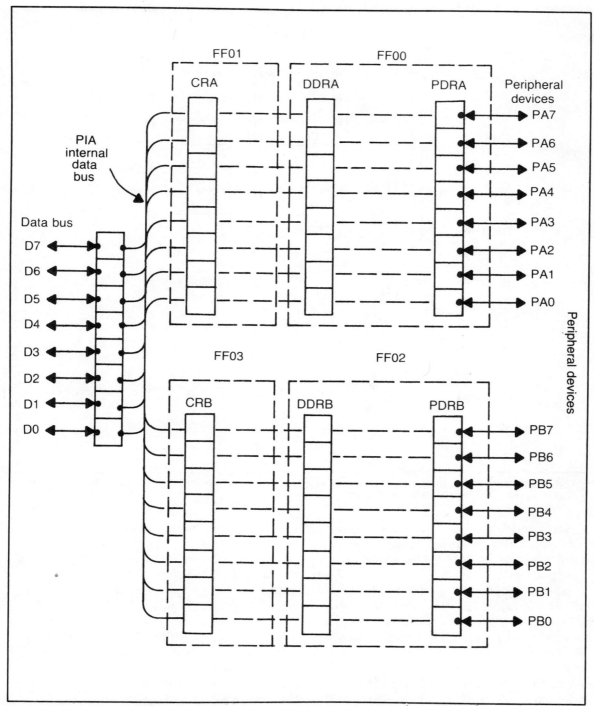

Fig. 16-2. The PIA activity is based around the six registers that have four addresses FF00-FF03.

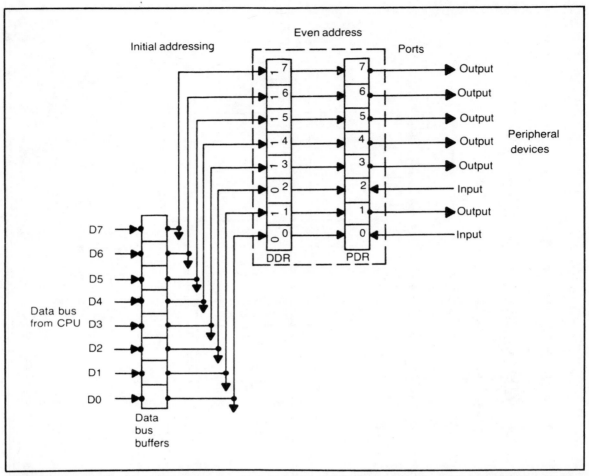

Fig. 16-3. The DDR and PDR registers share the same address. The DDR is addressed at the beginning of the operation then the PDR takes over and stays in control for the rest of the operation.

Once the PDR has the correct direction states it is ready to work. There will be more about this later. Meanwhile the DDR did its job and must be turned off. This is done in the following way. When the computer is powered up, bit 2 of the control register, CR, is given a 0. Bit 2 takes part in choosing between PDR and DDR. Remember, one address has to take care of both of these registers. The address choosing is accomplished with two signals in bits A1 and A0 of the address line. They are called register selects, RS1 and RS0, and are connected to two of the chip pins. RS1 and RS0 work with 2 of CR. Between RS1, RS0, and bit 2 of

the CR, there are eight possible combinations of 1s and 0s.

When bit 2 of the CR has a 0, then RS1, and RS0 choose the DDR register. After the DDR is made to do its job of configuring the PDR then the operating system installs a 1 in bit 2 of the CR. If an address comes down the address bus for PDR-DDR, with a 1 in bit 2 of CR, then DDR is no longer chosen. PDR gets chosen. The DDR is usually only the chosen one during initialization. Once the PDR is set up by the DDR it becomes the main address between the two registers.

Therefore, even though there are six registers

in PIA there are only four addresses. During checkout the chip select pins, CSs, and the register select pins, RSs, are the ones to test. In the back of your mind remember bit 2 of the CR is taking place in the action.

THE CONTROL REGISTER

Besides bit 2 there are seven other bits in the CRs. Bit 2, it was mentioned, attends to the choosing of DDR or PDR when an even PIA address is contacted (Fig. 16-4). There are three other control jobs the CR does in the PIA. The three jobs are all intertwined. Let's examine them.

There are two control pins CA1 and CA2 connected to the chip. CA1 is an input only line. It is used to set bit 7 if an interrupt is found to be needed. CA1 uses bits 0 and 1 to set bit 7 and to decide what to do with the interrupt.

CA2 is an input and output line. It uses bits 3, 4 and 5 to set bit 6 if an interrupt is needed. CB1 and CB2 do the same jobs on the control register on the B side as CA1 and CA2 lines do on the A side.

The actual setting of the control register is a machine language programming job and has little to do with servicing. There are many details and numerous steps to go through and these can be learned if you ever write a machine language program. The important parts of the control register to the servicer, are the four control lines that attach to the pins of the chip, CA1, CA2, CB1, and CB2. The status of these lines during servicing is necessary information. This will be covered at the end of the chapter.

THE PIA PINS

The power is supplied at pin 20, +5 V to ground at pin 1 (Fig. 16-5). The addressing is mainly done with the chip selects, *CS2, CS1, and CS0. Pins 24-22, and the register selects, RS1 and RS0, pins 35 and 36, with some help from bit 2 of the CR. The enable pin E, 25, holds the chip selects high during E.

The computer's data bus is connected to D7-D0, Pins 26-33. The R/W line 21, controls the direction of the data streams during the movement

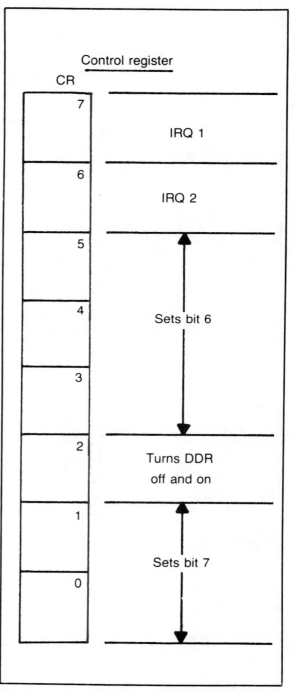

Fig. 16-4. The control register does a number of jobs. The CA and CB control lines receive their status from this register.

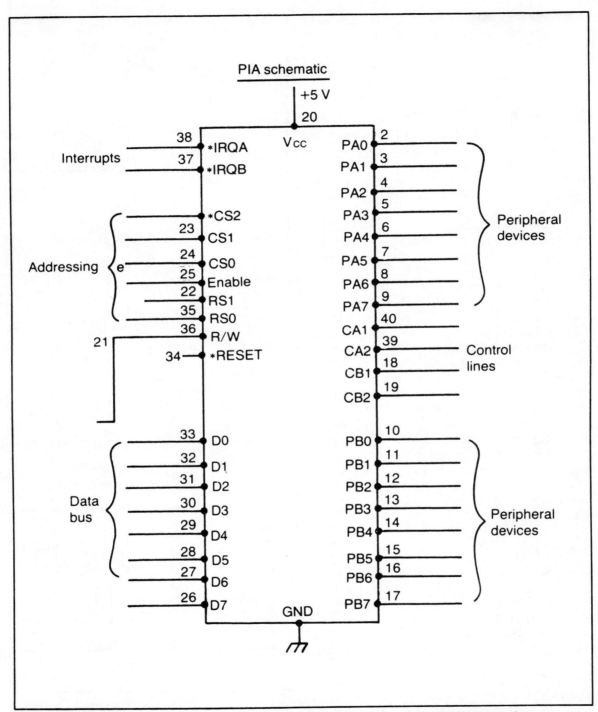

Fig. 16-5. The PIA schematic is usually drawn so that the various sections of the chip are best discerned.

of data. A high on the R/W line lets the CPU read from the PIA. A low on the R/W line lets the CPU write to the PIA.

Each PDR has its own one byte data output line. A PDR can both read and write to an external device over its output bus. It can't easily do both read and write like the data bus inside the computer can. The PDR gets configured on power up with 1s and 0s at the DDR. If a bit is going to be an input, then the bit gets set with a 1. Should the PDR bit be configured as an output, then it will be cleared with a 0.

The I/O bits in PDRA are attached to PA7-PA0 on pins 9-2. The I/O bits PDRB are connected to PB7-PB0 on pins 17-11. Pin 34 is the *reset line. It is activated during a reset when power that had been lost is restored. The reset will reinitialize all the PIA registers when it is activated after a power failure. While the computer is operating normally, *reset is held high, as the asterisk indicates. It only does its reset job when it is forced low.

Pin 25 is E from the clock circuit. It does the timing for the PIA activity. It is called enable and is an enable pulse. Pins 40 and 39 are the control lines CA1 and CA2. Pins 18 and 19 are control lines CB1 and CB2. Pins 38 and 37 are two interrupt lines IRQA and IRQB. They are normally held high till an interrupt occurs when they go low.

The PIA is a versatile chip and can do all sorts of I/O jobs. Let's check out the pins with a logic probe as the PIA does its work.

THE PIA IN ACTION

In the TRS-80 Color Computer two MC6821 PIAs are used with a 6809E CPU. The PIAs do all the I/O jobs. The input duties are handling the keyboard, joysticks, and cassette tape input. The output jobs are the color video output, the audio output, data for the printer and the cassette recorder.

The schematic (Fig. 15-4) shows two PIAs U8 and U4. We'll test U8 first, U8 is shown on the memory map (Fig. 16-6) as occupying addresses FF00-FF03. All four of these addresses are accessed simultaneously by the chip select action from the SAM. CS1 and CS0 are tied together and

held high. *CS2 is also held high except when the CPU wants to access U8. *CS2 is connected to pin 11 of U11 the decoder that works with SAM. When U8 needs to be accessed, the decoder forces *CS2 low and U8 is selected, all four addresses.

If you make a probe test of CS0, CS1 and *CS0 (Table 16-1) they will all read high, even though *CS2 is forced low, the static condition is being held high.

As U8 is being selected, there are four addresses to the chip. The PDR-DDRs are two of the addresses and the CRs are the other two addresses. The DDRs set the direction data can flow in the PDRs during initialization, so addressing the PDR-DDR combination of registers really addresses the PDR only. RS1 and RS0 can choose between the PDRs and CRs which are the four addresses inside the PIA.

RS1 and RS0 are tied to A1 and A0 of the address line. Therefore the SAM can address the register it wants by sending logic states out over the address line. If you check RS1 and RS0 with the probe, you'll see normal address pulses on the pins. That takes care of the addressing. The chip is selected and then the register is selected. Once the register is selected it is turned on and connected to the internal data bus.

If you read pin 34 the reset connection, it will be a high. The reset is held high during normal operation. When you test for the presence of E on pin 25, when it is there the probe will show a pulse as the timing signal keeps coming. Pins 20 and 1 will read high and low respectively since they are +5 V and ground.

The above probe readings are more or less universal for the MC6821 PIA. They are the normal addressing, operating voltages, timing signals and logic states that power and control the chip's operation. If you are making routine tests the probe results will quickly show a missing or abnormal condition. If you are working on a lot of the same boards you'd memorize the normal results and be able to spot abnormalities fast.

The rest of the pin readings have to do with the I/O jobs. Since the jobs vary with different PIAs you must know the jobs so you can intelligently inter-

```
FF00 – FF03            PIA    U8
```

FF00
- BIT 0 = KEYBOARD ROW 1 and right joystick switch
- BIT 1 = KEYBOARD ROW 2 and left joystick switch
- BIT 2 = KEYBOARD ROW 3
- BIT 3 = KEYBOARD ROW 4
- BIT 4 = KEYBOARD ROW 5
- BIT 5 = KEYBOARD ROW 6
- BIT 6 = KEYBOARD ROW 7
- BIT 7 = JOYSTICK COMPARISON INPUT

FF01
- BIT 0 — Control of the Horizontal
  - 0=IRQ to CPU Disabled
  - 1=IRQ to CPU Enabled
- BIT 1 — sync clock (63.5 microseconds) Interrupt Input
  - 0=Flag set on the falling edge of HS
  - 1=Flag set on the rising edge of HS
- BIT 2 = Normally 1:   0=Changes FF00 to the data direction register
- BIT 3 = SEL 1:   LSB of the two analog MUX select lines
- BIT 4 = 1   Always
- BIT 5 = 1   Always
- BIT 6 =   Not Used
- BIT 7 =   Horizontal sync interrupt flag

FF02
- BIT 0= KEYBOARD COLUMN 1
- BIT 1= KEYBOARD COLUMN 2
- BIT 2= KEYBOARD COLUMN 3
- BIT 3= KEYBOARD COLUMN 4
- BIT 4= KEYBOARD COLUMN 5
- BIT 5= KEYBOARD COLUMN 6
- BIT 6= KEYBOARD COLUMN 7
- BIT 7= KEYBOARD COLUMN 8

FF03
- BIT 0 — Control of the field sync clock
  - 0= IRQ to CPU Disabled
  - 1= IRQ to CPU Enabled
- BIT 1 — 16.667 Ms Interrupt Input
  - 0= sets flag on falling edge FS
  - 1= sets flag on rising edge FS
- BIT 2 = NORMALLY 1:   0= changes FF02 to the data direction register
- BIT 3 = SEL 2:   MSB of the two analog MUX select lines
- BIT 4 = 1   Always
- BIT 5 = 1   Always
- BIT 6 =   Not Used
- BIT 7 =   Field sync interrupt flag

Fig. 16-6 The PIA memory map closeup shows they each have four addresses (courtesy of Radio Shack, a division of Tandy Corporation).

pret the probe results. For instance, U8 handles the input from the joysticks and the joystick action output to the video display. Pins 2 and 3 which are the data register As bits 0 and 1 are shown on the schematic as PA0 and PA1. These are the inputs for the joystick fire buttons. Pin 9 is the input for the joystick itself. If you probe these three pins they should be all highs. This is because they

```
FF20 – FF23              PIA      U4
```

```
        ⎧ BIT 0 = CASSETTE DATA INPUT
        ⎪ BIT 1 = RS-232 DATA OUTPUT
        ⎪ BIT 2 = 6 BIT D/A LSB
FF20   ⎨ BIT 3 = 6 BIT D/A
        ⎪ BIT 4 = 6 BIT D/A
        ⎪ BIT 5 = 6 BIT D/A
        ⎪ BIT 6 = 6 BIT D/A
        ⎩ BIT 7 = 6 BIT D/A MSB
```

```
        ⎧ BIT 0 ⎧ Control of the CD        ⎧ 0 = FIRQ to CPU Disabled
        ⎪       ⎨                          ⎪ 1 = FIRQ to CPU Enabled
        ⎪ BIT 1 ⎩ RS-232 status Input      ⎨ 0 = set flag on falling edge CD
        ⎪                                   ⎩ 1 = set flag on rising edge CD
        ⎪ BIT 2 = Normally 1:    0 = changes FF20 to the data direction register
FF21   ⎨ BIT 3 = Cassette Motor Control:    0 = OFF    1 = ON
        ⎪ BIT 4 = 1        Always
        ⎪ BIT 5 = 1        Always
        ⎪ BIT 6 =          Not Used
        ⎩ BIT 7 =          CD Interrupt Flag
```

```
        ⎧ BIT 0 = RS-232 DATA INPUT
        ⎪ BIT 1 = SINGLE BIT SOUND OUTPUT
        ⎪ BIT 2 = RAM SIZE INPUT      LOW = 4K      HIGH = 16K
FF22   ⎨ BIT 3 = VDG CONTROL OUTPUT                 CSS
        ⎪ BIT 4 = VDG CONTROL OUTPUT                 GM0 & INT/EXT
        ⎪ BIT 5 = VDG CONTROL OUTPUT                 GM1
        ⎪ BIT 6 = VDG CONTROL OUTPUT                 GM2
        ⎩ BIT 7 = VDG CONTROL OUTPUT                 A/G
```

```
        ⎧ BIT 0 ⎧ Control of the cartridge   ⎧ 0 = FIRQ to CPU Disabled
        ⎪       ⎨                            ⎪ 1 = FIRQ to CPU Enabled
        ⎪ BIT 1 ⎨ Interrupt                  ⎨ 0 = sets flag on falling edge CART
        ⎪       ⎩ Input                      ⎩ 1 = sets flag on rising edge CART
        ⎪ BIT 2 = Normally 1:    0 = changes FF22 to the data direction register
FF23   ⎨ BIT 3 = Six BIT Sound Enable
        ⎪ BIT 4 = 1  Always
        ⎪ BIT 5 = 1  Always
        ⎪ BIT 6 =    Not Used
        ⎩ BIT 7 =    Cartridge Interrupt Flag
```

```
FF40 – FFBF              NOT USED
```

are all held high, since they were configured as inputs. They will hold the high logic state while you are making the test. If they are not high then there could be a configuration problem. The PIA either can't be configured properly, which means a new one is needed, or the initialization process if not being completed properly. This indicates problems in the CPU-ROM circuits.

Table 16-1. The Logic Probe and a Service Chart Like This One Will Checkout the Status of a PIA Quickly.

Pin Number		High (1)	Low (0)	Pulse
KEYBOARD PIA SERVICE CHECKOUT CHART				
Ground	1			
PA0	2	✓		
PA1	3	✓		
PA2	4	✓		
PA3	5	✓		
PA4	6	✓		
PA5	7	✓		
PA6	8	✓		
PA7	9	✓		
PB0	10	✓		
PB1	11	✓		✓
PB2	12	✓		✓
PB3	13	✓		✓
PB4	14	✓		✓
PB5	15	✓		✓
PB6	16	✓		✓
PB7	17	✓		✓
CB1	18	✓		✓
CB2	19		✓	
Vcc	20	✓	✓	
R/W	21	✓		
CS0	22	✓		
•CS2	23	✓		
CS1	24	✓		✓
ENABLE	25			✓
D7	26			✓
D6	27			✓
D5	28			✓
D4	29			✓
D3	30			✓
D2	31			✓
D1	32			✓
D0	33			✓
•RESET	34	✓		
RS1	35			
RS2	36			✓
•IRQB	37	✓		✓
•IRQA	38	✓		✓
CA2	39		✓	✓
CA1	40	✓		✓

The output devices for the joystick is the video display circuits. The output bits that connect to the video circuits are in the CR. Pins 19 and 39 are CB2 and CA2. These two control lines can be used as an output port if it is not being used in a control line capacity. In this computer they are used as the joystick outputs. The two lines are capable of choosing from four joystick outputs. The schematic shows the two lines exiting U8 at pins 19 and 39 and going to an analog multiplexer. From there the signals developed by the joysticks are directed into the video circuits. If you probe pins 19 and 39 you are reading the two bit 3s of the two CRs. In this case the bit 3s are cleared so you get lows.

The next input to the PIA is the keyboard. The PA6-PA0 lines, which are pins 8-2 are connected directly to seven rows of keys. The PB7-PB0 lines, which are pins 17-10 are connected directly to the eight columns of keys. Yes, the two fire button inputs are also connected to pins 2 and 3. However, the two inputs to a single pin rarely are both activated at once, and even if they are, there is no real harm done.

The seven bits 0-6 in the A data register are configured as inputs during the initialization process. If you probe the pins you'll get all highs. In order to get the data register bits to act as an input or output, a 1 must be installed in each bit. If the high isn't there on one or more of the bits, that could be a sign of trouble. The PIA might be defective or the initialization process could have problems.

As long as the highs are all on their pins the A register is ready for I/O duty. In this case the job is inputting the information about the keyboard rows to the internal data bus of the computer. If a row is shorted because one of the keys were struck, that row is connected to a register pin and the pin receives the message.

There are seven rows in the keyboard. On each row there are eight columns. Each column is connected to a pin in register B. Register B is configured as an output. When a key is struck it not only has a row, it also has a column. If the number of the column struck can be included with the number of the row struck, then the character of that key can be coded. Each individual key has its own combination of row-column. For instance the character T is row 3 and column 5. When T is struck, the fact that it is row 3 is automatically sent to the I/O port PA2. How about the column information?

The columns are looked over continually with a strobe signal derived from the clock. The signal pulses from PB0 to PB7 continually. It is an output pulse from the PIA. It is of course moving many times faster than the fastest human typist can go. Every time a key is struck, the pulse is momentarily shorted and it is recorded on the column struck. The signal state of the struck column is combined with the signal state of row affected and the resultant put back into the computer through the I/O port.

When you probe the pins of the B register, you will get a high since the register is set to be an output. In addition the probe will reveal the strobe pulse on each pin. Both the high and the pulse must be there if the B register is set ok. If the signals are not there, a clue to trouble has been found.

In the control registers CA1 and CB1 are used as interrupts for the video signal. CA1 which is pin 40 and CB1, pin 19 are both connected to the clock output signals on the video display generator chip. CA1 is arranged to interrupt the video after each line, like a horizontal sync signal. CB1 is set to interrupt the video after each screen of data, like a vertical sync signal. There will be more about them in the video chapters. If you probe pins 40 and 18 you should get highs and pulses. On pin 18, which is the vertical sync, you could reach both a high and low along with the pulse. The interrupts are down around 60 Hz and both logic states could be picked up by the probe due to the low frequency.

There are two other interrupts, pins 37 and 38, *IRQB and *IRQA. They are tied together, held high and are pulsed from the CPU. Under normal conditions, they will remain in that condition. They will cause an interrupt during computer malfunction and shut down the PIA. Normally the probe should show them high with a pulse. If they are not, a trouble is occurring and requires further checking. It could be a short in the PIA chip at the pins.

The final eight pins of the 40-pin PIA are the data pins D7-D0 that connect to the data bus of the computer. They can send data back and forth to the

CPU and constantly have a clock pulse working in them. The logic probe if touched down on pins 26-33 will show pulses if the data bus and the pins are intact. If a pulse is not there it probably is not the PIA causing the trouble but is elsewhere in the data bus circuits.

A DIFFERENT PIA APPLICATION

The other PIA in the Color Computer is also an I/O Port but conducts its business in a different manner. It must output to the video display circuits, the audio output, the cassette recorder and the printer output. It has to take an input from the cassette player, and an input from an RS-232 input. In addition it can control the motor on the cassette and manipulate the input of a ROM cartridge if it is plugged into use. Besides all that it has a couple of interrupts like the other PIA.

The pinout numbers are, of course, the same on both MC6821 PIAs (Table 16-2) but the logic probe readings are not necessarily the same. In fact, in this case there are a lot of different results mixed in with readings that are identical. Let's compare the results on the two PIAs that sit side by side on the print board and note which ones are the same and which readings are different.

First of all, there is the addressing. The four addresses of the U8, the chip that was just discussed, is hex FF00-FF03. The address of U4 is FF20-FF23. The addresses represent the four registers in the PIA that are active during the time the computer runs programs.

In both U8 and U4 there are three chip select pins. They are CS1 and CS0, pins 24 and 22, tied together. They are attached to a high, and the probe reads high. The third chip select, *CS2 at pin 23 is held high and the probe will read a high. When U8 is selected pin 11 from the decoder U11 sends a low. That turns on U8. If U4 is to be selected, pin 10 of the decoder sends a low. As a result the probe shows the held high position as a static reading.

The actual probe test however, in addition to the high, shows a pulse on U8's *CS2 but no pulse on U4's *CS2. This means when U8 is turned on it is pulsed on. When U4 is activated it receives a static low that stays there while the chip is in action. To

the servicer, the fact that U8 has a probe show a high-pulse and U4 only a high, is the important thing. The difference must be noted, so the different readings on the same type chip, doesn't throw the troubleshooting routine procedure off track and waste a lot of time.

As the probing continues, pin 21s on both chips, the R/W lines are both held high and read highs. The E pulses on the 25 pins are both timing pulses and the probe will show a pulse. The data bus pin connections 26-33, D7-D0, are the same throughout the computer, all pulses, and the readings on the PIAs are no different. The register selects, RS1-RS0 are both connected to the timing pulsing and they usually read as pulses too. The power into all PIAs is the same, a high at pin 20 and a low at pin 1. *reset on pins 34 are both held high.

The rest of the pins can have a lot of differences according to the PIA application. In U8 pins 37 and 38 the *IRQA and *IRQB are both held high as the asterisk indicates, but they are also being pulsed. The same pins on U4 are held high but are not being pulsed. The probe will show the highs with a pulse on U8 and the highs without a pulse on U4. The servicer must be aware of the different type readings on the different chips with the same numbers. The same type of situation is found on the control lines CB1 and CA1. U8 has them held high with pulses, U4 has them held high without pulses. To further confuse the readings CB2 and CA2 are the same on both U8 and U4, both low.

The reason it is so important to realize the differences is due to a favorite technique a lot of servicers use. When two chips of the identical type are mounted near each other, comparing the readings on the same pins can often indicate where troubles can be hidden. The technique works best if you compare the readings of a defective computer, with the readings in a good computer of the same type. Be careful of comparing the readings of the same type chips doing different jobs.

CHECKING THE I/O BYTES

There are 16 more pins on the PIA, 2-17. They are the I/O ports. In the U8 checkout, they were all found to be held high. Two through nine are pro-

Table 16-2. Even Though Both PIAs are Physically Identical,
The Different Applications Cause Different Logic States to Appear on the Same Pin Numbers.

Pin Number		High (1)	Low (0)	Pulse
D/A-VDG PIA SERVICE CHECKOUT CHART				
Ground	1		✓	
PA0	2	✓		
PA1	3	✓		
PA2	4		✓	
PA3	5		✓	
PA4	6		✓	
PA5	7		✓	
PA6	8		✓	
PA7	9		✓	
PB0	10		✓	
PB1	11			
PB2	12	✓		
PB3	13	✓		
PB4	14	✓		
PB5	15	✓		
PB6	16	✓		
PB7	17	✓		
CB1	18	✓		
CB2	19		✓	
Vcc	20	✓		
R/W	21	✓		✓
CS0	22	✓		
*CS2	23	✓		
CS1	24	✓		
ENABLE	25			✓
D7	26			✓
D6	27			✓
D5	28			✓
D4	29			✓
D3	30			✓
D2	31			✓
D1	32			✓
D0	33			✓
*RESET	34	✓		
RS1	35			✓
RS2	36			✓
*IRQB	37	✓		
*IRQA	38	✓		
CA2	39		✓	
CA1	40	✓		

grammed as inputs and read highs without pulses. Ten through seventeen are programmed as outputs and read high with pulses as the strobe keeps a constant check on the keyboard functions. All the pins were doing keyboard and joystick jobs.In U4 pins 2-17 are being used to communicate with all the other peripherals in the system. The U4 probe readings are almost entirely different.

Pins 2 and 3 are connected to bits 0 and 1 of address FF20. This peripheral data register has the cassette data input coming into bit 0. The RS-232 data output is coming out of bit 1 and goes to the printer. Both pins are held high to perform their jobs. When you probe them a pair of highs indicate they are configured properly and are operative. These readings are the same as U8 has for its fire button and keyboard input duties, two highs.

Pins 4-9 are connected to bits 2-7 of FF20. When I say connected, I mean through chip components like latches and buffers, but these components are ignored since they can't be tested directly. The testing must be input-output reasonings based on what the probe says is present on the chip pins.

Pins 4-9 are all output and send out an audio output through a circuit called, the six bit digital to analog signal. This circuit is covered in the audio section in Chapter 18. The pins are connected to six buffers with bit 2 being the LS bit and bit 7 the MS bit. When pins 4-9 are probed they should all read lows if ok. If one or more reads high, pulse or nothing that could be an indication of trouble nearby, perhaps a shorted buffer or defective PIA. The pins 4-9 on U8 all were held high, exactly the opposite of 4-9 on U4.

The other PDR is connected to pins 10-17. Its address is FF22. Bit 0 on pin 10 is held low. It is the RS-232 data input port. While the printer takes the serial output of the computer through the single bit 0 of FF20, the computer can also take a serial input, from a teletype machine or another computer through bit 0 of FF22. Pin 10 is held low for the input duties. The probe should show a low during normal checks.

Pin 11 is connected to bit 1. The single bit sound source is connected to the repeated output of the sound circuit and is isolated from the D/A six-bit sound. It is covered in Chapter 18. The probe reads nothing when touched down on pin 11.

Pin 12 is an input for the memory size jumper. When it is probed it reads a high. Pins 13-17 are the VDG chip's input. That means they are outputs. They all probe out as lows.

The other two addresses in the PIA are registers that are used for control rather than I/O, although they can be used as ports too. To read the contents of FF21 and FF23 you can't go directly to a pin and read what is in a bit. The control registers eight bits are controlled by two control lines each CA1-CA2 and CB1-CB2, at pins 40-39 and 18-19. CA1 and CB1 are used as I/O ports and you can check bits 0 and 1 of the addresses through them. CA2 and CB2 are used in the same way and bits 3, 4, and 5 can be checked by means of them.

CA1, pin 40 which controls bits 0 and 1 of the A control register is an input in this computer. It receives a status interrupt pulsing signal called CD. The pin is held high and should read high-pulse on the probe. CA2, pin 39 controls bits 3, 4 and 5 of CRA. It is an output and is used to turn the cassette motor off and on. Pin 39 is held low when it is normal. If either of these pins are not reading properly, you have a symptom of trouble.

Line CB1, pin 18 is the cartridge interrupt input. When the ROM cartridge is plugged in, pin 19, bits 0 and 1 of CRB are changed and this sets *IRQB, pin 37. Pin 37 and 38 are tied together and go to *FIRQ on the CPU. The CPU then interrupts the internal ROM that was in control and gives control to the cartridge ROM.

Line CB2, pin 19 is the control line for the sound output. It can turn the sound on and off. This will be covered in Chapter 18. When you probe pins 18 and 19 they should read high-low-pulse for 18 and low for 19.

THE CHIP PIN CHART

If any of you are TV, Radio, or any type of electronic technician, you are familiar with resistance and voltage charts that are found in service notes. For example, a tube voltage chart will list all the vacuum tubes in the gear on the left side and the pin numbers of the tubes across the top. Then the voltages that are found under normal operation are marked into the blocks of the chart. If a repair is tough, you take out the voltage chart and begin testing the voltages one by one. When an incorrect voltage is found, you have a clue. The clue could be indicative of the trouble or just a false lead. Either way you follow the lead till you uncover the trouble or conclude the lead is false. The charts are valuable servicing aids.

Using these charts are fairly easy and saves a lot of reasoning time. It is not really necessary that you know whether you are reading a cathode, grid, or plate. It is only necessary to compare the voltage on the test point with the called for voltage on the chart. In a similar way, if you had a chart of all test points on the computer board, the same type of testing could be done.

Instead of voltage or resistance charts, a logic probe chart would be more effective. Highs, lows, and pulses are the tests that should be made. Every chip has test nodes available. All you would have to do is carefully test pin after pin and check the probe results against the called for results. When a discrepancy is found, it could be a valid clue to the trouble.

Some manufacturers might provide some charts of this nature. I haven't seen very many. However, you could prepare your own charts like the ones in the illustrations. If you are repairing a lot of computers, especially the same models over and over again, the preparation is easy. Simply take a known good computer and do the charts.

If you are only going to be repairing your own computer, do the charts while the computer is operating properly. Then if it ever goes down, your service notes will tell you what type of signals should be present when the computer is normal.

Chapter 17

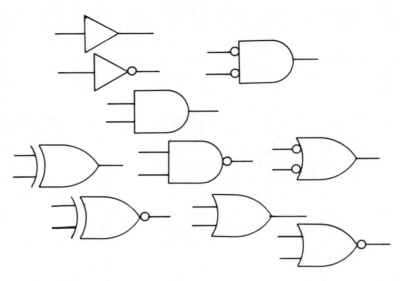

The Video Display Generator

As you type into a computer, the characters you strike appear on the TV screen. It seems instantaneous but we all know that a lot of complex electronic digital and analog processing takes place between the time you hit the key and the appearance of the character. The heart of all circuitry, between the keyboard and the TV monitor is the video display generator, known as the VDG (Fig. 17-1). The VDG is the chip that takes the video that is coded in digital and converts it to analog signals that the picture tube can display.

TYPICAL VDG INPUTS

If you look at the block diagram of the computer (Fig. 8-10) the VDG is seen to receive two major inputs. One is from the PIA and the other is the video RAM. The schematic of the Color Computer shows a lot more lines attached to VDG pins that are bringing in digital signals. Then, of course, there is the +5 V and ground return to power the chip (Fig. 17-2).

The system clock sends a 3.579545 MHz square wave into pin 33. For those of you who are

familiar with color TV, you will recognize the color oscillator signal. This is derived from the crystal oscillator frequency and is used to help build the composite color TV signal that will be the final output of the computer. With a sensitive expensive scope you could look at the signal, but the logic probe will read dead on pin 33 (Table 17-1).

The VDG clock signal enters pin 33 as an input, but also is inserted into the next stage, the video mixer chip at its pin 2. There is a bypass capacitor, 56 pF in the line.

At pin 22 there is a line called DA0. It operates with the 3.58 MHz color signal and helps keep the color in sync. If you probe that test node, the results will be a high-low-pulse as the activity keeps the probe lit.

The PIA U4 has 5 lines from its address FF22. The 5 lines are coming from bits 3-7 out of the pins 13-17. These are the lines that set up the display modes of the VDG. The modes are what the VDG is all about. The VDG in this computer has the ability to set up 16 modes. What is a display mode? We'll discuss that in the next section. Meanwhile, the five

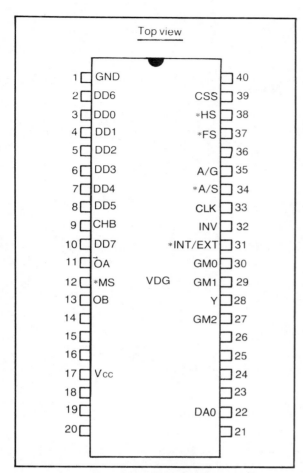

Fig. 17-1. The VDG chip contains a lot of ROM circuits that change the digital inputs to alphanumeric, semigraphic, and pure graphic video outputs.

PIA lines attach to six VDG pins. One line connects to two pins 30 and 31, * int/ext, and GMo. This line selects a mode called semigraphic 6. A probe of the line shows a low. Doublechecking with the vom reveals the low is about 0.5 V not 0 V, which means it is active not dead.

The next two lines are called GM1 and GM2. They operate with GM0 and are able to select one of eight modes. They are on pins 29 and 27, and the probe shows them as lows too. Another line at pin 35, A/G, selects between alpha-semigraphics and full graphic modes. It probes low too. The fifth line CSS also probes low.

While the VDG inputs from the PIA are there to set up modes, there is another group of lines that are coming from the video RAM. These lines are latched in this computer because the video RAM is not latched. Latch or not, the lines from the video RAM are data lines and are bringing data to the VDG. While the various modes set up the way the TV tube is to display the picture, the data is the information that is going to be in the picture (Fig. 17-3).

The data enters the VDG through the latch and is processed in the VDG. The data is changed from binary bits to analog signals that will turn light dots on and off in the display. The data enters lines DD7-DD0. In this computer, pin 32 is connected to DD6 and pin 34 is connected to DD7. These connections aid in the mode making. Pin 34 is called INV and pin 34 is *A/S. These will be covered in the next section. If you probe any of the DD lines a low-pulse result will be found if there aren't any troubles there.

VDG CHARACTER SET

The most used mode of the computer is called the alphanumeric inverted mode (Fig. 17-3). All that means is a black character is on a light background. It is the normal mode that appears when a computer is turned on (Fig. 17-4). It is called inverted because the picture tube is made to have a black background and then light will appear on the screen. This is the opposite of that arrangement. However, there is a second mode called alphanumeric non-inverted (Fig. 17-5) which does use the black background with light characters. This mode is useful and can be employed to show the difference between capital letters and lowercase. The non-inverted can display caps while the inverted can designate lower case.

Inside the VDG is a circuit called a character generator. It was mentioned earlier in the book that the computer display area in the color computer is composed of 512 blocks. There are 32 blocks on a row and 16 rows. Each block is able to display one character. The characters can be in the inverted mode or the non-inverted mode.

Each block is in turn made up of 96 tiny blocks

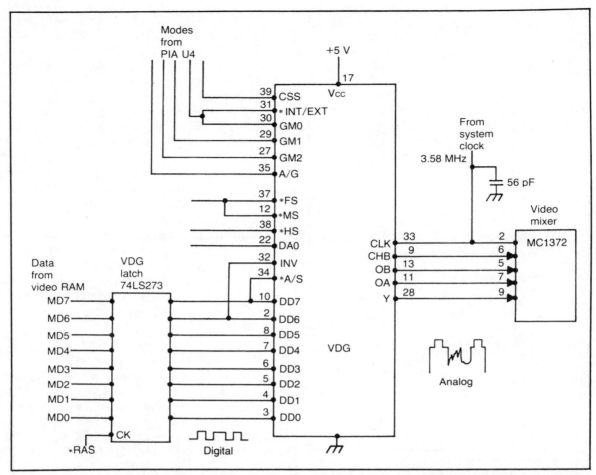

Fig. 17-2. The schematic drawing of the VDG chip shows the inputs from a PIA and video RAM to the output that goes to a video mixer.

called picture elements. These 96 blocks called pixels, which is short for picture elements, are arranged eight to a row and there are 12 rows of them (Fig. 17-4). The pixels can be lit or dark. The character generator is able to turn them on or off in that way.

In each character block the character generator operates on 35 of the 96 pixels. The 35 operating pixels are a group made up of a section of five pixels across and seven down. This leaves a buffer area of two pixels on the top, three on the bottom, one on the left and two on the right.

The character generator is able to turn the 35 operating pixels off and on. The result of this is the ability to form all the letters of the alphabet, numbers from 0 to 9 and all the other characters found on the computer keyboard. The character generator receives the data that tells the generator what character to display in a block, from the data lines DD7-DD0. The data lines feed the character generator eight binary bits. The generator circuits are built to decode these bits and convert them to the characters they represent.

VIDEO RAM INVOLVEMENT

The data that enters the VDG is coming from the video RAM. Video RAM is just ordinary RAM except it is reserved for the video display duty. In

260

		VDG			
					SERVICE CHECKOUT CHART
Pin Numbers		Logic Probe	Pin Numbers		Logic Probe
1	GND	Low	39	CSS	Low
2	DD6	Pulse	38	*HS	Low-Pulse
3	DD0	Low-Pulse	37	*FS	Hi-Low-Pulse
4	DD1	Low-Pulse	35	A/G	Low
5	DD2	Low-Pulse	34	*A/S	Low-Pulse
6	DD3	Low-Pulse	33	CLK	Nothing
7	DD4	Low-Pulse	32	INV	Pulse
8	DD5	Low-Pulse	31	*INT/EXT	Low
9	CHB	Nothing	30	GM0	Low
10	DD7	Low-Pulse	29	GM1	Low
11	0A	Low	28	Y	Scope (Very Weak)
12	*MS	Hi-Low-Pulse	27	GM2	Low
13	0B	Low			
17	Vcc	High	22	DA0	Hi-Low-Pulse

this computer there are 512 locations reserved for the alphanumeric mode. Location 1024 in decimal is the start of the RAM and 1536 is the end. Location 1024 corresponds with the upper left-hand block on the screen, while 1536 is the last lower right hand block.

Each location in RAM is able to hold the binary code for one character. The coding is called ASCII for *American Standard Code for Information Interchange*. These tables show an ASCII code modification for these inverted and non-inverted modes. The non-inverted modes are usually used as capitals and the inverted mode is lowercase when capitals are used. Note the non-inverted mode uses decimal numbers 0 to 63. The inverted mode uses decimal 64 to 127 (Tables 8-1, 8-2, and 8-3).

In binary, 0 to 63 is 00000000 to 00111111.

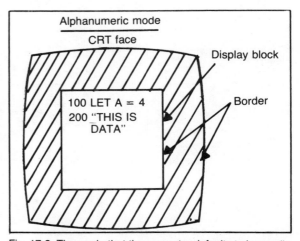

Fig. 17-3. The mode that the computer defaults to is usually alphanumeric. (The term "default" means the state the computer assumes automatically as it comes on.)

261

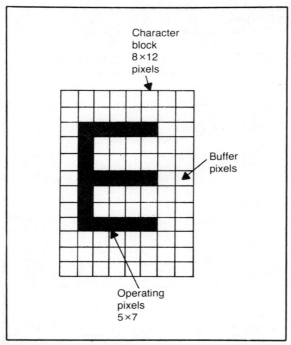

Fig. 17-4. In the alphanumeric mode the space a character occupies on the screen can be composed of 96 pixels (picture elements) arranged in this fashion. A character generator ROM in the VDG is able to turn each pixel off and on to create the characters.

Sixty-four to 127 is 01000000 to 01111111. The character generator is constructed to show light characters on a black background when the bits 7 and 6 are both clear. The character generator displays black characters on a light background when only bit 7 is clear.

Video RAM holds the binary code for the 512 blocks that are displayed on the TV screen. Video RAM is strobed by the address lines out of SAM. The strobing is synced in with the TV sweep. As the picture is scanned horizontally and vertically, the address lines strobe the video RAM. This places the binary data into the character generator as the cathode ray is passing across the block the data is put in. That is how the character appears on the TV screen in the alphanumeric modes.

There is exactly one character position on the screen for one 8-bit memory location in video RAM. As you hit a key, the computer forms the ASCII code for the character and sends it to video RAM. As long as you see the character on the screen, it is still in video RAM. Should the screen be filled and the character is moved up and out of view, the character is no longer in video RAM, but stored somewhere else in a RAM location. The video RAM is like a window that shows you what is inside. You

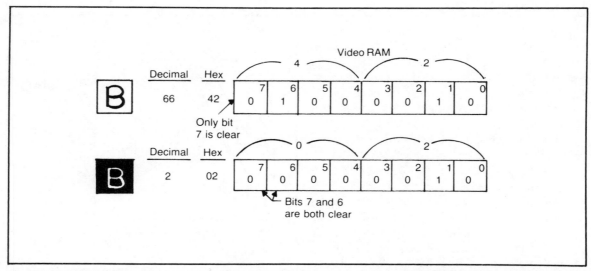

Fig. 17-5. The video RAM sends a byte to the character generator ROM. The code tells the ROM what character to display and what color background should be shown. If only bit 7 is clear the character is dark on a light background. When the byte has both bits 7 and 6 clear then the character is light on a dark background.

see the character that has been coded from the ASCII input.

THE OTHER MODES

There are two other types of modes besides alphanumerics. They are called semigraphics and true graphics.

THE SEMIGRAPHIC MODE

The inverted and non-inverted alphanumeric modes display ASCII characters. They are only two of many possible ways the TV screen is used. A second important set of modes is semigraphics. These modes are a form of graphics but not the pure form. Semigraphics, as the name implies, are a cross between alphanumerics and true graphics. There are five types of semigraphics available in this VDG. There are generator circuits in the VDG that can take the bits in the video RAM locations and produce different mode semigraphics on the screen, just as the alphanumeric character generator did.

With two of the semigraphic modes there are still only 512 video RAM locations. These locations match up with the 512 blocks on the TV face. The blocks are still composed of 8 by 12 pixels. There are two major differences. One, all of the 96 pixels are used to form the semigraphics, not 35 with a buffer around the group. Two, in a color computer,

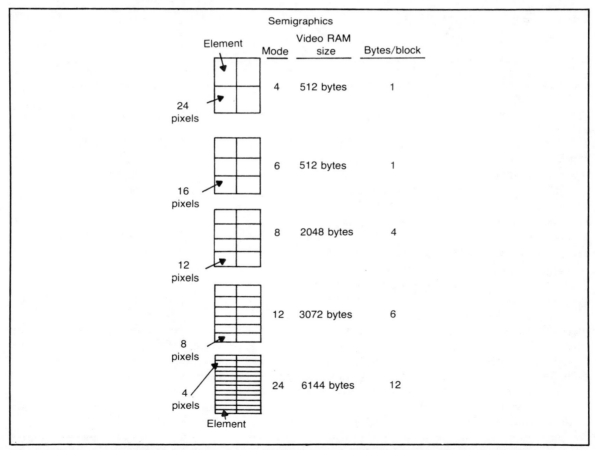

Fig. 17-6. The various semigraphic modes available in this VDG use the same size 96 pixel character block as alphanumerics but arrange the pixels differently. Also, these modes can change colors in a color computer.

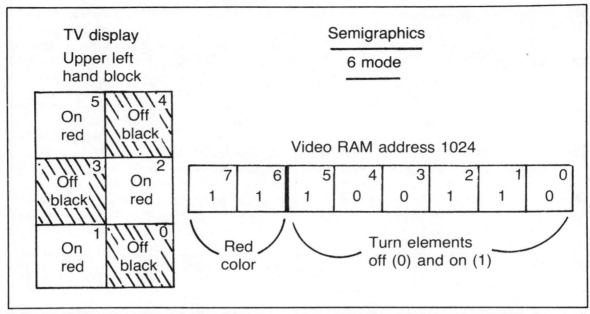

Fig. 17-7. In this semigraphic 6 mode the video RAM byte can choose a display color with bits 7 and 6, and turn the elements off and on with the other bits. Note how the bits 5-0 in the memory byte correspond with the 6 display elements.

colors are used besides the monochrome of light and black.

There are five semigraphic modes available in this VDG (Fig. 17-6). They are called 4, 6, 8, 12, and 24. The reason for the names is the way the pixel blocks are divided. All of the modes divide the blocks in half vertically. That is, the eight pixel wide block is divided into two sides that are four pixels wide each. Then the 4 mode has the two sides divided into 4 elements of 24 pixels each. The 6 mode divides the total block into 6 elements of 16 pixels each. The 8 mode divides the block into 8 elements of 12 pixels each. The 12 mode divides the block into 12 blocks of 8 pixels each, and the 24 mode divides the block into 24 blocks of 4 pixels each.

In each mode, the VDG circuits are able to turn each element, not each pixel, off and on. For example, suppose you were in the 6 mode. This activates the VDG circuit that divides the 512 blocks on the screen into 6 elements. There are a lot of designs you can arrange with this mode. What you decide to do is make the upper left-hand block look like a piece of a red and black checkerboard. With the 6

mode you can turn three elements in the block on and three off (Fig. 17-7).

Since the block corresponds with video RAM location 1024 you poke the following bits into that location. In the 6 mode six bits are used to do the job. The VDG is able to control the six element blocks with bits 5, 4, 3, 2, 1, and 0. The six bits are arranged 100110. The 1s turn on the elements and the 0s turn them off. This will produce the checkerboard effect.

There are two bits left in the memory byte, bits 7 and 6. Since two bits can form four combinations, these two bits can choose from four colors. The colors in this VDG that can be chosen are green 00, yellow 01, blue 10, and red 11. If these two bits are added to address 1024 then the byte will define a checkerboard pattern in a desired color. If you want a red and black pattern then the byte will be 11100110.

The 8, 12, and 24 element semigraphics can't make it with only the 512 locations in video RAM. The 8 mode needs four bytes of memory to control the 8 elements. It can't do the job with one byte. This means the TV screen requires 4 times 512

RAM locations, which is 2048 bytes of RAM. In turn the 12 mode needs six bytes per pixel block and the 24 mode requires 12 bytes to turn the colors off and on. This means the 12 mode uses 3072 bytes of RAM and the 24 mode a large 6144 bytes.

The alphanumeric and semigraphic modes work inside the 8 × 12 pixel character boxes. The alphanumerics occupy the center of the box with a buffer of pixels surrounding the formed character. The semigraphics use the entire 8 × 12 box to show the various graphic forms.

The alphanumerics and the semigraphic modes 4 and 6 use 512 bytes of memory to display the 512 character boxes on the TV face in this computer. Other computers could have a different number of character boxes on display. The 512 bytes here start with decimal addresses 1024 and go to 1535. Addresses 1024-1535 are called the video memory. They are also called the text screen. It is said that alphanumerics and semigraphic models 4 and 6 occupy the text screen.

On the memory map, the addresses above the text screen starting at 1536 can also be used as video memory. The VDG arranges the correct wiring when a mode is selected that needs more than 512 bytes to handle the video display chore. In semigraphic modes 8, 12 and 24, 2048, 3072, and 6144 bytes are needed to be video memory.

PURE GRAPHICS

When the VDG is made to form pure graphics, it dispenses with the 8 × 12 character box. The 512 boxes are all blurred into one large box. The eight different graphic modes all use the same display but change the number of pixels in each display (Fig. 17-8). In the crudest mode there are 4096 large pixels. That number is the result of a display that is 64 pixels across by 64 down. This display produces the thickest lines and the picture with the worst resolution. The finest mode has 49152 tiny pixels. This display has 256 across and 192 down. This display produces the finest resolution. The rest of the graphic modes lie somewhere in between. There is also a 128 × 64, a 128 × 96, and a 128 × 192. Each display type can choose to be a two or four color. With four display types, each able to be

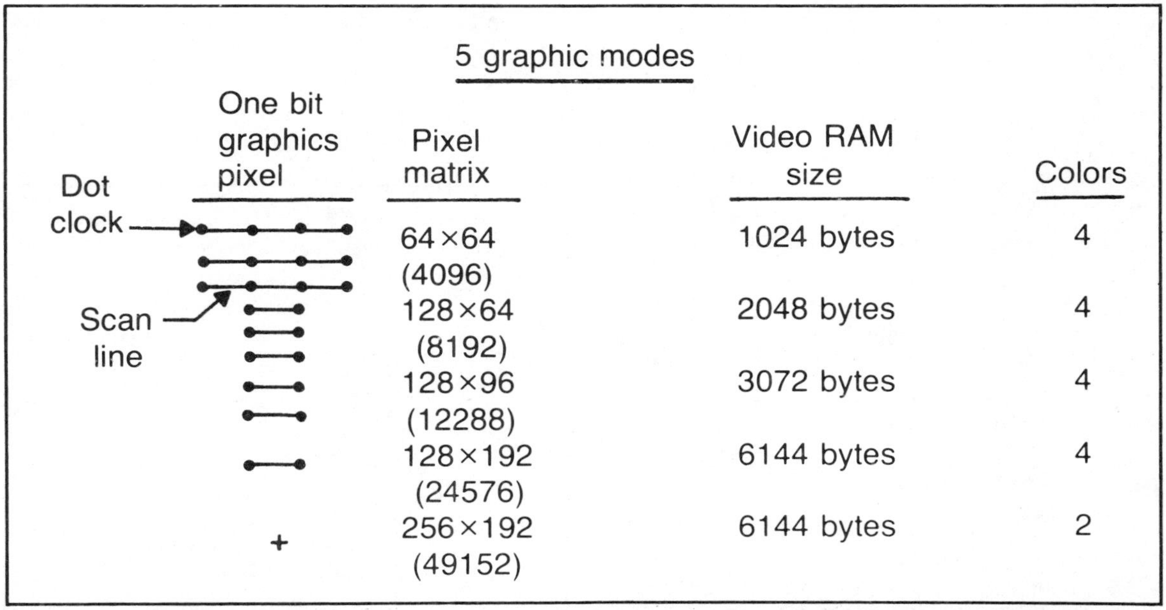

	One bit graphics pixel	Pixel matrix	Video RAM size	Colors
	5 graphic modes			
Dot clock		64×64 (4096)	1024 bytes	4
Scan line		128×64 (8192)	2048 bytes	4
		128×96 (12288)	3072 bytes	4
		128×192 (24576)	6144 bytes	4
+		256×192 (49152)	6144 bytes	2

Fig. 17-8. The pure graphic mode does not use the 96 pixel character block. It uses a matrix of individual pixels. In the matrix with the fewest pixels, 64 × 64, the picture has the crudest resolution since the pixels are large, with four dot clocks by three scan lines. In the matrix with the most pixels, 256 × 192, the picture has the finest resolution since the pixels are tiny, with only one dot clock by one scan line.

two or four colors, there are eight graphic modes available from this VDG.

With the eight graphic modes comes a choice of one of two color borders. Pin 39 CSS can be set or cleared. With CSS a high, one color border and four display colors are chosen. With CSS a low, another color border and the other four display colors are chosen.

The pixels in a graphic are thick or thin according to the resolution desired. A pixel is composed of two components. One is called a dot clock, the other is a scan line (Fig. 17-9). The dot clock is a spot on the TV screen. This special dot occurs during one half the period of the 3.58 MHz color signal. Each beat of the color oscillator produces dot clocks. This important timing is the key to the accuracy of the graphic display.

The other component is the scan line. The picture tube is being scanned by the CRT electron beam, one line beneath the preceding line. The scan lines produce line after line of dot clocks. In the finest resolution mode, a pixel consists of the tiniest element, one dot clock on one scan line. The crudest resolution mode has pixels that consist of four dot clocks by three scan lines.

The graphic modes have the ability to turn a pixel off and on. The modes also can make a pixel one of four colors. By being able to turn the pixels on and off, and also change each pixel's color, the mode is able to form pictures by filling the video memory with bits.

In the alphanumeric mode, one byte corresponded with one character. With the finest graphic mode, one bit corresponds with one dot clock, when only two colors are being displayed. Two bits correspond with one dot clock when four colors are being shown. Some of the possible graphic modes the VDG can produce are in Fig. 17-8.

THE VDG VIDEO OUTPUT

The VDG and the video memory along with the help of the other chips that set the modes in the VDG produce the various parts of the composite TV signal that is to be displayed. The signal is quite like the signal a TV station makes to send out over the airwaves. In this VDG there are seven output pins

that contain these parts of the total composite. These outputs are not digital. The VDG is a place in the computer where the digital signals are changed to analog. At the VDG output pins, old tried and true analog test methods can be used. An ordinary inexpensive service scope can pick up the analog output if they are there.

At pin 28 (Fig. 17-2) the Y signal, a composite video-sync signal can be found. The signal is weak, only about 1 volt peak to peak, but it is present (Fig. 17-10). The signal has sync peaks, blanking level, and black level. The video signal it contains is information on turning pixels on and off. There are four levels of brightness for the display.

At pin 11 is a three level analog signal called 0A. It is combined in the next stages with the Y signal and helps the Y signal to display one of eight colors. At pin 13 there is another signal called 0B. It is like 0A except it is a four level signal that helps Y and 0A specify one of eight colors. In addition 0B uses one level to time the color burst signal properly. Pin 9 is a color dc reference level to keep the signals tracking during variations in temperature.

The signals at pins 37 and 38 are the field sync, FS∗, and horizontal sync, HS∗. Field sync is vertical sync. The Y signal, 0A, 0B, FS∗, and HS∗ can all be viewed on the scope. They should look somewhat like the patterns in the illustrations. Pin 9 uses a dc low voltage and the scope will show nothing.

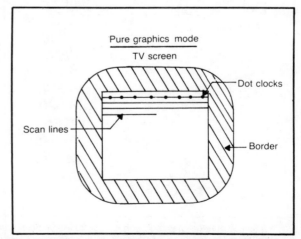

Fig. 17-9. The pure graphic modes use dot clocks, scan lines, and border color changes.

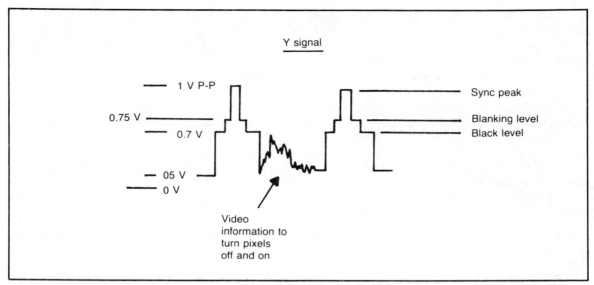

Y signal

1 V P-P

0.75 V

0.7 V

05 V

0 V

Sync peak

Blanking level

Black level

Video
information to
turn pixels
off and on

Fig. 17-10. The Y signal is nothing more than a black and white TV signal. It is weak but can be seen on an ordinary TV service scope.

CHECKING OUT THE VDG

During bouts of video troubles the VDG can be checked out with some input-output tests. The inputs respond well to the logic probe. The outputs show up nicely on the scope face (Table 17-1).

If you use the logic probe on the output pins, the probe will read highs, lows, and pulses. These indications though are meaningless as far as troubleshooting goes. Also you could test the input pins with the scope probe. You will see all sorts of video and spike waveshapes. Again, from a troubleshooting point of view, the results have no meaning. The input digital signals are best tested with a logic probe and the output analog waveshapes have meaning when seen on the scope.

If you are curious and start reading the unused pins on the VDG chip, with the logic probe and scope, lo and behold, there will be highs, lows, pulses, and scope waveforms. This is because during manufacturing all sorts of connections are made because connecting equipment is geared up that way. If the schematic doesn't show the connection though, ignore the findings. They have no use in the computer you are troubleshooting.

The way to test the chip is to have a chart like Table 17-1, that shows what should be on the pins when the computer is working normally. Then when the video trouble occurs, test each active pin and look for an abnormal condition. When one is found, that is a clue that could lead you to the trouble.

THE VDG OUTPUT

Once the VDG chip produces the Y signal, the rest of the video circuitry is nothing more than a form of television receiver. If the computer is a monochrome type the circuitry for the display shows a Y signal in light and dark. When the computer is a color type, like the one we have been discussing, then a color TV is needed to produce the alphanumerics or graphics.

In this computer, the VDG chip outputs four signals to produce a color display. The signals, Y, 0A, 0B and CHB are all sent to a typical color TV mixer chip (Fig. 17-11). The four signals enter at pins 9, 7, 5, and 6. The color clock signal also enters the chip at pin 2. The four signals are combined in the chip to make a wave shape that is color video with the color burst added. This signal emerges from pin 8 and is immediately ac coupled to pin 10 through a .01 capacitor. A 750 ohm resistor sets the *luminance to chrominance ratio*.

The composite color TV signal exits at pin 12. If you view it on the scope it looks exactly like a transmitted TV picture only it will display computer developed alphanumerics or graphics, not motion pictures. It can only show the digital bits that are in the video memory.

The composite video at this point though is actually too weak to display anything. It must be amplified. The amplification is accomplished with a conventional TV video amplifier transistor stage. The schematic shows such an amplifier based around transistor Q1.

Q1 is an npn configured to produce current gain. The video output is taken at the emitter and coupled directly into pin 1 of the rf modulator. There is a good strong video signal coming out of Q1 and it could also be coupled into a video monitor instead of the rf modulator. Both schemes are common in small computers (Fig. 17-12).

With the ordinary scope, you can trace the video signals from the output of the VDG to the input of an rf modulator or video monitor. The four signals leaving the VDG are weak. As they enter the video mixer chip, they do not get any stronger, but they are combined into one signal that emerges from pin 12. The other two pins 13 and 14, in this particular chip, usually do the job of being an rf oscillator when the chip is used in a TV receiver.

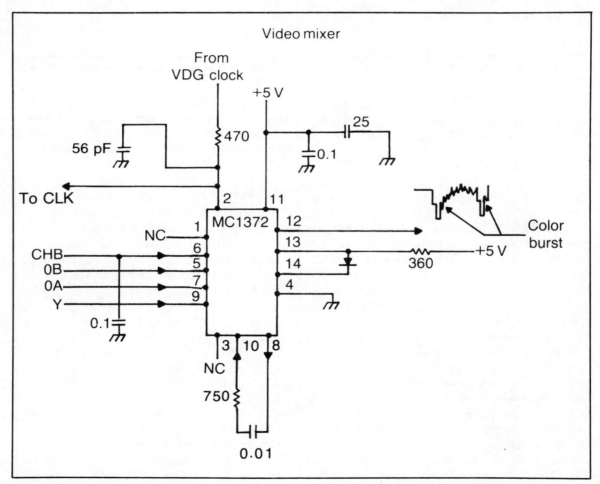

Fig. 17-11. The video mixer chip is also a TV product. Normal analog service tests are used to troubleshoot it.

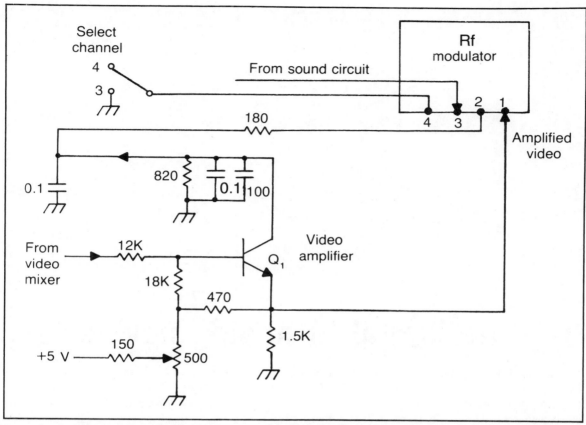

Fig. 17-12. The video mixer amplifies its output in a video amplifier before inserting the signal into the rf modulator.

The rf oscillator is not needed in the computer, since the clock takes care of all the timing duties. Therefore these two pins get a diode and resistor installed to dampen any attempt of the tank to start oscillating.

During servicing you must be careful with these extraneous type circuits. There are lots of circuits in chips that are not used at all in a particular computer design. These circuits do not cost extra, they just exist in the chips. It is often cheaper during design and manufacturing to purchase chips, off the shelf, with lots of extra circuits and not use the extras, than to have a special chip made to do a job. This mixer chip from TV design is a good example. Pin 1 is left with no connection to an oscillator that will never be used in this computer. Also pins 13 and 14 must have a diode and resistor installed, and all the components do is stop the rf tank from running. Not only is the tank not working, but the expense of the two extra components must be borne. Be careful of these extra circuits. They could lead you on a troubleshooting wild goose chase.

The video signal leaves pin 12 of the mixer chip and goes into a voltage divider in the base of Q1 (Fig. 17-12). The scope can still follow the video into the base and out at the top of the emitter resistor. The last place the scope will help in this circuit is at the input of the rf modulator. The video signal will be there. Once into the modulator the video gets installed onto a TV channel 3 or 4 carrier wave and the ordinary scope can't display the signal. If the video output signal is applied to a video monitor, the scope can troubleshoot the monitor.

Chapter 18

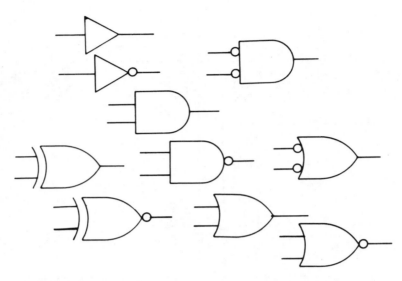

The Digital to Analog Devices

Any input to a computer must be in the form of binary numbers. The computer doesn't understand anything else. When the computer outputs, the output is also in the form of the same binary numbers. In the real world the binary numbers are meaningless. The world uses values like voltage and positions of switches and shafts. The binary numbers are of course, digital. Voltages, positions of switches and shafts, among other things, are analog values. They are not simply 1s and 0s with nothing in between. The voltages can have many values between 1 and 0. Shafts can have many positions between horizontal and vertical.

In order for a computer to perform analog jobs, the digital outputs must be converted to analog values. The circuits that perform the conversion are aptly called digital-to-analog converters. Conversely, any circuits that change analog to digital numbers are called analog-to-digital converters. Most home computers use both the D/A converters and the A/D converter. Actually the same circuitry can do both jobs. All that is needed is to reverse the direction of signal flow.

The VDG is a digital to analog device but is not the ordinary type. Since the VDG has to convert digital numbers to the complex analog composite color TV signal, it is a very complicated device. Most computer D/A circuits are really simple in comparison to the VDG. Typical examples of ordinary D/A circuits are computer audio and joystick devices.

COMPUTER AUDIO

There are a number of audio sources in the computer. One of the most familiar noises is the blasting of space craft that emanates continually from electronic arcades. This is computer sounds that are made by outputting an array of six voltage levels.

In one of the PIAs we discussed at address FF20 the six MSBs are called the 6-bit sound output (Fig. 18-1). They exit the PIA at pins 4-9 which are PA7-PA2. When they exit they go directly to a set of buffers. In the buffers the six logic states are impedance matched to the output analog circuitry. The output circuit begins with a voltage divider

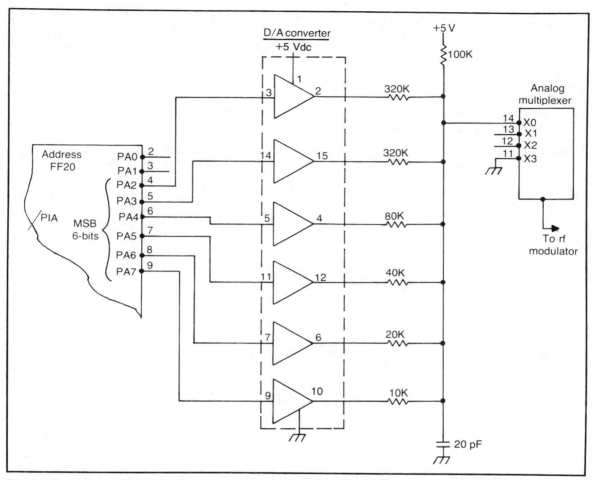

Fig. 18-1. The typical home computer D/A converter can be a set of buffers connected to a voltage divider. The bits leave the computer world, pass through the buffers and develop a voltage that is representative of the arrangement of the bits.

consisting of six series resistors and a 100 k parallel resistor in series with a 20 pF filter capacitor.

All the resistors are tied together and held high by +5 V on the far side of the 100 k. When all six bits are in a high state (111111), the resultant output voltage is near +5 V at +4.75 V. If all six bits are in a low state (000000), the resultant output voltage drops to near ground and measures at +0.25 V. There are 64 possible bit combinations so there are 64 possible voltage levels available to be developed in the voltage divider circuit. Each voltage can be converted into a different sound tone.

The resultant voltage is injected into pin 14 of the analog multiplexer. There the six-bit voltage is joined by other sound voltages. The job of the multiplexer is to choose from among the various audio voltages in the computer. In addition to the six-bit sound tones that are developed from the PIA, there is audio developed in the cassette, the ROM cartridges and a single-bit sound source.

The cassette can be holding audio signals. The cassette input is injected from a cassette input circuit to pin 12 of the analog multiplexer. The cassette has to have the input voltage given an average voltage of +2.5 V, and range between zero and +5 V, to operate correctly in the multiplexer. This is accomplished in a small matching network of a non-polarized capacitor and some resistors.

The cartridge ROM input is attached to pin 13 of the multiplexer. The signal comes directly from the ROM where it is originally designed to match the computer's audio circuit.

The last sound input, in the example circuit is called the single-bit sound source. The single bit, which produces a ray gun sound, is not attached to the multiplexer input. It is connected to the chip's output through an isolation 10k resistor. When the single bit sound is used, a select signal turns the multiplexer off. That way, none of the other sounds can interfere with the single bit.

Figure 18-2 shows how one of the sound sources can be chosen to the exclusion of the other

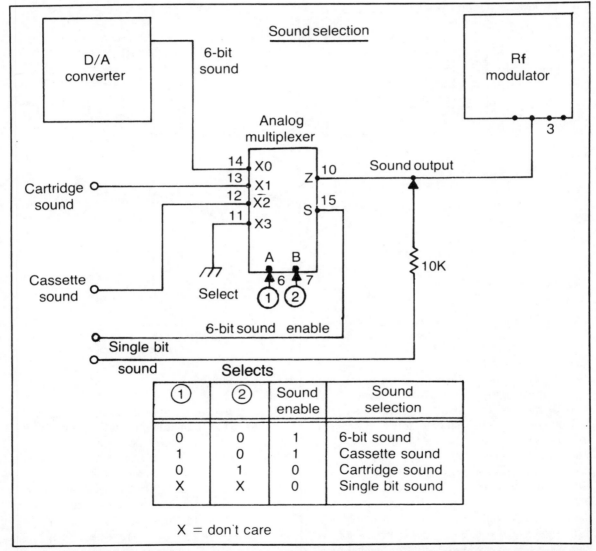

①	②	Sound enable	Sound selection
0	0	1	6-bit sound
1	0	1	Cassette sound
0	1	0	Cartridge sound
X	X	0	Single bit sound

X = don't care

Fig. 18-2. An analog multiplexer is able to receive the various audio outputs and with the aid of two select pins and an enable, choose one of the outputs for use.

three. There are two sound select pins and a sound enable pin. With three such pins it is easy to choose one out of four sound modes. Once chosen, the selected audio is attached to pin 3 of the rf modulator. In the modulator the sound is converted to the 4.5 MHz TV FM signal that can be used by the TV acting as the monitor.

CHECKING OUT THE SOUND CIRCUIT

On occasion the sound will quit. When that happens the sound circuit must be checked out to locate the defect. The first step is to analyze the symptoms closely. In the typical sound circuit like the one we have been discussing there could be four separate sound sources that all feed into the audio circuits. Each sound source must be exercised. If one of the sources cannot produce its own individual type of audio, then the trouble is indicated to be in the source circuits. Should all four sources fail to sound off, then the trouble is more likely to be in the output circuits that all four sources have in common.

The first audio type is the 6-bit sound. In lots of home computers there is, as was mentioned earlier, a diagnostic program that can be installed in the computer. More than likely the diagnostics will have an exercise for the 6-bit sound. All you have to do on my exerciser is press S on the keyboard, and the program puts a sine wave through the 6-bit sound circuit. The low to high sound frequencies then emanate from the TV speaker when the 6-bit D/A circuit is good. Immediately after the sine wave my exerciser puts out a short duration high frequency pulse that exercises the single-bit sound too. When these two audio signals are heard normally, then the two circuits are exonerated as troublemakers. Should one of them not perform then the circuit is indicated as containing a defect.

If you do not have an exerciser, then you could use a program line in the resident language of the computer. The actual line you would originate would depend on the computer you were working on. If the computer has BASIC as its language a typical line could be SOUND 250,10: SOUND 125,10: SOUND 25,10. This would test the 6-bit sound by running three tones, one high, one me-

dium and one low. If they sounded off the circuit is probably ok.

The cartridge and cassette audio circuits can be exercised by simply trying a cartridge with sound and a cassette tape with sound. If they work then their circuits are ok. If one doesn't operate then you have pinpointed a possible bad circuit.

Once the ailing circuit is found then the circuit must be analyzed using the logic probe in the digital sections and the vom in the analog areas. For instance, if the 6-bit sound is deemed inoperative, the trouble is indicated to be somewhere between the PIA output pins 4-9 and pin 14 of the analog multiplexer. The vom can test the +5 V input, the resistors in the voltage divider, and the 20 pF capacitor. The logic probe can check out the hex buffer chip. The trouble should be located among those components.

The other three sound sources can also be tested individually. The cartridge input on pin 13 comes directly from the cartridge through the cartridge 40-pin connector. Either the connector or the cartridge contains a trouble if the cartridge won't make its usual noises.

The cassette input comes through an analog circuit consisting of a non-polarized capacitor and some adjoining resistors and a capacitor. In addition there is a connection to a comparator circuit. All of these components could possibly be causing trouble and are covered in Chapter 19 in the Cassette section.

When the entire sound section is down, and the TV is completely silent, the trouble is where all the audio types travel together. The analog multiplexer is suspect. The two selects and the enable are also to be tested.

THE JOYSTICK INTERFACE

The popular joystick circuit, that is the electronic game player's delight, is a device that is able to change the position of a shaft into a voltage. As you move the spaceships across the TV screen, the joystick is varying a voltage. This voltage is then injected into an analog to digital circuit and the voltage levels are changed to binary bits. The bits are sent into a PIA address and from there to the

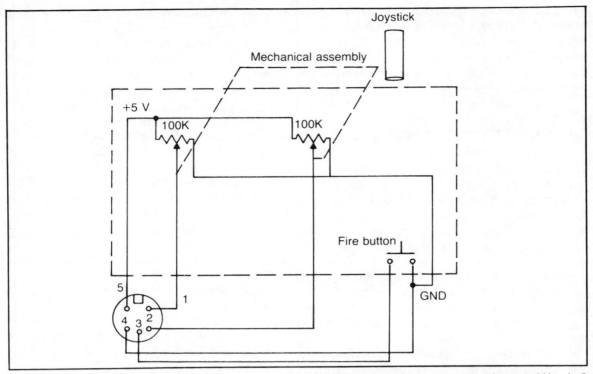

Fig. 18-3. A joystick assembly can be two ordinary potentiometers attached together that varies a voltage between 0 V and +5 V. The fire buttons are simply grounding buttons.

data bus. Once in the data bus the joystick signal is operated on, placed into video memory, and causes the spectacular TV effects.

To be more exact, the joystick shaft has one end held by your fingers and the other end connected to a pair of potentiometers like ordinary volume controls (Fig. 18-3). As you propel your spaceship, the two pots are varied at the same time. There is +5 V to ground across both pots. The center wipers therefore can output 0 V to +5 V as the shaft is moved.

The two varying voltages, one from each center wiper is sent to two terminals on an analog multiplexer. In most computers there are two identical joysticks. The second one is hooked up in the same way to two more pins of the same multiplexer. The multiplexer, by means of two select pins is able to choose one of the four joystick inputs. The multiplexer voltage output is then fed to a comparator chip (Fig. 18-4).

Meanwhile, down at the D/A converter circuit, the same one that is used for the 6-bit sound, the circuit is perking along. The system clock keeps the circuit pulsing as long as the computer is operating. The D/A circuit is able to produce what is known as a stairstep waveform at its output (Fig. 18-5). A sample of the stairstep is tapped off at the voltage divider output and sent to the same comparator chip the joystick voltage was injected into. The comparator chip therefore has two inputs, the joystick voltage and the stairstep waveshape.

The joystick voltage output varies between 0 V and +5 V according to the positions of the joysticks. This analog output cannot be used by the computer to move spaceships across the outer space of the TV screen. The stairstep waveform is a result of the voltage divider in the D/A buffer output being activated by the system clock causing constantly changing bits coming out of the PIA into the buffers. Each bit change causes a different out-

274

put voltage that shows up in total as a stairstep. The stairstep is rising and falling between +0.25 V and +5 V.

The joystick output enters one comparator input pin and the stairstep enters the other input pin. The comparator does not activate as long as the two voltage inputs are different. The comparator has no output in those cases. However, when both input voltages are the same, the comparator produces a logic state out of its output pin. The logic

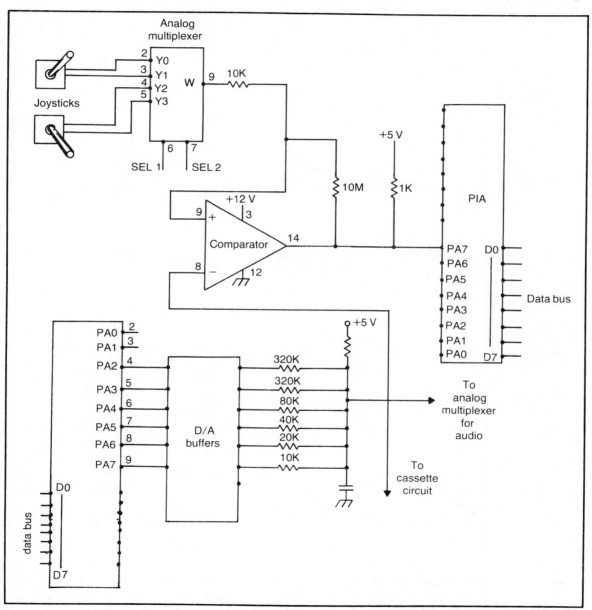

Fig. 18-4. The joystick voltage variations are converted to digital switch signals in a comparator circuit that compares the joystick voltage to a stairstep waveshape from the D/A converter.

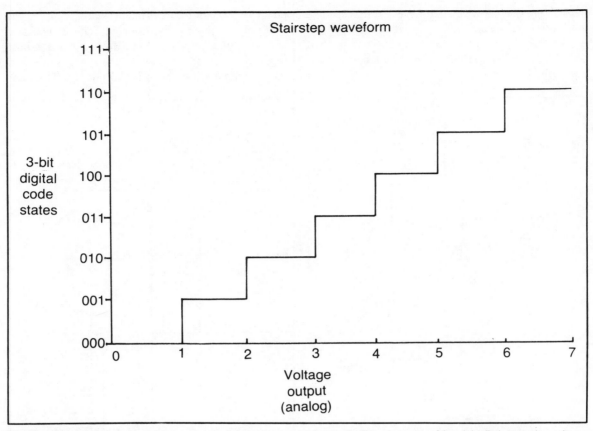

Fig. 18-5. If one 3-bit digital code state enters a digital to analog converter, it will produce one of the eight distinct analog voltage steps, at the output.

state is injected into PA7 of the PIA, where it is sent to the data bus where it can go to work. The comparator is actually an analog to digital converter. It produces a logic state as it compares two analog voltage outputs.

In addition to the potentiometers, joysticks have fire buttons. A fire button is only a grounding button. When you press the fire button, you ground a direct connection to a PIA bit that is normally held high. The sudden low the grounding causes activates the bit. The activity can easily be directed into the computer display to produce a visual explosion and into the audio to hear the single-bit sound.

CHECKING OUT THE JOYSTICK INTERFACE

One of the commonest troubles in the home computer is a broken joystick. Sometimes the constantly used joystick gets broken in an obvious way. Other times the device can develop internal breaks or shorts that are not easily noticed. Before digging into the computer when a joystick stops working be sure to try new joysticks. When the new ones won't work either, then you can consider the computer circuits.

To check out the joystick circuit you should have the D/A circuit producing a stairstep waveform. If you have an exerciser program, put it on since it will get the stairstep working for the joystick test. Other ways to get the test underway is to use a game cartridge that uses the joysticks during the game.

Once the test program is in operation you can

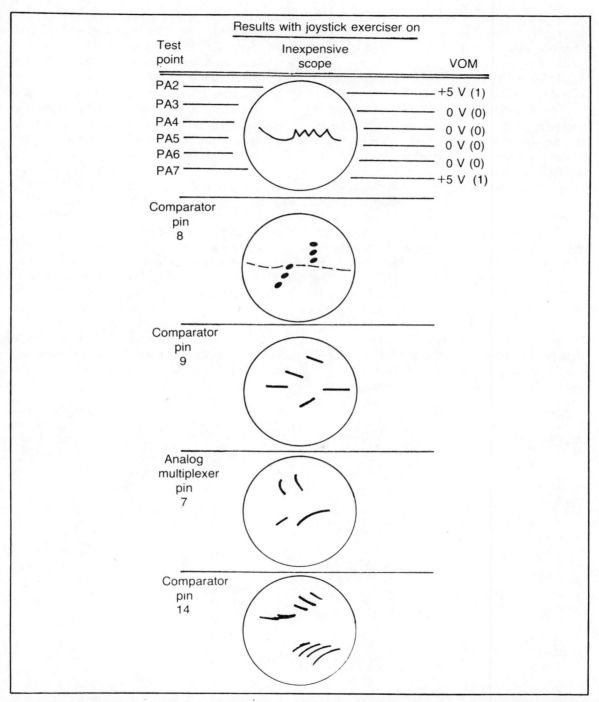

Fig. 18-6. Touching down on the various test points with a scope or vom can produce these results when the joystick exerciser is on.

test the circuits with a cheap scope and a vom. The first test area is the PIA outputs to the hex buffers, in our test example that is pins 4-9. The stairstep should be present. The scope will display it as a jaggedy line as seen in Fig. 18-6. If the waveform is there then the PIA is exonerated.

Next stop is the output of the D/A which can be checked at pin 8 of the comparator chip. There the stairstep should be more viewable. If it is present then the D/A circuit is in good shape. Should the waveform be missing the D/A circuit is probably defective. Check the buffers and the voltage divider. The voltage divider, when shorted or open will mess up the stairstep causing uneven steps. Be on the lookout for this eventuality. When the stairstep is present and not distorted, then the entire pin 8 input circuit to the comparator looks good.

The next check is the output of the analog multiplexer. The scope should display the four dc voltage outputs from the four joystick pots. The dcs appear as four haphazard lines. As you vary each pot you should disturb its line in the scope display. When you can do this then the circuits to that spot, from the joysticks, are deemed ok. If one of the dc or all of the dc lines do not act in this manner, it is time to test the input of the analog multiplexer.

Touch down on all the input pins including the select pins. The dc voltages should be present. If they are at the inputs but not at the outputs, then the multiplexer chip is probably defective.

When the entire circuit checks out ok, it then is time to test the comparator chip. You know the comparator inputs are good. All that is left to test is the output at pin 14. There should be a waveshape there that is a form of the dc inputs and the stairstep. If the waveshape is missing then the comparator could be in trouble. It could be bad and need replacement, but be sure it is getting +12 V to ground before passing final judgment. The +12 V could be gone and need restoration.

In this example home computer, the D/A circuit is used to change digital bits to analog voltages in the 6-bit sound circuit. The D/A is also used to change analog joystick voltages into digital bits, with the aid of a comparator circuit. The circuit is a doorway between the digital world and the analog world. The servicer must be prepared to use digital techniques on the computer side of the door and analog techniques on the outer world side of the door.

Chapter 19

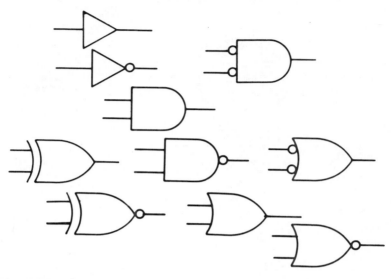

The Cassette and RS-232 Interfaces

Two plugs that are invariably found on the back panel of home computers, are to connect to a cassette recorder and to a line printer. Both peripherals are forms of memory. The cassette memory is electronic and the printer is old fashioned hard copy. Both are entirely different than the data bits that the computer keeps in RAM or ROM. The interfaces between the computer innards and the external storage forms has the job of converting the computer digital bits into analog audio waves for the cassette and transferring digital bit instructions and data to the printer. These type of I/O ports are subject to mechanical and electronic failure. They get a lot of heavy wear. Fortunately they are small circuits and can be repaired quickly once you get the indication there is trouble in that area.

THE CASSETTE INTERFACE

Motor Control. The cassette environment can lose four different functions. The first item in the cassette circuit that could fail is the motor control circuit. The cassette motor is completely under the control of ROM software. The motor is instructed when to turn on and when to turn off. There is one output control line in the PIA that is connected into an npn control transistor (Fig. 19-1).

The transistor acts like a switch. It will go from saturation to cutoff and back according to whether the PIA control line outputs a 0 V or a +5 V. The collector of the transistor is connected to +5 V through a relay coil. The relay coil opens and closes its switch. When it closes, the cassette motor turns on and when it opens, the motor goes off. A diode is placed across the coil to shunt out any voltage surges that occur when the coil switches. There are two more diodes and a .02 capacitor that do the same type of shunt job on any voltage spikes that happen when the switch opens and closes.

The closed circuit connects a voltage to the motor in the cassette through pins 1 and 3 of the cassette plug. When the motor of the cassette stops working the first step is to try another cassette. No sense in pulling the computer apart and have a bad motor in the cassette all the time. If a known good

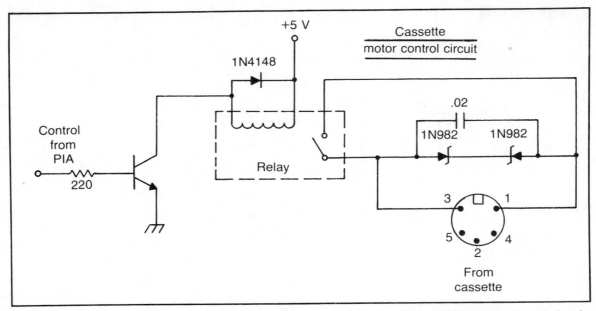

+5 V

Cassette
motor control circuit

1N4148

Control
from
PIA

220

Relay

.02

1N982   1N982

3 ☐ 1

5 · · 4
2

From
cassette

Fig. 19-1. The motor control circuit is turned off and on by applying a logic state to an npn control transistor. The transistor in turn activates the off-on relay.

replacement cassette also does not work, then the computer motor control circuit is indicated.

Try the MOTOR ON and MOTOR OFF commands of the operating language of the computer. At the same time test the collector of the npn transistor. If the collector is switching from 0 V to +5 V and back then the transistor and the PIA output are ok. When the transistor is not switching then the transistor or PIA area contains the defect.

If the npn is switching, chances are good the relay is broken. The relay switch gets a lot of action and is subject to failure. It is possible one of the diodes is shorted too. They will on occasion short out.

Cassette Audio. In the sound section the cassette audio was mentioned. Now this is normal audio such as speech or singing that is recorded along with a program on cassette tape. It is different in intelligibility than the cassette storage of logic states. If you listen to logic states you will hear whines, buzzes, and what have you. When you hear audio it is probably your voice that you recorded with program.

The audio enters the computer through pin 4 of

the plug along with the program that is written in logic states (Fig. 19-2). The audio passes through a 10 μF non-polarized capacitor. The capacitor removes the level of the voltage. The amount of voltage is still the same but the level is no longer between 0 V and +5 V. There are two 4.7 k resistors in series between +5 V and ground. They rearrange the voltage level of the audio, still in a range of 5 V, but varying around a midpoint of 0 V and going to +2.5 V and −2.5 V. This voltage is then attached to the audio analog multiplexer at pin ×2, where it becomes one of the audio group.

When the audio stops operating, the cassette is otherwise ok, then this audio line becomes suspect. There are only a few components and the starting test point is +5 V at the top of the series 4.7 k resistors. If it is present and the resistors are good, then check the 10 μF and the multiplex chip.

Cassette Input. When the cassette won't input the contents of a tape into the computer, and you know the cassette and the tape are good, and the other cassette circuits are operating, then the cassette input circuit is indicated as containing the defect. The input circuit is a form of analog to digital

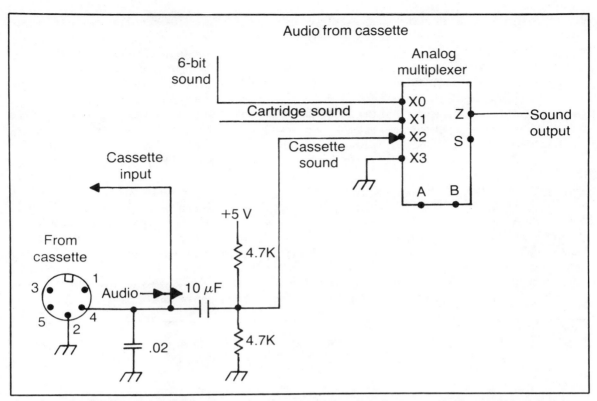

Fig. 19-2. Any intelligible audio on the tape can enter the computer audio network through a 10 μF non-polarized capacitor.

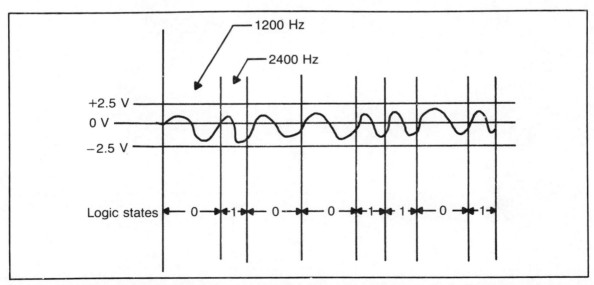

Fig. 19-3. The logic states must be coded into sinewaves before they are sent to the tape recorder. The code is a sinewave of 1200 Hz to represent a 0 and 2400 Hz to represent a 1.

converter. On the cassette tape are sinewaves (Fig. 19-3) that represent logic states rather than square waves. How is that done? Well there are two different kinds of sinewaves used. One type is a sinewave with a frequency of 1200 Hz. The other one is a frequency of 2400 Hz. One cycle of the 1200 Hz represents a 0 and one cycle of the 2400 Hz represents a 1. The sinewave oscillates around a midpoint voltage of 0 V and varies from about +2.5 V to −2.5 V. The cassette input circuit feeds the sinewave into a comparator. The comparator switches slowly when a 1200 Hz cycle arrives and switches quickly when a 2400 Hz cycle is applied. The software is able to interpret the 1200 Hz as a 0 and the 2400 Hz as a 1. The output of the cassette input circuit is sent to a pin on a PIA where this interpreting can begin to take place.

The input circuit enters the computer through pin 4 of the plug, like the audio input (Fig. 19-4).

However the cassette input branches away before the 10 μF and goes to another circuit. If the 10 μF is shorted the cassette input could be missing but so would the audio input. Therefore, if only the cassette input is gone and the audio is still present, then the cassette input is indicated.

The cassette input is coupled to pin 10 of the comparator over a 220 ohm resistor that terminates the cassette input line. There is also a pair of series resistors, 8.2 k and 6.8 k, that along with the 56 k to +5 V, biases the comparator pin 10 at 1 volt.

At pin 11 there are two more resistors, a 15 k and 56 k to +5 V, that biases pin 11, also at 1 volt. In this bias condition the comparator's output is low. It stays low while there is no input from the cassette. When the cassette sends signal to the comparator the following happens (Fig. 19-5). As the ac signal appears at pin 10, it goes positive and negative. During the negative part of the cycle, the diode in

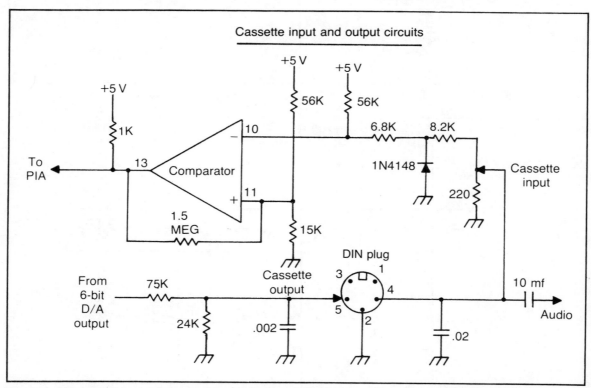

Fig. 19-4. The cassette tape contents inputs the comparator circuit through pin 4 of the DIN plug. The computer data that is to be recorded exits through pin 5 of the same DIN plug.

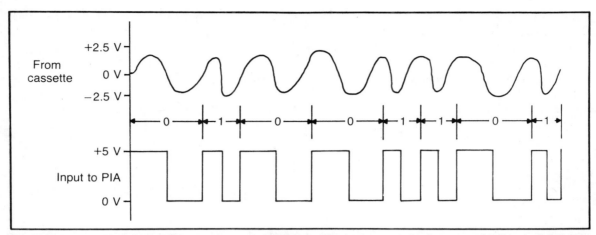

Fig. 19-5. The signal that leaves the cassette tape is in the form of a sinewave, varying between +2.5 V and −2.5 V. The comparator changes the signal to a square wave that has a high of +5 V and a low of 0 V.

the line conducts. This changes the voltage at pin 10 to about 0.5 volts. Pin 11 is still 1 volt so the comparator switches to a high output. As the input signal goes positive the diode turns off and the voltage on pin 10 rises above 1 volt. The comparator then switches back to low.

The output of the comparator is held high by attaching it to +5 V through a 1 k resistor. There is a 1.5 meg resistor across pins 11 and 13 that dampens any attempt of the comparator to start oscillating.

Cassette Output. The cassette output circuit consists of only three components attached between the D/A converter and pin 5 of the cassette plug (Fig. 19-4). The two resistors, a 75 k and 24 k, and the .002 capacitor are simply a voltage attenuator network to set the D/A output to 1 volt so the cassette recorder circuit can use it.

It was mentioned in the Cassette Input section that the magnetic impulses recorded on the tape were not digital highs and lows but analog sinewaves of 2400 Hz and 1200 Hz representing the highs and lows. In other words the highs and lows are coded into the two separate frequencies. When you purchase a software tape for your computer, the software manufacturer has done the coding for you, and as you play the tape into your computer, the input circuit decodes the data by using an analog-to-digital arrangement based around the com-

parator chip. What about the times you want to record the program or data you place into memory? Your computer is going to have to take the highs and lows in memory and code them into 2400 Hz and 1200 Hz, so the recorder can put them on tape properly. How is this accomplished?

In the ROM in your computer is software to help you do this. The software produces a code for the highs and lows that can be fed to the D/A converter (Fig. 19-6). The code is simple. For a 1 the code is 10 for one cycle. For a 0 the code is 1100 for a single cycle. As you can see the 10 occurs in ½ the time a 1100 happens. If the 10 is happening at a 1200 Hz rate the 1100, which is twice as many logic states has a 2400 Hz rate.

The logic states that are in the memory are then coded by the software and sent to the PIA. From the PIA the data is put into the D/A converter. The D/A outputs a varying voltage according to the input. The input 10 produces a sinewave at 2400 Hz and the input 1100 produces another sinewave but slower at 1200 Hz.

The output of the D/A is set by the voltage divider to be between 0.25 V and 4.75 V. This is connected to the little attenuator network and is reduced to 1 volt. Then the signal is applied through pin 5 of the plug to the recorder.

When you desire to play the data back into memory, the recorder sends it back through pin 4 of

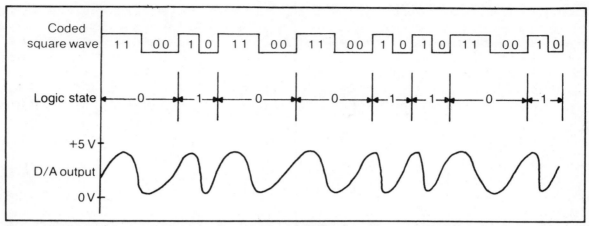

Fig. 19-6. The coded square wave is applied to the D/A converter. The converter changes the square wave to a sinewave that varies between 0 V and 5 V. This signal is then sent to the cassette recorder.

the plug and into the input circuit. The signal from the recorder is raised to a peak-to-peak voltage of about 5 volts but varys around zero volts, +2.5 V to −2.5 V. This, as previously discussed, is compared in the input chip, changed from analog sinewave to digital squarewave and sent to the PIA for the rest of the processing.

When the cassette input circuit doesn't work,

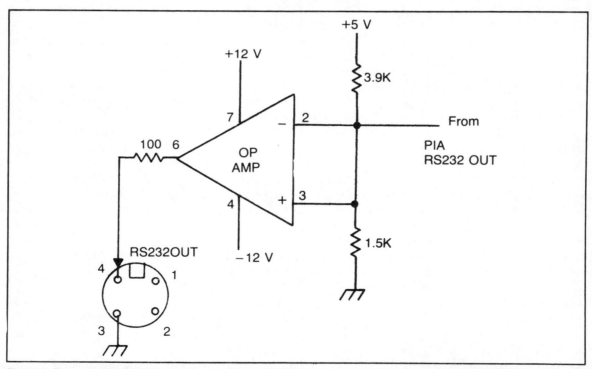

Fig. 19-7. The op amp is able to change the input from the RS232OUT pin on the PIA, from a +5 V, 0 V high, low to a +3 V, −3 V high, low. This can be applied to pin 4, the RS232OUT pin of the plug.

284

you can record ok but can't return the signal to the computer. If the cassette output circuit doesn't operate the signal can be placed into the computer but you can't record. It follows that if you cannot send data from the recorder to the computer test the circuit with the comparator chip. When you can't send data from the computer to the recorder check out the circuit attached to the D/A converter.

The comparator can be checked by running a long tape into the computer. Then test the comparator output to see if you are getting a squarewave as a result of the sinewave you are sending in. The ordinary service scope will show it. When the input to the comparator is a sinewave and the output is missing the comparator could be defective. If it is ok then a component by component test will have to

be made taking into consideration the three +5 V inputs.

To test the cassette output circuit, the first step is to make sure the D/A converter is operating. This can be done with the joystick or the 6-bit sound. If they work ok the D/A is fine. If they are not operative either, then the D/A is causing the trouble. Once the D/A is declared good then there are only the three little components attached to pin 5 of the plug, as valid suspects.

THE RS-232C TYPE INTERFACE

The RS-232C type interface is some hardware to pass the RS-232C signal. The signal consists of digital highs and lows, but the high is defined as a voltage larger than +3 volts. The low is defined as a

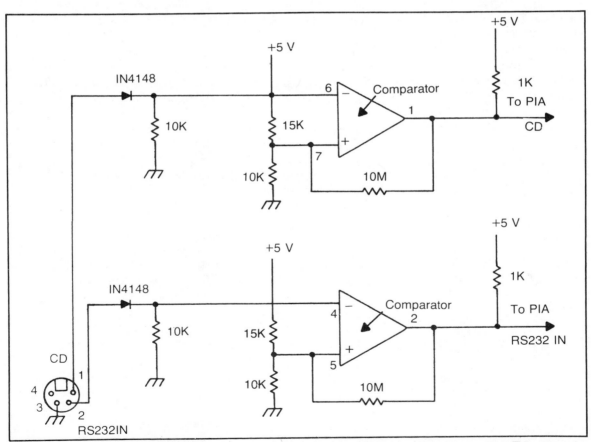

Fig. 19-8. The inputs to an RS232C circuit can enter through Pins 1 and 2 the CD and RS232IN connections. The comparator circuits then adjust the voltage levels so the PIA's can use the signals.

285

voltage less than −3 volts. The hardware has the job of receiving the usual highs and lows, such as +5 V and 0 V, and changing their level to +3 V and −3 V.

The typical line printer used with a home computer is interfaced with an RS-232C system. The components though, only have to output the highs and lows to the line printer. Once the digital signals get to the printer, circuitry and mechanical devices in the printer change the digital bits to characters printed on paper. There is no return signal from the printer to the computer. The PIA to RS-232C circuit is all that is needed.

The RS-232C interface though, is used to connect telephone modems and other computers to the home computer. With these devices, in addition to the output signal, the units send signals back to the computer. Therefore, in the interface, input circuits are installed. The first piece of hardware to the outside world is the RS-232C plug. It can be a 4-pin DIN connector. The four pins are a serial output, a serial input, a status input and a ground zero voltage pin.

RS-232OUT. The output from the computer to the printer can be changed from a +5 V, 0 V high, low to a +3 V, −3 V with an op amp that has input supply voltages of +12 V and −12 V (Fig. 19-7). Into pin 2 of the op amp is the signal from the PIA for the printer. Into pin 3 is attached +5 V through the two referencing resistors, a 3.9 k and a 1.5 k. This sets a reference dc of 1.4 V on pin 3.

This reference voltage causes the op amp to be able to swing between the +12 V and −12 V as the op amp switches states. From there the output goes to pin 4 of the output plug and then on to the line printer.

RS-232IN and CD. When a modem has to send signal into the computer it uses the RS-232IN and CD pins 1 and 2 of the plug (Fig. 19-8). These two pins are connected to two identical circuits. Both circuits operate in the same way. They both receive RS-232C signals and they are to change the voltage levels on these digital signals for PIA use.

The two diodes act as a form of detector. As the input signals go positive the diodes conduct and send an impulse to pins 4 and 6 of the twin com-

Table 19-1. The Little Test Program Sets Decimal Address 65312, Bit 1, FF20 In Hex. Then the Program Marks Time so a Test can be Seen. Then the Program Clears FF20, Bit 1. The Program Then Marks Some More Time and Starts the Same Operation Over and Over Again. This Activity Causes the Op Amp and Comparators, Which are Connected Together for the Test to Each Switch as the PIA Bit is Set and Cleared. The Service Chart Shows you What Should be on the Test Points as the Program is Run. If any of the Predicted Results are Missing, That is a Valid Clue Which Will Help You Pinpoint the Defective Part.

Service Chart			
OP AMP	TEST POINT	SCOPE	VOM
INPUT	2	SWITCHING	
OUTPUT	6	SWITCHING	+11 TO −11
COMPARATORS			
INPUT	4	SWITCHING	0 TO +10
INPUT	6	SWITCHING	0 TO +10
OUTPUT	1	SWITCHING	
OUTPUT	2	SWITCHING	

parators. When the signal swings negative the diodes shut off and there is no signal applied to the comparator. The comparators have their pins 5 and 7 referenced at $+2$ V by the two resistors in series with $+5$ V. That way if a voltage of $+2.6$ is applied to pins 4 and 6 the comparators switch on and the PIA gets signal.

When the printer or modem stops working and the devices are ok, the interface is indicated as a suspect. The quickest way to check out this type of interface is all at once. The voltage levels of the inputs and the outputs are all identical. If you can send some signal out of the PIA into the op amp, and then attach the op amp output to the comparator circuit inputs, you can see if they are all operating. The indication of operation will be at the following test points: pin 2 of the op amp, pin 6 of the op amp, pin 4 of the comparator, pin 6 of the comparator, pin 1 of the comparator, and pin 2 of the comparator.

The test operation is to first short pin 4 to pins 1 and 2 of the plug. Then the following program can be used. This circuit we are discussing is drawn from the TRS-80 Color Computer. In their service manual they recommend this program in their Color Basic language.

```
5   POKE 65312,2 — SETS RS232OUT ON PIA
10  FOR X=0 TO 10:NEXT X — MARKS TIME
15  POKE 65312,0 — CLEARS RS232OUT ON
    PIA
20  FOR X=0 TO 10:NEXT X — MARKS SOME
    MORE TIME
25  GO TO 5 — CONTINUES SETTING AND
    CLEARING
```

With this program installed and running the test points should show the results on the service chart (Table 19-1). If they do not, there is a defect in the RS-232C circuits. Test the components near the test point with the incorrect result.

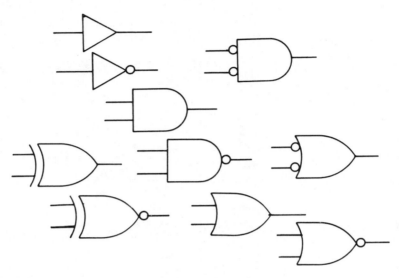

Chapter 20

Reset and the Power Supply

There is on occasion some confusion between the reset button and the computer power supply. Both circuits have a button control that are often identical. However, the control in the power supply is the off-on switch, while the reset button has an entirely different job to do.

THE RESET CIRCUIT

The computer is built so that the program counter increments after every addressing. This forces the computer, unless commanded otherwise, to go from address to address in numerical order automatically. The computer will go about this business no matter what. The printer could jam, the cassette could keep on running where it should have stopped or other emergencies could occur. You don't want to turn the computer off. All of the RAM contents would disappear. What can you do? Press the reset button. The CPU will stop the program in operation and jump back to a previous address and revert to a ready mode. Then you can look the emergency over and decide what to do.

In order to get into a reset ready mode, all operations must be put on hold by the pressing of the reset button (Fig. 20-1). For example, there could be a reset terminal on a lot of the chips excluding RAM. On the CPU, PIAs VDG, and SAM a *reset terminal is installed. *reset is wired internally to place the chip into a special hold position when activated. *reset is held high. A low coming from the reset button will turn *reset on.

The reset circuit is based around the button. One side of the button is attached to +5 V through a 100 k resistor. The other side connects to ground. While the button is dormant the circuit is held high since no current flows through the 100 k. However, when the button is pressed the circuit goes low as it is connected to ground and the 100 k blocks off the +5 V as some current flows through it.

There are two sections to this reset circuit. Each section provides a different time duration to the two output pulses. One section is based around the 0.1 μF capacitor and its series 100 k to +5 V. It provides a 10 millisecond pulse to SAM's terminal

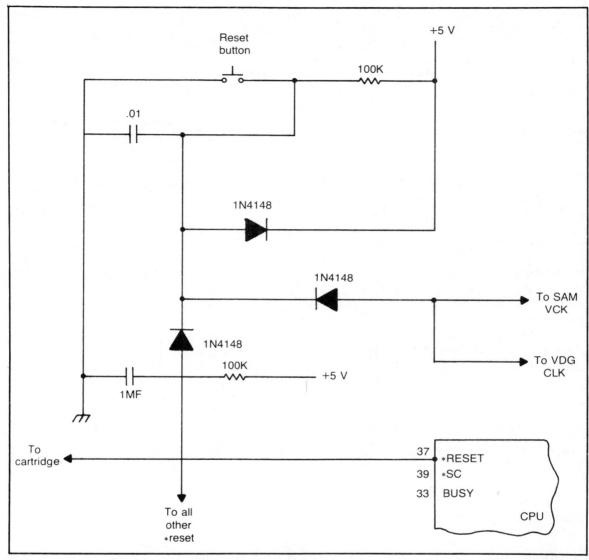

Fig. 20-1. The reset button can stop operations during an emergency and place the computer back into the original ready mode. If there are any programs installed in RAM they usually remain intact.

vck and the VDG's terminal clk. The diode in their output line is there to isolate the reset circuit from the chips.

The other reset pulse is timed by the 1 μF capacitor and its series 100 k into the other +5 V supply line. They time the pulse to about 0.1 second. This is the pulse that enables *reset on the

CPU, PIAs and any other circuits that have to be reset.

The diode between the two RC networks isolates one from the other. The diode in parallel with the 0.1 capacitor and its 100 k allows quick discharge of the capacitor in case a number of fast multiple resets are needed.

The main symptom a bad reset circuit causes is inability of the reset to operate properly. Most of the time the reset button itself will be the problem due to mechanical failure. If the button is good, test the diodes first and the capacitors and resistors last. It is an easy discrete component analog circuit to check out.

THE POWER SUPPLY

The typical voltages needed to power the home computer are +5 V, +12 V, −5 V and −12 V. The most demanding voltage is the +5 V. The current requirements for +5 V is usually heavy in comparison to the other voltages. It is the main supply to most of the chips. It could provide a total of as much as 2 amps to the computer.

The next largest current drain is given to the +12 V line, although it only supplies a fraction of the current the +5 V line does. It could supply about 500 milliamps as an example, if the +5 V line is providing 2000 mils. The −5 V and −12 V lines provide the least amount of current.

The Fuse and Power Transformer. The input to the computer from the 110 volt house line enters a polarized plug. The two active lines send the 110 to a power transformer that is fused in the high input line (Fig. 20-2). The ground connection is attached to the computer chassis ground. There are some HV capacitors across the lines to insure noise immunity.

The secondary windings are centertapped to ground. There are two of them that put out 16 Vac at 1 amp for the +5 V line and 33.5 Vac at 0.35 amps for the other voltage needs. There are a pair of rectifier diodes to change some of the ac to a pulsating dc. This is the transformer section of the supply and is subject to all the typical power supply troubles that technicians are familiar with in radios, TVs, and other home electronic gear.

The fuse can blow, the rectifiers short or open, and the transformer can open or start smoking from internal shorts in the windings. When this happens the computer acts dead. With a dead computer the first testing should be in this circuit. In some computers this part of the power supply is isolated physically from the rest of the computer. You can spot it quickly because of the fuse and power transformer.

The +5 Volt Line. In this example circuit, the input to the +5 V system is over top of a 10,000 microfarad filter (Fig. 20-3). The line is then attached to a pnp transistor emitter biased by a base to emitter 68 ohm resistor. This transistor is in control of how much current can flow into the +5 V line.

The transistor in turn is controlled by a 723C

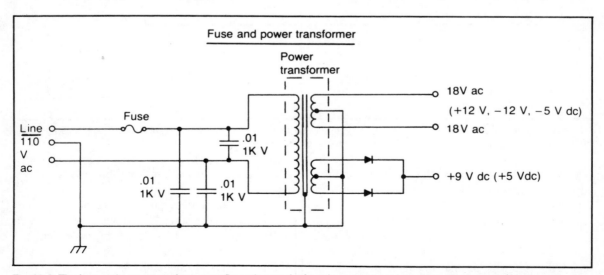

Fig. 20-2. The fuse and power transformer configuration can be found on a separate board away from the rest of the computer.

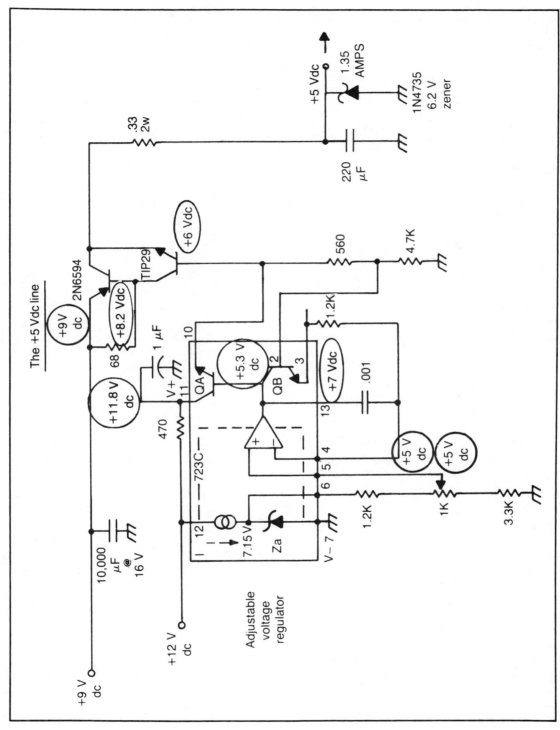

Fig. 20-3. The +5 volt system is much more complex than the other dc voltage supply circuits. Regulation is typically supplied by a 723C chip and accompanying pass and buffer transistors.

chip that is an adjustable voltage regulator. Coming out of pin 10 of the 723C is a regulator voltage. It is applied to the base of the npn transistor which is a buffer that is driving the pnp transistor. The output of the pnp then goes to the .33 ohm collector resistor. From there the voltage passes over a 6.2 V zener diode and 220 microfarad filter. It emerges from the circuit as the desired +5 V, able to supply 1.35 amps. The zener diode is normally off. It is only there in case a short develops between the +5 V line and the +12 V line. It will start conducting at 6.2 volts and not let any higher voltages get into the +5 V rated circuits.

The 723C is vital to keep the +5 V system closely regulated. The illustration shows the block diagram of the 723C regulator. The chip is powered from the +12 V system. The +12 V is applied at pin 12, passes through a coil and arrives at zener diode Za. The diode is rated at 7.15 V and this is applied to pin 6. This is the voltage reference for the chip and it can be adjusted slightly by a 1 k pot in series with a 1.2 k and 3.3 k resistors in series to ground, out of pin 6.

The reference voltage is set to exactly +5 V and connected to pin 5. Pins 4 and 5 are the inputs to a comparator circuit. Pin 13 is an output of the comparator and has a frequency compensating capacitor for the comparator.

The output of the comparator controls the npn Qa which is driving the regulator output through pin 10. There is another transistor Qb that is also providing some control over Qa. Qb is controlled at its base through the current limit set by the 560 and 4.7 k resistors in the base line of the npn attached to pin 10.

The net result of the circuit is if the comparator senses a rising or falling voltage leaving the supply to the computer, it will adjust the output voltage of the pnp pass transistor to readjust the output to exactly +5 V.

The power transformer uses one centertapped winding for the +5 V line since the amperage requirements are so large. The other centertapped winding is used for all the other voltages, +12 V, −12 V and −5 V. The +12 V is derived from the 18 Vac at the top of the winding, while the −12 V and −5 V is made from the 18 Vac that is at the bottom of the winding. The two winding outputs are connected to the bridge diodes in a CSB20. The top winding output is attached to a + of the diodes, while a − of the bridge gets the bottom winding output.

The +12 Volt Line. The 400 milliamp current the +12 volt line is required to supply can be regulated easily with a 7812 12 V regulator (Fig. 20-4). The regulator has three connections, input, output, and ground. The input receives +23.5 Vdc output from the bridge. The dc is filtered by a 1500 microfarad capacitor at 35 V. There is a diode attached across the regulator chip for protection. The output of the regulator is +12 V filtered some more by a 220 microfarad capacitor at 16 V and a .1 microfarad capacitor.

The Negative Voltages. The −12 V and −5 V lines are both drawn from the negative dc output from the bridge diodes. The bridge outputs −23.5 Vdc. Both lines use the same filter capacitor a 470 microfarad at 35 V. After the filter the line is split in two. One line goes directly to a 7912 12 V regulator. The other line goes to a 1.2 k current limiting resistor and then to a 7905 5 V regulator. The 1.2 k resistor drops the −23.5 Vdc to −20 Vdc.

The −12 V regulator circuit shows the protection diode installed opposite to the +12 V protection diode and the polarities of the capacitors are reversed. Otherwise the circuits are identical except for the 1 microfarad capacitor bypassing the input of the regulator. It is needed since both negative lines are using the same 1.2 k current limiting resistor.

The −5 V line has a similar configuration except the protective diode and the 220 microfarad capacitor output filter are not needed. The −5 V line is only required to draw 100 microamps and the regulator can handle that without the additional components.

POWER SUPPLY REPAIRS

The most obvious symptom in a supply like this is a dead computer. The vom can then be used at the outputs of the regulators or any of the test points that the voltages are applied to. Most of the

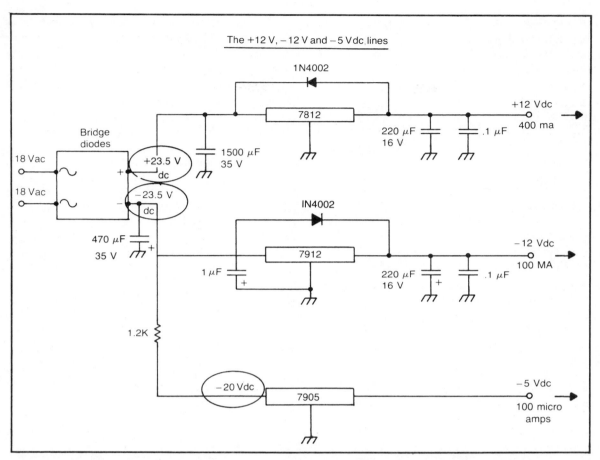

The +12 V, −12 V and −5 Vdc lines

Fig. 20-4. The +12 volt dc supply is derived from the top of an 18 Vac secondary winding of the power transformer. The −12 volt supply and the −5 volt are both derived from the same 18 Vac output from the bottom of the same secondary transformer winding.

time, when the supply has broken down, one of the lines is in trouble. The vom will pick out the line that is no longer providing its assigned voltage. For instance, if you discover that the −12 V line is no longer putting out −12 volts, then that line probably contains a defective component.

However, the troubleshooting is not always as simple as that. First of all, the +12 V line supplies some voltages to the +5 V line. Secondly, zener diodes like the 6.2 V type in the +5 V output line will automatically short to ground if more than 6.2 V is applied to the line. This could be confusing and lead to false troubleshooting paths that go nowhere.

Therefore, if there is no voltage coming out of

the +5 V line, test the +12 V line first. If the 12 V is present you can eliminate that possibility from your mind. Next disconnect the 6.2 V zener diode. If a voltage returns the diode is being overloaded and is killing the +5 V. Find out where the overload is coming from. It could be the regulator circuit in the +5 V area. Disconnect the .33 ohm 2 watt resistor, to avoid overloading computer components and test the regulator.

When there is no voltage in any of the lines, disconnect the line plug and check the resistance from the supply to ground, it could be a short to ground, either a shorted component or a board short.

If none of the above methods bear fruit, then turn on the unit and begin tracing the voltages from test point to test point. The bridge diodes can be checked to see if the voltages are passing as prescribed. If both the +23.5 Vdc and the −23.5 Vdc are missing, the bridge is probably defective. If only one of the voltages is missing then the filter capacitor or the regulator has broken down.

The +5 V line can be traced by following the voltage from the +9 Vdc input to the +5 Vdc output. As soon as you arrive at a wrong voltage you are near the bad component.

Chapter 21

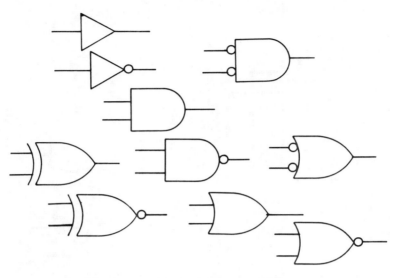

The TV Display

In the video display generator chapter (Chapter 17), the discussion ended with the video signal entering an rf modulator. In the modulator the video was mixed with a carrier wave at channel 3 or 4's frequency and then directed to a conventional TV receiver. The TV set in that case is completely separate. The TV set treats the incoming computer video as simply another TV transmitter input. There are no electrical connections between the computer and the TV display. When a trouble occurs in the computer, it is treated as a separate entity. If a trouble happens in the TV, it needs an old fashioned TV repair not a digital checkout.

There are a lot of popular home computers that do not use the TV receiver as a TV display. Good examples are the Heathkit H-89A and the TRS-80 Model III. They have the TV display circuits installed inside the case along with the digital computer circuits. They use the same general power supply and share a number of other circuit voltages and signals (Fig. 21-1). When a trouble occurs the troubleshooting must take into consideration the TV display circuit areas as well as the computer circuits.

These TV display circuits are like their counterparts in the home TV receiver. However, only a few of the home TV set circuits are present in the computer TV display. The computer produces a composite TV signal. If the computer was transmitting the signal over the air to the display, it would have to install the signal on a carrier wave like channel 3 or 4. The receiver would then need a tuner with a channel selector, a strip of i-f amplifiers, a detector, and all the other circuits needed to process the transmitted signal until it was able to be applied to the video output circuits.

When the TV display is installed in the computer case all this transmitting and reception equipment can be dispensed with. The composite TV signal can be coupled directly from the video display generator circuits to the video output circuits. The video can then be quickly transferred to the cathode of the CRT and be displayed.

Since the cathode ray tube is part of the com-

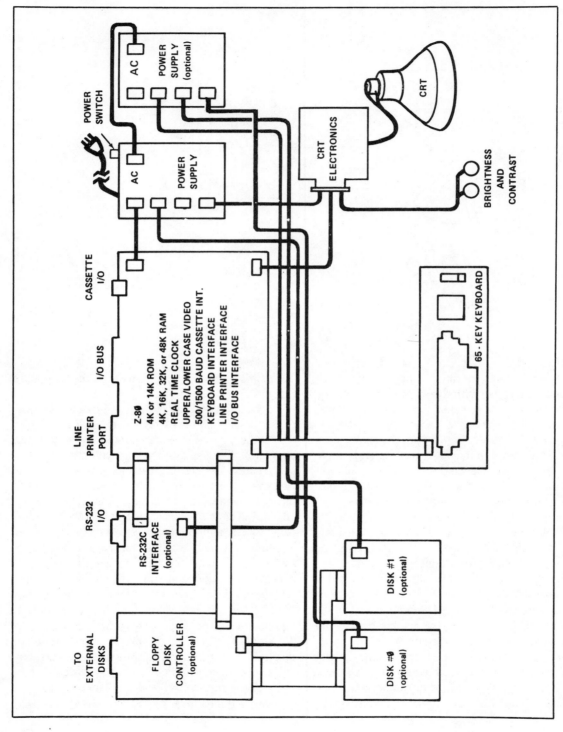

Fig. 21-1. Troubleshooting computers with a built-in TV display system requires considering the TV section as well as the computer circuits (courtesy of Radio Shack, a division of Tandy Corporation).

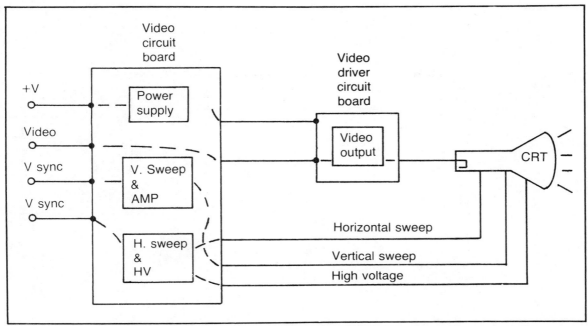

Fig. 21-2. The TV type troubleshooting is confined mostly in the sweep, high voltage, and video output circuits.

ter, the circuits such as the vertical sweep, horizontal sweep and high voltage generation must be in the computer case too. This makes some of the possible troubles fall into the category of TV repairs. When troubles occur in these combination computer-TV units the overall troubleshooting is a potpourri of digital and analog considerations. Let's examine the Heathkit H-89A TV display circuits. The circuits are all contained on a video circuit board, a video driver circuit board and the CRT (Fig. 21-2).

THE VIDEO CIRCUIT BOARD

Power Supply. The video circuit board performs six jobs. First of all, it has a power supply line to produce two source voltages that are needed to run the transistors and chips on the board. There is +53 volts for the transistors and +6 volts for the chips (Fig. 21-3).

The power lines receive an input of +65 volts from the computer's primary power supply. The voltage is applied to a four transistor network that acts as a voltage regulator. The transistors Q201,

Q202, Q203, and Q204 output a regulated +53 volts and +6 volts. The two voltages are used in both the video and video driver boards.

When trouble happens in this power supply the following symptoms could appear. If the collector of Q204 shorts to the heatsink the main fuse will blow shutting down the entire unit. When you change the fuse and the new fuse also blows this could be your problem.

When the symptom of no brightness occurs, check for the presence of +53 V. When it becomes defective the entire TV display section stops. If +53 V is missing trace it back to +65 V till you encounter the break in the line. The potential troublemakers are the four transistors and the two diodes.

The Vertical Oscillator. The vertical sweep frequency the computer uses for its display is 60 Hz. The vertical oscillator, which is based around a unijunction transistor Q205 (Fig. 21-4) is designed to operate as a free running oscillator at 50 Hz. A 60 Hz sync pulse from the CPU circuit, is applied to the gate of the oscillator through C206 and D204. This

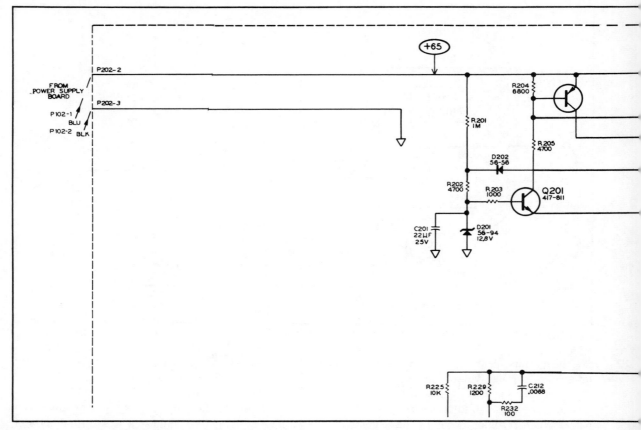

Fig. 21-3. The TV display section can have its very own power supply, derived from the primary supply (© 1981 Heath Company, Reprinted by Permission of Heath Company).

forces the oscillator to run at 60 Hz. The oscillator continues at this 60 Hz pace as the logic control board keeps generating the vertical sync pulse and applying it to the sweep circuit. After the 60 Hz is produced it is sent to Q206 a voltage follower. There is some feedback from the emitter of Q206 through a vertical linearity control, to linearize the sawtooth vertical waveshape.

When trouble strikes in the vertical oscillator, the vertical sweep could collapse into a bright horizontal line across the screen (Fig. 21-5A). This no vertical sweep symptom happens when the oscillator stops running. This could happen if the vertical sync pulse from the logic board doesn't arrive, if one of the oscillator transistors, Q205 or Q206 fails, or one of the related components conks out.

Between Q205 and Q206 are C208 and C209. They have the job of charging up to the full +53 V through R221. This generates the sawtooth waveshape. If one of these should short or change value the frequency will become unstable. This produces a symptom of vertical jitters on the screen.

The vertical size pot is in the +53 V line going to the coupling between Q205 and Q206. Troubles in this circuit area can cause too little or too much height (Fig. 21-5B and C).

The Vertical Output. The transistors Q207, Q208, Q209, Q211, and Q212 make up the vertical output amplifier. Their output is fed through C216 to the vertical windings of the deflection yoke. The sawtooth waveshape in the vertical yoke takes vertical control of the cathode ray and draws it up and

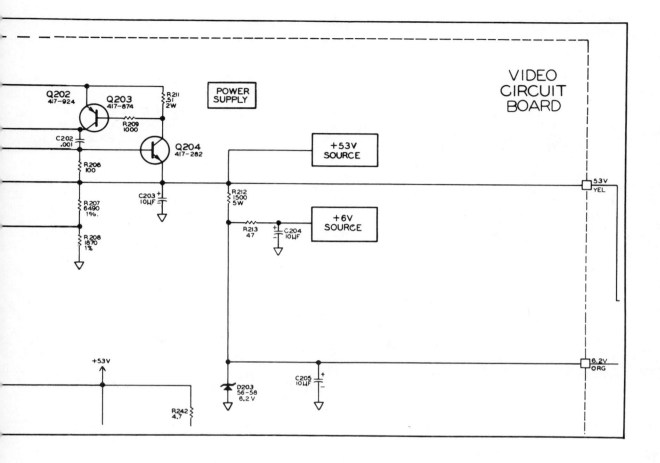

down the TV face at the 60 Hz rate. Failure in the vertical output circuit also can cause the no vertical sweep symptom. In addition the likelihood of too much vertical sweep is possible, due to defective components here too.

The Horizontal Oscillator. Q213 is a horizontal sweep driver transistor that is connected to T201, the driver transformer. The transistor is there to amplify a sawtooth waveform of approximately 15,750 Hz that is produced in two flip-flop like chips. They are timers acting as monostable multivibrators. The two chips U201 and U202 are triggered into oscillation by a horizontal sync pulse that is coming from the CPU logic board (Fig. 21-6).

The horizontal centering control is in a +6 V line attached to U201. Adjusting the control adjusts

the width of the U201 output pulse. The output timing of U202 is determined by C233 and R249. They cause the output pulse from pin 3 to have a 20 microsecond interval. With the pulse having a specified width and specified time delay, it is then transferred to the horizontal output circuit through Q213 and T201.

If trouble should occur in the horizontal oscillator circuit the two main symptoms are no horizontal sweep or the horizontal centering will not work. If there is no horizontal sweep, there could be a bright white line down the center of the screen, much like the no vertical sweep symptom where the white line is side to side. Mostly though the loss of horizontal sweep will kill brightness altogether. Either way, the horizontal sweep is gone, but the

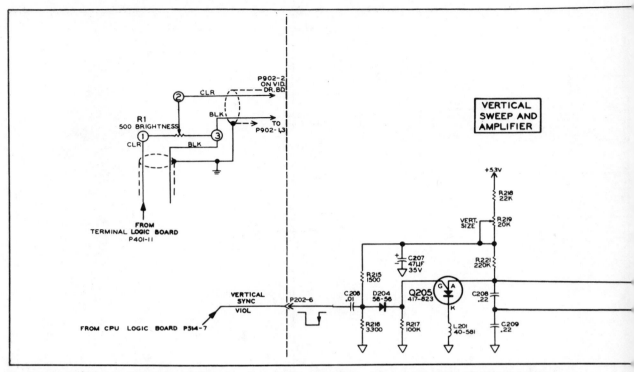

Fig. 21-4. This vertical oscillator is based around a unijunction transistor that runs free around 50 Hz (© 1981 Heath Company, Reprinted by Permission of Heath Company).

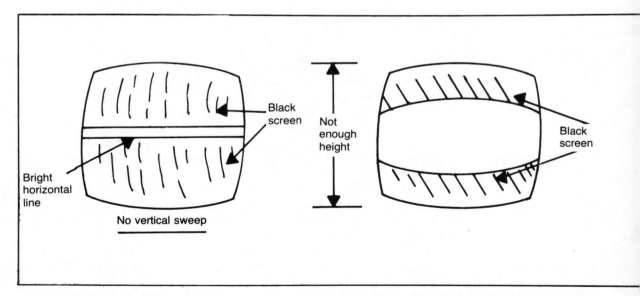

Fig. 21-5. When the vertical sweep circuit fails, the picture could collapse into a bright horizontal line (A), shrink at the top or bottom (B), or expand causing a whitish haze foldover at the bottom (C).

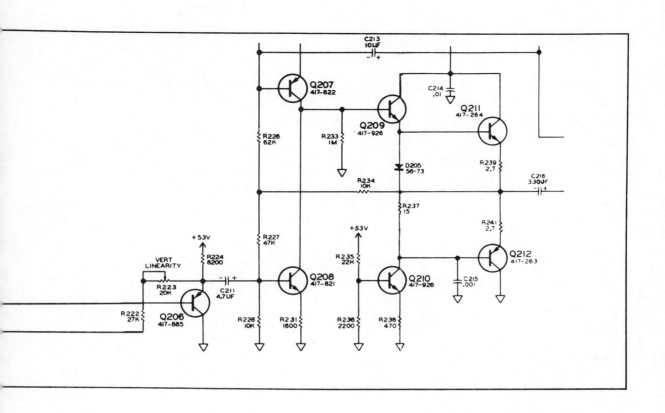

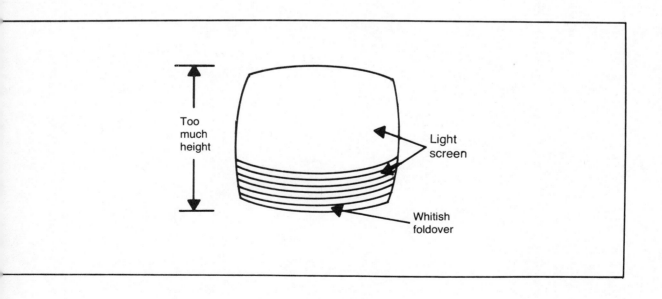

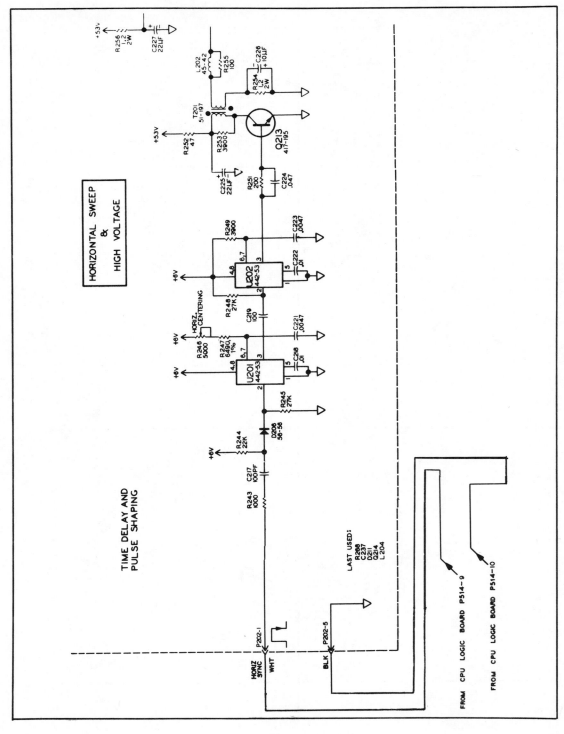

Fig. 21-6. The horizontal oscillator is based around two IC timer chips that are triggered by a horizontal sync pulse from the CPU logic board (© 1981 Heath Company, Reprinted by Permission of Heath Company).

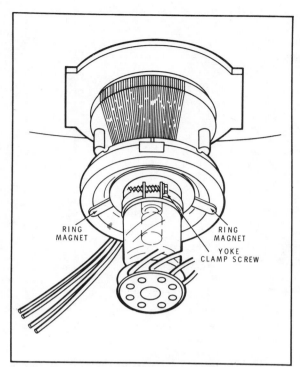

Fig. 21-7. The deflection yoke around the CRT neck takes control over the cathode ray as it passes through the center yoke (© 1981 Heath Company, Reprinted by Permission of Heath Company).

RING MAGNET

RING MAGNET

YOKE CLAMP SCREW

horizontal sync pulse, coming from the logic board will still be present at the input pin P202-1. The components that can cause no horizontal sweep are any of the components from R243 to Q214. Especially vulnerable are D206, U201, U202, Q213, Q214, T201, C226, and the resistors in the +6 V and +53 V lines.

When the centering control is inoperative, the centering control itself rarely breaks but its series components, C221 and R247 might let loose. The timer chip U201 also could develop a defect causing poor centering control.

Horizontal Output. Once a well shaped pulse, correctly timed enters the horizontal output transistor Q214 through T201, Q214 starts turning off and on since it is a switch that controls the flow of current through the horizontal output transformer, T202 and the horizontal windings of the deflection yoke (Fig. 21-7).

As Q214 switches on, current flows from the +53 V supply through the primary winding of T202, through the deflection yoke, L203, L204, and C232 to ground. During this interval, the yoke current is increasing in a linear fashion and causes the cathode ray, that is passing through the yoke, to be deflected to the right side of the screen. The ray is being drawn all the way to the edge of the screen, not the end of the display block the computer uses as its window into the video RAM (Fig. 21-8).

When the ray reaches the right edge, Q213 turns on and the output transistor Q214 switches off. This transfers the energy that was stored in the yoke to C228. The energy takes the form of a halfwave voltage pulse with an amplitude of 550 volts. As the yoke then goes to zero, the cathode ray returns to its original position at screen center. C228 now discharges current back into the yoke. The current going the other way, draws the cathode ray to the left side of the screen.

As the voltage in C228 discharges to zero, C228, the yoke and the primary of T202 form a resonant circuit that tries to ring. As it tries to oscillate the energy that has been transferred to the yoke now draws the ray back toward screen center. The damper diode D208 aids in the sweep action by damping the oscillation and charging C228 for the first half of the scanning line.

The width coil L203 is in series with the yoke and can adjust the total current through the yoke. The amount of current can spread or shrink the scan somewhat. The horizontal linearity coil L204, though, provides a fixed amount of linearity correction.

As mentioned, the scan lines developed by the vertical and horizontal sweep systems, are drawn from one side of the CRT to the other. As the horizontal sweep pulls the cathode ray from side to side, the vertical sweep is pulling the ray down and up. This is identical to the way the sweep is conducted in a TV receiver. The complete scanning produces 525 lighted scanning lines known as a raster. The raster is largely a product of the TV display circuitry, except for the triggering vertical and horizontal sync signals, that are sent to the TV display circuits by the CPU logic board.

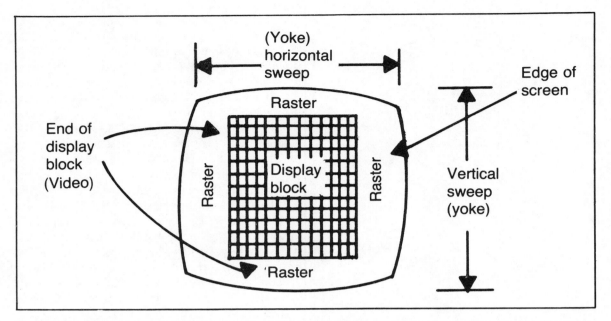

Fig. 21-8. The display block is a window into the video RAM. The display block is composed completely of video. The raster, that contains the display block, is produced by the horizontal and vertical sweep circuits and the yoke.

High Voltage. In order for the cathode ray to be attracted to the phosphor screen fast enough to smack the phosphor and light up the pixels, an anode voltage of +15,000 volts must attract the electrons in the ray. This high voltage is developed as a byproduct of the horizontal output transformer T202. The horizontal output transformer is also known as the flyback.

The flyback activity produces a voltage pulse that is developed during the horizontal retrace. The retrace is the time between the end of one scan line and the beginning of the next scan line. That is when the scan line has ended on the right side and is drawn back to the beginning on the left side. The brightness is off during that time.

The primary of the flyback transformer is coupled to three secondary windings (Fig. 21-9). The top winding at P203-1 is the high voltage. The flyback pulse out of the collector of Q214 is stepped up to 15,000 volts. This is rectified by D1 and applied to the CRT anode (Fig. 21-10). The internal capacitance of the CRT anode is about 500 pF and acts as the filter for the HV. The +15,000 volts can then do its attraction job.

The bottom flyback winding is 6.3 V to supply the CRT with a filament voltage of 450 milliamps. The center winding is for a −100 volt dc supply. D207 and C229 rectifies and filters the −100 V. Another flyback related output is a tap into the Q214 collector line. It provides +500 volts and is rectified and filtered by D211, and C231. This voltage is needed by the screen grid of the CRT (G2) as an acceleration voltage for the cathode ray. Resistor R265 and focus control R264 are a voltage divider between +500 and −100 and they feed the focus grid (G4) of the CRT. And still another voltage divider of D209, R261, G1, control R262, between +53 V and the −100 V, gives the control grid, G1, an adjustable bias voltage.

These assorted voltages provide the CRT with the following voltages and abilities. The 6.3 V filament voltage heats up the cathode. The cathode emits the ray which passes through the control grid, G1. The control grid is adjustable which varies the intensity of the ray and subsequently the brightness. The ray is then accelerated by the +500 V on G2 and is narrowed into a well focused beam by the adjustable G4. The ray then passes through the

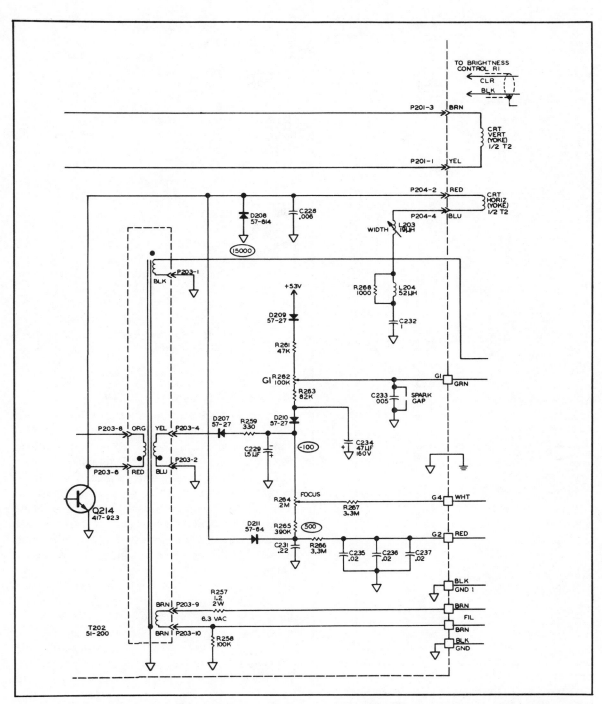

Fig. 21-9. The primary of the flyback transformer, T202, is coupled to three secondary windings (© 1981 Heath Company, Reprinted by Permission of Heath Company).

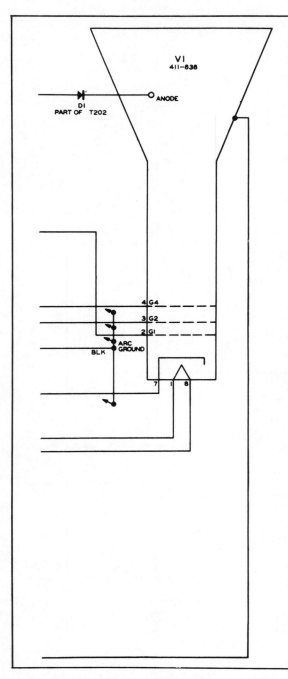

V1
411-838

D1
PART OF T202

ANODE

4 | G4
3 | G2
2 | G1

ARC
GROUND

BLK

7   1   8

Fig. 21-10. The 15,000 volt ac developed by the flyback is rectified by D1 into dc and filtered by the internal capacitance of the CRT anode (© 1981 Heath Company, Reprinted by Permission of Heath Company).

center of the yoke windings, where it is scanned across and back by the horizontal windings and down and up by the vertical windings. The HV then attracts the beam and has it impinge on the phosphor to produce the raster.

When trouble strikes in the horizontal and HV circuits the symptom is usually no brightness. Due to the complex interaction between all the circuits from the IC timers to the anode of the CRT, most of the components in the circuits could be suspects. Therefore it would be a good idea to narrow the search area down before checking individual components. This can be done with a neon bulb, a HV probe, and a test horizontal output signal substitution. The neon bulb will light up if the rf of the flyback pulse is active.

The HV probe is used to check to see if the +15,000 V dc is on the anode. A signal substitute can be obtained from test equipment that is usually in a TV service shop. Once the circuit area is narrowed down a bit, the components in the suspect area can then be tested with normal analog measures.

THE VIDEO DRIVER CIRCUIT BOARD

The video driver board is a small print board with only two transistors (Fig. 21-11). The two transistors, Q901 and Q902 act as a conventional cascade analog amplifier. The amplifier receives a steady stream of composite TV waveforms from the computer at P902-2. The signal is applied to the board through a brightness control on the back panel of the computer. The signal enters the base of Q902. The signal then is transferred to the cathode of the CRT through R904. L901, a high frequency compensation choke maintains the frequency response of the video through the circuit.

In the CRT cathode the stream of video modulates the cathode ray. Two of the elements of the video information are the horizontal and vertical sync pulses in the composite that construct the display block in the raster.

Each TV raster frame consists of 264 scan lines. Only 192 scan lines are lit up to show the display block. There are 72 scan lines blacked out at top and bottom to form the top and bottom border.

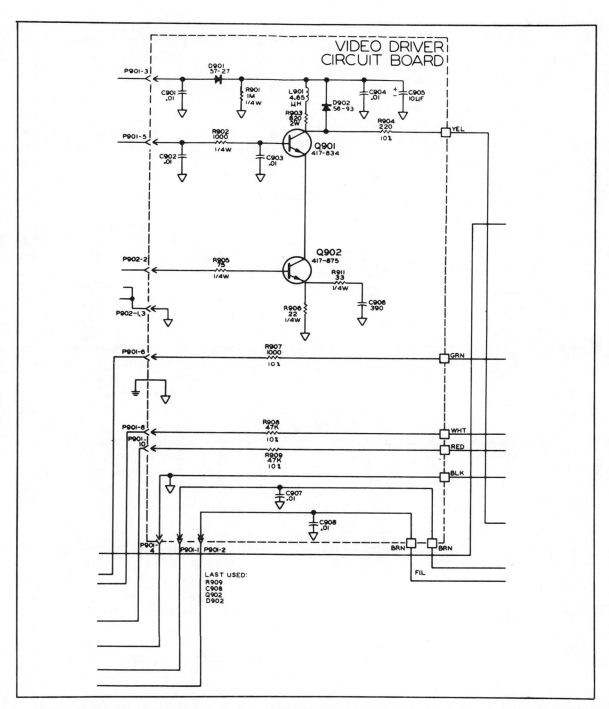

Fig. 21-11. The video driver board contains a cascade video amplifier consisting of Q901 and Q902. It is also a routing area for the CRT electron gun voltages (© 1981 Heath Company, Reprinted by Permission of Heath Company).

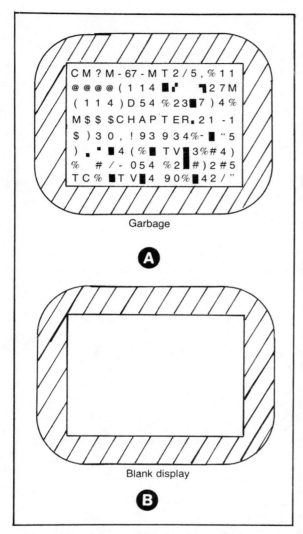

```
C M ? M - 6 7 - M T 2 / 5 , % 1 1
@ @ @ @ ( 1 1 4 ■ ▪    ▀ 2 7 M
( 1 1 4 ) D 5 4 % 2 3 ■ 7 ) 4 %
M $ $ $ C H A P T E R ▪ 2 1 - 1
$ ) 3 0 , ! 9 3 9 3 4 % - ■ " 5
) ▪ ▀ 4 ( % ■ T V ■ 3 % # 4 )
%   # / - 0 5 4 % 2 ■ # ) 2 # 5
T C % ■ T V ■ 4   9 0 % ■ 4 2 / "
```

Garbage

A

Blank display

B

Fig. 21-12. The symptom of "garbage" happens when the computer logic circuits develop troubles (A). Another form of garbage is a blank display block. It too indicates the failure of logic circuits (B).

In addition the beginning of each scan line and the end is blacked out to form the side borders of the display block. The sync information on when to light the scan lines and turn them off, is contained as pulses in the composite video. The video also con-

tains the logic information that directs the lighting and extinguishing of pixels. Between the sync and the logic in the video the display block and its contents are specified.

When there is trouble in the logic circuits, it shows up in the 192 lines inside the display block. The commonest trouble is seen by the symptom called *garbage* (Fig. 21-12A). Garbage is the condition of the display filling up with meaningless characters, symbols and numbers. The entire block could fill up or only sections will show the nonsense. Another variation of the same sort of trouble is the appearance of a blank display block (Fig. 21-12B). Whichever version does appear, the symptom indicates troubles in the logic areas of the computer. This includes all the sections that use binary, and the video display generator.

If the display block itself should disappear and only a raster remain, then the horizontal and vertical sync signals are gone and the display block cannot be constructed. This could possibly happen in the sync circuits in the computer. However, this trouble is more likely to occur due to failure in the cascade video amplifier section of Q901 and Q902. More than likely, the entire composite video is not getting past the video driver board. Start testing there.

Testing the video amplifiers is a straightforward analog operation. The scope will show the inputs and output and the missing signal is quickly traced. The dc collector and base voltages are also easily checked and missing voltages located. The circuit extends from the board input to the cathode of the CRT.

Besides being the video output, this board routes all the CRT electron gun voltages to their correct grids. There are a couple of rf bypass capacitors, C907 and C908, attached to the 6.3 V CRT filament on the board. The board also has a common ground attached. The ground forms an arc path to the chassis to eliminate any possibility of electrical sparks upsetting the operation of the computer.

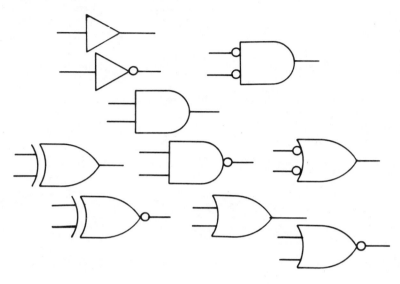

Index

A

Accumulator, the, 181
ACIA, 10, 39, 53, 58, 120
Address and data bus testing, 221
Address bus, 215
Addresses, 129
Addresses, assigning, 219
Addressing, 115
Address lines, 46, 69, 217
Alphanumeric display mode, 49
Alphanumeric mode, 52
Alphanumerics, 14
Alpha semigraphics, 14
ALU, 180
American Standard Code for Information Interchange, 261
Analog multiplexer, 272
AND, 132, 142
AND gate, 90, 143, 144
ANDing, 174
Anode, 76
ASCII, 124, 125, 261
Assemblers, 197
Assembly language, 146
Asynchronous communications interface, 10
Asynchronous communications interface adapter, 39, 53

B

BASIC, 146
Binary addresses, 71
Binary counter, 162, 165
Buffer, 84
Buffers, 82
Buffers, tristate, 86
Byte, 54, 168

C

Cabinet removal, 21
Cassette audio, 280
Cassette input, 280
Cassette interface, 279
Cassette output, 283
Cathode, 76
CCR, 183, 185
Central processor unit, 39
Chip location guide, 27, 34
   drawing your own, 28
   important parts of the, 36
   using the, 37
Chip pin chart, 256
Chips, changing, 99
Chip select, 220
Chip troubles, common, 100
Cleaning and inspection, 24
Clearing and complementing, 172

Clock, 121, 205
Clock, testing the, 212
Clock circuit, 205
Clock functions, 208
Clock signal, 210
CMOS, 106
CMOS chips, 109
COBOL, 146
Column address strobe, 239
Columns and rows, 72
Complementary MOS, 108
Component layout guide, 20
Computer, simple, 113
Computer audio, 270
Computer block diagram, 113
Computer repair, start to finish, 5
Computers, styles of, 18
Computer system, 41
   block diagram of a, 6
   typical, 7
Computer troubles, general categories of, 14
Control lines, 44
Control register, 247
Counter, binary, 162
CPU, 12, 39, 40, 42, 64, 113, 123
CPU, checking out the, 176
CPU, inside the, 178

CPU addressing circuits, 198
Crystal-controlled oscillator, 206

D

Data bus, 45, 115, 215
Data bus, digital components in the, 216
Data lines, 43, 215
DDR, 246
Decoders, 88
Deflection yoke, 303
Device selection, 239
Diagnostic program, 3
Digital logic circuits, 132
Digital logic probe, 136
Digital logic states, 134
Digital registers, 160
Digital states, 87
Digital to analog devices, 270
Diode-transistor logic, 99
DIP, 109
Disassembly, repairing by, 22
   step-by-step, 22
DTL, 99, 101

E

Electricity, static, 24
Enable, 83
Enable terminal, 152
Encoders, 88
EPROM, 77, 80
EPROM, MOSFET, 79
Erasable programmable ROM, 77
Exclusive NOR, 132, 155, 158
Exclusive NOR gate, 93
Exclusive OR, 148
Exclusive OR gate, 92

F

Factory seals, 19
FET, 105
Fetch and execute, 47
Flip-flop, 132, 163
   basic, 161
   R-S, 160
Flyback transformer, 305
FORTRAN, 146
40-pin DIP, 176
Full graphics, 14, 49

G

Garbage, 15, 308
Gate testing, 159
Graphics, pure, 265

H

Hand assembly, 196
Hexadecimal, 167
Hex 3-state bus driver, 137
High voltage, 304
Home computer, exploded view of a, 17

Horizontal oscillator, 299, 302
Horizontal output, 303

I

IC extraction technique, 109
IC insertion technique, 110
IGFET, 107
Incrementing and decrementing, 172
Index register addressing, 201
Input-output chips, 119
Inspection and cleaning, 24
Instruction register, 183, 186, 193
Instruction set layers, 192
Integrated circuits, 2
Internal wiring, 81
Inverters, 139
I/O bytes, 254
I/O port, 11

J

Joystick assembly, 274
Joystick interface, 273, 276
JUMP instruction, 191

L

Latches, 85
Least significant bit, 167
Logical states, three, 132
Logic gates, 89
Logic gates, servicing, 132
Logic probe, 136
Logic symbols, 91
LSI, 109
LSI, typical, 39
LSI chips, 39

M

Master frequency, 205
Memory, upgrading, 78
Memory map, 198, 204
Metal-oxide semiconductor, 24
Metal oxide silicon, 105
Metal oxide silicon field-effect transistor, 77
Microcomputer block diagram, 9
Mnemonics, 195
Modulator, 93
Monitor, 122
MOS, 24
MOS chips, 104
MOSFET, 77
Most significant bit, 167
MSI, 109

N

NAND, 132
NAND gate, 92, 104, 149, 157
NMOS, 105
No color, 15
NOR, 132
NOR gate, 94, 153
No sound, 15

NOT, 132
NOT gate, 92, 140, 141
Nybble, 166, 167
Nybble, LS, 170
Nybble, MS, 170

O

Octal D flip-flop, 85
Op code, 197
Operand, 197
Operating system, 122
OR, 132, 145
OR gate, 91, 94
ORing, 174

P

Parallel interface, 55
PASCAL, 146
PDR, 246
Peripheral interface adapter, 10, 39, 243
PIA, 10, 39, 42, 49, 123, 243
PIA application, 254
PIA I/O chip, 120
PIA memory map, 250
PIA pins, 247
PMOS, 108
Power supply, 288
   computer, 97
Power supply repairs, 292
Power supply voltages, 38
Power transformer, 290
Print boards, 30
Problems, isolating, 4
Program, assembling a, 194
Program, diagnostic, 3
Program counter, 131, 174, 185
Programmable ROM, 77
PROM, 77

R

RAM, 9, 60, 64, 116, 123
RAM, dynamic, 63
RAM, 1K, 61
RAM address, 67
RAM chips, 67
RAM register, 66
RAM test, 4
RAM wiring, 74
Random-access memory, 9, 60
Read-only memory, 10, 65
Reassembly, step-by-step, 25
Registers, 59
Regulators, 97
Relative addressing, 200
Reset circuit, 288
Resistor-transistor logic, 99
Resoldering, 112
Rf modulator, 96
ROM, 10, 60, 65, 117, 119
ROM chips, 68
Row address strobe, 240

Rows and columns, 72
RS-232 interface, 279, 285
RTL, 99, 102

S

SAM, 39, 50
SAM block diagram, 227, 239
SAM chip, 206, 226, 230
SAM chip, checking the, 240
SAM schematic, 226
Scope traces, 277
Semigraphic mode, 263
Serial interface, 57
Service checkout chart, 179
Service notes, 27
Shift register, 171
Shift registers, 169
Shorts, 23
Sockets, 29
Soldering precautions, 111
Sound circuit, 273
Source program, 197
SSI, 109
Stack pointer, 203
Static electricity, 24

Symbols, 133
Synchronous address multiplexer, 39, 50, 226
System timing, 237

T

Timing diagram, 207
Transformer, flyback, 305
Transistors, 2
Transistor-transistor logic, 24, 99
Tristate, 102, 135
Tristate buffers, 218
Trouble analysis, 13
Truth table, 138
TTL, 24, 99, 101
TTL family, 103
TV display, 295
TV signal, rf modulated composite, 8

V

Vacuum tubes, 2
VDG, 39, 48, 51
VDG, checking out the, 267
VDG character set, 259
VDG inputs, 258

VDG output, 267
VDG video output, 266
Vertical oscillator, 297
Vertical output, 298
Vertical sweep, 300
Video circuit board, 297
Video display generator, 39, 258
Video driver circuit board, 306
Video mixer, 93
Video mixer chip, 268
Video mixer circuit, 96
Video RAM, 118, 128, 260, 262
VLSI, 108

W

Warranty, 16
Wired memory, 73
Write operation, 75

X

XNOR gate, 95

Y

YES, 132
YES gate, 136